CONTENTS

To my mother and the memory of my father—Louise and Albert Carron

Social Psychology Of Sport

ALBERT V. CARRON
UNIVERSITY OF WESTERN ONTARIO
LONDON, ONTARIO

SOCIAL PSYCHOLOGY OF SPORT

Copyright© 1980 by Mouvement Publications

Artwork by: Graphic Works, Ithaca, N.Y.

Production by Gary Marsden

Typeset by Strehle's Computerized Typesetting, Ithaca, N.Y.

Printed in the United States of America by Wilcox Press, Inc.

First Edition

International Standard Book Number: 0-932392-06-7

SOCIAL PSYCHOLOGY OF SPORT

Albert V. Carron
University of Western Ontario
London, Ontario

Mouvement Publications
102 Irving Place
Ithaca, N.Y. 14850

18 Kilmorey Park
Chester CH23QS
United Kingdom

Box 26 Torquay
Victoria 3228
Australia

PREFACE

This textbook was prepared for senior undergraduate and graduate students in physical education interested in the area of sport psychology. Its basic purpose is to outline in detail those social psychological parameters which influence behavior and performance in sport and physical activity.

Social psychology, as a discipline, is characterized by its emphasis upon the *individual* in society and the impact of *social influence processes* upon individual behavior. Thus, from a perspective which encompasses the social psychological dimensions of sport and physical activity, I have focused on the *athlete* as well as the predominant social factors which affect the athlete's behavior—the *coach*, the *team* and *spectators*.

It should also be noted, however, that the content ot this book is not always consistently social psychological. I did not feel committed to adhere to any perceived boundaries separating social psychology from sociology or other areas of psychology. Thus, whenever material from other related disciplines seemed pertinent, it was also incorporated.

Upon the completion of this project, I am faced with a complex series of emotions and feelings. Obviously, relief and satisfaction that my work is now finished are among these. But, possibly my two most dominant impressions are illustrated in Alfred Tennyson's poem, *Ulysses:*

> *...I am a part of all that I have met;*
> *Yet all experience is an arch wherethro'*
> *Gleams that untravell'd world whose margin fades*
> *For ever and ever when I move.*

The first line aptly summarizes my first general set of impressions. (Ironically perhaps, I first became aware of this line in another author's work. It seemed so applicable to my own case that I then went to Tennyson's work where I became aware of the suitability of the total quote presented above.) An examination of the list of references should clearly demonstrate that while this text is "my work" in the sense that I compiled, organized and interpreted it, it truly originates from the hundreds of researchers and scholars who have literally spent thousands of hours carefully designing their experiments, collecting data, analyzing results and preparing their articles for publication. This text evolved from that body of literature and hopefully the extent of my indebtedness is clearly evident.

The second portion of the quote from Ulysses is also most appropriate. Although an attempt has been made here to present "what we know in the social psychology of sport and physical activity," I am struck by just how little that actually is. Any social scientist attempting to understand and predict human behavior must begin that quest with a feeling of humility and be resigned to the reality of personal limitation. Otherwise, the complexity which characterizes man can only lead to a sense of frustration. Over 40 years ago, Chester Barnard (The functions of the executive, Harvard University Press, 1938) stated that "It seems to me quite in order to cease encouraging the expectation that human behavior in society can be anything less than the most complex study to which our minds may be applied." This sentiment seems equally applicable today.

I do owe a great personal and professional debt to a number of individuals and institutions who encouraged, assisted and supported my work. The University of Western Ontario and Dean W. J. L'Heureux of the Faculty of Physical Education supported my application and plans for a sabbatical leave and this provided me with the time to undertake the research and writing required.

The Canada Council also supported this project and my general sabbatical plans through a Leave Fellowship and Research Grant. It is doubtful whether I would have been able to complete my work without their assistance.

Dr. Don Anthony of the Center for International Sport Studies in London, England and Mr. Peter Simons of Avery Hill College readily welcomed me and provided me with a base and excellent facilities from which to operate.

The graphic work in the text reflects Mr. Sandy Welland's technical skill. Also, I must acknowledge the efforts of my two typists who were responsible for the original draft of this manuscript—L. C. and B. C. They demonstrated quite conclusively that reduction in speed is not necessarily accompanied by an increase in accuracy.

Particular thanks are due to my colleague, Dr. P. Chelladurai. He helped in so many ways that to specifically list any would be to risk understating his involvement.

Drs. Dan Landers, Ed Burke and Bill Straub read and reacted to an earlier draft of this manuscript. Their comments and suggestions were invaluable.

Finally, it isn't possible to become involved in the preparation of a book without that project having a significant impact upon the total family. Thus, I am appreciative of the understanding and encouragement of my wife, Lynne, and my children, Wendy, Brett, Patrick and Christopher.

A.V.C.
London, Canada
October, 1979

SECTION I
INTRODUCTION

The unexamined life is not worth living.

Plato

When you cannot measure it, when you cannot express it in numbers, your knowledge is of a meager and unsatisfactory kind.

Lord Kelvin

The psychologist and the athlete or coach have always been uneasy partners. Neither the psychologist [nor] the athlete/coach has had much understanding of the long-term concerns of the other, and hence they have had little respect for each other.

J. H. Salmela

What can I wish to the youth of my country who devote themselves to science?
Firstly, gradualness. About this most important condition of fruitful scientific work I never can speak without emotion. Gradualness, gradualness and gradualness. From the very beginning of your work, school yourselves to severe gradualness in the accumulation of knowledge.

Ivan Pavlov

It is Facts that are needed; Facts, Facts, Facts. When facts have been supplied, each of us can try to reason from them.
James Bryce

A SOCIAL PSYCHOLOGICAL PERSPECTIVE OF SPORT AND PHYSICAL ACTIVITY

Physical activity and sport are basic and universal elements within virtually all cultures from highly industrialized societies to developing countries. This pervasive influence has yielded advantages and disadvantages insofar as the development of sport in general is concerned. Two of the more apparent advantages are associated with the inherent popularity of sport and physical activity. That is, as a general rule, there has been a strong motivation on the part of all individuals to participate or become involved in sport. Also, that involvement is viewed favorably and enjoyed by most members of society. As a result, sport must be viewed as a significant social institution in society.

However, one disadvantage which parallels this natural, ready-made interest and motivation is that the development of a scholarly, scientific study into sport and physical activity has been relatively slow. There has been a strong traditional tendency to regard sport and physical activity as an *art* form—*an ability or skill which can be acquired through practice and observation*. An argument advanced implicitly in this regard is that there is no need to study something so simple and self-evident.

The selection of coaches in both amateur and professional sport clearly illustrates this viewpoint in operation. Any individual who has participated and acquired the requisite abilities or skills through experience and practice is regarded as an authority in that sport. Indeed, it is typically concluded that those individuals who have demonstrated the greatest skill as participants will develop into the most suitable coaches.

A second, somewhat related disadvantage has been that even in those instances where the evidence from empirical research is available and utilized, where the approach to physical activity and sport is scientific in nature, the scope of that approach has usually been severely restricted. For example, it has not been atypical for those coaches who draw upon physiological or biomechanical principles in order to develop appropriate training programs for an athlete, to either ignore or treat the psychological aspects of participation as an art form which has either already been mastered or can be perfected through experience.

This latter viewpoint may be a reflection of a number of factors. Certainly, as Vanek and Cratty (1970) concluded after reviewing the history of sport psychology in Europe and North America, "it is apparent that sport psychology is one of the younger disciplines within the larger area of psychology." It is also apparent that sport psychology is one of the younger subdisciplines within the relatively young discipline of physical education.

Historically, the initial scholarly interest shown toward physical activity and sport was in medical schools and physiology departments. Even today, the general public more closely associates participation in sport and physical activity with physiological concerns such as cardio-respiratory fitness and strength development. The psychological area simply has not yet progressed to the same state as the physiological area. If this is coupled with the fact that the concepts and terminology of sport psychology (e.g., "stress", "motivation", "cohesion", "personality") are highly familiar to the general public as a result of having received extensive treatment in newspaper articles and popular literature, it is probably not so surprising that most coaches and the general public consider themselves experts in this area.

Fortunately, however, there has been a marked increase in recent years in the interest and emphasis placed upon the psychological correlates of sport and physical activity. Certainly, within the past decade, the quantity and quality of research in the area of *sport psychology*[1]—which includes motor learning, child development, psychometrics and social psychology—has improved dramatically. And, as Singer (1972a) observed "research is one of the keys to progress and is being utilized to a greater extent than ever before in all aspects of coaching".

Although the research from various areas within sport psychology is, to a large extent, interrelated, one area which might be said to encompass all of the others is *social psychology*. There are two features which define social psychology. The first is its interest in the *individual*—the individual as a participant within a social situation. The second is the emphasis placed upon understanding the *underlying processes* associated with the impact that the social situation has upon individual behavior (Hollander, 1971).

The interrelationship of social psychology with sport and physical activity is obvious. The individual—the child participating in movement skills—is our focal point. But, an individual participating in sport and physical activity does so in a social context—in the presence of teammates, competitors, coaches, officials and/or spectators. And, each of these has an influence upon the individual's behavior. The focus of this book is on the social psychology of sport—the individual in sport and physical activity and the nature of those social influences which affect behavior and performance.

However, in order to provide an overall perspective of the social psychological dimension, it is necessary to consider initially the general nature and purposes of science; then the scope of the science of sport and physical activity; and finally, a theoretical model pertinent to the study of the social psychology of sport and physical activity.

THE NATURE OF SCIENCE

Science may be defined as *a systematized body of knowledge which is acquired: (1) when events are observed and measured; (2) when those observations and*

---

1. There is some debate in North America and Europe concerning whether sport psychology and motor learning should be considered separate, independent areas of investigation or whether one of these (and there is no concensus which one it is) is a subfield of the other. The position implicitly adopted here is, of course, that motor learning as a field of psychological inquiry, should be subsumed under the umbrella term "sport psychology."

measurements are then categorized and classified; and finally, (3) when those categorizations and classifications are then used to generate theories, principles and laws.

The goal of science is to obtain an *understanding* of those phenomena germane to its interests and concerns. To arrive at an understanding implies that there will be a successful completion of two individual but interdependent processes: *description* and *explanation (prediction)* of the phenomena.

There are four phases or sequential stages associated with the processes of description and explanation/prediction (Hardman, 1973). In the first phase, the *descriptive phase*, an attempt is made to identifiy or define the essential characteristics which relate to the phenomena. Thus, if our interest is in the behavior and performance of elite basketball players, the descriptive phase might involve establishing a summary profile from one or a number of different perspectives such as the *physiological* (e.g., by assessing maximal oxygen uptake, muscular strength and endurance); the *anthropometric* (e.g., by assessing height, weight, relative percentage of body fat, body somatotype); the *sociological* (e.g., by obtaining demographic data such as birth order, parental socioeconomic status); and the *psychological* (e.g., by determining the predominant personality dispositions present).

In the *hypothesis development phase* which follows, an attempt is made to explain why. Consequently, hypotheses are generated in an effort to provide reasons for the findings obtained in the descriptive phase. Thus, for example, if elite basketball players as a group are found to have considerably higher levels of achievement motivation than the general population, it might be hypothesized that this trait is essential for success at the highest levels of athletic competition.

In the third phase—the *empirical analysis phase*—the hypotheses generated to explain the observed pattern of results are subjected to rigorous scientific investigation. For the example outlined above, research might be undertaken to determine the achievement motivation levels in elite wrestlers, field hockey players, business executives and medical doctors to determine whether this personality disposition is present in all exceptional achievers. Or, the performance of individuals with high and low levels of achievement motivation might be compared in a laboratory experiment.

In the final *predictive phase*, the knowledge obtained from the previous phases is used in a *predictive* fashion. Thus, if level of achievement motivation is strongly associated with elite basketball ability, a decision might be made to initially screen competitors on this personality dimension prior to permitting tryouts for a national team. (Aside from the serious moral and philosophical implications of this type of a decision, it is doubtful that anything as complex as elite athletic performance will ever be predicted from information on one dimension! Consequently, it should be obvious that this example is only used to illustrate a total process).

Within the science of sport and physical activity, the principal phenomena of interest are *behavior* and *performance* in movement activities. These two constructs are similar since as Alderman (1974) has stated:

> *. . .Behavior can be defined as the total aggregate of human responses that the person makes to both internal and external stimuli. Though very much a stimulus-response viewpoint, this definition is useful in that it places a behavioral approach to the psychology of sport in a context in which everything the participant does, thinks and feels should be examined. Performance, on the other hand, is usually interpreted as that relatively short*

term aspect of behavior which is marked by activity toward the execution of an obser-
vable, identifiable discrete task. Individual behavior in physical activity and sport thus
becomes all-encompassing in scope within which individual performance is only one
aspect.

Although this latter suggestion of Alderman's seems quite reasonable, nevertheless, a clear distinction is made in this book between behavior and performance. The principal reason for this is that the basis for evaluating the two is markedly different. In sport and physical activity, the criteria for performance effectiveness are usually well defined—performance, as goal-directed behavior, may be improved or worsened, more or less successful, and so on. Thus, the question of what detrimental or beneficial effect social influence[2] processes have upon performance is significant. For example, is team performance better or worse if the group is cohesive?

On the other hand, with the possible exception of those instances where there are excesses or extremes in behavior, where behavior fails to conform to broad social norms (e.g., deviancy), value-oriented judgements are not appropriate for behavior. Behavior is the unique response of the individual participant within the sport situation. Thus, the principal questions are essentially descriptive in nature (e.g., introverted versus extroverted? high versus low anxiousness? socially adjusted? and so on).

GENERAL MODELS FOR THE SCIENCE OF SPORT AND PHYSICAL ACTIVITY

If the emphasis is on behavior and performance within the science of sport and physical activity, then there must be a logical general theoretical framework within which these can be examined. A number of authors have emphasized this point via the models they have proposed for performance effectiveness. For example, four categories of variables were advanced by Cratty (1967) as having an influence upon indiviudal performance: *physiological, social, body structure* and *psychological*. This schema is illustrated in Figure 1.1.

Cratty pointed out that "physical activity, both proficiency levels and the types selected, is influenced by, and reflected in, various kinds of social behavior". He also proposed that these social influences could be direct and immediate to the performance situation (such as is the case with an audience); indirect but in close social proximity through the influence of various subcultures (such as the family or peer group); or, indirect and removed from the individual, (such as societal expectations).

In a similar fashion, Singer (1972b) proposed a model comprised of a series of foundational blocks (stages) which were viewed as leading to athletic proficiency. In Singer's heirarchical model, it was assumed that *genetics, childhood experiences, personal goals, environmental influences* and *interactions* (e.g., athlete and coach, athlete and teammates) contribute in a sequential manner to the development of performance excellence (see Figure 1.2).

Alderman (1974), in a model which has some similarities to Cratty's, suggested that four major classes of variables underlie skilled performance. These include the dimensions of *fitness, skill, physical endowment* and the *psychological* (see Figure 1.3).

---

2. According to Martens (1976) "social influence occurs whenever one individual responds to the actual or implied presence of one or more other individuals."

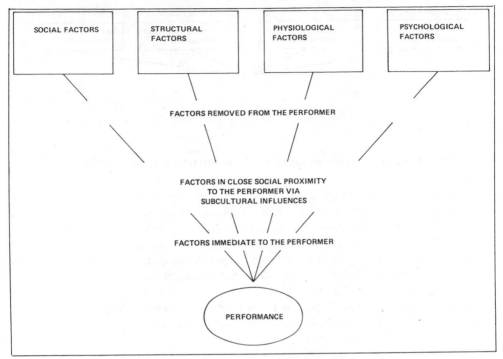

Figure 1.1. The modifiers of motor performance (Adapted from Cratty, 1967).

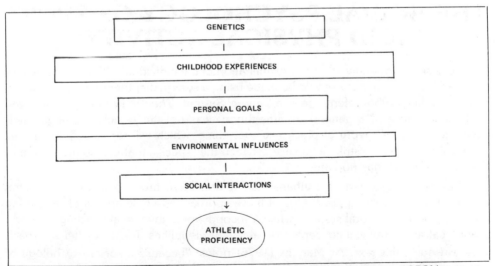

Figure 1.2. The determinants of athletic proficiency (Adapted from Singer, 1972b).

These dimensions were viewed by Alderman as being interdependent with skilled performance, being a function of the meshing of the four.

It might be apparent from the preceeding discussion that if the objective is to obtain an understanding of behavior and performance in sport and physical activity, then the

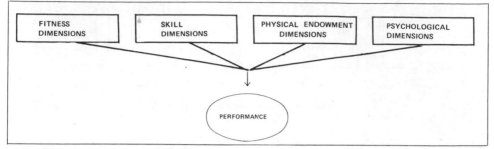

Figure 1.3. The underlying dimensions for athletic performance (Adapted from Alderman, 1974).

comprehensive picture proposed by Cratty, Singer, and Alderman should be considered. However, while a holistic, multivariate approach would be preferable, it is beyond the scope of the present level of understanding within human motor performance. Thus, as Holtzman (1964) has pointed out in his discussion of the dilemmas in personality assessment "A major limitation is that in any practical situation one must make rather arbitrary choices and exclude all but a small portion of the general model".

That small portion in the case of this book is, of course, the social psychology of sport and physical activity. Thus, the focus here is on the *individual* as a social entity interacting with other individuals and groups within the social institution of sport.[3]

A GENERAL SYSTEMS APPROACH FOR THE SOCIAL PSYCHOLOGY OF SPORT AND PHYSICAL ACTIVITY

It does seem imperative that any examination of the individual within the context of sport and physical activity should be made using a systematic, theoretical framework; what Boulding (1956) referred to as a *General Systems Theory*. Boulding emphasized that the purpose of a general systems theory was not "to establish a single, self-contained 'general theory of practically everything' which will replace all the special theories" but rather to strike a balance between the "specific that has no meaning and the general which has no content."

It has been suggested by Luthans (1973) that there are two ways that general systems theory can be applied. One of these approaches would consist of structuring a hierarchy of behavioral systems while a second would involve abstracting common theoretical and empirical concepts from relevant disciplines. It is this latter approach that is used in this text. As Martens (1976) notes: "because a social psychology of physical activity has no theories of its own, . . . it is appropriate and parsimonious to borrow social psychological theories and determine their applicability to physical activity."

3. While a number of authors (e.g., Edwards, 1973; Loy, 1968; Luschen, 1967; Snyder and Spreitzer, 1974) have proposed differing definitions of *sport*, no attempt is made here to delineate the limits of this construct. Rather, the term *sport* is used in its broadest context to encompass organized and nonorganized physical activity.

A GENERAL SYSTEMS MODEL FOR PERFORMANCE

It was pointed out earlier that a distinction is made in the text between behavior and performance. Thus, the models used to examine each are slightly different. From a social psychological perspective, the individual athlete's performance may be considered an *output* (i.e., a dependent variable) which is influenced or affected by various *input* variables (i.e., independent variables). This is illustrated schematically in Figure 1.4. A question of some interest then is what are the principal independent variables, factors, parameters—the inputs or social influences—which influence athletic performance?

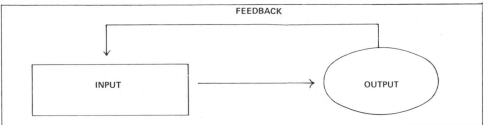

Figure 1.4. A feedback loop.

Also however, the output (motor performance) can, in turn, feedback and reciprocally influence the input (see Figure 1.4). Thus a second question of interest is what subsequent effect does performance have upon various social psychological parameters?

Carron and Chelladurai (1978) utilized this concept of a feedback loop in their proposal that from a social psychological perspective

> . . .there are four interdependent classes of variables which are related to athletic performance. These may be categorized under broad classifications: team, athlete, coach and spectator and a number of psychological parameters contained within these four dimensions have either a direct or indirect influence upon ultimate athletic performance. And in turn the athletic performance itself has psychological implications for the team, athlete, coach and spectator.

A schematic illustration of the general model for performance which is used in this text is outlined in Figure 1.5.

The influence of team cohesiveness provides a good example of this general feedback loop in operation. The level of team cohesiveness—represented in Figure 1.5 as the interaction of the athlete and team dimension—serves to contribute to performance effectiveness. In turn, the success or failure the team experiences, also "feeds back" and serves to enhance the feeling of team cohesiveness and personal satisfaction.

A GENERAL SYSTEMS MODEL FOR BEHAVIOR

When behavior itself is the focus, then it is again necessary to consider those classes of variables which have a direct influence upon it. The classic formulation advanced by Kurt Lewin (1935) is still appropriate, namely that *behavior* is a product of the *person* and the *environment*, or

$$B = f (P,E)$$

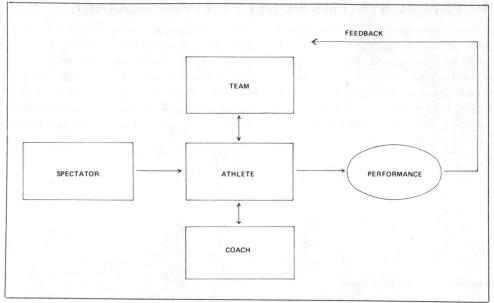

Figure 1.5. A social psychological perspective for performance effectiveness (Adapted from Carron and Chelladurai, 1978).

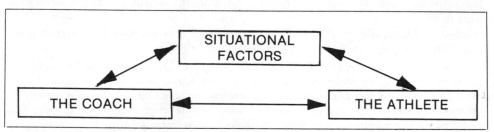

Figure 1.6. Interpersonal behavior as a product of person and situation (From Carron and Chelladurai, 1978). Reproduced with permission of the publisher.

Carron and Chelladurai (1978) presented a schematic illustration of this Lewinian formula with specific reference to the interpersonal behavior of a coach and athlete (see Figure 1.6).

They emphasized that implicit in the interrelationships suggested within this illustration is the proposition that an athlete's interpersonal behavior is a product of three general sets of forces: (1) factors specific to the *situation* or *environment* (including the role expectations operative, the task demands, the influence of other members of the team and spectators); (2) factors specific to the *coach* (including factors such as his/her personality, attitudes and need dispositions); and, (3) factors specific to the *athlete* (including personality, need dispositions, attitudes etc).

If a comparison is made between Figure 1.6 and the extreme left hand component of Figure 1.5, two points would be evident. The first is that these two components or aspects of the models are highly similar. If the athlete's behavior is the focus, then the spectator and team dimensions would represent some of the environmental forces affecting that behavior. A second point which can be emphasized is the distinction made in this text between performance and behavior. In Figure 1.5, the focus is on the output (performance) while in Figure 1.6, the focus is on the specific behavior of the athlete.

PROLOGUE

The text is organized into four main sections which correspond to the following dimensions: athlete, coach, team and spectator. The *Athlete* is discussed in the next section, Section II.

A considerable amount of research effort has been directed toward the topic of *personality* and its relationship to sport and physical activity. The principal orientation has been that of *description;* what are the unique, identifiable personality characteristics which differentiate athletes from nonathletes? In Chapter 2, the topic of personality is the focus. The nature of personality is outlined and then the present status or level of understanding of personality within sport and physical activity is discussed.

Motivation is the psychological construct which is used to represent the energy and purpose underlying behavior. In Chapter 3, a summary of the predominant theories of motivation is presented and their application to the context of sport and physical activity is explored.

Section III, the *Coach* dimension, begins with a discussion of the dynamics of leadership in Chapter 4. Historically, the study of leadership has centered upon the traits or behaviors of leaders with each of these being considered as either universal or situational in nature. (Generally, the approach in sport and physical activity research has been restricted to one of these orientations—a *universal trait approach*. In this regard, a predominant concern has been with the question of whether coaches as a group have characteristic personality profiles, e.g., authoritarian?, uninvolved emotionally?, etc.) An overview of the various theories of leadership and their application to sport and physical activity is presented.

In Chapter 5, a number of models for examining coach-athlete interaction are presented and examined with respect to performance and behavior. The concern with whether coaches-as-a-group have a unique personality profile is largely motivated by an interest in the effect that that personality has upon athletes in the sport environment. But the athlete is not a passive recipient of the coach's behavior—a coach-athlete relationship is characterized by reciprocity and mutual dependence. In short, the coach-athlete relationship should be considered as a *social interaction system* and examined within that framework. This is done in Chapter 5.

Section IV centers on the *Team* dimension. In Chapter 6, the initial chapter within that section, the *nature of groups* is discussed with particular reference to group structure, the process of group development, and the impact of group structure and communication upon behavior, performance and group conformity.

Chapters 7 and 8 deal with the issue of group dynamics. The term *dynamics* has a connotation of energy, force, activity and change. In the context of the group, the designation *group dynamics* has come to represent those processes underlying the changes associated with group involvement—the two major processes being *locomotion* (i.e., activity of the group in regard to its objectives) and *cohesiveness* (i.e., activity of the group relating to the development and maintenance of group solidarity). In Chapter 7, the focus is on the former. Specifically, the factors of group-oriented motivation and aspiration, the attributions ascribed for causality of performance outcome, the distinctiveness of the individual versus the group in behavior and performance characteristics, and the competitive versus the cooperative process are discussed.

The topic of cohesiveness is analyzed in Chapter 8: its properties, how it is assessed, its determinants and consequences. Also, the implications of cohesiveness for sport and physical activity (particularly with reference to performance effectiveness) are discussed.

Section V deals with the *Spectator* dimension. One of the most extensively examined topics in the social psychology of sport and physical activity has been *social facilitation* and this work is examined and summarized in Chapter 9.

SUMMARY

Physical activity and sport are basic and universal elements of all societies. Two advantages which accrue to sport as a result of this are that individuals are strongly motivated to participate in sport, and that participation is viewed favorably and enjoyed. However this has had disadvantages for the development of a scholarly scientific study into sport generally, and the social psychological dimensions of sport and physical activity specifically.

Science may be defined as a systematized body of knowledge which is acquired when events are observed and measured; those observations and measurements are then categorized and classified; and finally, those categorizations and classifications are then used to generate general theories and principles. The goal of science is to obtain an understanding (through the description and then explanation/prediction) of those phenomena germane to its interests.

Within the science of physical education the phenomena of interest are behavior and performance and a general theoretical framework comprising sociological, psychological, physiological and structural dimensions is necessary in order to logically examine these. However, since this is beyond the scope of the present level of understanding within human motor performance, each of these dimensions must be pursued independently through the use of a general systems approach.

If motor performance is considered, the independent variables, factors, parameters—the social influences—which affect individual performance comprise the athlete, the coach, the team and spectators (Figure 1.5). In turn, performance effectiveness has psychological implications for the athlete, coach, team and spectators. Similarly, when behavior is the focus, both the individual and the social environment must be taken into consideration (Figure 1.6).

SECTION II
THE ATHLETE

Man is not the creature of circumstances. Circumstances are the creatures of men.

Benjamin Disreali

It is the spirit we bring to the fight that decides the issue.

George C. Marshall

A man can be destroyed but not defeated.

Ernest Hemingway

PERSONALITY AND THE ATHLETE

2

As was pointed out in the previous chapter, a fundamental goal for the science of sport and physical activity is to gain an understanding of behavior. Since "personality is an abstraction or hypothetical construction from or about behavior" (Martens, 1975), it is not surprising that historically one of the most popular and extensively discussed issues in sport psychology has been the relationship of personality to participation in sport and physical activity. While the specific topics pursued have been varied, the experimental work can be classified within two broad, general categories according to the research strategy utilized (see Figure 2.1).

√ One strategy has been oriented toward the process of *explanation/prediction*. In this regard the main interest has been in exploring general cause-effect relationships: the *cause* being a specific personality dimension (which has then been varied with situational or environmental variables of interest) and the *effect* being performance outcome. Illustrative of the type of research question which has been examined in this regard is "Do those individuals who exhibit a high degree of anxiousness perform better or worse in highly stressful situations than do those individuals characterized by a low degree of anxiousness?" Through the substitution of other personality characteristics for anxiousness (e.g., need achievement, aggressiveness, tough mindedness, dominance) and in combination with any of a number of situational conditions (e.g., easy versus difficult task; individual versus team sport; early versus late in the learning process), the list of examples could be expanded markedly. The basic point to be stressed here however, is that in this particular experimental paradigm, the personality dimensions and situational factors represent independent variables; performance outcome, the dependent variable. Thus, if the models presented in Chapter 1 are considered, this experimental paradigm is associated with Figure 1.5. In the next chapter, the research which has used this particular experimental paradigm is discussed.

√ A second strategy which has been utilized is related to the process of *description* (again, see Figure 2.1). In this approach, the emphasis has been on determining whether there are individual differences in personality which are associated with participation in specific sports or physical activities. Thus, as an example, a characteristic

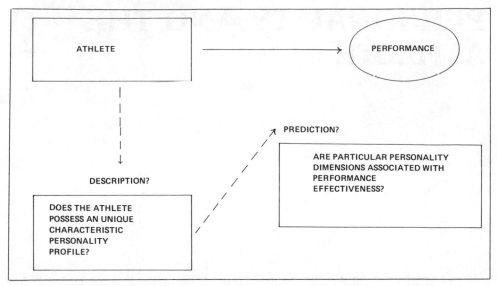

Figure 2.1. Research strategies used in personality research in the social psychology of sport and physical activity.

research question which has been pursued in this regard is "Do athletes as a group possess common personality characteristics which differentiate them from nonathletes?" If this question is considered in relationship to Figure 1.6, involvement in sport and physical activity would be a situational variable to which athletes would be exposed and to which nonathletes would not. If this situational variable, sport and physical activity, has had a significant impact, then athletes and nonathletes might exhibit different personality characteristics.

Again, the list of illustrations could be easily expanded since any of a number of different groups could be contrasted for possible personality differences; e.g., male versus female athletes, team versus individual sport athletes, elite versus lower skilled athletes. In this experimental paradigm, the various groups are the independent variables under test while personality is the dependent variable. The present chapter deals with this general area of research.

There have been a large number of overview articles written in which research in the social psychology of sport and physical activity has been discussed, summarized and/or critiqued (Carron, 1975; Cofer and Johnson, 1960; Cooper, 1969; Fisher, 1974; Hardman, 1973; Kane, 1964, 1978; Kroll, 1970; Martens, 1975; Morgan, 1969, 1972, 1978; Ogilvie, 1968; Rushall, 1975; Ryan, 1974; Singer, 1967; and, Smith, 1970). These have been drawn upon extensively here. However, in order to more fully appreciate the discussion, it is initially necessary to understand personality generally and the specific theoretical viewpoints endorsed.

THE NATURE OF PERSONALITY

DEFINITIONS

The exact origin of the term personality is not clear. However, the Latin words *per sonae* which translate as "to speak through" (and denoting the masks worn by actors in ancient Rome), and the Greek word *personae*, also denoting a theatrical mask, are the most frequently endorsed. Viewed from this perspective, personality would be considered as that facet, role or aspect of the individual which is presented to the public.

While this may be one valid view of personality, it is somewhat restrictive. And, an examination of both the number and nature of different definitions advanced for personality clearly shows that personality is conceived of as being much broader than a role presented publicly. For example, some representative definitions are:

. . . the sum total of an individual's characteristics which make him unique [Hollander, 1967].

. . . a person's unique pattern of traits [Guilford, 1959].

. . . the more or less stable and enduring organization of a person's character, temperament, intellect, and physique which determines the unique adjustment to the environment [Eysenck, 1960].

. . . the dynamic organization within the individual of those psychophysical systems that determine his unique adjustments to his environment [Allport, 1937].

. . . a stable set of characteristics and tendencies that determine those commonalities and differences in psychological behavior (thoughts, feelings and actions) of people that have continuity in time and may or may not be easily understood in terms of the social and biological pressures of the immediate situation alone [Maddi, 1968].

As Kluckhohn and Murray (1949) have stated, each individual is like all other men, like some other men, like no other men. The above definitions reflect this view in their emphasis on *uniqueness* as well as on *commonality*. The complexity of personality is also illustrated by the emphasis on *stability* as well as on *change and adjustment* and, on the *physical* as well as the *psychological*. Above everything else though, the different definitions point to the diverse and varied nature of both personality itself and the various theoretical views advanced to explain it.

THEORIES OF PERSONALITY

Psychodynamic Theories. The origins of psychodynamic theories were in the clinical environment; the earliest researchers being physicians with their focus being the abnormal or deviant behavior of disturbed people. Although Sigmund Freud developed psychoanalysis and is most readily associated with the psychodynamic approach to personality, a number of other individuals such as Carl Jung, Alfred Adler, Erich Fromm and Eric Erickson have made significant contributions. Two distinguishing characteristics of the psychodynamic approach have been its concern with the examination of the whole individual in depth (i.e., usually in the clinical setting) and its emphasis upon unconscious motives as the source for observed behavior.

For example, the main tenets of Freud's (1955) theory are the *id, ego* and *superego* which are conflicting personality constructs. The id, representing the *unconscious* instinct, is viewed as comprising two dimensions which are in constant conflict with each other: the life or pleasure instinct and the sexual-aggression instinct. Freud refered to the *conscious*, logical, reality-oriented aspect of man as the ego. Since the ego serves to interpret reality for the id through intellect and reason, the two are in constant conflict. Finally, the superego was considered by Freud to serve the function of a *conscience*. Thus, it was proposed that societal and personal norms, values, attitudes, and morals are absorbed into the superego which then aids in the resolution of conflicts between the id and ego. Essentially, Freud advocated a *conflict theory of personality* (see Figure 2.2) in which unconscious sexual and aggressive instincts are major determinants of behavior.

In a departure from Freud, other psychodynamic theorists (e.g., Fromm, 1941;

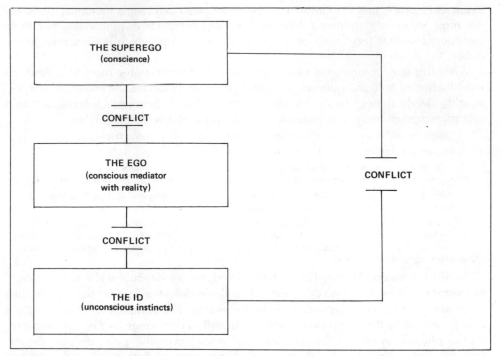

Figure 2.2. The Freudian conflict theory of personality.

Erickson, 1968) have proposed more social and interpersonal interpretations for behavior — less emphasis is placed upon the instinctual forces emanating from the id and greater emphasis is placed upon the role of the ego and superego. Despite these modifications in general orientation, the basic psychodynamic approach which comprises informal observation, clinical intuition and a reliance on intrapsychic dynamics has remained intact (Mischel, 1973).

Phenomenological Theories. In contrast to the instinct – based, conflict theories and the output oriented social behavior (social learning) theory of personality (which is discussed subsequently), proponents of a *humanistic* concept of man (such as Abraham Maslow, Carl Rogers, George Kelly and Gordon Allport) developed a more positive, free-will oriented interpretation for human behavior.[1] Maslow (1943) emphasized this aspect when he stated "the general point of view to which one must come in the study of personality . . . is holistic rather than atomistic, functional rather than taxonomic, dynamic rather than static, dynamic rather than causal, purposive rather than simple-mechanical."

In Maslow's theoretical approach, five levels of a need hierarchy were proposed as underlying human behavior: *physiological needs* (which are the most basic needs and include hunger, thirst, sleep, sex); *safety needs* (which correspond to emotional and physical well being and safety); *love needs* (which include the need for affection and affiliation); *esteem needs* (including achievement, power and status); and, *the need for self actualization* (which reflects self-fulfillment). This is illustrated in Figure 2.3. In

1. While the humanistic view does not reject unconscious motivation or the effects of conditioning, an emphasis is placed upon intellect and reasoning (i.e., free will) in contrast to conditioning and/or the instinctual drive for pleasure and gratification.

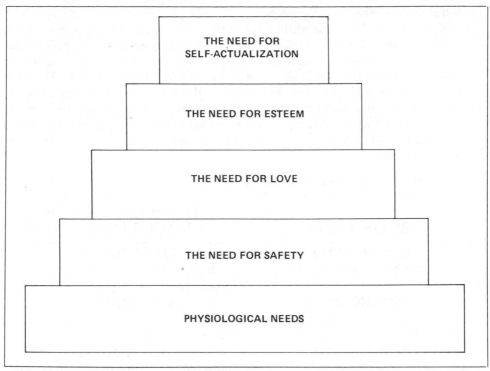

Figure 2.3. Maslow's (1943) hierarchy of needs.

this hierarchy, prior to the safety needs assuming importance, the physiological needs must be satisfied; prior to love needs assuming importance, the safety needs must be satisfied and so on.

While the various phenomenological theories of personality are diverse, they do universally stress the concept of self-change, growth and maturation toward a self-fulfillment. This is well illustrated in Rogers' (1964) theory on the development of a valuing process (i.e., behavior in which preference is shown for one object or objective rather than another). Rogers initially proposed that there is a change in value orientations from infancy to adulthood and from adulthood to a state of psychological maturity. He then outlined a sequential series of propositions: namely that:

> . . . there is an organismic basis for the valuing process within the human individual; that this valuing process is effective to the degree that the individual is open to his experiencing; that in persons relatively open to their experiencing there is an important commonality or universality of value directions; that these directions make for the constructive enhancement of the individual and his community, and for the survival and evolution of his species [Rogers, 1964].

Although the phenomenological theories of behavior have had some appeal (undoubtedly due in part to their humanistic orientation), a major limitation has been the inability to test the theories via a strong scientific approach.

Constitutional (Body Type) Theories. A third approach which could be discussed because of its impact upon sport and physical activity is the *constitutional* or *body type theory* of personality which is usually associated with Stanley Kretschmer and William Sheldon. The underlying rationale adopted is that individuals possess specific physiques or body types, largely genetically determined, which serve as a predisposing factor toward behavioral consistency.

In Sheldon's (1942) schema which is the most familiar, three primary dimensions of body structure were isolated: *mesomorphy* (muscularity), *endomorphy* (roundness, fatness) and *ectomorphy* (linearity, thinness). Each of these dimensions was associated[2] with a specific personality type or temperament (see Table 2.1). Thus, the personality type associated with mesomorphy, *somatotonia*, was characterized by the love of adventure, risk taking and the need for violent physical activity. *Visceratonia*, the type associated with endomorphy was characterized by affection, love of comfort and sociability. And, *cerebrotonia* was related to tenseness, social restraint, inhibition and social isolation.

Table 2.1. Sheldon's body type schema for personality.

BODY TYPE	TEMPERAMENT OR PERSONALITY FACTOR
ECTOMORPHY	**CEREBROTONIA**
Characterized by linearity, tallness, leanness	Characterized by tenseness, social restraint, inhibition, social isolation
ENDOMORPHY	**VISCEROTONIA**
Characterized by plumpness, fatness, roundness	Characterized by affection, love of comfort, sociability
MESOMORPHY	**SOMATOTONIA**
Characterized by muscularity	Characterized by love of adventure, risk taking, the need for violent physical activity

The body type theories have never received a wide acceptance. As even Sheldon noted, "to try to explain a personality from a constitutional pattern alone is as futile as to attempt such an explanation solely from the life history of the individual" (Sheldon and Stevens, 1942).

Trait Theories. The theoretical approach having the strongest impact upon personality research in psychology has been the *trait* view. This impact has also extended to the social psychology of sport and physical activity since as Carron (1975) pointed out "researchers in physical education engaged in a search for identifiable personality characteristics in athletics have implicitly or explicitly supported the trait view . . ."

The personality trait itself has been perceived in a variety of ways. For example, Allport (1964) referred to it as "a neuropsychic structure having the capacity to render many stimuli functionally equivalent and to initiate and guide equivalent (meaningfully consistent) forms of adaptive and expressive behavior."

While Guilford's (1959) view of the trait is substantially in agreement with Allport's, he did emphasize the need for a broad perspective and did caution against the inherent limitations which exist in a trait description. That is, he pointed out that since the study of personality is the study of individual differences, inevitably an analytical process must be undertaken. However, as a result of the analytical process, individuals must be characterized by their properties (e.g., "tall", "vigorous", "sociable",

2. Although Sheldon reported rather high correlations between his physical and temperament dimensions (i.e., .79, .83 and .82 between endomorphy/viscerotonia, ectomorphy/cerebrotonia and mesomorphy/somatotonia respectively), subsequent research has not replicated these findings.

"thin") and "properties are abstractions that come by way of analysis from totalities . . . no one can therefore truthfully claim that his abstractions, however numerous have exhausted the object or ever completely account for it" (Guilford, 1959). Within the restrictions and scope of this framework, Guilford then suggested that "*a trait is any distinguishable, relatively enduring way in which one individual differs from others.* 'Trait' is then a very broad, general term."

An essential factor, however, is that no matter how the trait is defined, a universal aspect of all definitions is the connotation of *enduring tendency.* Within trait theory, a fundamental assumption is that the trait is a general, underlying cause or dispositional tendency which contributes to behavioral *consistency* and *generalizability* — that is, the trait contributes to a stability in behavior both over time and across a variety of different situations. As a logical extension of this fundamental assumption, trait theorists have attempted to isolate and identify the basic personality traits, dimensions or factors which account for behavioral consistency.

Although the actual process of isolating traits is both complex and laborious, the basic concept is relatively straight-forward. Initially, an extensive cross-section of characteristic behavioral situations are developed and compiled as items within an inventory or questionnaire. (As an example, one of the items of an anxiety questionnaire might be "I am nervous in crowds.") This inventory is then given to representative or random samples of the ultimate target population (e.g., "athletes," "college students," "children," "psychotics") and each individual in that sample responds to the various items, indicating the degree (e.g., "true versus false" or "very much so versus not at all") to which the behavior is characteristic of him or her. Through factor analysis of the responses, clusters or groupings of those specific items (behaviors) which are most highly interrelated are then obtained. These clusters, groupings, factors or traits are usually given a name or label which intuitively summarizes the specific class of behaviors.[3]

J. P. Guilford, Raymond Cattell, Gordon Allport, Hans Eysenck and, more recently, Douglas Jackson, have all made significant contributions to the trait theory of personality. And, Cattell's *Sixteen Personality Factor Questionnaire (16PF)* has been the most extensively used in sport and physical activity research.

In Cattell's approach, personality is viewed as comprising a hierarchical structure of traits. Thus, initially, through factor analysis, 171 *source traits* were identified. These source traits, considered as a totality, were viewed as contributing to the uniqueness of individual behavior. That is, the relative degree to which each individual possesses each of the various source traits accounts for his/her unique pattern of behavior.

In turn, the 171 source traits fall within 16 categories, factors or clusters called *surface traits.* These are listed in Table 2.2 While individual behavior itself is a result of the source trait, the *overt* manifestations of behavior are a result of the interactions of the various surface traits.

Cattell also isolated a number of second-order and third-order factors. The surface

---

3. It might be evident that since each trait theorist constructing an inventory of personality develops and analyzes independent lists of behaviors, the specific clusters of items obtained through factor analysis would be different. Thus, even though two inventories contain a trait with a highly similar or identical label, it would be incorrect to assume equivalency in factors across different personality tests. For example, while the *Edwards Personal Preference Schedule* and Cattell's *Sixteen Personality Factor Questionnaire* both include a trait of *dominance,* the construct is not identical.

Table 2.2 Cattell's primary and second order factors from the 16 PF.

PRIMARY FACTORS			SECOND ORDER FACTORS	COMPONENTS@
A	Warm, Sociable	vs Aloof, stiff	High Anxiety/	C, H, L, O, Q3, Q4
B	Mentally Bright	vs Mentally Dull	Low Anxiety	
C	Mature, Calm	vs Emotional, Immature		
E	Aggressive, Competitive	vs Mild, Submissive	Extraversion/	A, E, F, H, Q2
F	Enthusiastic	vs Prudent, Serious	Introversion	
G	Conscientious	vs Casual, Undependable		
H	Adventurous	vs Shy, Timid	Tough Poise/Tender	A, C, E, F, I, M, N
I	Sensitive, Effeminate	vs Tough, Realistic	Minded	
L	Suspecting, Jealous	vs Accepting, Adaptable	Emotionality	
M	Imaginative	vs Practical		
N	Sophisticated	vs Simple, Unpretentious	Independence/	A, E, G, M, O, Q2
O	Timid, Insecure	vs Confident, Self-Secure	Subduedness	A, E, G, M, O, Q2
Q1	Radicalism	vs Conservatism		
Q2	Self-Sufficiency	vs Group Adherence		
Q3	Uncontrolled, Lax	vs Controlled		
Q4	Phlegmatic, Relaxed	vs Tense, Excitable		

@The components or primary factors which comprise the second order factors.

traits which contribute to the most interesting of the second-order factors (i.e., interesting from the perspective of sport and physical activity involvement) are also outlined in Table 2.2.

In Chapter 1, it was pointed out that behavior has traditionally been viewed as a product of the person and the environment (see Figure 1.6) or

$$B = f (P,E)$$

While trait theory generally[4] and Cattell's approach particularly does take into account the importance of environmental factors, a major focus is on the *person* dimension; an attempt is made to account for the broad underlying dimensions (traits) which are reflected in the similarities and differences in individual behavior.

Social Learning (Social Behavior) Theories. In contrast to trait theory, social learning theory "is highly committed to the importance of the psychological situation. It is emphasized that behavior varies as the situation does" (Rotter, Chance and Phares, 1972). Thus, in the social learning approach to personality, the focus is on actual behavior itself and the environmental conditions and situations which influence it; not on theoretical constructs (e.g., intervening variables such as traits, instincts or drives) which must be *inferred* from behavior.

---

4. The emphasis placed upon environment factors is evident in the writing of Allport (1937), one of the earliest major contributors to trait theory. For example, he cautioned that no single trait—nor all traits together will determine behavior all by themselves.

Early pioneers in the behavioral school include Ivan Pavlov, the Russian physiologist, John Watson and Clark Hull while more recently, B. F. Skinner, Albert Bandura and Walter Mischel have made significant contributions.

Although the earliest theoretical approaches in behaviorism were rather simplistic — almost mechanistic in orientation (i.e., a basic S-R operant conditioning approach) — more recently, the emphasis has been on learning, learning as a consequence of reinforced behavior. For example, Mischel (1968, 1973) pointed out that social behaviors result in positive consequences in some instances, negative in others. Since each individual has a unique, individualistic social learning background, the interpretations and meanings attached to specific stimuli or events will be individualistic. Thus, the specificity evident in behavioral dimensions is a reflection of man's discriminativeness.

Mischel attributed individual differences in behavior to individual differences in specific response potentials which are activated by specific stimulus situations. Five categories of *person variables* which contribute to the individual differences in response potential were identified by Mischel. These person variables were an attempt to account for the fact that different individuals differ in: *construction competencies*

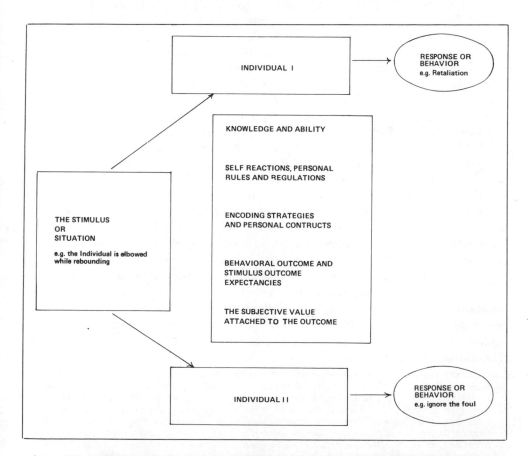

Figure 2.4. The influence of *person variables* (Mischel, 1973) upon behavior. As a result of the individual differences in these person variables, different responses could occur to the same stimulus or situation.

(what a person knows and is capable of doing); *encoding strategies and personal constructs* (how individuals perceive themselves and label or encode the stimulus events of the situation); *behavioral outcome and stimulus outcome expectancies* (the expectancies individuals associate with particular responses or stimuli; *subjective stimulus values* (the subjective values that are attached to the outcomes of the situation); and, *self-regulatory systems* (the self reactions, personal rules and regulations brought to the situation). In Figure 2.4, an example is presented in which two individuals, faced with the same stimulus/situation, could behave differently because of differences in these person variables.

In a further discussion, which seems particularly relevant to sport and physical activity, Mischel (1973) noted that if the "psychological nature" of the situation was sufficiently powerful or significant, the wide individual differences in these person variables would be reduced and a behavioral consistency across individuals might be expected. In an extension of this point to athletics, Carron (1975) noted that "competitive athletics contains numerous instances where the 'psychological situation' or 'treatment' is sufficiently powerful, where the stimulus event is of sufficient magnitude that relatively consistent behavior is displayed by a total group . . . [for example] . . . the range of individual differences in competitiveness is reduced and heightened competitiveness is demonstrated universally in all football players when their one-on-one encounter is isolated and viewed by all coaches and teammates."

If the Lewinian formula, $B = f (P,E)$, is examined in light of the social learning/social behavior theory of personality, it is evident that while P, the person dimension is taken into account, the predominant emphasis is placed upon situations, the environmental factor E, as the significant predisposing factor for behavior.

Interactionist Model for Behavior. In an attempt to resolve the issue of whether situations or persons were of the greatest relative importance insofar as determining behavior, Endler and Hunt (1962, 1966, 1968, 1973) developed a series of self report inventories (e.g., the *S-R Inventory of Anxiousness*). These inventories provided the subject with a number of different situations (e.g., "You are about to take a final examination for a course in which your status is doubtful"). With each of these situations, the subject was provided with a number of possible modes of response (e.g., "hands trembling," "can't concentrate"). As a result, Endler and Hunt were able to separate the relative impact of the *situation*, the *person*, the *mode of responses* and the *interactions* between each of these upon the variability in test responses (behavior). It was observed that neither the individual differences (the person) nor the situations contributed in a major way to the variability in the anxiousness responses (see Figure 2.5). Rather, the interactions between these as well as their interactions with the mode of response contributed nearly one-third of the variability in behavior. The authors concluded that:

> . . . the finding that neither individual differences across situations or situations per se contribute heavily to the total variance lends confirmation to the conclusion . . . that this issue of the relative importance of subjects and situations is but a pseudo-issue . . . If such findings hold for such other common traits as hostility and honesty, they have implications for personality description in general. First, they imply that attempting to devise better instruments with which to measure individual differences in traits across situations is doomed to the failure epitomized by validity coefficients ranging from .2 to .25. Second, they imply that it may be possible to save some of the loss of validity for personality description in general where specifying particular situations may be unfeasible . . . it should be feasible to move in a fruitful direction by categorizing both situations and the response-indicators of the traits in question [Endler and Hunt, 1973].

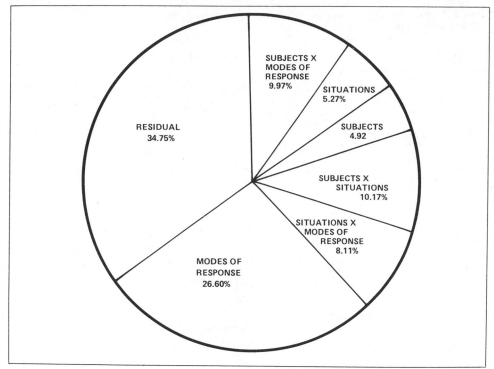

Figure 2.5 The partition of total response variability (Adapted from Endler and Hunt, 1973). The percentages reflect median values for 21 samples of subjects tested on five forms of the S-R Inventory of Anxiousness.

Anxiety has been the characteristic behavior focused upon by Endler and Hunt. It is now necessary to determine whether these same general findings also apply to other characteristics or traits.

PERSONALITY AND SPORT AND PHYSICAL ACTIVITY

INTRODUCTION

In what was possibly the earliest comprehensive, definitive paper in the area of personality and athletics, Kroll (1970) listed five options which comprise the possibilities for a relationship between the personality dimension and the dimension of sport and physical activity (see Table 2.3). The first was a *common preliminary core alternative* which reflects the situation in which there may be a set of personality characteristics which motivate individuals to select and participate in specific sports. A popular stereotype which reflects this alternative is that extraverts select team sports while introverts show a preference for individual sports. Thus, those individuals with the requisite personality characteristics would select a sport while those individuals lacking these charactristics would not.

The *modification and attrition alternative* underscores the fact that while there may be no characteristic pattern or personality type which enhances initial entry into a

Table 2.3. Models for the possible relationship of personality to involvement in sport and physical activity (Kroll, 1970).

MODEL	DESCRIPTION
Common Preliminary Core	Those individuals with specific personality traits select and participate in specific sports
Modification and Attrition	No common personality characteristics initially but through modification and attrition, only those individuals with suitable characteristics persist
Common Initial Interests/ Dissimilar Final Interests	There is a common personality pattern among beginners but through participation and attrition, veterans possess dissimilar personality characteristics
Neophytes Opposite to Veterans	Veterans in a sport possess personality traits which are completely opposite to rookies
No Relationship	Personality is unrelated to involvement in sport and physical activity.

sport, either by modification of the existing personality or through the attrition of inappropriate personality patterns, only those individuals possessing a suitable pattern would persist and achieve success. In this alternative, sport beginners would be dissimilar in personality profiles but veterans would be similar. Thus, we might assume that as a result of their experiences, all elite race drivers as a group would eventually demonstrate uniformly high levels of toughmindedness.

A third possibility is the *common initial interests/dissimilar final interests alternative*. This alternative takes into account the possibility that there may be a common personality pattern among beginners but as a result of participation and attrition, veterans possess dissimilar and nondiscriminant personality patterns. A situation which highlights this point is where all neophyte karate participants might exhibit high aggressiveness, a characteristic which is neither uniformly present nor absent in accomplished veterans.

In the *neophytes opposite to veterans alternative,* Kroll takes into account the possibility that performance could result in dramatic changes in personality characteristics of an individual. "Under this scheme the presence of certain traits in novice participants could indicate that just the opposite traits were required for success and characteristic of veteran performers" (Kroll, 1970). A situation which illustrates this is one in which all athletes attracted to a particular sport are introverted. However, because of the specific task demands or performance requirements of that sport (e.g., high teamwork and interaction), all veterans would come to reflect the same trait of extraversion.

The final possibility is a *no relationship alternative;* neither beginners nor veterans possess discriminant personality characteristics. This alternative recognizes the possibility that there may not be a relationship between the personality dimension and sport and physical activity.

PRESENT STATUS?

In the social psychology of sport, the question of whether personality and athletics are related has been a controversial issue with Kroll's first and second alternative representing one polar view with the fifth alternative being the other. Morgan (1978) succinctly summed this up, noting that:

> . . . there are basically two personology camps in contemporary sport psychology, and the members of these two camps espouse either a credulous or a skeptical viewpoint concerning the prediction of athletic success from psychological data. The credulous psychologist would lead us to believe that psychological data are extremely useful in predicting success, whereas the skeptical would argue that psychological data are of little or no value whatsoever.

From a chronological point of view, the credulous viewpoint has had the earliest support in sport and physical activity. Kroll (1970) emphasized this point when he observed that "a basic premise of almost quasi-mystical potency for personality research in athletics is that athletes possess unique and definable personality attributes different from nonathletes. It is commonly held, moreover, that in addition to differentiation from nonathletes, athletes in one sport can be distinguished from athletes in another sport."

This credulous perspective has been rejected recently in favor of a skeptical viewpoint by a number of researchers. Some representative viewpoints are as follows:

> . . . it is nearly impossible to find any consistent results in the literature. Few investigators report reliable evidence and those that do are of questionable validity. Unfortunately, after years of study we know little about personality as related to sport [Martens, 1975].

> . . . any honest appraisal of the work in athletic personality must conclude that the picture is unsettled. Only clinical interpretations have been able to come up with anything approaching a definite conclusion while studies with objective measurements of personality continue to offer conflicting results [Kroll, 1970].

> . . . after all the years of research no clear findings are available. Physical education and sports personality researchers are not yet off the ground. It is evident that the investigative process must be restored in new directions, utilizing new techniques and designs, adopting theoretically sound bases . . . [Rushall, 1972].

> . . . the research in this area has largely been of the 'shot gun' variety. By that I mean that investigators grabbed the nearest and most convenient personality test, and the closest sport group, and with little or no theoretical basis for their selection fired into the air to see what they could bring down. It isn't surprising that firing into the air at different times and at different places, and using different ammunition, should result in different findings. In fact, it would be surprising if the results weren't contradictory and somewhat confusing [Ryan, 1968, quoted in Martens, 1975].

However, Morgan (1978), commenting upon the credulous-skeptical debate has rejected both perspectives as extreme. He argued that:

> . . . neither position is acceptable . . . success in athletics is dependent in part on selected psychological states and traits, but the relationship between various psychological measures and success is far from perfect.

As an alternative, a more positive, middle-of-the-road perspective was advanced. Since a text represents a general summary or *state of the union* presentation, it might be beneficial to examine both the positive and the skeptical perspectives and the factors which contributed to them.

A SKEPTICAL PERSPECTIVE

As indicated previously, a number of literature reviews, summaries and critiques have appeared in the 1970s. Many of these endorsed a skeptical or *no relationship* conclusion insofar as the relationship of personality to sport and physical activity is concerned. An overview of these skeptical summaries and critiques reveals that the conclusion of "no relationship" is based upon three main considerations (categories of factors). These are (1) the lack of consistent patterns or trends in research results; (2) the lack of utility of much of the research which has been carried out because of various limitations in the general research design; and (3) inadequacies in the different theoretical models advanced to account for personality.

LACK OF GENERALIZABILITY IN THE AVAILABLE RESEARCH

The difficulty of generalizing across a wide cross – section of studies is that as Hardman (1973) has observed:

> . . . research workers have used a wide variety of measurement techniques and it is not always possible to equate one directly with another. Cofer and Johnson (1960) draw attention to this point and Hardman (1968) gives some indication of the range of techniques in reporting studies using Cattell's 16 P.F. questionnaire, the California Personality Inventory, the Minnesota Multiphasic Inventory, the Maudsley Personality Inventory and the Bernreuter Personality Inventory. Difficulties arise from the fact that some of these instruments measure source traits while others measure surface traits and, in addition, some researchers have used projective and physiological techniques.

A more preferable approach is to compare the results from studies which have used the same personality test — but, even this approach is not without its limitations since there is no assurance that the samples tested are comparable, the methods used were identical and so on. In Table 2.4 a summary, which was compiled by Hardman (1973), is presented for 42 different athletic samples that were tested with Cattell's 16 P.F.[5]

Scores on the 16 P.F. are represented as *sten scores* — a standardized score on a 10-point scale which Cattell (1970) described as follows:

> . . . the conventional s-sten ('Standard-score-based sten') scale takes the raw score mean of the population as the central value, (which is, therefore, exactly midway between sten 5 and sten 6), and steps out one sten for each half standard deviation of raw score. Thus, the mean of the scale has the precise value of 5.5 stens. Any raw score falling between this mean (at 5.5) and a point one-half a standard deviation downward translates to a sten point of 5; and one falling correspondingly within the limits of a sten half a sigma upward of the mean point gets 6. Thus, the range of what we would essentially call 'average, normal' scores, namely a one-sigma range, centered on the mean, is represented by stens 5 and 6. Consequently only when we get to stens of 4 and 7 should we begin to think of a person as definitely 'departing from the average.'

There is no evidence of a consistent *athletic personality profile* in the data presented in Table 2.4. It is apparent that there is a wide range of sten score values for any personality trait across the various samples listed. *And, these values represent group means.* Thus, for example, within the sample of wrestlers tested by Kroll (1967), it might be expected that some heterogeneity would be evident in each of the different

5. The reader may wish to again refer to Table 2.2 where a term or brief description of each factor is presented.

Table 2.4. mean scores of criterion athletic groups on Catell's 16 PF Questionnaire (From Hardman, 1973). Reproduced with permission of the publisher.

PERSONALITY FACTOR	A	B	C	E	F	G	H	I	L	M	N	O	Q_1	Q_2	Q_3	Q_4	Anxiety	I/E
1. ATHLETICS																		
Heusner (1952)																		
i. 41 Olympic Athletes	56	6.0	7.6	78	6.4	8.9	7.5	6.5	4.7	5.6	5.0	3.3	4.9	5.1	5.9	6.1	4.2	7.9
Kane (1964)																		
ii. 23 British Olympic Athletes	5.1	8.6	5.9	4.6	6.5	4.0	4.5	6.4	5.1	6.0	4.7	5.8	6.3	5.8	5.8	6.0	5.7	5.1
Hardman (1968)																		
iii. 10 Club Athletes	7.2	7.2	4.1	6.4	7.0	4.7	5.2	6.1	7.1	5.9	5.6	6.1	5.0	5.4	4.2	6.5	6.8	6.8
2. CROSS COUNTRY																		
Hardman (1968)																		
i. 22 Top Class British Cross-Country Runners	5.6	8.2	4.5	6.1	5.8	4.9	4.2	6.5	6.2	5.7	4.1	6.6	6.2	6.3	5.4	6.4	6.7	5.2
Hardman (1968)																		
ii. 13 Club Cross-Country Runners	5.2	7.9	4.9	5.5	5.2	5.4	3.9	6.6	5.9	6.3	3.5	5.9	6.5	7.4	5.4	5.3	5.8	4.4
3. SWIMMING																		
Kane (1964)																		
i. 11 British Olympic Swimmers	5.0	8.3	4.6	5.2	7.0	4.4	4.6	5.6	5.7	4.7	4.7	6.5	4.7	6.6	5.5	6.5	6.5	5.4
Hardman (1968)																		
ii. 10 British Olympic Swimmers	5.8	8.4	5.0	7.3	7.3	3.4	6.2	5.1	6.8	5.5	4.3	5.6	6.0	4.6	5.2	5.8	5.9	8.0
Hardman (1968)																		
iii. 10 Club Swimmers	5.9	7.4	4.5	7.1	6.2	4.6	4.9	4.5	5.9	5.2	4.6	6.5	6.3	5.3	5.0	6.5	6.6	6.0
Hendry (1968)																		
iv. 126 British Swimmers	5.5	7.5	4.4	7.0	5.3	4.3	3.3	5.7	6.3	5.6	7.3	6.0	6.5	6.0	3.7	6.1	6.9	4.8
Rushall (1967)																		
v. 57 American Swimmers	5.5	6.2	5.5	6.5	6.1	5.4	5.7	5.2	5.9	6.3	5.2	5.7	5.9	5.5	4.7	5.8	5.7	6.1
4. GYMNASTICS																		
Hardman (1968)																		
i. 10 Top British Gymnasts	6.0	8.0	5.9	7.3	6.8	5.7	5.9	5.0	6.4	6.0	4.8	5.5	5.6	5.7	6.2	6.0	5.6	6.9
ii. 10 Club Standard Gymnasts	5.9	7.6	4.8	5.2	6.7	4.5	4.8	6.3	5.9	5.7	4.0	6.2	5.4	5.3	5.0	5.5	6.1	5.7
5. CLIMBING																		
Jackson (1967)																		
i. 10 Top Class British Climbers	4.5	8.5	5.2	7.8	6.4	3.6	4.4	6.4	6.5	6.9	3.9	6.5	6.5	7.5	4.5	7.1	7.1	5.5
Hardman (1968)																		
ii. 10 Club Standard Climbers	4.7	6.5	3.6	6.2	7.2	3.9	4.8	6.3	7.2	5.6	3.9	6.9	6.1	6.7	4.5	6.5	7.3	5.8
6. TENNIS																		
Jones (1968)																		
15 Champion Players	7.6	5.0	5.1	5.0	8.0	5.0	4.0	4.5	6.0	6.0	4.9	6.5	6.5	5.2	3.4	5.7	7.0	5.3
7. TABLE TENNIS																		
Whiting & Hendry (1969)																		
7 Internationals	6.0	6.0	4.3	5.1	6.4	4.0	4.7	4.7	7.4	5.7	5.3	5.6	6.1	6.1	4.7	6.4	6.6	5.3
8. RIFLE SHOOTING																		
Hardman (1968)																		
i. 10 Internationals	6.0	7.6	4.9	6.1	4.6	6.1	4.3	4.3	6.7	5.2	6.0	5.7	5.3	5.6	6.5	5.7	6.0	4.4
ii. 10 Club Riflemen	4.2	7.6	4.6	7.3	4.3	4.7	4.0	4.1	6.1	5.6	5.2	6.4	5.5	7.7	5.2	7.2	6.6	4.3
9. GOLF																		
Hardman (1968)																		
i. The British Walker Cup Team	6.3	8.0	4.5	5.1	5.7	4.0	4.4	6.0	5.4	6.1	4.2	6.5	5.4	6.2	4.3	6.5	6.6	5.8
ii. 10 Golfers (H'caps 10-18)	5.5	7.8	4.0	6.4	4.4	4.3	4.6	4.5	6.8	5.3	5.4	7.4	4.8	6.6	5.5	6.6	7.1	4.7
iii. 30 Golfers (H'cap 0-4)	6.3	—	4.5	7.3	5.8	7.6	6.0	3.9	6.3	6.0	6.0	5.5	6.3	6.2	6.8	5.5	5.6	6.5
iv. 30 Golfers (H'cap 13-16)	6.0	—	5.3	5.6	5.5	8.0	6.2	3.3	5.8	5.3	7.3	4.5	5.8	6.2	6.5	5.2	5.0	6.1
10. JUDO																		
Hardman (1968)																		
i. 10 Leading Scottish Players	6.1	6.4	3.8	6.1	6.6	3.3	4.1	6.2	7.0	5.8	3.5	7.6	5.3	5.7	3.8	7.3	7.9	5.6
ii. 10 Club Players	5.9	7.0	3.7	6.4	7.2	3.4	4.9	6.0	7.3	5.6	4.1	6.7	5.9	6.3	4.0	7.0	7.5	6.2
11. WRESTLING																		
Kroll (1967)																		
i. Superior Wrestlers	6.3	5.9	5.8	6.5	5.7	6.1	5.3	4.0	4.9	5.6	5.3	5.4	5.7	5.7	6.0	5.4	5.0	6.0
ii. Excellent Wrestlers	5.8	5.8	5.6	6.3	6.3	5.4	5.5	4.2	6.3	5.6	5.1	6.2	5.4	5.2	5.1	6.3	5.8	6.3
iii. Average Wrestlers	5.6	5.8	5.6	5.3	5.4	5.7	4.6	4.3	5.7	5.5	4.4	5.7	4.7	5.7	5.6	5.7	5.8	5.2
12. KARATE																		
Kroll & Carlson (1967)																		
i. Advanced Players	5.6	6.1	5.4	5.8	6.1	6.0	5.6	6.0	6.3	5.8	5.7	5.8	6.4	6.3	5.8	6.5	6.2	6.0
ii. Intermediate Players	5.0	6.1	5.7	5.8	5.3	6.7	5.2	5.2	4.8	5.8	5.5	5.3	6.0	7.0	5.7	5.7	5.3	4.9
iii. Elementary Players	6.0	6.2	5.7	5.9	5.3	6.4	5.4	5.8	5.3	6.2	5.8	5.8	5.8	6.5	6.0	6.0	5.4	5.1
13. ASSOCIATION FOOTBALL																		
Kane (1966)																		
i. Professionals	6.8	6.1	5.1	5.8	5.3	4.2	5.2	5.8	6.1	6.5	5.9	6.5	6.0	5.1	6.0	6.0	6.3	5.6
ii. Young Professionals	5.8	5.7	6.0	4.0	6.3	5.1	5.8	5.4	5.2	5.0	5.9	5.5	4.8	5.8	6.7	4.7	4.5	5.5
iii. Amateur Internationals	5.7	7.8	4.5	5.7	6.7	4.8	3.6	5.4	6.0	4.5	5.0	6.0	5.8	5.8	5.4	6.0	5.4	5.6
iv. 13 Club Players	5.7	6.5	4.0	6.2	7.3	4.3	5.8	4.5	5.3	5.6	3.7	6.9	5.5	4.9	3.6	7.3	7.1	6.8
14. RUGBY FOOTBALL																		
Hardman (1968)																		
i. The England XV	6.7	7.7	4.6	6.1	6.7	4.0	4.5	6.1	6.4	5.6	4.5	5.6	5.8	5.7	4.2	6.3	6.5	5.9
ii. 17 Club Players	5.4	8.4	3.5	6.5	7.4	3.6	5.5	5.7	6.9	6.2	3.9	6.7	4.9	5.4	4.1	7.1	7.2	6.8
Sinclair (1968)																		
iii. 32 Internationals	6.4	—	6.0	6.7	5.9	6.7	6.4	3.8	5.7	5.6	6.0	4.3	5.6	5.5	6.5	4.5	4.8	6.5
iv. 48 Country & 1st Class	6.8	—	5.5	6.8	7.3	6.6	6.7	3.7	6.3	6.1	7.5	3.6	6.7	5.4	7.5	4.7	4.0	7.3
v. 52 Junior Club Players	4.3	—	5.8	6.9	7.1	5.6	6.4	3.5	7.1	5.8	7.4	4.4	6.5	6.6	6.2	5.3	4.9	6.4
15. AMERICAN FOOTBALL																		
Kroll & Petersen (1965)																		
139 Players	6.1	5.8	6.0	5.9	5.6	5.6	5.3	5.5	6.0	5.3	5.2	5.7	5.2	5.6	5.4	6.0	6.0	5.8
16. BASKETBALL																		
Hardman (1968)																		
i. The England Squad	5.9	8.1	5.1	6.5	6.5	5.2	5.1	5.5	5.6	6.1	4.3	6.5	6.1	4.9	5.4	6.3	6.3	6.5
ii. 17 Club Players	5.6	7.5	4.2	5.3	6.2	3.9	4.2	5.5	5.4	6.4	3.4	7.6	5.5	5.2	4.7	7.3	7.5	5.1

traits assessed — there would be individual differences in personality since each wrestler would not have an identical score on each of the different traits.

The extent to which intragroup variability does exist was discussed by Hardman (1973). He pointed out that there is a:

> . . . danger inherent in trying to establish an athletic personality type . . . through the use of mean scores. Only rarely does a researcher give the range of scores obtained in an investigation. Usually the mean score is given which can lead the reader to the conclusion that the group is a homogeneous one. Hardman (1968) and Whiting & Hendry (1969) have shown that this is not so, and that some members of athletic groups seem to succeed despite a wide divergence from the group mean.

In summary, it is reasonable to assume that in addition to the marked intergroup heterogeneity in personality, there is also a large degree of intragroup heterogeneity.

Table 2.5 clearly illustrates the degree to which intergroup heterogeneity is present in the data summarized by Hardman. The range reflects the range of group mean values reported for the 42 samples presented in Table 2.4. In addition, the number of group means which were either in the average range (i.e., a sten score between 5.00 and 6.00), above average (i.e., a sten score greater than 6.00) or below average (i.e., a sten score less than 5.00) is also indicated.

The results for Factor G which reflects conscientious, persistent on one end of the continuum versus casual, undependable on the other end, serve as a useful illustration. The range of sten score values for the 42 samples was 3.3 to 8.0 with 11 studies

Table 2.5. Overview of the 16PF results from 42 athletic samples (Adapted from Hardman, 1973).@

FACTOR	RANGE	AVERAGE	ABOVE AVERAGE	BELOW AVERAGE
A	4.2-7.6	27	11	4
B	5.0-8.6	8	29	0
C	3.5-7.6	20	1	21
E	4.0-7.8	16	24	2
F	4.3-8.0	12	27	3
G	3.3-8.0	11	8	23
H	3.3-7.5	15	6	21
I	3.3-6.6	17	10	15
L	4.7-7.4	18	21	3
M	4.5-6.9	30	10	2
N	3.4-8.0	17	5	20
O	3.3-7.6	18	19	5
Q_1	4.7-6.7	22	14	6
Q_2	4.6-7.7	23	16	3
Q_3	3.4-7.5	20	8	14
Q_4	4.5-7.3	18	21	3
Anxiety	4.0-7.9	15	22	5
Introversion/ Extroversion	4.3-8.0	21	15	6

@The designation average represents a sten score value between 5.0 and 6.0 while above average is>6.0 and below average is < 5.0.

reporting results in the average range, 8 above average and 23 below average. Thus, the studies in which these three dramatically different classes of findings were obtained would be characterized by three quite different types of conclusions: namely,

(1) athletes do not differ from the general population on the personality disposition characterized by conscientiousness, persistence or casualness, lack of dependability,

versus

(2) athletes are characterized by a high degree of conscientiousness, persistence, dependability,

versus

(3) athletes are characterized by a high degree of casualness, undependability.

The one primary source trait[6] which did show a consistent pattern across all samples of Table 2.5 was *intelligence* (Factor B). In all 37 samples in which this factor was assessed, the sten score obtained was either in the average or above average range. Hardman (1973) observed that "whatever the reason, present results would indicate that the unintelligent do not choose organized sport as a form of recreation at adult level." Thus, in summary, with the exception of the trait of intelligence, no evidence of a general trend is evident in the literature summarized by Table 2.4.

LIMITATIONS IN THE RESEARCH DESIGNS IN SPORT PERSONALITY RESEARCH

The second major consideration or class of factors contributing to the skeptical perspective concerns the lack of utility of much of the previous research (see Table 2.6). This lack of utility arises from problems in various aspects of the general research design of some personality research — in the *planning, testing, analysis* and *interpretative stages.*

Martens (1975) referred to these as *methodological* and *interpretative* problems; Rushall (1975), as *methodological* and *conceptual* errors. Rushall stated that if the studies with conceptual and methodological errors were ignored/removed from further consideration, this procedure would eliminate the majority of published work so that the small number of remaining studies would not be sufficient to permit generalization.

The Planning Stage. Four types of problems have been associated with the planning/preparation phase of a research project in the area of personality. One of these was referred to by Rushall (1975) under the term *inbreeding* and two prevalent problems were listed. One of these was that many summary articles and bibliographies only include those studies which support a conclusion that personality and sport are interwoven while the second was that the bibliographies of successive research articles are principally repetitious. That is, studies in which positive findings were reported are cited while other studies are ignored. While this is undoubtedly not conscious or deliberate, the result is that a pattern of consistency is often suggested which is not supported by all of the available literature.

A third problem in the planning or preparation stage could be referred to as the *popularizing of findings.* The general public is usually impatient and unsatisfied with the scientist's attempts to qualify his findings. There are strong pressures to produce an

6. The second order traits are discussed subsequently (see p. 37-39).

Table 2.6. Limitations in the research design aspect of sport personality research.

STAGE IN THE RESEARCH PROCESS	PROBLEM-LIMITATION
PLANNING	**INBREEDING** a) Reviews highlight positive findings b) Positive findings exclusively, repeatedly cited **POPULARIZING OF FINDINGS** **SUMMARIES ARE** **NONCRITICAL PRESENTATIONS**
PROCEDURE	**SUBJECTS** a) Classification of subjects inadequate b) Random sampling ignored **DEPENDENT MEASURES** a) Inappropriate use of inventories b) Use of single assessments c) Clinical assessments lack reliability and validity
ANALYSIS	**STATISTICAL ANALYSES** a) Use of multiple t tests vs. analysis of variance or discriminant function analysis b) Use of univariate vs. multivariate analysis
INTERPRETATION	**MISPLACED SOPHISTICATION** **CAUSATION INFERENCES FROM** **CORRELATIONAL DATA** **POSITIVISM**

overview or summary statement and the summary statement "we don't know" is not typically suitable. Further, it has very little commercial value for books or magazine articles. Thus; it is often easier to reconcile conflicting results, trends and so on with a positive conclusion emanating from one or two isolated studies. This possibility may have been the case in sports personality.

A fourth, somewhat related point is that many reviews have been *noncritical summaries;* the presentation of the research completed to that date. "Reviewers must be aware that published research is not necessarily infallible or valid. Conscientious screening of reports may reduce the perpetuation of erroneous postulations" (Rushall, 1975).

The Procedure Stage. Within the actual studies themselves, there have been methodological problems which fall within two broad categories: *subjects* and the *dependent measures* (Martens, 1975; Morgan, 1972; Rushall, 1975). The *classification* schemes adopted and the *sampling* procedures utilized are two problems which lie within the subjects category.

The *classification* problem has been one of the most frequently listed limitations of sport personality research. Martens (1975) termed it the "inability to clearly operationalize important variables." Essentially, this issue revolves around the question of what is an athlete, a question which may be as fundamental (and as perplexing) as the question of what is sport (e.g., are the Sunday jogger, the senior citizen lawn bowler, the high school basketball player, the professional race driver, etc. all athletes?) but also could include the questions of the degree of affiliation required (e.g., should the individual who practices with a team but is not sufficiently skilled to compete be classified as an athlete?) and the multiple group participant (e.g., is the boy who boxes and plays basketball a team versus individual versus combative versus noncombative athlete?). It is obvious that "it is difficult to determine whether athletes differ on personality characteristics if an athlete cannot be clearly distinguished from a nonathlete" (Martens, 1975).

The *selection of the sample* has also been a problem since most researchers have opted for the convenience of using intact groups (e.g., a football team from one school) rather than obtaining a random sample of subjects from the population of interest (Morgan, 1972; Rushall, 1975). As a consequence, any conclusions must be restricted to the group tested, School X football players, rather than the general class or category (i.e., football players in general). However, an examination of specific studies and/or general literature reviews clearly reveals that this has not been the case; conclusions have been generalized repeatedly to the population.

The *dependent measures utilized* (the actual personality test) have represented another source of confusion in sport personality research (Martens, 1975; Morgan, 1972; Rushall, 1975). As one example, there is a problem relating to the appropriateness or *validity* of particular tests for the sport context. "Many scales that have been used for measuring normal athletes were not developed for measuring normality but for identifying abnormality" (Martens, 1975). The *Minnesota Multiphasic Personality Inventory (MMPI)* is probably the most readily apparent and frequently mentioned illustration of this point (Kroll, 1970; Rushall, 1975).

A second concern associated with the dependent measures utilized is that most studies have used a *single test* for assessing personality whereas a more reliable procedure would be to incorporate a number of different techniques in the assessment process (Rushall, 1975).

A third factor, the use of *clinical assessments* of personality as a means of predicting athletic success, was discussed by Martens (1975):

> . . . this problem is isolated to only a few individuals, Bruce Ogilvie and Thomas Tutko being the best known. Ogilvie and Tutko (for example, 1971) have received wide public acclaim through their assertion that they have been able to identify with the Athletic Motivation Inventory unique personality profiles of very successful athletes. On the basis of that assertion they offer for a fee to assess athletes' personalities and from this information to predict success as well as suggest to the coach ways to 'handle' an athlete so that the athlete may maximize his potential. This dubious enterprise is unsubstantiated by any reported data by Ogilvie and Tutko . . .

An inherent limitation in clinically derived conclusions is that these are based upon the insight and expertise of the clinician. Thus, questions which must be answered are the extent to which these insights are consistent over time — the issue of reliability — and, the extent to which these insights would be in agreement with those of other clinicians — the issue of *validity*. There is strong evidence that the insights characteristic of clinical interpretations are neither very valid nor reliable (e.g., see the discussion and results of Goldberg and Werts, 1966). As Cattell and Bucher (1968) warned "it is necessary to distinguish insight from fantasy by rigorous empirical methods."

The Analysis Stage. The *statistical analysis* used in sport personality research has also been questioned (Martens, 1975). Two of the more frequent statistical errors listed have been (1) the use of multiple *t* tests to examine for differences between the individual traits of an inventory rather than discriminant function analysis or analysis of variance and (2) the inappropriate use of univariate analyses rather than multivariate analyses. The rationale underlying both of these is similar and might be illustrated with a single example.

When the experimental method is used, the investigator usually examines the data using a statistical test. The basic purpose of this test is to determine within a particular level of confidence, certainty or probability whether the differences observed between the two groups tested are simply a function of chance (i.e., the two groups are to all intents and purposes identical) or are real and significant reflecting some underlying systematic effect or condition. Traditionally, the probability level used in research has been either .95 or .99 (out of 1.00). Therefore, the researcher who reaches the conclusion that there is a difference between the groups tested, does so within these probability limits. If an investigator compares athletes and nonathletes on the trait of aggression, analyzes the data statistically using a t – test and finds that the groups are different according to this test, it could then be concluded that "athletes are more aggressive than nonathletes." However, implicit in this conclusion is the addendum "I'm 95 percent sure that I'm right."

Therefore, it must be emphasized that since this conclusion is a probability statement, it could be in error. In the above example, there is a 5 percent chance that the conclusion emanating from the comparison of the aggression scores is in error. This possibility could be referred to as the *error rate per comparison* (Ryan, 1959). It would be identical for each of the different comparisons made within a study. In the above example, if the investigator had compared athletes and nonathletes on 100 different traits (admittedly, an extreme example, but one which does illustrate the problem) and used a t – test for each trait comparison, the error rate per comparison in each of the 100 individual instances would be the same as that within the aggression comparison.

However, there is second consideration which, in terms of scientific validity is even more important. That is, the total experiment is a package, a totality or unit which contains 100 conclusions concerning the differences between athletes and nonathletes. What degree of confidence is there in this totality; what is the probability that there are no errors of conclusion within the experiment as a whole? This degree of confidence or probability can be referred to as the *error rate per experiment* (Ryan, 1959). Since 100 comparisons were made in the athlete versus nonathlete study, it could be expected (it would be probable) that 5 would be in error; that the statistical test would support a conclusion that there is a real difference between the groups when, in fact, the differences obtained were simply chance. In short, if enough comparisons are carried out by an investigator, there is a good probability that some differences will be found.

However, it is possible statistically to reduce the likelihood of an incorrect conclusion in the experiment. Since the 100 comparisons conceivably could be completed in one analysis using discriminant function analysis or analysis of variance, only one comparison would be made in the study. Thus, the error rate per comparison and the error rate per experiment would be identical. And while the investigator's conclusion could still be in error, there would be a much lower probability that this would be the case.

The Interpretation Stage. Various reviewers have also queried the way in which the actual results of sport personality research have been interpreted (e.g., Fisher, 1974; Martens, 1975; Rushall, 1975). For example, one point which has been emphasized is what Fisher (1974) referred to as the *fallacy of misplaced sophistication*. While a difference between two groups could be statistically significant, this information might be of little practical value. That is, as was just pointed out in the previous section, a statistical test permits the investigator to conclude within some level of certainty or probability that the differences obtained are not simply a reflection of chance variation. But, "does it make much sense to state that the mean differences between aggression of athletes and nonathletes reached statistical significance at the .05 level, when the mean difference is extremely low?" (Fisher, 1974). A more critical factor is whether the differences obtained are of sufficient magnitude to be *practically useful*.

Another prevalent problem in the interpretation of sport personality research has been the tendency to infer *causation from correlational evidence* (Martens, 1975). Thus, if research evidence repeatedly showed that athletes were more dominant than nonathletes, there still would not be any basis for a conclusion that athletic experience enhances the development of the trait of dominance. The characteristic of dominance is present (associated) with athletic performance but it may be that only dominant individuals select or remain in sport and not that sport participation "caused" that dominance.

A final interpretative problem, *positivism* (Rushall, 1975), was mentioned earlier — the investigator as a result of preexperimental expectations may be more readily inclined to accept positive, supportive evidence at face value. Rushall (1975) has suggested that results supporting a conclusion that personality and sport participation are not related are either not published (or are not accepted since research journals do have a tendency to favor studies in which significant findings are obtained) or explained away as being a function of sampling error, control etc.

THEORETICAL ISSUES IN SPORT PERSONALITY RESEARCH

The third major consideration, the ongoing debate in psychology concerning the nature of personality and its assessment, has also had an impact upon sport personality research. Solely for purposes of organization (since these do not necessarily fall into independent, discrete classifications), the major concerns in this regard can be presented under three headings: *general personality theory, trait versus social learning interpretations of behavior* and *sport specific concerns*. These are summarized in Table 2.7.

General Personality Theory. In his discussion of the *Recurring dilemmas in personality assessment,* Holtzman (1964) pointed out that the most fundamental current problems affecting the development of a theory and technique of assessment for personality have been longstanding. He observed that "much of what I see as recurring dilemmas in personality assessment was recognized by Murray [in his classic publication 'Explorations in Personality'] although their manifestations take a different form today than 25 years ago." Six unresolved issues were listed by Holtzman.

In discussing the first issue which he referred to as *the meaning of personality,* Holtzman observed that the way in which personality is viewed (and assessed) depends upon the theoretical model endorsed by the investigator. So, for example, the view of personality which is held by a psychodynamic theorist such as Freud is markedly different than that held by a constitutional theorist such as Sheldon or a social learning theorist such as Skinner. And, even in those instances where in-

Table 2.7. Theoretical Concerns in Personality theory and assessment.

CATEGORY	ISSUE
General Personality Theory	The Meaning of Personality The Measurement of Personality The Separtion of Method from Personality Variance The Culture-Bound Nature of Assessment Procedures The Need for a Systematic, Comprehensive Empirically Linked Theory of Personality The Moral Dilemma of Personality Assessment
Trait vs. Social Learning Interpretations of Behavior	The divergent Perceptions Between Actor and Observer on the Cause of Behavior The issue of Reification The issue of Tautology The Empirical Limitation of Traits The Empirical Limitation of Situationism
Sport Specific Concerns	The Problem of Salience

vestigators subscribe to the same theoretical viewpoint, differences in conception and definition persist. An illustration of this latter point is that while many trait theorists include 'extraversion' as a dimension of personality and assess it via their inventories, the theoretical basis and characteristic behaviors thought to reflect it are different.

In his second point, Holtzman emphasized the *complexity of the individual personality* and the difficulty in understanding personality on the basis of a limited number of traits, situations, etc. He noted that:

> . . . if indeed it is true that a large amount of past and present information about an individual must be properly digested, together with detailed knowledge of the future circumstances likely to prevail, then it is highly unlikely we will ever reach a very satisfactory level of understanding in the sense of prediction from personality assessment. While I'm inclined to think we can still achieve efficient differential prediction of important things about a person by improving our techniques of assessment, I must admit that this belief is based largely upon faith rather than hard evidence.

In the third dilemma presented, the *difficulty in separating method variance from personality variance*, it was pointed out that the assessment of a personality trait is as much a function of the methods used as it is of the underlying theoretical construct. That is, individuals develop response sets (such as the tendency to acquiesce or social desirability) and these are confounded with the personality trait being assessed. If, for example, I'm taking a personality test, I may want to appear in a good light. Consequently, I might not answer the questions according to the way in which I actually behave but, rather, in a more idealistic or positive manner. The problem then facing the investigator is whether an underlying predisposition has been tapped or a transient mood or inclination.

A fourth concern is that the theories and techniques of assessment of personality may be *culture-bound* within western, industralized societies. If this is the case, and there is some evidence to support the suggestion, then the scope of personality psychology is very restricted.

In the fifth dilemma outlined, Holtzman questioned whether a *systematic, comprehensive personality theory* could ever be developed which is closely linked with empirical data. It was noted that personality theories are characterized by diversity, disagreement, lack of formal clarity and a lack of demonstrated empirical utility.

A sixth concern expressed was with the *moral dilemmas created* by the need for personality assessment. That is, there is a basic, fundamental conflict between an individual's right to maintain privacy and his personality without threat of intrusion versus the need for experimentation and investigation of that individual's personality in order to achieve an understanding of human behavior.

Trait versus Social Learning Interpretations of Behavior. The dilemmas presented by Holtzman (1964) reflect the larger, more philosophical concerns in general personality theory and assessment. Within the past 30 years the most predominant theoretical models, particularly insofar as an empirical analysis of behavior is concerned, have been the trait and social learning theories. A number of issues concerning these have been summarized and discussed by Fisher (1974), Kroll (1970) and Martens (1975) particularly.

A paradox, which lies at the very center of personality assessment, is that there are *divergent perceptions of the causes of behavior.* A respondent has the tendency to explain behavior in terms of situational determinants (e.g., "I hit him because . . .") while an observer has the tendency to explain that same behavior in trait terms (e.g., "he hit him because he's aggressive"). Fisher (1974) referred to this as a "misplaced concreteness" but possibly Jones and Nisbett (1972) summed the problem up best:

> . . . the actor's perceptions of the causes of his behavior are at variance with those held by outside observers. The actor's view of his behavior emphasizes the role of environmental conditions at the moment of action. The observer's view emphasizes the causal role of stable dispositional properties of the actor . . . there is a pervasive tendency for actors to attribute their actions to situational requirements, whereas observers tend to attribute the same action to stable personality dispositions.

While Jones and Nisbett were not discussing an athletic situation, their comment seems equally appropriate in this context. While coaches, spectators, journalists, etc. tend to use global, dispositional terms to describe an athlete's behavior (e.g., "coachable," "aggressive," "dominant,") the athlete, explaining the same behavior, does not. Rather, the athlete emphasizes "the situational constraints at the time of action — the role limitations, the conflicting pressures brought to bear, the alternative paths of action that were never open or that were momentarily closed — and to perceive his actions as having been inevitable" (Jones and Nisbett, 1972). Thus, depending upon whether you are the actor or the observer, you might subscribe to a social learning view of behavior — situational factors are critical — or to a trait view of behavior — person factors are critical.

Earlier in the chapter, a quote by Kroll (1970) was presented in which he commented upon the fact that a fundamental assumption "of almost quasi-mystical potency" is that athletes possess unique, identifiable personality attributes. Possibly this assumption has arisen in part from the natural tendency on the part of observers to interpret behavior in terms of stable dispositions?

Fisher (1974) listed two additional concerns which have been leveled against trait theory. He referred to these as the *fallacy of reification* and the *fallacy of tautology* and then used a quote by Janis, Mahl, Kagan and Holt (1969) which illustrated both:

> *. . . the key terms* personality *and* trait *have been defined in two apparently different ways: in terms of observable patterns of ongoing behavior and in terms of inferred dispositions to behave in pattern-ed ways. Though dispositions refer to future actions and sound somehow more intrinsic to a person than do behavior patterns, the difference is only verbal. To say that a person is disposed to be punc-tual or that he has been observed to show up promptly time after time amounts to the same thing. A trait, therefore, is a description, not an explanatory concept. The failure to grasp this point exposes us to dangers of two fallacies — that of* tautology *or thinking in circles, and that of* reification *. . . To say that a person is prompt because he has a trait of punctuality is an excellent example of a tautology in which what looks like an explanation adds nothing to the original observation.*

Possibly the most serious of the criticisms directed toward a trait theory explanation for behavior has been *empirical* — typically, the amount of variance accounted for by traits has been less than 15 percent. In short, traits, as global underlying dispositional tendencies have not been very effective as a means of explaining behavior.

A number of limitations are also present in the social learning theory of personality and Martens (1975), (in some cases drawing upon a review by Bowers, 1973), has summarized many of these. Many of the limitations have also had an *empirical* basis. For example, any studies in which an environmental condition has been manipulated and nonsignificant results have been outlined, are evidence against a social learning theory of behavior. The rationale for this is that a central assumption of social learning theory "is that individuals behave differently across situations and that behavior across subjects in similar situations is minimally different" (Martens, 1975). However, there is evidence that this is not the case; that behavior is not consistent within situations across subjects. When a statistical analysis is utilized, individual differences within the situa-tion are reflected in the error variance. Thus, if this error variance is relatively large and nonsignificant results accrue, this is potential evidence that individual behavior is not consistent across situations.

A second empirical example is more direct. It was pointed out earlier that Endler and Hunt (1973) regard the question of the relative importance of persons versus situations as largely a pseudo-issue since both account for only a minimal (and highly similar) portion of the response variance — usually under 15 percent. The variance unaccounted for is typically a major component of the total variance. Kroll (1970), in discussing this fact, observed that *"it may be time for athletic personality researchers to recognize that the unaccounted for variance characteristic in general personality research constitutes a more important challenge than the duplication of accounted for variance."*

Sport Specific Concerns. A theoretical problem with particular application for sport and physical activity is the question of *salience* (Fisher, 1974; Kroll, 1970; Rushall, 1975) — the applicability of general personality assessment techniques for sport and physical activity. Many of the dispositions (traits) assessed in general per-sonality inventories may not be pertinent to an athletic context. As Fisher (1974) pointed out:

> *. . . of course correlations are low when behaviors formulated in some rather innocuous, uninvolving situations are contrasted with behaviors formulated in salient situations . . . some of the questions on the paper-and-pencil personality inventories are not tapping salient areas of the individual's behavior. When one then compares or attempts to predict future sport behavior from these inven-tories, what chance for success is there?*

"We have, in effect, gone fishing for minnows with a nomological net designed for whales and have no right to complain about the poor catch." (Kroll, 1970).

A POSITIVE PERSPECTIVE

Primarily in response to the growing skepticism in sport psychology, a more positive perspective concerning the general trait model of personality and the relationship of personality to sport and physical activity was advanced by both Morgan (1978) and Kane (1978). Neither Kane nor Morgan endorsed what Morgan referred to as the credulous viewpoint — that personality data are extremely valuable in predicting success in athletics. However, both questioned the validity of an exreme skeptical viewpoint — that there is no relationship between the personality dimension and sport and physical activity. As was pointed out previously, Morgan argued that "neither the credulous nor the skeptical arguments are scientifically defensible." And, in fact, it does appear that a reasonable case can be made for a more positive perspective if some of the methodological limitations (which are summarized in Table 2.6) are taken into consideration.

METHODOLOGICAL CONCERNS

It was pointed out in the discussions of the "skeptical perspective" that Rushall (1975) suggested that if the studies with methodological and conceptual errors were removed, this would eliminate the majority of published work. And, as a result, the small number of studies remaining would not be sufficient to permit generalizations.

However, it might be argued that this same rationale could be used in support of a positive perspective. There is the axiom "the difference between an optimist and a pessimist is that the former considers the glass *half-full* while the latter views it as *half-empty*." Thus, if the methodological limitations negate the possibility of concluding that "there is a relationship," they also negate the possibility of concluding that "there is no relationship." In short, additional, more scientifically rigorous investigation is necessary. (One study which satisfies this criterion — a comprehensive, well designed, well analyzed investigation reported by Schurr, Ashley and Joy (1977) — did reveal some clear relationships between the personality dimension and the sport dimension. That study is discussed in detail in a subsequent part of this chapter.)

Morgan (1978) has listed *response distortion* as a possible methodological consideration which has not been controlled and which might have contributed to the skeptical perspective:

> . . . it is quite conceivable that groups of Ss differing in physical ability may not differ on selected psychological traits simply because of response distortion. The transparent nature of questions contained on most inventories makes this a clear possibility, and this may represent the primary basis for the skeptical position. (Morgan, 1978)

One instance of response distortion was illustrated (see Figure 2.6). Subjects were given the scale of Speilberger's State-Trait Anxiety Inventory (STAI) and instructed to "fake good" or "fake bad."

It is apparent that these instructions had a major impact upon the nature of the results obtained. Whether response distortion has been a factor in sport personality research (causing athletes to respond in *stereotypic, good, bad,* or *random* ways) is, of course, impossible to evaluate at this point.

Another possible reason for the failure to find a relationship between physical performance and personality is the tendency for researchers to concentrate on primary

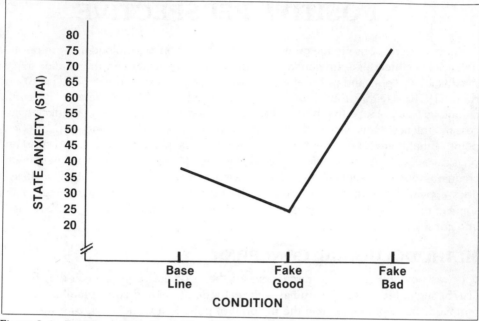

Figure 2.6. Response distortion with a 20-item scale (From Morgan, 1978).

(source) traits and to ignore second-order factors (see Table 2.2 again). Morgan (1978) pointed out that previous research by Kane (1970) and Rushall (1970) was consistent in supporting a no relationship conclusion when their analyses on the first order factors were compared. "It was only when Kane analyzed the second order [factors] that a relationship between physical ability and personality was observed . . . the most important and consistent second order factor in Kane's study was extroversion" (Morgan, 1978).

It has also been suggested that the choice of statistics used in the majority of pervious research — for example, whether the experimental method or the correlational method were used and/or whether the resulting data were analyzed with univariate or multivariate statistics — might account for the apparent lack of relationship between sport involvement and personality. Commenting on the former (i.e., the use of an experimental method versus the correlational method), Kane (1978) observed that "surprisingly few correlational studies have been reported attempting to tease out the nature of the personality/physical performance relationship. If and where a relationship exists it would seem that appropriate correlational procedures could best demonstrate the circumstances under which it is maximized and this in turn could give rise to a better understanding of the nature of the relationship."

Also, however, the "appropriate correlational procedure" might have to be *multivariate* — that is, one which permits for a large number of personality and sport participation variables to be analyzed simultaneously. Drawing upon the results from his earlier research, Kane (1970, 1972, 1976) noted that the magnitude of the correlation coefficient increased when the type of analysis utilized proceeded from simple, bivariate techniques (correlating one personality variable with one physical performance variable) to more complex, multivariate techniques. "A number of these

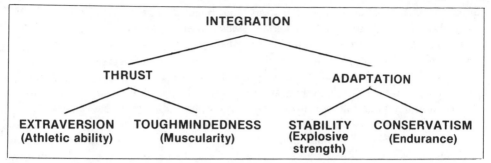

**Figure 2.7. Personality — athletic ability — hierarchical factor structure (From Kane, 1978).
Reproduced with permission of the publisher.**

analyses with multivariate vectors have produced significant coefficients averaging about 0.7 and in many cases permitting a clear interpretation of tough-minded, stable extraversion going with general athletic ability" (Kane, 1978). The personality-athletic ability hierarchical factor structure outlined by Kane is illustrated in Figure 2.7.

Hardman (1973) did carry out a comprehensive analysis of some of the second-order factors of the 16 P.F. using the data presented in Table 2.4. In fact, two of these second-order factors, anxiety and introversion-extraversion, have also been listed in summary fashion in Table 2.5.

In the case of anxiety, it was observed that the predominant pattern was for the scores to be average or above average with the top class athletes tending to be much closer to the population norm (i.e., stable and nonanxious) than less competent players. Hardman (1973) stated that:

> . . . in light of these results it is surprising that the claim that games players are stable or non-anxious is pursued . . . a comparative lack of anxiety has been a characteristic of good players and this has led to the belief that such players have a degree of stability greater than the norm of the total population.

The general pattern of findings for the second-order factor of introversion-extraversion is similar to that for anxiety — the bulk of the group mean values tended to be in the average or above average range (see Table 2.5). However, Hardman found that the degree of introversion-extraversion present tended to be very sport specific and thus, "the claim for a positive correlation between extraversion and performance in sport should be linked only to specific sports."

The last point of Hardman's highlights what may be the most critical consideration in the search for a sport participation-personality relationship — the *classification* problem discussed earlier (see page 2.32). But, the classification of individuals must be made on at least two levels. In the first instance, it is necessary to differentiate an *athlete* from a *nonathlete;* in the second instance, it also seems essential to separate athletes according to sport type; male-female; team-individual; combative-noncombative; and so on.

A study by Schurr, Ashley and Joy (1977) did seem to overcome most of the procedural and methodological problems which have been mentioned. A large sample of subjects (1,956 college males) were tested on Cattell's 16 P.F. These subjects were classified as athletes or nonathletes (an athlete was defined as any male who participated in the University Intercollegiate Athletic program) and then, the athletes were further subdivided according to first, their level of success (letter winners versus non-letter winners) and, secondly, their sport type. Second-order factors from the 16 P.F. were then analyzed using a multivariate statistical analysis.

The classification scheme used to differentiate the athletes according to sport type is presented in Figure 2.8 Schurr, Ashley and Joy utilized a team versus individual sport dichotomy because it has received wide traditional support in the sport participation-personality literature. The subdivision into direct and parallel events resulted from "the observation that in certain sports (football, soccer, etc.) direct aggression against one's opponent is possible, whereas in other sports no direct aggression is expressed against the opponent" (Schurr, Ashley and Joy, 1977) and as a consequence, the personal qualities needed should be different. The third classification method utilized involved distinguishing the individual parallel sports according to whether they were of a long duration (e.g., cross country) or short duration (e.g., gymnastics.).

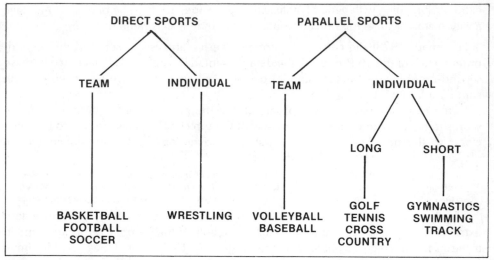

Figure 2.8. Classification of sport types (Adapted from Schurr, Ashley and Joy, 1977).

The authors found that no single personality profile distinguished all athletes from nonathletes. However, when the athletes were categorized according to sport type, a number of interesting differences were observed — not only in comparison to the nonathletic sample but also among the various sport types themselves. Some of the major findings are summarized in Table 2.8. It is apparent that a number of findings conform to "traditional" or "stereotypical" personality profiles for athletes. For example, team sport athletes were found to be more extraverted and more dependent than individual sport athletes; individual sport athletes were found to be less anxious and more independent and objective.

While the Schurr, Ashley and Joy results are significant in their own right in terms of any attempts to understand the relationship of personality to sport involvement, they are especially important because they suggest possible new directions for sport personality research. As the authors pointed out:

. . . given the generally dismal picture portrayed by the literature regarding studies of simple relationships between personality and sport participants, the results . . .conformed fairly well to several previous hypotheses.

. . . confirming the two sport classifications should be encouraging to sport psychologists in that they may well explain inconsistencies in previous research. The findings indicate the importance of classification techniques when comparisons of athletes and nonathletes are made . . . studies not dealing with a number of groups or not considering the additive effects of factors will not take into account all possible sources of variation.

. . . another finding is that the second stratum factors detected hypothesized relationships among sport groups . . .

. . . would results of other studies be as inconsistent if 16 P.F. second stratum factors had been emphasized? [Schurr, Ashley and Joy, 1977].

It is, of course, not possible to answer this question until previous research has been reanalyzed or further research is carried out.

A final methodological consideration which has been discussed is the need to assess both the psychological *traits* and *states*[7] of athletes in order to fully account for their

Table 2.8. An overview of some differences in personality that are present (1) between athletes from different sports and non-athletes and, (2) between athletes from different sports (Adapted from Schurr, Ashley and Joy, 1977)

REFERENCE GROUP	COMPARED TO	PERSONALITY PROFILE
Team Sport Athletes	Non-Athletes	less abstract reasoning more extraverted more dependent less ego-strength
Individual Sport Athletes	Non-Athletes	less abstract reasoning less anxious more dependent more objective
Direct Sport Athletes	Non Athletes	less abstract reasoning more extraverted more objective more independent
Parallel Sport Athletes	Non-Athletes	less abstract reasoning less anxious less independent more ego-strength
Letter Winners	Non-Letter Winners	no differences
Individual Sport Athletes	Team Sport Athletes	less dependent less anxious less extraverted less emotional more objective
Direct Sport Athletes	Parallel Sport Athletes	more aggressive*

*This difference was inferred—the basis of the inference was the primary traits which contribute to and comprise the second-order factors of Dependence and Superego strength.

7. A discussion of the state-trait approach proposed by Speilberger (1966) is outlined in Chapter 3

behavior (Morgan, 1978). Thus, for example, each individual athlete has an inherent or dispositional level of anxiety (the *trait*) which consistently exerts an influence upon behavior across a variety of different situations from athletics to social gatherings. And, in turn, each of these various situations is different in regard to its perceived threat or stressfulness — in regard to the level of *state* anxiety evoked. Consequently, if behavior is to be understood-explained, an understanding of both the state and trait are necessary.

Morgan (1978) pointed out that it has been "convincingly demonstrated that states and traits taken in concert will always account for more of the variance than either employed alone. Hence, abandoning trait psychology is . . . seen as an error in judgment."

THEORETICAL ISSUES

A predominant theme in the skeptical perspective has been that trait theory should be abandoned because of its inability to account for a sufficiently large proportion of behavioral variance. Both Morgan and Kane have taken exception to this suggestion.

Morgan (1978) argued that the specific trait model has not been adequately examined in sport personality research:

> . . . rather than discard trait theory, or develop new situation-specific inventories, it seems imperative that sport psychologists first demonstrate that existing theory and instrumentation is, in fact, inadequate. Most existing personality theories (e.g., Cattellian or Eysenckian) and their operational extensions (e.g., 16 P.F. and EPI) have been misused to a greater extent than they have been used. That is to say, these particular instruments have often been used inappropriately, and in many cases sport psychologists have ignored the theoretical underpinnings of the inventories. In other words, the inventories represent extensions of the theories, but investigators have chosen to employ the 16 P.F. and EPI atheoretically rather than using the inventories within the context of Cattellian or Eysenckian theory specifically.

A similar point was made by Kane (1978). He pointed out that the increasing emphasis upon the *person* and the *situation* is completely consistent with the viewpoints advocated by both Cattell and Eysenck:

> . . . neither Cattell nor Eysenck . . . would deny the impossibility of fully and accurately predicting an individual's behavior in all circumstances on the basis of measurement of broad personality characteristics, such as extraversion and anxiety, or on simpler ones like those incorporated in the 16 P.F. Indeed [Eysenck has constantly insisted] on the need for researcher's to be sensitive to changes in situational parameter values when interpreting their finding in behavioral experiment. Moreover, Cattell (1950, 1957, 1965) whose research and development in the area of personality traits is unmatched has distinguished clearly between 'source traits' (the relatively stable underlying causal entities that determine behavior) and 'surface traits' (the relatively varying and superficial elements that reflect behaviour in special circumstances), and has suggested the use of 'specifications equations' such as —
> $R(esponse) = S_1T_1 + S_2T_2 + \ldots S_nT_n$ where T_1T_2 etc. are traits and S_1S_2 etc. the weights relevant to each trait for a given situation.

Thus, it is not necessary to abandon trait models to emphasize an interactionist approach.

A PROLOGUE FOR FUTURE RESEARCH

Where should or can personality research in sport and physical activity go from its present status? It might be obvious that if dilemmas have persisted in general personality theory and assessment for over 35 years, there are no cook book answers.

However, it should also be emphasized that the empirical examination of the interrelationship of personality with sport and physical activity has only received concentrated attention within the past 10 years. Thus, in this period of accelerated growth, it might not be surprising that errors of interpretation and/or research design have occurred; the more comprehensive the information (in combination with hindsight), the greater the insight. In any event, the errors of interpretation and research design do not appear to be the major concern.

The theoretical issues would appear to be more difficult to resolve. A number of alternatives have been advanced. One proposal I suggested previously (Carron, 1975) would be to *utilize a social learning model in sport and physical activity*. The basis for this suggestion was that the trait approach had not proved to be highly effective and behavior across subjects in many situations in athletics is remarkably consistent. It was pointed out:

> . . . *a possible reason for the persistent view that athletics and personality are interwoven is the repetitively verified, subjective observation that athletics* are characterized by a unique consistency of behavior in the athletic event itself. *However, it would appear that this consistency of behavior is a function of the specific response situation, not of the underlying consistent generalizable personality dispositions of the athletes themselves. If we are to understand and predict behavior in a sport context, we must have greater understanding of the psychological characteristics of the specific response situations in athletic events [Carron, 1975].*

While there are advantages in obtaining an understanding of the psychological characteristics of the athletic situation, any suggestion that the trait approach be abandoned in favor of a social learning approach is unwarranted. It should be reemphasized that the trait view does not exclude the importance of the situation nor does the social learning view exclude the person. Also, the work of Endler and Hunt (1973), discussed previously, leads to a conclusion that *situations* considered in isolation are not better than *individuals* considered in isolation in terms of explaining the variability in behavior.

A second alternative — the *development of assessment techniques specific to sport* — seems promising (Kroll, 1970; Rushall, 1975). There has been some progress in a number of areas, not solely restricted to personality. The common focus has been an interest in the behavior of individuals participating in sport and physical activity. Some examples are Kenyon's scale for measuring attitudes toward physical activity; Kroll's (1976) scale for assessing sportsmanship; the Alderman and Wood (1974, 1976) scale for incentive motivation of athletes; Rushall's (1974) *Inventories for the Psychological Assessment of Swimmers;* and Martens' (1977) *Sport Competition Anxiety Test (SCAT).*

The work of Schurr, Ashley and Joy (1977) and Kane (1978) suggests yet a third alternative. That is, in order to tease out the complex relationship of personality to athletic participation, it may be necessary to begin examining the athletic dimension and the personality dimension in more specific — less global ways. All athletes (and the behavior they exhibit in the various sport situations) are not identical and, thus, the problems of classification must be taken into account. Also, human behavior is exceedingly complex and in order to more fully understand it in a sport context, the levels of analysis — second order factors versus surface traits and/or univariate versus multivariate statistical analyses — must be modified.

Finally, Endler and Hunt (1971) proposed that "personality description in general might be improved considerably by categorizing both situations and modes of response and then by describing individuals in terms of the kinds of responses they tend to manifest in various kinds of situations."

SUMMARY

Personality can be viewed as a hypothetical construction or abstraction from or about behavior. It is a complex construct and this complexity is mirrored in the number of definitions advanced to explain it and their diverse and varied nature. The uniqueness and yet generality of personality, its stability and yet susceptibility to change and its physical as well as psychological aspects have all been expanded upon. Perhaps in looking for a summarizing statement, it is difficult to improve upon the general and very imprecise suggestion of Kluckhohn and Murray that personality is the factor that makes each individual like all other men, like some other men and like no other men.

A number of theories have been advanced to account for personality. In the *psychodynamic* or conflict theory, an emphasis is placed upon the role of instinctual sexual and aggressive drives as the major determinants of behavior. On the other hand, the more humanistic *phenomenological* theories have emphasized a positive, free-will oriented approach; behavior is interpreted as being the product of intellect, reason and planning and not of nonconscious drives or mechanistic conditioned responses. In the *constitutional* theory, it is proposed that the individual possesses a specific physique or body type, largely genetically determined, which serves as a predisposing factor toward behavioral consistency.

A fundamental assumption of the *trait* theories is that personality is composed of distinguishable, relatively enduring characteristics (called factors or traits) which are the underlying causes or tendencies for behavior. Thus, individual differences in these traits contribute to the individual differences in behavior.

In contrast to the trait view, the *social learning* theories of personality emphasize the psychological nature of the situation. Behavior is thought to vary with the situation; the differences between subjects in similar situations being minimal.

In an *interactionist* interpretation of behavior, the conflict between the social learning and trait approaches is downplayed since neither of these alone explain as large a proportion of the variability in response as do the various interactions between persons, situations and modes of response. In sport and physical activity research, the trait view has been the predominant theoretical model adopted.

Kroll (1970) proposed five possible ways in which the personality and physical ability dimensions might be related: a common preliminary core alternative; a modification and attrition alternative; a common initial interests/dissimilar final interests alternative; a neophytes opposite to veterans alternative; and, a no relationship alternative.

The first two alternatives have been one popular view while the fifth alternative has been another. Although a large number of individuals have come out in favor of the *no relationship* alternative in the 1970s, a more positive viewpoint emphasizing a relative degree of relationship has also been advocated.

Two alternative approaches suggested for future sport personality research are the development of assessment techniques specific to sport and the use of the interactionist paradigm in sport and physical activity — an approach which does not disregard trait theory.

PSYCHOLOGICAL MOTIVATION AND ATHLETIC PERFORMANCE

3

The origin of the term *motivation* is generally ascribed to the Latin word *movere* which means "to move." In a modern psychological context, motivation has been used to represent the energy or intensity underlying behavior. Thus, quite simply, without motivation, there could be no behavior. Consequently, it should be apparent that any attempt at explanation/prediction of athletic performance (the output of Figure. 2.1) must include an understanding of its motivational bases.

However, as Littman (1958) observed "*There are many different kinds of motivational phenomena. It is simply not the case that the analysis of one kind of motivational phenomenon provides us with the analysis of all, or even a substantial portion, of other motivational concepts. Motivation is not a unitary phenomenon in the sense that all motivational things have the same properties and enter into the same laws in the same way.*" An examination of the various texts which attempt to account for motivation from physiological, biochemical or psychological viewpoints serves to illustrate this point. Further support is provided when the number of different conceptual perspectives within each of these disciplines is considered.

Since motivation is such a complex construct, there is no way that it can be discussed and outlined comprehensively in a single chapter. Trade-offs and decisions on relative priority have to be made. This is the case in the present chapter. Only those major theories which have had the most significant theoretical impact upon research in sport and physical activity are presented. These include drive theory, achievement theory, the optimal level theory, attribution theory and the theory of sport competition anxiety.[1]

DRIVE THEORY

Drive theory[2] must be viewed as *the* most influential theory of motivation in terms of

---

1. That is, they are predominant in the sense that they have been most frequently utilized in research studies concerned with the performance and learning of motor skills.
2. For reasons which should become more obvious from the discussion which follows, drive theory has also been referred to as *S-R reinforcement theory*, *drive-reduction theory*, and *Hullian-Spence drive theory*.

impact upon the field of social psychology of sport and physical activity. Historically, it was the earliest theoretical model used and it has continued to have a major impact. As one example, it has been the primary model used in the research studies concerned with the effect of *psychological stress* and/or the personality dimension of *anxiety* upon the performance and learning of motor tasks. (This research is discussed subsequently in the present chapter.) As another example, it has been the catalyst in a recent resurgence of interest in the influence that spectators and coactors have upon performance and learning (Zajonc, 1965). This research, which falls within the domain of *social facilitation* is summarized in Chapter 9.

THE MODEL

Drive theory is a mechanistic interpretation of motivation and learning which was originally developed by Clark Hull (1943, 1951, 1952) on the basis of his research at Yale Unversity. However, since Kenneth Spence (who was originally a student of Hull's, later an associate) of the University of Iowa also made a series of highly significant contributions and modifications to the original model (e.g., Spence, 1956), it is now widely ascribed to both Hull and Spence.

While the theory itself is exceedingly complex,[3] it is described as *mechanistic* because it is essentially a stimulus-response (S-R) interpretation of behavior (Weiner, 1972). Complexity arises in the form of the highly integrated postulates, theorems and corollaries developed by Hull to link the stimulus condition(s) to the overt response(s). Thus, the theory is not solely an S-R view but rather an S-O-R interpretation for behavior:

$$S — f — (O) — f — R \tag{1}$$

Input variables (S, the stimulus events) are linked to output variables (R, the response or responses) by means of a set of *intervening variables* (the 0 factor). These intervening variables represent unobservable entities which can only be inferred from the overt events.

In any theoretical model, the intervening variables are only theoretical constructs. If Formula 1 is used as an example, the S factor might reflect an antecedent condition such as the number of hours the organism has been without food. This stimulus situation could be systematically varied as an independent variable, e.g., 0, 4, 8 hours without food, to assess its influence upon the speed (i.e., the R, factor or response) with which rats solve a maze task and locate the food. Any theoretical constructs such as degree of motivation, the rate of learning, etc. which are proposed to link the differences in performance to the differences in the levels of the stimulus condition would be intervening variables.

It should also be pointed out that if any theory is to be scientifically useful, its intervening variables must be verifiable, logical, noncontradictory and interrelated. These qualifications are evident in Hull's theory. An overview of some of the general

3. A major problem in any attempt to summarize and present drive theory is its complexity. Using a mathematico-deductive approach adapted from Newton, Hull presented an interrelated series of postulates, theorems and corollaries in both a mathematical and verbal form. Further, he continued to revise these until his death. The final result, *A behavior system: An introduction to behavior theory concerning the individual organism,* is exceedingly difficult to understand without a background in psychology and mathematics. Consequently, it should be emphasized that what is presented here is only a highly simplified, incomplete translation.

features of drive theory is presented in Table 3.1. It should be noted that this is an overview. The system presented here has been simplified with the resultant consequence that some of Hull's precision has been sacrificed (see Footnote 2 again). Thus, only those intervening variables most pertinent to a discussion of motivation and its impact upon motor performance and learning have been included.

Table 3.1. Selected features of Hull's system of behavior (Adapted from Hilgard and Bower, 1966).

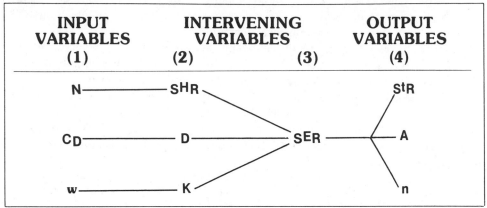

In the Hullian system, the input conditions (column 1) comprising those objective conditions which can be manipulated as independent variables include: *the number of prior reinforcements* (N); the *drive condition* (C_D); and, the *amount or weight of the reward* (w).

As Table 3.1 illustrates, each of these antecedent conditions is linked to a specific intervening variable (see column 2). The number of prior reinforcements effects *habit strength* ($_SH_R$), the drive condition effects *drive* (D) and the amount or weight of the reward effects *incentive motivation* (K).

In turn, these three intervening variables from column 2, in combination, determine the *excitatory potential* ($_SE_R$). Hull viewed their interaction as a multiplicative function, or

$$S \text{---} \boxed{_SE_R = f(_SH_R \times D \times K)} \text{---} R \qquad (2)$$

However, Spence, who had a major impact on Hull's thinking in regards to the influence of incentives (and, as a consequence, the symbol K is generally thought to represent Spence's first name), postulated that drive and incentive were additive, or

$$S \text{---} \boxed{_SE_R = f(_SH_R \times (D + K))} \text{---} R \qquad (3)$$

The final stage in the system, the response or output variables, are also verifiable in an experimental context. These included the *reaction latency* ($_St_R$), *reaction amplitude* (A) and the *number of nonreinforced trials to extinction* (n).

Drive (D). The underlying basis for Hull's drive theory was *need reduction* — the organism responds only because of an unsatisfied need which is referred to as a drive.

48

If there is no need, there is no behavior. In discussing this point, Hull (1943) suggested that:

> . . . since a need, either actual or potential, usually precedes and accompanies the action of an organism, the need is often said to motivate or drive the associated activity.

A number of important points evolve from the interrelationship of drive and drive reduction. First, while drive was originally (Hull, 1943) viewed as arising solely from a *tissue deficit,* such as hunger or thirst, this interpretation was later modified (Hull, 1951) and expanded to include acquired or learned drives. It is the acquired or learned drives such as competitiveness, affiliation, aggression, and so on which have the greatest relevance to sport and physical activity.

Secondly, drive was subsequently viewed by Hull as a *nondifferentiated energizer* of behavior. That is, drive was considered to be a general state which is contributed to by all the need states acting on the organism at a given time. Thus, if an individual's drive level is increased — for example, as a result of some psychological threat — this heightened state of drive was expected to energize *all* behavior. As a result, the individual would eat quicker, run faster, talk more rapidly and so on. As an *energizer,* drive serves to activate or motivate but it cannot determine the *direction* that behavior takes. Brown (1961) clarified this point:

> . . . in current discussions of motivation it is commonplace to encounter the word 'drives.' For certain writers, this term apparently conveys the idea of multiple directedness. The hunger drive is said to be directed or to direct behavior toward food, the thirst drive toward water and so on. But, this terminology is confusing if . . . it is desirable to limit the function of a drive to that of a motivator. If this latter position is adopted, drive can never be directed toward any specific goal, nor can it selectively activate one type of associative tendency to the exclusion of others, since this would indirectly involve a directive function. To speak of 'drives' implies that the constructs so designated are alike, yet different. If they are exactly alike when functioning as motivators, then identical processes must be involved in all cases, and all drives, as activators, become one. If they are not alike as motivators, then each must be motivating but in an unique way. Just what these different yet comparable ways might be is difficult for one to imagine. One might suppose, of course, that drives are all alike save that each is the result of its own distinctive motivational variable. But if this is the case, then we no longer have different drives as behavior determinants, but only different sources of drive.

Thus, it should be apparent that it is necessary to distinguish between the variable(s) which activate and motivate behavior (serve an energizing function) and the variable(s) which represent the direction that behavior takes. In its essential form, drive theory may be reduced to the following model (Weiner, 1972):

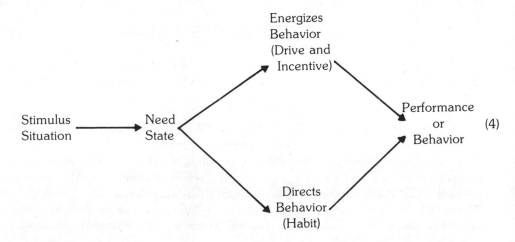

(4)

In drive theory, the variables which represent the magnitude or level of energy which the organism displays are drive and incentive motivation while the specific direction behavior takes is accounted for by the variable of habit strength. *Both energizing and directing constructs are necessary conditions for behavior but neither is sufficient alone.* A given response could be the product of a strong drive[4] and a weak habit or a weak drive and a strong habit. Further, it is not possible from an observation of behavior to determine the relative contributions of either.

A third point is that *reinforcement* is fundamental to drive theory schema: when a need state arises in the organism, it leads that organism to respond; when that response is appropriate (i.e., correct), it leads to a reduction in the need or drive; this drive reduction is reinforcing; and, as a result, a bond or strengthened association — a habit — develops between the stimulus situation and the specific response. Or, stated in a slightly different way, there is *learning.*

Also integral to this latter point is an understanding that in any response situation there are *competing response tendencies.* For example, if our previously discussed starving rat is introduced into a two-choice maze (T-maze), any of a number of responses are possible. Many of these are not competitional in nature; they can be done concurrently while the rat seeks out the goal box, e.g., head turning while moving along the maze. However, at the junction of the maze a choice is required — either a left or right turn may be made but not both simultaneously. Hence, they are in competition. Further, one is appropriate or correct insofar as it leads to the goal box and food while the other is incorrect. These two responses represent a *hierarchy of competing response tendencies* (see Figure 3.1).

On the first trial, both responses would be equally dominant in the hierarchy. However, with repeated trials and subsequent reinforcement, the correct response would become dominant. As Cottrell (1972) explained:

> . . . the learning process can be viewed as the modification of the hierarchy of competing responses elicited by the task stimuli. At the beginning of learning, the correct response has a low probability of

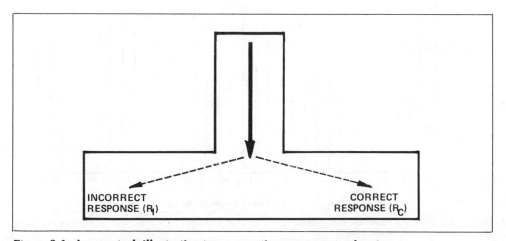

INCORRECT RESPONSE (R_I)

CORRECT RESPONSE (R_C)

Figure 3.1. A maze task illustrating two competing response tendencies.

4. Since drive and incentive are both components contributing to the energizing function it has become customary to combine them under the term drive.

50

emission. Some other response is dominant and so the subject's overt responses are mostly the wrong ones. As learning progresses, the response to be learned is strengthened and moves to the dominant position in the hierarchy, and the subject emits the correct response more and more frequently.

Indirect evidence that the dominant response is an incorrect response early in learning is provided by the fact that performance is relatively ineffective. With repeated practice and consequent reinforcement of the appropriate/correct response, the habit hierarchy changes — the correct response becomes dominant.

Habit ($_SH_R$). Since habit and drive are interrelated constructs insofar as the determination of behavior is concerned, most of the points raised above concerning drive also indirectly or directly relate to habit strength. However, some specific aspects of the latter should also be discussed to highlight its nature.

The first is that habits are *learned behaviors.*[5] A prerequisite for learning is the contiguity of stimuli and responses under conditions of reinforcement. Hull emphasized this point when he used the symbol $_SH_R$ to represent the habit construct. The S and R, representing the stimulus and response, are linked with H thereby reflecting their learned or habitual association — given the stimulus condition, it is reasonably probable that the response will occur.

Also, the level or degree of learning (which could also be referred to as the strength of the association between the stimulus and the response) was considered by Hull to be a function of the number of previous reinforcements. This point was also made previously, of course, in the discussion of competing response tendencies. In Hull's schema, the growth of habit strength was represented by a negatively accelerating curve. This is presented in Figure 3.2. A comparison between the proposed growth curve for habit strength and an actual learning curve typical of motor tasks serves to emphasize the fact that the habit construct in Hull's theory represents the learning

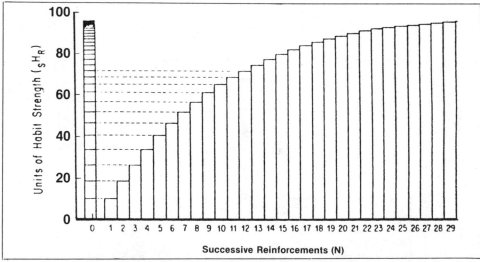

Figure 3.2. A diagrammatic representation of habit strength as a function of successive reinforcements (From Hull, 1943).

5. When drive theory is discussed in a context with other learning theories, the habit construct is given a greater emphasis. On the other hand, when it is presented with theories of motivation, the drive construct is emphasized.

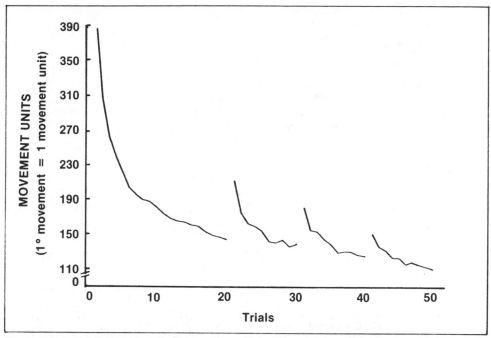

Figure 3.3 A stabilometer performance curve illustrating the increments in performance as a function of practice trials. The breaks in the curve (with accompanying performance decrements) represent rest intervals of 24 hours duration or longer. (From Carron and Marteniuk, 1970). Reproduced with permission of the publisher.

component. Figure 3.3 contains a learning curve for the stabilometer. The breaks in the curve represent 24 hour rest periods and the curve is descending rather than ascending but the similarity is obvious.

Incentive Motivation (K). The final construct from column 2 of Table 3.1 is incentive motivation (K). It is the reinforcement associated with the goal response — the quantity and quality of the reward. In his original formulations, Hull (1943) proposed that incentive motivation directly influenced the growth of habit strength. That is, he felt that reinforcement had a very direct impact upon learning; without reinforcement learning would not proceed. However, this suggestion later had to be modified since it could not be reconciled with the results from studies demonstrating *latent learning*.

The research of Tolman and Honzik (1930) clearly illustrates the latent learning phenomenon. Three groups of rats were tested: a no reward group which was permitted to wander about the maze but were given no reward in the goal box; a regularly rewarded group; and, a group that was not rewarded with food in the goal box until the eleventh day. As Figure 3.4 shows, this latter group demonstrated a dramatic improvement in performance after the introduction of the reward. In short, learning had been occurring throughout practice but it was not evident in performance until the reward was introduced. As a result of the various experiments demonstrating latent learning, Hull revised his thinking in 1951 so that incentives became a determinant of performance, not of learning.

It was pointed out that the specific interaction of incentive motivation with drive and habit was viewed differently by Hull and Spence as a comparison of Equations 2 and 3

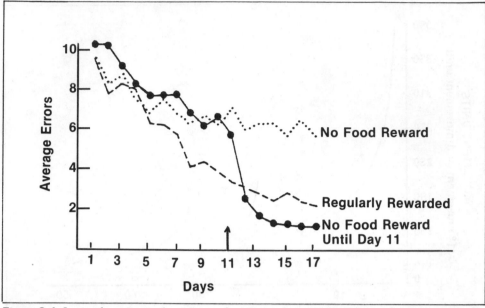

Figure 3.4. Latent learning in the maze performance of rats (From Hilgard and Bower , 1966. based on the results of Tolman and Honzig, 1930). Source: Ernest R. Hilgard and Gordon H. Bower, THEORIES OF LEARNING, ©1966, p.200. Reprinted by permission of Prentice-Hall, Inc., Englewood Cliffs, New Jersey.

clearly shows. However, both were in agreement that drive and incentive motivation contributed to the energizing function (drive being analogous to a "push;" incentive motivation to a "pull"). Therefore, Equations 2 and 3 can be modified as follows:[6]

$$S \text{———} \boxed{sE_R = D \times sH_R} \text{———} R \qquad (5)$$

Excitatory Potential (sE_R). Excitatory (or reaction) potential, as the name implies, is a potential, a threshold or level of excitation which contributes to the speed and vigor of response. According to Hull, habit strength is energized into excitatory potential by drive (which is, of course, the formula presented in Equation 5 above). If the level of drive is too low, the threshold for excitation is not reached and the response does not occur.

Since a learning situation is characterized by competing response tendencies, each of the possible responses has its own associative habit strength. This can be illustrated by converting the example presented in Figure 3.1 to a drive theory orientation using Equation 4 as a basis. The correct (R_c) and incorrect (R_i) responses are then represented by the two following equations:

$$S \text{———} \boxed{sH_{Rc} \times D = sE_{Rc}} \text{———} R_c \qquad (6)$$

$$S \text{———} \boxed{sH_{Ri} \times D = sE_{Ri}} \text{———} R_i \qquad (7)$$

The same stimulus may elicit either of two responses which can be viewed as being in competition with each other.

6. See Footnote 4 again.

It might also be evident from Formulas 6 and 7 as well as from the above discussion that not only does each response has its own associative habit strength, but it also has its own associative excitatory potential. Which of these two responses — the correct one (R_c) or the incorrect one (R_i) — might be expected to occur in a situation of psychological stress?

According to drive theory (i.e., drawing upon the outline just presented), the following proposals are tenable:

- drive (D) is a nondifferentiated energizer which simply serves as a numerical multiplier; it does not determine the specific response which will occur.
- the presence of psychological stress results in an increase in drive level.
- the direction that behavior takes (the specific response that occurs) is largely a function of habit strength.
- the strength of a habit is a product of previous reinforcements — the number of successive times that there has been reinforcement of the specific stimulus — response sequence.
- the performance situation is characterized by competitional responses. These responses reflect an underlying habit hierarchy comprising the correct habit ($_sH_{Rc}$) and the incorrect habit ($_sH_{Ri}$) or habits.
- drive energizes habit strength into reaction potential (as Equations 6 and 7 illustrate).
- the relative strength of the two reaction potentials — the relative strength of $_sER_c$ versus $_sER_i$ in the present example — affects the probability that a given response will occur. If the correct habit is dominant, with an increase in drive, it is probable that the correct response will occur.

Two corollaries evolve logically from the above:

(a) in unlearned or highly complex tasks — tasks in which the habit strength for the correct is weak — the dominant habit is incorrect and, therefore, an increase in drive resulting from the introduction of a psychological stressor (threat, presence of an audience etc.) is disruptive to performance.

(b) in well learned or very simple tasks — tasks in which the habit strength for the correct response is strong — the dominant habit is stronger in the habit hierarchy and, therefore, an increase in drive leads to performance improvement.

This represented the general framework or underlying rationale for a large number of studies. Many of these studies are outlined in Chapter 9.

DRIVE THEORY AND LEARNING AND PERFORMANCE

The Manifest Anxiety Scale (MAS). Drive theory was originally tested in animal research and with exceedingly simple tasks. Not surprisingly, there was also considerable interest in determining whether the model could be used to account for human learning and performance. Thus, subsequently, the theory was also extended to experimental situations involving human subjects. One significant impetus associated with this development was the work of Janet Taylor (1953, 1956) and Kenneth Spence (1956, 1958).

Taylor (1953) devised the Manifest Anxiety Scale (MAS) in order to differentiate individuals on the basis of their tendency to respond emotionally to aversive stimuli — in

54

short, to differentiate individuals according to the personality trait of anxiety. Thus, high anxious persons (HA) — those individuals who characteristically exhibit relatively high levels of anxiety across a wide variety of daily situations — are viewed as more emotionally responsive than low anxious persons (LA). And, in turn, these differences in emotional responsiveness are thought to reflect innate differences in drive level. In the drive level framework, HA can be viewed as a high drive (D) condition; LA, as a low drive (D) condition.

Initially, the MAS, as a measure of drive level, was utilized in conditioning experiments. The underlying rationale was quite straightforward. Since a conditioned response, e.g., an eyeblink conditioned to a puff of air, is simple, containing few competing response tendencies, it would be predicted that HA individuals, as a result of their inherently greater drive level, would show greater conditioning performance. There was considerable support for this prediction in the experimental work which was carried out. As Spence (1964) noted in his review of this research, "the results of 21 of 25 comparisons were [in the predicted direction]. If there actually were no relation between the MA scale and conditioning performance, the probability of obtaining such a percentage of differences (84 percent) in the same direction by chance is less than [one chance in 100]."

The analysis of drive theory in consort with the MAS was also extended to verbal learning tasks. While the pattern of findings was not quite as consistent, there was again considerable support for the interrelationship of the MAS (as a measure of emotional responsiveness, D) and drive theory. Figure 3.5 contains a summary of the findings from one study — a study by Spence, Farber and McFann (1956) concerned with the learning of easy and difficult paired-associates by HA and LA subjects.

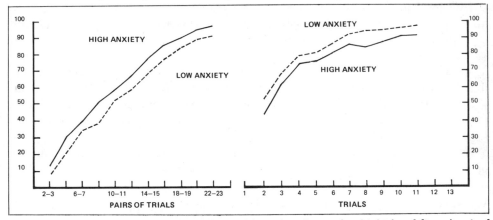

Figure 3.5. Performance on simple (left hand figure) and complex (right hand figure) paired associates lists by HA and LA individuals (Adapted from Spence, Farber and McFann, 1956).

Consistent with the rationale in the conditioning experiments, it was predicted that HA would be superior on the easy paired-associates task. Each stimulus-response pair was quite different and the responses required were synonyms of the stimuli presented. Consequently, the correct habit was already present and dominant. Therefore, the HA, as a result of their higher drive level should perform better than the LA. This was the case as Figure 3.5a shows.

In the case of the difficult paired-associates task, it was predicted that LA would be superior. That is, in the total list of paired associates, there was a great deal of similarity (interference) among the various stimulus-response pairs. Consequently, the correct habit was weak and this factor, in combination with the higher drive of HA, would be expected to lead to inferior performance. Again, this was the case as an examination of Figure 3.5b reveals.

The MAS and Motor Tasks. A number of studies were also carried out in which individuals scoring at the two extremes of the MAS were tested on a motor task. In some cases, psychological stress conditions were also incorporated into the research design in an attempt to further influence the drive level of the subjects.

The results from these various studies have not fallen into any consistent pattern however. For example, Table 3.2 contains a summary made by Martens (1971) of the research on motor tasks with the MAS when no psychological stressor was used. The equal sign (=) was used to signify no differences between HA and LA while the greater than sign (>) represented those instances where the performance of one of these groups was better than the other. An attempt was also made to interpret the results: whether they supported drive theory (positive), were opposite the predicted direction (negative), failed to show differences (none), or were uninterpretable. (According to Martens (1971) the classification of uninterpretable was not meant to imply "that the studies were necessarily deficient in experimental methodology. Rather, it indicates the difficulty in accurately predicting the effect of anxiety in a learning situation involving more than one response. This problem arises because it is difficult, if not impossible, to establish habit hierarchies for motor response." This specific issue is discussed in detail in Chapter 9).

It is apparent from Table 3.2 that 13 different findings were consistent with drive theory, 15 showed no differences between the two groups (and consequently might also be interpreted as contrary to drive theory expectations), while the remaining 7 were classified as uninterpretable. Thus, the general pattern of findings in motor skills research are highly equivocal leading to a suggestion that there is no relationship between the MAS dimension and motor behavior — at least in the absence of any psychological stressor. Martens noted that "these equivocal findings do not, however, preclude the possibility that in situations where a stressor is deliberately introduced, differences in motor performance among groups varying in anxiety may support drive theory notions."

This qualification is based upon a suggestion of Spence and Spence (1966). In a paper published in 1958, Spence noted that two alternate hypotheses were tenable in regard to the MAS: the *chronic hypothesis* and the *emotional reactivity hypothesis.* According to the chronic hypothesis, HA would respond more emotionally in a chronic fashion to all behavioral situations. On the other hand, the emotional reactivity hypothesis implies that HA have a lower *threshold* of emotional responsiveness and respond with a stronger emotional reaction to those situations involving some degree of stress. Thus, with the first hypothesis, differences in drive level would be expected in all mild, nonthreatening situations whereas, according to the second, no differences should be expected.

In 1966, on the basis of the results from a wide cross-section of studies, Spence and Spence strongly endorsed the emotional reactivity alternative. They felt that the presence of a psychological stressor such as competition or a threatening stimulus should be incorporated into the research design in order to increase the probability that

Table 3.2. Summary of the research on the MAS and motor behavior in the absence of a stressor (From Martens, 1971). Reproduced with permission of the publisher.

INVESTIGATOR(S)	SAMPLE	TASK	RESULT	INTERPRETATION
Axelrod et al. (1956)	College males & females	Stylus maze	LA = HA*	None
Baker (1961)	College males	Matching foot patterns while walking	HA>LA	Uninterp.
Carder (1965)	College footballers	Football ability	LA = HA	None
Carron (1968)	College males	Stabilometer	*Early* LA = HA	None
			Late LA>HA	Uninterp.
Castaneda et al. (1956)	5th grade boys & girls	Perceptual-motor discrimination	EASY TASK	
			HA>LA	Positive
			DIFFICULT TASK	
			LA>HA	Positive
Desiderato (1964)	College males & females	Response time	LA = HA	None
Diehl (1965)	High school girls	Agility, balance and coordination	LA = HA	None
Duthie & Roberts (1968)	College males	Time estimation	Learning Phase	
			LA>HA	Positive
			PERF. PHASE	
			LA = HA	None
Farber & Spence (1953)	College males & females	Stylus maze	LA>HA	Positive
Farber & Spence (1956)	College males & females	Response time	LA = HA	None
Grice (1955)	College males	Response time	LA>HA	Uninterp.
Hammer (1967)	College males	Sport achievement	LA = HA	Uninterp.
Hammer (1968)	High school and college males	Sport achievement	LA = HA	Uninterp.
Hammes & Wiggins (1962)	College males & females	Tracking	LA>HA	Positive
Kamin & Clark (1957)	Military men	Response time	LA>HA	Negative
Martens (1969)	College males	Coincident timing	Learning Phase	
			LA = HA	None
			PERF. PHASE	
			HA>LA	Positive
Martens & Landers (1969)	College males	Coincident timing	Learning Phase	
			LA>HA	Positive
			PERF. PHASE	
			LA = HA	None
Matarazzo & Matarazzo (1956)	Male VA patients	Pursuit rotor	LA = HA	None
McGuigan et al. (1959)	College females	Stylus maze	LA = HA	None
Meisels et al. (1967)	College males & females	Stylus maze	EASY	
			error	
			HA>LA	Positive
			time	
			LA>HA	Negative
			DIFFICULT	
			error	
			LA>HA	Positive
			time	
			LA>HA	Positive
Nash et al. (1966)	College females	Stylus maze	LA = HA	None
Palermo et al. (1956)	4th grade boys and girls	Perceptual-motor discrimination	LA>HA	Positive
Ryan & Lakie (1965)	College males	Ring-peg	LA = HA	None
Singh (1968)	High School males	Tracking	LA = HA	None
Vaught & Newman (1966)	College males	Steadiness	LA = HA	None
Wenar (1954)	College males	Response time	HA>LA	Positive
Wiggins et al. (1962)	Male VA patients and college males	Tracking	LA>HA	Positive
Wright et al. (1963)	College males	Writing letters	EASY	
		Inverted	LA>HA	Uninterp.
			DIFFICULT	
			HA>LA	Uninterp.

*LA = low anxious; HA = high anxious

HA and LA would differ in emotionality (and hence, drive level) in the experimental situation.

Therefore, Martens also reviewed the studies in which a stressor was introduced during performance on a motor task. An overview is presented in Table 3.3. Again, an inconsistent pattern of findings is evident: 3 of the findings were in the direction predicted from drive theory; 1 was in the opposite direction; 8 showed no differences (and, again, might be interpreted as also contrary to drive theory predictions); and, 6 were assessed as uninterpretable.

On the basis of the overall pattern of results presented in Tables 3.2 and 3.3, two proposals were advanced by Martens. One of these was that drive theory be abandoned as a theoretical model in motor skills research. However, Marteniuk (1971), Spence (1971) and Landers (1975) have all argued that this suggestion was unwarranted. They observed that the wide cross section of studies reviewed by Martens involved markedly different tasks, measures of psychological stress, subjects and pro-

Table 3.3. Summary of research investigating the interaction effects of the MAS and stress on motor behavior (From Martens, 1971). Reproduced with permission of the publisher.

AUTHOR	SAMPLE	TASK	STRESSOR	RESULT	INTERPRETATION
Baker (1961)	College males	Matching foot patterns while walking	Shock	LA > HA	Uninterpretable
Carron (1968)	College males	Stabilometer	Shock	STRESS EARLY LA > HA	Positive
				STRESS LATE LA & HA inferior	Uninterpretable
				DELTA SCORE LA = HA	Uninterpretable
Carron & Morford (1968)	College males	Stabilometer	Shock	LA = HA	Uninterpretable
Castaneda (1956)	High school boys and girls	Response time	Auditory stimulus	HA > LA	Positive
Diehl (1965)	High school girls	Agility, balance & coordination	Perf. filmed for evaluation	LA = HA	None
Farber & Spence (1956)	College males and females	Response time	Shock	LA = HA	None
Hammes & Wiggins (1962)	College males and females	Tracking	Illumination intensity	LA = HA	None
Kamin & Clark (1957)	Military men	Response time	Shock	LA > HA	Negative
Martens (1969)	College males	Coincident timing	Audience	ERROR LA = HA	None
				TRIALS-TO CRITERION HA > LA	Uninterpretable
Martens & Landers (1969)	College males	Coincident timing	Competition and failure	LA = HA	None
Nash et al. (1966)	College females	Response time	Shock	LA = HA	None
Price (1951)	College females	Pursuit rotor	Failure	LA = HA	None
Ryan & Lakie (1965)	College males	Ring-peg	Competition	LA > HA	Positive
Vaught & Newman (1966)	College males	Steadiness	Competition	LA > HA	Uninterpretable
Wenar (1954)	College males	Response time	Stimulus intensity	LA = HA	None

cedures, operational measures of habit strength and so on. Consequently, the lack of consistency evidenced could easily reflect these methodological and procedural differences.

A second proposal advanced by Martens was that alternatives to the MAS be explored — particularly alternatives which emphasize a *situational anxiety approach*. One such approach is Spielberger's (1966) conceptual distinction between state and trait anxiety and the resultant development of a measurement scale, the State-Trait Anxiety Inventory, STAI (Spielberger, Gorsuch, Luschene, 1970). The motor skills research related to the STAI is discussed in the next section. A second approach (which was developed by Martens, 1977) focuses on competitive trait anxiety and the Sport Competition Anxiety Test (SCAT) was developed to assess this construct. This approach is also outlined in a subsequent section of the chapter.

The STAI and Motor Skills. The distinction made by Spielberger (1966) between anxiety as a state versus anxiety as a trait essentially reduces to a distinction between a transitory response to the demands of a specific situation versus a relatively permanent personality disposition. Thus, state anxiety refers to "an empirical process or reaction which is taking place now at a given level of intensity . . . [and is] characterized by subjective consciously perceived feelings of apprehension and tension, accompanied by or associated with activation or arousal of the autonomic nervous system" (Spielberger, 1966). Consequently, state anxiety can be considered synonomous with psychological stress.

On the other hand, trait anxiety "indicates a latent disposition for a reaction of a certain type to occur if it is triggered by the appropriate (sufficiently stressful) stimuli . . . [it is defined as] a motive or acquired behavioral disposition that predisposes an individual to perceive a wide range of objectively nondangerous circumstances as threatening, and to respond to these with state anxiety reactions disproportionated in intensity to the magnitude of the objective danger" (Spielberger, 1966).

Thus, given a stressful stiuation, high trait individuals would be expected to exhibit markedly greater A-state reactions than low trait individuals. And, this pattern of differences in A-state elevation was observed in studies of computer assisted learning with college males (O'Neil, Spielberger and Hansen, 1969) and junior high school students (Spielberger, O'Neil and Hansen, 1971).

Klavora (1975) assessed the A-state reactions of male junior and senior high school football and basketball players who differed in A-trait. These results are contained in Figure 3.6. However, although athletes high on A-trait had greater A-state scores in practice, regular season and play-off games, their elevation (increase in magnitude) in A-state was the same as those for athletes low on A-trait.

Not surprisingly, the state portion of the STAI has been incorporated into a number of studies in an attempt to secure an objective measure of drive or arousal. However, the results have been mixed. When Griffen (1972) tested female competitors from three age categories (12-13 years, 16-17 years and 19 years), it was observed that the precompetition A-state level showed progressive decreases with increasing age. Also, Carron and Bennett (1976) found that individuals practicing in the presence of a coactor had higher A-state levels than individuals practicing alone. And, Iso-Ahola and Roberts (1977) reported that individuals working on a novel task had higher A-state levels than was the case with individuals working on a familiar task.

On the other hand, Landers, Brawley and Hale (1977) found no differences in

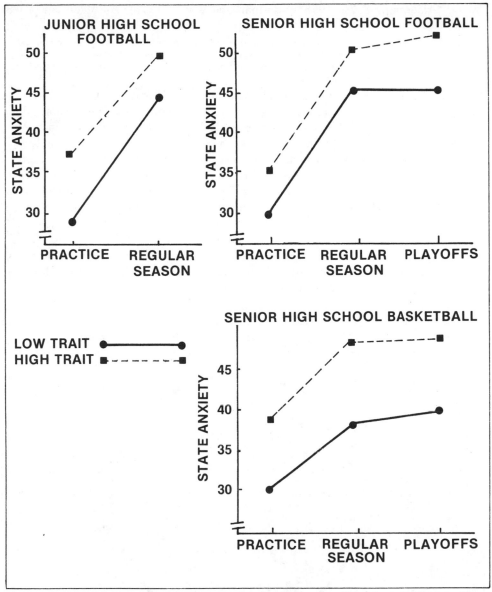

Figure 3.6. Precompetitive state anxiety of individuals who differ in trait anxiety (From Klavora, 1975). Reproduced with permission of the publisher.

A-state between a coaction or audience condition versus an alone condition. Similarly, Roberts (1975) obtained no differences in A-state level for subjects practicing under the apprehension of evaluation versus no evaluation. And, Moxley and Butcher (1975) found that the introduction of a competitive situation influenced performance but had no effect upon A-state level.

Incentive Motivation and Athletic Involvement. An interesting and potentially productive examination into motivation in sport has been initiated by Alderman and

Wood (Alderman, 1976, 1978; Alderman and Wood, 1976). As Alderman (1978) stated:

> . . . the focus is on discovering what it is about the sport itself (particularly its nature and demands) that motivates a young athlete to persist in his particpation. Incentive motivation simply refers to the incentive value a young athlete attaches to the possible outcomes or experiences he perceives as being available to him in a particular sport.

Drawing upon drive theory schema, Alderman and Wood (1976) noted that the amount of incentive (K) in a situation is a product of the organism's perceptions of the relative attractiveness of the various goals available and the outcomes possible. Also, however, incentive cannot be considered in absolute terms — the amount and type of incentive attached to a particular goal could vary markedly from one person to another. Since each person is constantly faced with alternatives (e.g., play basketball versus read versus practice music versus sleep, etc.), the choice of action the individual selects and persists with "comes about partially because of the *kind* of incentives that are particularly attractive to him at that moment in time, and the value which he attaches to them" (Alderman and Wood, 1976).

Seven major incentive systems were identified for sport: *power, independence, affiliation, stress, excellence, aggression,* and *success.*[7] These are illustrated schematically in Figure 3.7 while the specific definition for each is presented in Table 3.4.

Alderman and Wood analyzed the incentive motives of 425 young (between the ages of 11 and 14 years) ice hockey players. These results are presented in Figure 3.8.

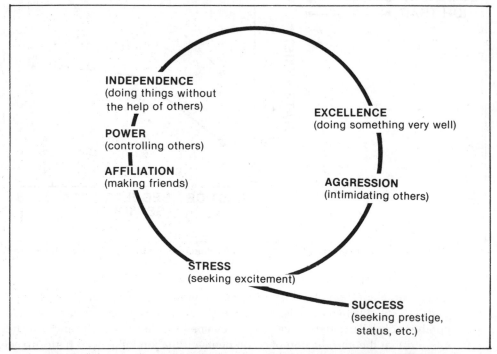

Figure 3.7. Major incentive systems in sport (From Alderman and Wood, 1976). Reproduced with permission of the publisher.

7. On the basis of their initial results (Alderman and Wood, 1976), some modifications were made. Two of these involved renaming the systems called *arousal* and *esteem* to *stress* and *success* respectively.

Table 3.4. The major incentive systems in sport (Alderman and Wood, 1976; Alderman, 1978).

INCENTIVE SYSTEM	CONSTRUCT
AFFILIATION	Incentives revolving around opportunities for social intercourse or being socially reassured that one is acceptable or worthwhile by the making of friends or maintenance of already existing friendships.
AGGRESSION	Incentives revolving around opportunities to subdue, intimidate, dominate or even injure other people.
EXCELLENCE	Incentives revolving around opportunities to do something very well for its own sake or to do it better than anyone else.
INDEPENDENCE	Incentives revolving around opportunities to do things on one's own without the help of other people.
POWER	Incentives revolving around opportunities to influence and control other people, particularly their attitudes, interests and opinions.
STRESS	Incentives revolving around opportunities for excitement, tension, pressure and pure action that sport can provide.
SUCCESS	Incentives revolving around the opportunity to obtain the extrinsic rewards that sport can provide; status, prestige, recognition and social approval.

When these results were considered in combination with the findings obtained from several thousand athletes from different sports (ages 11 to 18 years), a pattern of consistent findings emerged:

1. The two strongest and most consistent incentive conditions for young athletes are affiliation and excellence . . .

2. Stress incentives run a consistent third.

3. Aggression and independence incentives consistently lack any strength, even in the individual and physical contact sports.

4. Children are basically motivated by the same incentives *regardless* of their age, sport, sex and culture [Alderman, 1978].

These generalizations do have very direct practical implications since the sport environment should reflect the athlete's incentive motives.

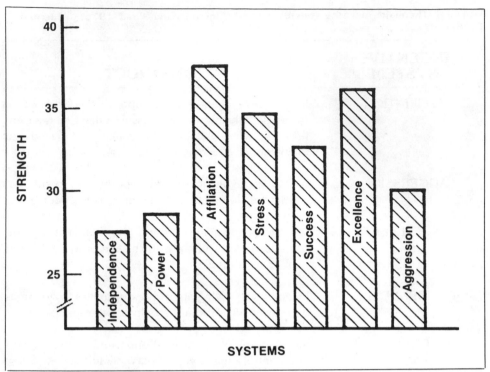

Figure 3.8. Strength of various incentive systems for 425 young hockey players (From Alderman and Wood, 1976). Reproduced with permission of the publisher.

OVERVIEW

As indicated earlier, drive theory has had a significant impact upon research concerned with motivation and learning of motor skills. There have been numerous criticisms of the theory and its limitations. In the motor skills literature, one of the major criticisms advanced has been in regard to the intervening variable of habit strength. Because of the difficulty of assessing the habit hierarchy in motor tasks, it has been suggested that the theory cannot be adequately tested.

Another concern is with drive theory's mechanistic S-R view of human behavior. Can a theory which had its origin as an explanatory model for the behavior of animals, account for the complex behavior characteristic of man?

Despite these limitations, the theory has repetitively evidenced explanatory power in human and animal learning. And, it is certainly an understatement to state that drive theory is firmly entrenched in motivation and learning psychology. As Weiner (1972) pointed out "Hull's influence on psychology was so pervasive that in a recent poll psychologists voted him the most important contributor to psychology during the two decades 1930-50 . . . this pool also revealed that Hull is considered second only to Freud in importance to the field of psychology." It is extremely doubtful that drive theory will be readily abandoned in the immediate future.

OPTIMAL LEVEL THEORY

Although the heading for this section implies that there is one comprehensive theory which draws upon the principle of an *optimal level*, this is not, in fact, the case. Rather, there are a number of different theoretical approaches which can be loosely grouped within two broad categories. One of these categories comprises the theories proposed by Berlyne (1960), Duffy (1962), Hebb (1949), Leuba (1955), Malmo (1959), and Walker (1964).

In their essential form, each of these theories within this category contains the proposal that *every person has an optimal level for stimulation, complexity, or arousal*. In turn, and as a corollary to this proposal, three principles are advanced. One is that every individual, having an optimal level for external stimulation, strives to maintain it by adjusting the level of stimulation present in the environment — increasing environmental complexity if there is too little stimulation; decreasing it if there is too much. Thus, environments characterized by either stimulus deprivation or stimulus overload are equally unsuitable to the organism.

A second is the *simplification principle* — as a result of repeated exposures, stimuli or situations become less complex, less stimulating and/or less arousing. For example, a record played at high speeds is unintelligible initially but, over time, it becomes coherent.

And finally, a third principle is the *habituation principle* — those individuals who are more experienced with a stimulus or situation show greater preference for an increase in complexity than individuals who have less experience (Arkes and Garske, 1977). By way of overview, this category of theories can be said to relate to the *state of the organism*.

The second broad category of optimal level theory is not concerned with a preferred state within the individual per se but rather with the effect of arousal level upon performance effectiveness. This approach evolved from the pioneer work and formulation of Yerkes and Dobson (1908). As a result, the underlying principle has come to be referred to as the *Yerkes-Dobson Law* or *inverted-U hypothesis*. Since the general objective of the present chapter is to examine those factors which influence output — athletic performance — the inverted U hypothesis is the approach discussed here.

THE MODEL

In its essential form, the inverted-U hypothesis contains the proposal that *there is a curvilinear relationship between the intensity of arousal and the effectiveness of performance*. With progressive increases in arousal level, there are associated increases in performance effectiveness until a critical point is reached. Further increases in arousal beyond this point result in progressively worsening performance. This is illustrated in Figure 3.9.

It is also evident from an examination of Figure 3.9 that the task dimension is superimposed on this schema. That is, the optimal level of arousal for a very difficult/complex task would be less than that for a moderately difficult or simple task.

The model seems quite simple and straightforward. However, Landers (1978) cautioned that the arousal-performance relationship is more complex than appearances might suggest — it is undoubtedly mediated by a number of other factors. One of those mentioned was *individual differences* in susceptibility to arousal. The personality trait of anxiety discussed in the drive theory context is one obvious example. Also, *level of experience* would be another. Since individual athletes differ in their degree of experience, it could be expected according to the principle of habituation and the prin-

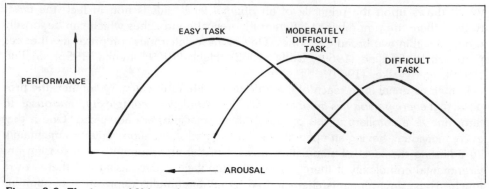

Figure 3.9. The inverted-U hypothesis.

ciple of simplification that there would be individual difference in response to a stressful or arousing situation. In short:

> . . . there are differences between subjects in their reactions to similar or identical 'stressful' environments. Some subjects show a marked anxiety reaction to the stressor while others appear to be unconcerned. Further, one condition may prove to be stressful or anxiety producing to a subject while another situation (judged equally threatening by an independent observer) may have no effect [Carron, 1971].

Another mediating factor suggested by Landers was the *task*. It was noted that "there is much conjecture concerning the mediating effects of task difficulty . . . but few studies conducted on its effects." It was also noted that research with measures of movement time have failed to show the predicted curvilinear relationship between arousal and performance. Movement time is apparently one type of task in which progressive improvements occur with increasing levels of arousal — there is no decrement in performance.

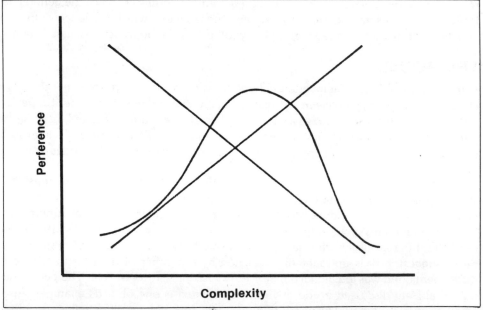

Figure 3.10. Three relations between preference and complexity, all of which are permitted by optimal level theory (From Arkes and Garske, 1977).

However, Arkes and Garske (1977) have observed that this type of finding is *not inconsistent* with an inverted-U hypothesis. In fact, three types of curves are permissible (see Figure 3.10) or, at least, are not inconsistent with an inverted-U prediction. Thus, it might be argued that with further increases in arousal, the ascending-descending curves in Figure 3.10 would plateau and then show a worsening effect. This could also be the case with movement time.

AROUSAL AND PERFORMANCE

The minimal experimental condition necessary in order to test the inverted-U hypothesis consists of at least three levels of the arousal condition. Consequently, the great majority of studies carried out in sport and physical activity cannot be examined from an inverted-U perspective. One study which does satisfy the criterion was carried out by Martens and Landers (1970). High-, moderate- and low-trait anxiety preadolescent boys were tested on a motor steadiness task under three arousal conditions: a low, moderate or high probability of receiving an electric shock. As the level of stress progressively increased (and this was assessed by palmar sweat masures), the performance level showed an inverted-U pattern — an increase followed by a decrease (see Figure 3.11).

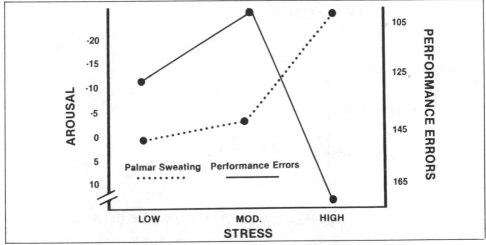

Figure 3.11. Relationship between palmar sweating, task performance and stress induced by threat of electric shock (From Landers, 1978, based on results from Martens and Landers, 1970). Reproduced with permission of the publisher.

Even more impressive support was obtained by Klavora (1977). Figure 3.12 outlines the theoretical curve advance by Klavora to depict the relationship between precompetition state anxiety and performance effectiveness in athletics. It was observed that *outstanding performance* (OP) would be associated with only one level of precompetition anxiety (i.e., an optimal level). On the other hand, a *poor performance* (PP_1 and PP_2 on Figure 3.12) and an *average or expected level of performance* (AP_1 and AP_2 of Figure 3.12) each could be the product of either of two precompetition levels — arousal slightly above the optimum or arousal slightly below the optimum.

This theoretical model was analyzed using high school basketball players. Precompetition anxiety was assessed through the state anxiety measure of the STAI while performance effectiveness was judged by the athlete's coach. The results are presented in Figure 3.13.

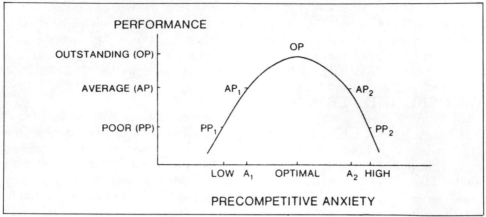

Figure 3.12. A theoretical model showing the relationship between precompetitive levels of state anxiety and performance in athletics (From Klavora, 1977). Reproduced with permission of the publisher.

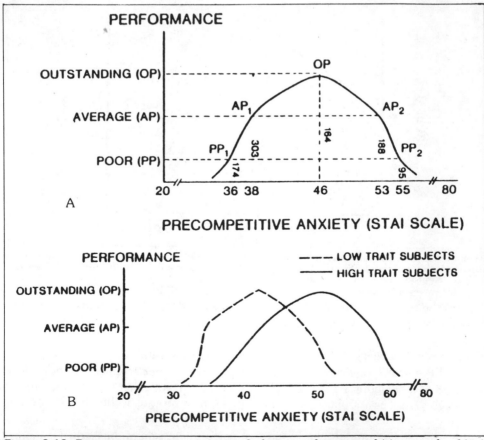

Figure 3.13. Precompetitive state anxiety and playing performance of (a) a sample of high school basketball players (figure on the top and (b) that same sample subdivided according to level of trait anxiety (figure on the bottom). (From Klavora, 1977) Reproduced with permission of the publisher.

As Figure 3.13a shows, the mean state anxiety score for the 164 athletes judged to have had an outstanding performance was 46.2. In the case of the average performers, the mean state anxiety score for the 188 athletes scoring above the *optimal* — the state anxiety score of 46.2 — was 53.1; for the 303 scoring below, it was 38.2. Finally, in the case of those basketball players who were judged by their coaches to have had a poor performance, the 174 scoring below the optimum had a mean state anxiety score of 36.3; the 95 above, a mean score of 55.5.

Klavora further analyzed the state anxiety-performance data using an identical procedure but with the outstanding, average and poor performers subdivided according to their *trait anxiety* levels. This analysis is presented in Figure 3.13b.

Commenting upon the individuals at the lower end of the activation (precompetitive anxiety) continuum, Klavora stated that:

> . . . *[low] A-trait subjects were found to be psychologically underactivated on the precompetitive A-state scale and played poorly 15.57% of the time. This percentage was slightly higher for the high A-trait subjects (22.86%) indicating that they were underactivated more often than were the low A-trait subjects . . .*
>
> *These findings have important implications in sport psychology. It has been believed that high A-trait athletes are usually overaroused in competition, whereas the opposite is true for low A-trait subjects. Therefore, high A-trait subjects have to be calmed down and low A-trait subjects have to be activated to achieve optimal performance . . . to the contrary, the findings of this study suggest that both the low and the high A-trait subjects have to be approached in the same way [Klavora, 1977].*

A number of other studies have provided additional support for the inverted-U hypothesis: Samuel, Baynes and Sabeh (1978) with an anagram task; and Courts (1942), Kennedy and Travis (1948), and Wood and Hokanson (1965) when activation was induced by varying the level of muscle tension of the subjects. However, there have also been other studies which have failed to show direct support (Pinneo, 1951; Kling and Schlosberg, 1959; Teichner, 1957; Marteniuk, 1968; Basler, Fisher and Mumford, 1976).

PRACTICAL IMPLICATIONS FOR THE INVERTED-U

The inverted-U has an intuitive appeal in terms of explaining the relationship between arousal and performance. The athlete who is unaroused, not interested, poorly motivated, will not perform well. And, conversely, an athlete who finds the situation excessively stressful also will not perform well. Consequently, the critical factor is to try to strike a balance somewhere between the two extremes. But where is that optimal level? Since the optimal level is thought to vary as a function of task complexity and individual differences, it is difficult for the coach or teacher to determine what degree of motivation should be attempted with different individuals in different sports.

In an attempt to provide some guidelines on the task complexity dimension, Oxendine (1970) arrayed a number of sports along a continuum comprised of five categories. This is illustrated in overview in Figure 3.14. One extreme included those activities or sports which place a high premium on speed, strength and endurance but a low premium on complexity, fine muscle control and judgment. Included in this group were weightlifting, blocking and tackling in football and strength items such as push-ups.

At the other extreme of the continuum were those activities or sports which place a high priority on fine muscle control and judgment but a low premium on strength, speed etc. Included in this group were golf putting, figure skating, bowling and archery.

68

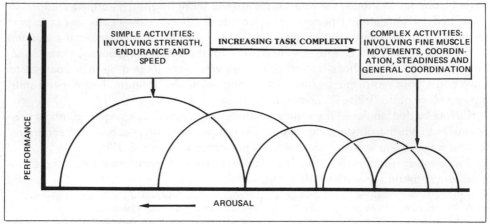

Figure 3.14. The relationship of arousal to performance in sport and physical activity (Adapted from Oxendine, 1970).

The assumptions underlying the designation of the various sports to the five categories along this continuum were that:

1. A high level of arousal is essential for optimal performance in gross motor activities involving strength, endurance and speed.

2. A high level of arousal interferes with performance involving complex skills, fine muscle movements, coordination, steadiness and general coordination.

3. A slightly above-average level of arousal is preferable to a normal or subnormal arousal state for all motor tasks [Oxendine, 1970].

This schema does have some very useful implications. However, Landers (1978) has questioned the validity of the first and third assumption. He stated that (1) not all speed of performance events show improvements with arousal increases (i.e., fastest reaction time is associated with an intermediate rather than high level of arousal); and, (2) there are few nonlaboratory situations in which a high level of arousal is beneficial to performance. Landers then suggested that "what is missing from Oxendine's analysis is the role that attention plays in most skills, including those involving speed, endurance and strength . . . one of the most commonly reported effects of arousal is its effect on the narrowing of the visual field."

As an addendum to the inverted-U hypothesis, Landers submitted the model illustrated in Figure 3.15. Thus, with increases in arousal from a low to a moderate level, there is a corresponding increase in perceptual selectivity — task irrelevant cues are eliminated and performance improves. However, with further increases in arousal, the "tunneling effect" becomes more pronounced and performance deteriorates.

The football quarterback provides a useful example. Under a low arousal condition such as a practice drill, a variety of peripheral cues (the coach, spectators, etc.) vie for attention and either through a lack of concentration or low selectivity, irrelevant stimuli are attended to by the QB. With moderate arousal levels (e.g., a practice scrimmage), the increased arousal is accompanied by increased perceptual selectivity which in turn contributes to effective performance. At extremely high levels (e.g., the first interscholastic game as a starting quarterback), the perceptual field becomes so restricted that performance deteriorates. The quarterback may focus on one pass

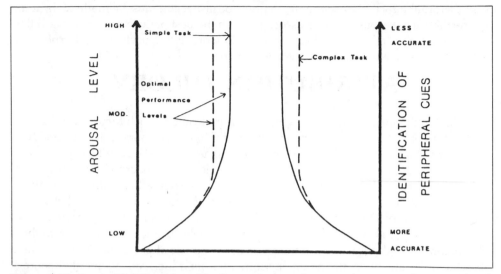

Figure 3.15. Arousal level and breadth of attention to relevant task cues as a function of task difficulty. *Note.* **The point of optimal performance is higher on the arousal continuum for simple tasks than for complex tasks (From Landers, 1978). Reproduced with permission of the publisher.**

receiver exclusively for example.

Within Lander's proposal, task complexity was considered to be a function of the breadth of perceptual cues the athlete must attend to in performance. In this regard, a distinction was made between *open* and *closed skills*.[8] The former consist of those skills in which the individual must attend to and respond to a rapidly changing environment. The games of tennis, basketball and soccer and the task of the hockey goalkeeper all serve to illustrate open skills. On the other hand, closed skills are carried out in an environmental situation in which the stimuli are relatively unchanging. Sports such as the sprint events in track and swimming and tasks such as high jumping and shot putting illustrate this category.

Individuals involved in closed sports, "the sports demanding narrower attentional focus can tolerate higher levels of arousal since there are fewer task cues and, therefore, less chance of task-relevant cues being eliminated through the perceptual narrowing process" (Landers, 1978). While Landers has provided an interesting addition to the inverted-U hypothesis, it has not yet been tested empirically.

OVERVIEW

Although the previous discussion does highlight the fact that the inverted-U hypothesis is a reasonable explanatory model for the arousal-performance relationship, it does have limitations. One of these is that "an inverted-U relation allows so many possible curves that the theory is difficult to refute. Any theory not susceptible to disproof is worthless" (Arkes and Garske, 1977). Figure 3.10 shows one result which directly confirms the inverted-U relationship and two other curves (the ascending and descending curves) which, at worst, do not disprove it. In fact, these results might even be interpreted as "partial support."

A second, related limitation is the difficulty of designating the optimal arousal a

8. Footnote 3 of Chapter 5 contains a further elaboration on the distinction between open and closed skills.

priori (before-the-fact). Consequently, a post hoc inspection must be made of the data to determine what arousal level is associated with the best performance result and this level becomes the "optimal." While this procedure provides a useful way of *explaining* the results, it is of little value for *predictive* purposes.

ATTRIBUTION THEORY

Attribution theory[9] is a cognitive approach to motivation which focuses on the way in which people form causal interpretations for their personal behavior and the behavior of others. Heider (1944, 1958), the originator of attribution theory, describ- ed it as *common sense* or *naive psychology* since it is not concerned with theoretical abstractions such as drives, instincts, internal forces etc. but rather with the "theories" that people use in everyday situations to understand, explain and predict behvaior.

A cornerstone of Heider's theory was that every person strives for prediction and understanding of daily events in order to impose a stability and predictability into their interpersonal and physical environments. Thus, an athlete after competition, a student following an examination and a person returning from a social engagement all share a common desire to understand *why* the particular outcome occurred as it did. And, when each of these individuals analyzes their situation, it is not through the use of complex constructs such as *need for achievement, habit hierarchy, optimal arousal,* and so on, but with straightforward concepts such as *effort, difficulty, ability* and *fatigue.* In short, people do not concoct elaborate, comprehensive scientific theories for *everyday* experiences. They utilize a relatively small number of factors — factors which are either perceived to be under personal control or which are a product of the situation itself — in order to account for the outcome.

However, Heider (1958) pointed out that there are some very direct parallels bet- ween scientific psychology and the processes used in common sense psychology:

> . . . in common-sense psychology (as in scientific psychology) the result of an action is felt to depend on two sets of conditions, namely factors within the person and factors within the environment . . . one may speak of the effective force (ff) of the person or of the environment when one means the totality of forces emanating from one or the other source.
>
> The action outcome, x, may then be said to be dependent upon a combination of effective per- sonal force and effective environmental force, thus: x = f (ff person, ff environment).

There are very obvious parallels between this formula suggested by Heider and the formula for behavior advanced by Lewin, $B = f (P,E)$. But, there is also an important distinction between the two. With his formula, Lewin was attempting to account for the *underlying causes for behavior.* On the other hand, Heider was interested in the *perceived causes* of a previous outcome.

Thus, the unsuccessful athlete, student and date each might conclude that a per- sonal factor such as the amount of effort expended was primarily responsible for the poor outcome. While the athlete and student might attribute their failure to a lack of ef- fort ("I just didn't try hard enough"), the unsuccessful suitor could attribute the out- come to too much effort ("I came on too strong"). Or, all three could also conclude that the outcome was largely a product of factors within the situation which were

---

9. This possibly should be amended to the plural form — attribution theories — since there is no single, comprehensive model for attribution. Rather, there are three major viewpoints: Heider's (1944, 1958) outline, and Weiner's (1972) modification of it; the Jones' and Davis' (1965) theory of correspondent inferences; and Kelley's (1967, 1971, 1972, 1973) multiple causation model. Only the former is presented here.

beyond personal control — such as luck for example ("It simply wasn't in the cards today"). Or, finally, the situation and personal factors could be held equally responsible ("I didn't try as hard as I should have but with any kind of luck . . .").

THE MODEL

Fritz Heider. The model for causal attribution proposed by Fritz Heider (Heider, 1944, 1958) is presented in Figure 3.16. As is evident in this illustration, and consistent with the above discussion, Heider proposed that behavioral outcomes (success and failure for example) are attributed to *effective personal force* and *effective environmental force*.

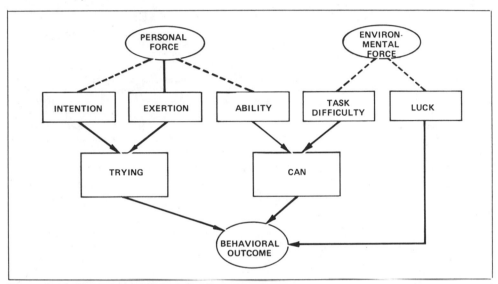

Figure 3.16. Heider's model for causal attribution.

The effective personal force was considered to be comprised of two components: the *power* and the *motivation* of the individual. The former was thought to consist primarily of *ability* while the latter (which was represented as *trying*), was thought to consist of *intention* and *exertion*. Intention was used to represent the qualitative dimension of motivation (what the individual was attempting to do) while exertion was used to reflect the quantitative dimension (how hard the individual was attempting to do it). Both were thought to reflect motivation since the athlete who intends to compete may do so with great or minimal effort.

Thus, ability and trying together were considered integral components of effective personal force — a high school basketball player, no matter how motivated, cannot compete professionally; there is simply not sufficient ability. Effective personal force may be represented as follows:

$$\text{Personal Force} = f \,(\text{Ability} + \text{Trying}) \tag{8}$$

Heider also proposed that the situational or environmental force used to account for behavioral outcomes was comprised of two components: *task difficulty* and *luck*. The most important of these is task difficulty. As Figure 3.16 shows, task difficulty and ability were also thought to interact to yield a dimension referred to as *can*. Thus, if the task is extremely simple or the individual possesses a great deal of ability, that task *can* be accomplished successfully. Conversely, either an extremely difficult task or low ability would mean that the task *cannot* be carried out successfully. While these two factors of ability and task difficulty are interrelated to some extent, it will be evident in the subsequent discussion that the pattern of causal attribution to each is markedly different after successful versus unsuccessful outcomes.

The highly variable, unpredictable factors within a situation (and over which the individual has no direct control) were encompassed within a category called *luck*. Thus, the effective environmental force can be represented as follows:

$$\text{Environmental Force} = f \text{ (Task Difficulty + Luck)} \tag{9}$$

Bernard Weiner. A number of significant contributions to the understanding of causal attribution in achievement situations were made by Bernard Weiner and his associates (e.g., see Weiner, 1972). These contributions were made largely within Heider's basic schema. As Weiner (1972) stated:

> . . . *following Heider, it is postulated that there are four perceived causes of success and failure at achievement tasks: ability (power), effort, task difficulty, and luck. This is not an exhaustive list. Surely individuals often assign causality to sources not readily classifiable within these four categories. For example, failure might be attributed to fatigue (which is distinguished from effort expenditure), bias (which is distinguished from task difficulty), misread instructions (which is distinguished from bad luck), and so forth. It is contended, however, that the four causal elements listed above generalize to all achievement tasks, and account for the major sources of variance when considering the perceived causes of success and failure.*

What Weiner then did with Heider's schema was to restructure the four factors[10] within two main causal dimensions: *stability* (fixed attributes versus variable attributes) and *locus of control* (internal attributes versus external attributes). This is outlined in Figure 3.17.

	Internal	External
Stable	Ability	Task Difficulty
Unstable	Effort	Luck

Figure 3.17. Weiner's classification scheme for the causal attributes.

Although Weiner did present research evidence in support of this classification scheme (e.g., Weiner, 1972; Weiner, Freize, Kukla, Rest and Rosenbaum, 1971), it also possesses inherent face validity. That is, one of the personal attributes, ability, is categorized as internal and stable; the other, effort, as internal but unstable. In an achievement situation such as competitive wrestling for example, the athlete with suffi-

---

10. The overwhelming majority of researchers have used these four categories of causal attributes. Thus, the present discussions focus on this schema. However, it should be noted that Freize (1976) did test the assumption that ability, luck, effort and the task have the most relevance to achievement situations. Subjects were given the outcome of an achievement-oriented situation and asked to state why they thought each event occurred. The format was open-ended — no possibilities were suggested. Freize concluded that her "open-ended studies . . . validated the types of causal attributions typically employed to explain the causes of success and failure." However, she also pointed out that (1) *luck* was very infrequently cited; and that (2) *mood* and *other people* attributions were suggested frequently enough to suggest their inclusion in attribution studies.

cient experience in the sport, retains a relatively unchanging (stable) perception of personal ability. However, the perceived effort expended in successive competitions could vary markedly and is, therefore, unstable.

Similarly, one of the enviornmental attributes, task difficulty, is categorized as external and stable; the other, luck, as external but unstable. Again, by way of example, the ability of the wrestler's opponent (and we'll assume that it's the same person), which would represent the task difficulty in this example, would not change markedly from one competition to the next—it would remain relatively stable. On the other hand, the degree of luck experienced would be unstable and variable over time.

The causal attribution model outlined by Heider and Weiner has been examined in a variety of achievement situations including athletics.

CAUSAL ATTRIBUTIONS IN ACHIEVEMENT SITUATIONS

Past Experience. Past experience is a major determinant in the attributions made to causality. Figure 3.18 illustrates the pattern of causal attributions made when a success or failure outcome occurs following differing amounts of previous success (i.e., past success varying from 0 to 50 to 100 percent). The results presented here are from studies by Freize and Weiner (1971)

It is evident that the greater the discrepancy between the immediate outcome and prior performance, the larger the attributions to unstable factors. That is, when a success occurs following 100% previous failures or a failure occurs following 100% previous success, the unstable factors of luck and effort are most strongly endorsed. Similarly, a reverse pattern occurs with the stable attributes of ability and task difficulty. These two are most strongly endorsed when the outcome is most consistent with previous experience — a success following a history of previous successes or a failure following a history of previous failures.

There is an inherent reasonableness in this pattern of findings. A tennis player who has been constantly successful against an opponent or a student who has repetitively obtained an A standing in schoolwork would be inclined to view a failure as an isolated phenomenon resulting from bad luck or a decline in personal effort — not to low ability or the difficulty of the task. Similarly, these same two generally successful individuals would be inclined to attribute another success to personal ability and/or the relative simplicity of the assignment rather than extreme luck or exceptional effort.

This general pattern of findings reported by Freize and Weiner has also been replicated in a number of studies dealing with attributions made in the nonlaboratory context of sport. For example, Spink (1977, 1978), using high school basketball players analyzed the attributions made to ability, the task, effort, luck and officiating. The latter factor was included because "officials often play a dominant role in athletics. Consequently, athletes might view this as a distinct cause of their success or failure"[11] (Spink, 1978).

The results are presented in Figure 3.19. An outcome which was consistent with a previous outcome — success after a success or failure after a failure against the same opponent — was attributed to the stable factors of task and ability. On the other hand,

11. Spink's results did show that officiating was not strongly endorsed as a causal factor in athletic outcomes. He suggested that this result might have been the product of either good officiating, a subsuming of this factor under the category of "luck," or that officiating is not considered to be an important component contributing to the outcomes in high school basketball.

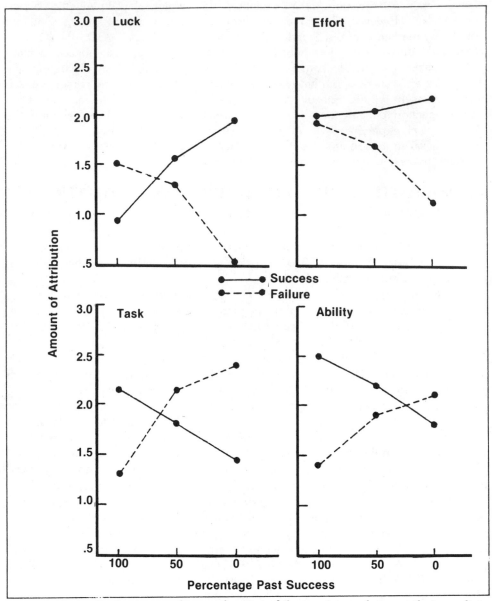

Figure 3.18. Attribution to causality as a function of the consistency between the immediate outcome and past performances (From Weiner, 1972, based upon results from Freize and Weiner, 1971). Reproduced with permission of the publisher.

when the result was inconsistent — failure following a success or success following a failure — the unstable factors of effort and luck were endorsed (Figure 3.19a).

This interaction between past history and mode of attribution is more strongly highlighted in Figure 3.19b. The same factors are utilized here (excluding officiating since it is not actually a component in Weiner's model) with the stable dimension being, of course, ability and the task; the unstable dimension being effort and luck. These general findings have also been reported by Roberts (1975) and Iso-Ahola (1975) with

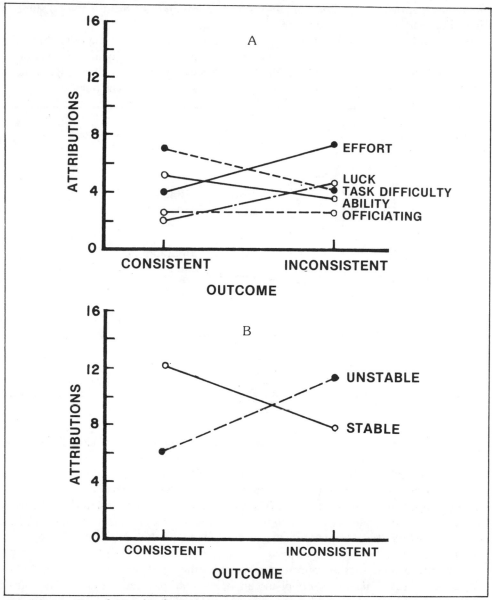

Figure 3.19. The relationship between consistency of outcome and (a) attributions to luck, ability, task difficulty, effort and officiating and (b) attributions to stable (ability and task difficulty) versus unstable (effort and luck) factors (From Spink, 1977). Reproduced with permission of the author.

Little League baseball players.

Previous experience apparently serves to provide the individual with a frame-of-reference within which to understand/explain behavioral outcomes. In novel, unfamiliar situations, this frame-of-reference is lacking and the ascription of outcomes (either success or failure) to stable factors decreases. This was illustrated in an experiment reported by Iso-Ahola and Roberts (1977) with college males. A group of subjects with previous experience on a motor maze were given success or failure feedback following performance. Their attributions were compared to those made by subjects who had had no previous experience with the task.

Figure 3.20 contains a summary of the results. With previous experience on the task, the stable attributions were more strongly endorsed to explain the outcome. However, the attributions to the stable factors showed a decline while the attributions to unstable factors showed an increase when the task novelty was high.

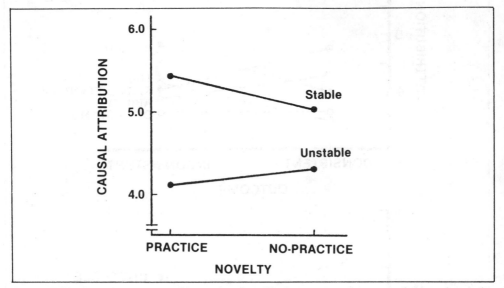

Figure 3.20. Attributions to stable versus unstable factors as a function of the task novelty (Adapted from Iso-Ahola and Roberts, 1977).

Egocentricism in Causal Attributions. Although the individual's past experiences do provide a frame-of-reference for understanding behavioral outcomes, there is also strong evidence which suggests that individuals use ego-enhansive and ego-defensive strategies in their attributions for causality in achievement situations. There is a tendency to ascribe successful outcomes to personal/internal factors while unsuccessful outcomes are attributed to environmental/external factors. In short, *I am responsible and accept credit for the success* whereas, on the other hand, *The loss was out of my control.*

The two explanations advanced to account for the egocentric pattern of attribution have been a *self serving bias model* and an *information processing model*. The former in its most elemental form was outlined by Heider (1958) who noted that the "tendency to raise the ego level will structure causal units in such a way that only good acts and not bad ones are attributed to the person." Thus, the self serving bias model emphasizes the presence of an egocentrically-oriented motive on the part of the individual which emanates from the need to maintain or enhance self esteem (Heider, 1958, Kelley, 1967).

In the information processing model (Bem, 1972; Miller and Ross, 1975), the notion of a biased, self-serving motive is discounted in favor of an explanation which emphasizes the logical basis for egocentric perceptions. That is, if the individual has had a history of previous successes, then success in a given task might be logically attributed to personal factors and failure to external factors. Miller and Ross (1975) noted that since the type of subjects commonly used in research (i.e., college students, athletes) have had a history of general success, personal attributions in achievement situations while appearing to reflect a self serving motivation, might be, in actuality, a conclusion arrived at logically from the available information.

The studies which have either directly or indirectly attempted to compare the plausibility of these two models have found greater support for the self serving bias model. Some of this research is summarized in a section dealing with group attributions in achievement situations (see Chapter 7).

Whatever the underlying cause, a pattern of egocentric attribution has been observed consistently in a variety of achievement and role playing situations (e.g., Arkin, Gleason and Johnston, 1976; Beckman, 1970; Feather and Simon, 1971; Freize and Weiner, 1971; Gilmor and Minton, 1974; Simon and Feather, 1973; Weiner and Kukla, 1970; Wolosin, Sherman and Till, 1973; Wortman, Costanzo and Witt, 1973).

Similarly, it has also been shown in a number of studies relating to attributions in athletics. Figure 3.21 outlines the results obtained by Spink (1977, 1978) in his study with high school basketball players. As Figure 3.21a shows, the internal dimension (effort and ability) was more strongly endorsed than the external dimension (luck and the task) when the outcome was successful. However, following a loss, there was a decrease in internal attributions and a corresponding increase in external attributions.

Gilmore and Minton (1974) found that the most extreme scores on an anagram test — scores reflecting highly effective or highly ineffective performance — were attributed to internal factors (ability or lack of ability). However, as performance (whether successful or unsuccessful) more closely approximated the pass-fail criterion, external attributions showed an increase.

As Figure 3.21b reveals this was not the case in the Spink study. Attributions to a decisive win and a close win were internal. In the loss condition (both decisive and close), there were no differences in the level of internal and external attributions.

A self-enhancing pattern of attributions to causality has also been noted by Iso-Ahola (1977a, 1977b) and Roberts (1975) with Little League baseball players and Iso-Ahola and Roberts (1975, 1977) with college students on a novel motor task. However, one exception to this pattern was a study by Duquin (1977). When an open-ended questionnaire was administered in elementary school physical education classes (grades 5 to 8), it was found that both success and failure were attributed internally. Over 90% of the students who were successful and 60% of those who were unsuccessful perceived the outcome to be a result of internal factors (ability, mood, effort).

Pride and Shame Associated With Perceived Causality. Weiner (1972) has hypothesized that affective or evaluative reactions to task outcomes are a function of the perceived reasons for the outcome. The athlete who loses but perceives the result to be due to bad luck or the exceptional play of an opponent experiences less shame than an athlete who fails and perceives this to be a product of low effort. Conversely, an athlete who perceives success to be the result of luck, experiences less pride in that outcome than one who attributes an outcome to ability.

Figure 3.22 contains a summary of the Weiner proposal. It was hypothesized that when attributions for success and failure are made, to internal, personal factors — ef-

78

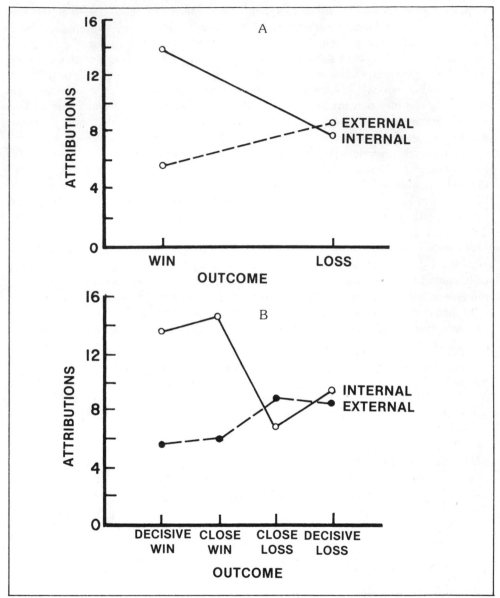

Figure 3.21. The relationship between (a) win and loss outcomes and attributions to internal versus external factors and (b) the decisiveness of the outcome and attributions to internal and external factors (From Spink, 1977). Reproduced with permission of the author.

fort and ability — there is more affect than attributions to external factors — task difficulty and luck. Also, as Figure 3.22 indicates, Weiner suggested that within the internal dimension, greater affect is associated with perceived effort than with perceived ability.

Weiner and Kukla (1970) provided direct support for these latter proposals (see Figure 3.23). Student teachers were asked to reflect on their feelings of pride or shame following various achievement performances which were a result of four combinations

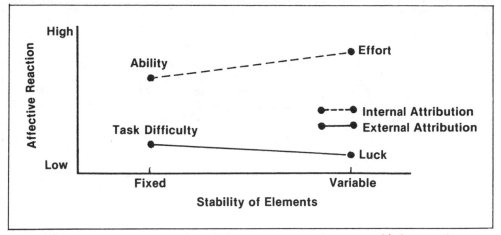

Figure 3.22. Hypothesized magnitude of affective reaction to success and failure as a function of causal ascriptions (From Weiner, 1972). Reproduced with permission of the publisher.

of the personal factors of ability and motivation: ability and motivation; ability and no motivation; no ability and motivation; and no ability and no motivation. The greatest amount of pride was associated with a successful outcome that was attributed to effort while the greatest shame accrued from a failure outcome resulting from a lack of effort. Also, when no motivation was present (ability and no motivation and no ability and no motivation), there was generally more pride associated with success and less shame associated with failure when the individual possessed less ability. On the basis of these findings, Weiner (1972) concluded that "the clearest empirical result in these data is that perceived effort is the most important determinant of affective reactions to success and failure."

Iso-Ahola (1976) obtained a similar pattern of findings in a study concerned with the effect associated with team outcomes. This study is discussed in Chapter 7 (see Figure 7.6).

Subsequent research by Nicholls (1975, 1976) has led to the suggestion that there may be mediating factors to the generalization contained in Weiner's conclusion and the relationship depicted in Figure 3.23. In one experiment, Nicholls (1975) found that when children attempted a novel task and were successful, resulting attributions made to ability were associated with greater pleasure than resulting attributions made to effort. Apparently, the children derived satisfaction from the knowledge that since they possessed the stable attribute of ability, they were assured of additional pleasure at some future date. Success resulting from the unstable attribute of effort did not provide any real assurance that the individual would encounter more success at some subsequent achievement activity.

In a second experiment, Nicholls (1976) had college students indicate what type of person they would prefer to be: one who did well (or poorly) with some ability and little effort or one who did well (or poorly) with little ability and much effort. The students were also asked to indicate the degree of pride or shame they would attach to outcomes reflecting these conditions.

Nicholls found that consistent with the Weiner and Kukla findings, pride over success was associated with low ability and high effort while shame over failure was associated with low effort and high ability. However, in response to the question regar-

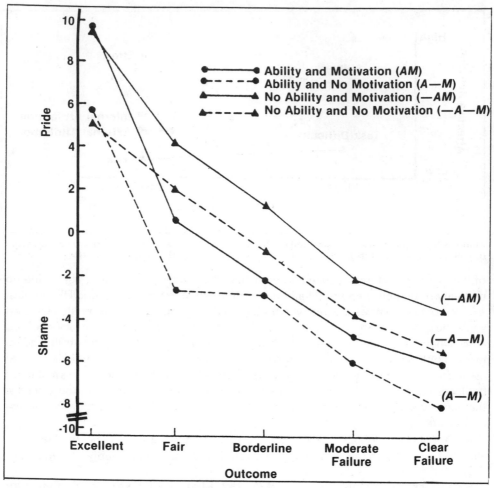

Figure 3.23. Perceived pride and shame attached to outcomes resulting from different combinations of ability and effort. Source: Weiner, B. and Kukla, A. An attributional analysis of achievement motivation. *Journal of Personality and Social Psychology,* 1970, 15, 1-20. Copyright, 1970 by the American Psychological Association. Reprinted by permission.

ding what type of person they would prefer to be, a preference was shown for high ability rather than high effort. As Nicholls observed, the "students indicated that shame over failure would be occasioned by the very circumstances (high ability and low effort) they would prefer when presented with a choice."

Nicholls reasoned that the effect associated with effort and ability is related to whether the person will have to carry out the task at some future date. Looking back reflectively, the tennis player can derive greatest satisfaction from a victory in which her low ability was overcome by an outstanding effort. On the other hand, since, as indicated above, pleasure is associated with victory, not defeat, in anticipating future performances, greater pleasure would be associated with the knowledge that she possessed high ability. The chances for future reward would be greater than if she simply possessed high levels of motivation.

OVERVIEW

The great strength of attribution theory is its simplicity and adaptability to a wide cross-section of situations — not simply to the achievement situations highlighted here. The fact that it emphasizes cognition rather than intervening variables or theoretical constructs has also held a wide appeal to many researchers. And, while the initial interest and work with the theory has been in regard to the factors used to explain previous behavior, the model has also been extended by Weiner to outline the conditions under which attributions influence subsequent behavior. This is outlined in some detail in Chapter 9. Because the impact of attribution theory has been relatively recent, there has been a great deal of interest in testing its applicability to a wide range of situations. There is no doubt that the theory has a number of attractive features.

Arkes and Garske (1977) have pointed out that the very advantages of "attribution theory — breadth of explanation and cognitive emphasis — also create shortcomings." One of these is its scope. "Paradoxically, the advantage of globalness can also be a bane. Other massive theories, such as psycholanalytic theory, also have the ironic distinction of being *too* explanatory. This feature, of course, is not at all problematic if a theory is as adept at predictive explanation as it is at postdictive description. But attribution theory is not" (Arkes and Garske, 1977).

A second limitation of attribution theory is that there is no strong evidence to suggest that a cognitive analysis of the causes of an outcome will necessarily lead to behavior (Arkes and Garske, 1977). These limitations notwithstanding, attribution theory has had the most significant impact upon the psychology of motivation since the introduction of the work of Hull-Spence and Atkinson-McClelland.

THEORY OF ACHIEVEMENT MOTIVATION

The general context of sport and physical activity is essentially *achievement oriented*. Whether the athlete is performing alone (which could be the case in the game of golf or during a cross country run for example) or as a member of a group (which would be the case in team sports such as soccer, hockey, basketball, etc.), a number of standards of excellence are available against which personal achievement may be evaluated. These standards might be *personal* (a previous performance), or *normative* (the degree of difficulty in a dive or the par on a golf course) or *environmental* in nature (an opponent). In some instance, and the game of golf provides a good example, all three standards could be present. For some individuals, such an achievement oriented situation is pleasurable and is readily entered into; for others, the situation is viewed unpleasantly and avoided if possible. Why is this the case? What are the factors which account for the wide individual differences in behavior in achievement situations?

The theory of achievement motivation — which originally emanated from the work of David McClelland and John Atkinson — was developed to account for behavior in *all* achievement related situations. According to Atkinson (1964), an achievement situation comprises those instances where an individual "knows that his performance will be evaluated (by himself or by others) in terms of some standard of excellence and that the consequences of his actions will be either a favorable evaluation (success) or an unfavorable evaluation (failure)."

The scope of achievement theory — or, more accurately, the wide variety of areas in which attempts have been made to extend the theory — is impressive. As might be expected, it has been used in obvious achievement situations such as sport (e.g, Ryan and Lakie, 1965), industry (e.g., Block, 1962), and academic settings (e.g., Cox, 1962). However, it has also been utilized to compare sexual, cultural and racial differences in achievement motivation (e.g., Feather and Raphelson, 1974; Weston and Mednick, 1970); analyze the developmental pattern for the growth of achievement motivation in children and adults (e.g., Winterbottom, 1953; McClelland and Winter, 1969); chart the economic growth of various countries in the world (e.g., McClelland, 1961); examine the basis for choices in college majors (e.g., Mahone, 1960); contrast the effectiveness of United States presidents (Donley and Winter, 1970); and, even postdictively chart the growth, climax and decline of early Greek civilization as well as the economic growth of England over the 350 year period from 1500 to 1850 (McClelland, 1961).

But, this diversity should not be interpreted as evidence that the theory has had universal acceptance as an explanatory model for motivated behavior. On the contrary, the theory of achievement motivation has also been the object of strong criticisms — particularly in reference to its reliability and validity (e.g., Entwhistle, 1972; Fineman, 1977; Klinger, 1966). When viewed from this total perspective — potentially wide applicability versus potentially serious psychometric limitations — it is easy to appreciate that the theory of achievement motivation has had a major impact on the study of motivation.

THE MODEL

Introduction. In a manner which is consistent with the Lewinian prescription that $B = f(P,E)$, McClelland and Atkinson considered achievement-oriented behavior to be a product of the two factors of person and environment. Within the environment dimension, the principal component incorporated is the incentive value of a goal or objective. However, a second component is intimately interrelated to the goal's incentives/rewards — the expectancy or perceived probability that that goal can actually be attained.

Thus, in its essential form, the Atkinson-McClelland approach is an *expectancy-value theory* of motivation — the extent to which an individual is motivated toward a goal depends upon the incentive value of that goal (the rewards associated with it) and the perceived expectation that its attainment is at least possible. The interrelationship between incentive and expectancy is obvious. For example, an intermediate-level tennis player would attach great value to beating the club professional while viewing this goal as quite improbable. Conversely, that same player's expectations for success against a beginner would be very high but the associative incentive value would be minimal.

Considered within the person dimension are two independent personality dispositions (i.e., traits) reflecting individual differences in motivation toward achievement situations. One of these, the *need to achieve* (which is represented as "n Achievement," "n Ach" and "M_s"), is a measure of the strength of an individual's motive to enter into and achieve success in achievement situations. A person's n Ach is typically assessed[12] by means of the Thematic Apperception Test (TAT) — a projective personality test developed by Murray (1943). In this test, the individual is shown a series of pictures and asked to write stories concerning:

1. What is happening? Who are the persons?
2. What has led up to the situation; that is, what has happened in the past?
3. What is being thought? What is wanted; by whom?
4. What will happen? What will be done? [Atkinson, 1964].

The stories are then scored for their degree of achievement-related content.

The second personality disposition toward achievement situations which is present in all individuals is the *motive to avoid failure* (which is represented as M_{af}). As the name implies, it is a disposition to delay or avoid entering into achievement situations. The motive to avoid failure is typically assessed[13] by means of the Sarason and Mandler Test Anxiety Questionnaire (TAQ). This self-report inventory measures the degree of anxiety experienced in various achievement (test situations. Thus, the rationale is that the higher the degree of test anxiety present, the stronger the motive to avoid failure.

Prior to outlining the general theory itself, three important points relating to these two achievement motives should be emphasized. The first is that both dispositions are present (in varying degrees) in every individual. The second is that they are independent. That is, M_s and M_{af} are not correlated. Consequently, knowing the degree to which one is present in an individual does not provide any indication of the degree to which the other is present; high M_s could be present with high, medium or low M_{af}. And finally, since they are personality dispositions, they are *transituational* — the individual with high M_s and low M_{af}, for example, should show a characteristic pattern of motivated behavior which is relatively consistent over time and generalizable across a wide cross-section of different achievement situations.

The Tendency to Approach an Achievement-Oriented Goal (T_s). One of the two main components of the theory, the tendency to approach an achievement-oriented goal (T_s), is the general motivation an individual has to enter into achievement activity. It is a multiplicative function of three factors: (1) the strength of the individual's dispositional motive for success (M_s) — which is assessed through the TAT personality test; (2) the perceived probability for success in the task (P_s); and, (3) the incentive value of success (I_s). This is expressed as:

$$T_s = M_s \times P_s \times I_s \qquad (10)$$

Table 3.5 contains as summary of these constructs.

As pointed out above, since M_s is an inherent personality disposition, its influence is consistent across all achievement situations. However, both the incentive and the probability associated with attaining it are situation specific. Also, incentives are considered to be the inverse of probability; if incentive is high, probability is low and vice versa. This is expressed as:

$$I_s = 1 - P_s \qquad (11)$$

12. A number of other tests have subsequently been used to measure the achievement motive (e.g., French 1958; Jackson, 1967; Lynn, 1969) but the TAT was the first used by Atkinson and McClelland.
13. Other personality tests have also been used to assess the motive to avoid failure (e.g., Taylor, 1953; Cowen, 1957).

Table 3.5. Achievement motivation constructs.   —

FACTOR	DESCRIPTION	SYMBOLIC REPRESENTATION
Motive for Sucess	The individual's dispositional motivation to engage in achievement tasks.	M_s
Motive to Avoid Failure	The individual's dispositional motivation to avoid or delay entering into achievement tasks.	M_{af}
Perceived Probability for Success	The estimate or judgement made by the individual that performance will be successful.	P_s
Perceived Probability of Failure	The estimate or judgement made by the individual that performance will be unsuccessful.	P_f
Incentive Value of Success	The rewards, incentives and perceived satisfaction associated with a successful outcome.	I_s
Incentive Value of Failure	The perceived dissatisfaction, shame and displeasure associated with failure. It is always a negative value.	I_f
Tendency to Approach an Achievement-Oriented Goal	The disposition, inclination or tendency to engage in an achievement-oriented task. It is a multiplicative function of the individual's personality (M_s), the probability of success (P_s) and the incentives attached to that success (I_s).	T_s
Tendency to Avoid an Achievement-Oriented Goal	The disposition, inclination or tendency to avoid or delay entering into achievement situations. It is a multiplicative function of the individual's personality (M_{af}), the probability of failure (P_f) and the pride, displeasure and dissatisfaction associated with that potential failure (I_f).	T_{af}
Resultant (Net) Achievement Motivation	The difference between the tendency to approach and the tendency to avoid an achievement oriented task is the resultant (net) achievement motivation.	T_r

The example with the tennis player again illustrates this relationship. The higher incentive value attached to beating a superior player is associated with a lower expectation that this is possible.

Since these three factors are thought to combine in a multiplicative manner (as Equation 10 shows) and since incentive and probability are thought to be inversely related (as Equation 11 shows), the theory of achievement motivation yields some very specific predictions concerning the types of achievement situations most preferred by individuals of high M_s versus low M_s.

Table 3.6 contains an overview of the motivation toward achievement (T_s) evidenced by a high M_s person[14] (for example, a M_s score of 8) and a low M_s person (for example, a M_s score of 2) in situations where the perceived probability for success (P_s) varies from a virtual assurance of success (for example, a probability of .90) to certainty of failure (for example, a probability of .10). The incentive value (I_s) for these situations also varies accordingly.

Table 3.6. The motivation to engage in achievement-oriented tasks (T_s shown by a high n Ach ($M_s = 8$) and a low n Ach ($M_s = 2$) person faced with various situations which differ in their incentive-probability (I_s and P_s).

P_s	HIGH M_s (8) $M_s \times P_s \times I_s = T_s$	LOW M_s (2) $M_s \times P_s \times I_s = T_s$
.10	$8 \times .10 \times .90 = .72$	$2 \times .10 \times .90 = .18$
.30	$8 \times .30 \times .70 = 1.66$	$2 \times .30 \times .70 = .42$
.50	$8 \times .50 \times .50 = 2.00$	$2 \times .50 \times .50 = .50$
.70	$8 \times .70 \times .30 = 1.66$	$2 \times .70 \times .30 = .42$
.90	$8 \times .90 \times .10 = .72$	$2 \times .90 \times .10 = .18$

It is apparent from an examination of the various T_s values in Table 3.6 that both individuals show a preference for achievement situations in the intermediate range of difficulty ($P_s = .50$). Also the greater the motive for success ($M_s = 8$), the greater the absolute motivation toward the task.

The Tendency to Avoid an Achievement-Oriented Goal (T_{af}). The outcome of an achievement situation will evoke pride and pleasure if the outcome is favorable. However, it is also possible that the goal may not be achieved and the result of that outcome would then be shame and displeasure. Consequently, while achievement situations produce a motivation to approach or engage in the activity (T_s), they also produce a tendency to avoid the activity; this is referred to as the tendency to avoid failure (T_{af}). A summary of this construct is also presented in Table 3.5.

The tendency to avoid failure (T_{af}) is the motivation to avoid or delay entering into an achievement situation. It is the product of three factors: (1) the strength of the individual's personality disposition to avoid failure (M_{af}) — which is assessed through the TAQ personality test; (2) the perceived probability of failing (P_f); and, the incentive value attached to failure (I_f). This is expressed as:

$$T_{af} = M_{af} \times P_f \times I_f \tag{12}$$

14. The protocol which is illustrated in the example presented in Table 3.8 is actually the correct approach. The examples presented in Table 3.6 (and also subsequently in Table 3.7) serve the purpose of outlining the rationale within the theory in a relatively simple context.

The interrelationship of the three factors contributing to T_{af}, the motivation to avoid failure, is identical to that within T_s, the motivation to engage in achievement tasks. That is, each person brings the disposition M_{af} to an achievement situation. In addition, when faced with the specific goal, the person forms a subjective probability that performance can lead to failure (P_f). In turn, that potential failure is associated with a certain degree of shame or displeasure — the incentive value for failure (I_f).

The level of I_f is always less for extremely difficult tasks — there is less shame attached to a lack of success in a virtually impossible situation than when the situation is extremely easy. Thus, as was the case with I_s and P_s, the incentive value of failure is considered to be inversely related to the probability of failing, or:

$$I_f = -(1 - P_f) \qquad (13)$$

As Equation 13 reveals, the incentive value of failure is always expressed as a negative value.

Table 3.7 includes T_{af} values for two individuals — one with high M_{af} (M_{af} score of 8); the other with low M_{af} score of 2). In contrast to the person who is high in M_s, the individual who is high in M_{af} is most strongly *motivated away from* achievement tasks of intermediate difficulty. A greater preference is shown for tasks which are either extremely easy $(P_f = .10)$ or extremely difficult $(P_f = .90)$. In the former instance, success is virtually assured — an outcome which is entirely compatible with a motive to avoid failure. In the latter case, the task is virtually impossible (but it has a high incentive value) and, therefore, there is very little shame or displeasure associated with failure. In fact, the situation can be best summed up as "everything to gain and nothing to lose."

Table 3.7. The motivation to avoid achievement-oriented tasks (T_{af}) shown by a high M_{af} and a low M_{af} person (scores of 8 and 2 respectively) faced with various situations which differ in their incentive-probability (I_f and P_f).

P_f	HIGH M_{af} (8) $M_f \times P_f \times \quad I_f =$	T_{af}	LOW M_{af} (2) $M_f \times P_f \times \quad I_f =$	T_{af}
.10	$8 \times .10 \times -.90 =$	$-.72$	$2 \times .10 \times -.90 =$	$-.18$
.30	$8 \times .30 \times -.70 =$	-1.66	$2 \times .30 \times -.70 =$	$-.42$
.50	$8 \times .50 \times -.50 =$	-2.00	$2 \times .50 \times -.50 =$	$-.50$
.70	$8 \times .70 \times -.30 =$	-1.66	$2 \times .70 \times -.30 =$	$-.42$
.90	$8 \times .90 \times -.10 =$	$-.72$	$2 \times .90 \times -.10 =$	$-.18$

The Resultant (Net) Achievement Motivation (T_r). Since each individual possesses both personality dispositions, the two tendencies of T_s and T_{af} are *always* present in all achievement situations. As a negative quantity, T_{af}, the tendency to avoid the achievement goal, detracts from T_s, the positive tendency toward that goal. The difference between the two is referred to as the net or resultant tendency to approach an achievement-oriented task (T_r), or:

$$T_r = T_s + (-T_{af}) \qquad (14)$$

This is basically a conceptual formula; a very simple formula which is identical mathematically, can be derived for practical purposes by combining Equations 8 and 10. The result is the following:

$$T_r = (M_s - M_{af}) (P_s \times I_s) \qquad (15)$$

In discussing the specific implications of this formula and net or resultant achievement motivation (T_r) Weiner (1972) observed:

> . . . it is reasonable for the reader to ask such questions as: 'How can one be classified as high or low in the resultant tendency to strive for success? How can the strengths of M_s and M_{af} be compared, for they are conceived as independent dimensions and assessed with different instruments?' The procedure generally followed by Atkinson and other researchers in this area is to assign each individual standard scores, or Z-scores, on the basis of his TAT and TAQ score deviations from the means of the population under investigation. By transforming scores on both the TAT and TAQ into Z-scores, it is possible to compare the relative strengths of these motives within any individual. Thus, if an individual scores high on the TAT relative to his comparison group, and low on the TAQ relative to this group, he is classified as high in resultant achievement motivation, or one in whom $M_S > M_{AF}$.

Table 3.8. T_r values in situations of varying difficulty and incentive for individuals high, medium and low in resultant achievement motivation.

P_f	HIGH ($M_s=8$, $M_{af}=2$) $M \times P \times I = T_r$	INTERMEDIATE ($M_s=4$, $M_{af}=3$) $M \times P \times I = T_r$	LOW ($M_s=2$, $M_{af}=8$) $M \times P \times I = T_r$
.10	$6 \times .10 \times .90 = .54$	$1 \times .10 \times .90 = .09$	$-6 \times .10 \times .90 = -.54$
.30	$6 \times .30 \times .70 = 1.26$	$1 \times .30 \times .70 = .21$	$-6 \times .30 \times .70 = -1.26$
.50	$6 \times .50 \times .50 = 1.50$	$1 \times .50 \times .50 = .25$	$-6 \times .50 \times .50 = -1.50$
.70	$6 \times .70 \times .30 = 1.26$	$1 \times .70 \times .30 = .21$	$-6 \times .70 \times .30 = -1.26$
.90	$6 \times .90 \times .10 = .54$	$1 \times .90 \times .10 = .09$	$-6 \times .90 \times .10 = -.54$

In Table 3.8, hypothetical data is presented for three individuals: one who is *high* in resultant achievement motivation (as a consequence of a M_s score of 8 and a M_{af} score of 2); a second who is *low* in resultant achievement motivation (as a consequence of a M_s score of 2 and a M_{af} score of 8); and, a third who is *intermediate* in resultant achievement motivation (as a consequence of a M_s score of 4 and a M_{af} score of 3).

The implications of the results presented in Table 3.8 are completely consistent with those presented in conjunction with Tables 3.6 and 3.7. That is, individuals who are $M_s > M_{af}$ (the individuals referred to as *high* and *intermediate*) show the greatest preference for tasks in the intermediate range of difficulty. This is evident when the T_r values associated with $P_s = .50$ are contrasted with the values associated with $P_s = .10, .30, .70,$ or $.90$.

Also, the greater the discrepancy between M_s and M_{af}, the greater will be the net resultant achievement motivation brought to the specific situation. This is evident when any of the T_r values for the *high* person are compared with the corresponding T_r values for the *intermediate* person. The absolute amount of T_r is always greater for the *high* individual.

In addition, an individual who is $M_{af} > M_s$ (the individual referred to as *low* in Table 3.8) shows the least preferences for tasks of intermediate difficulty. As the tabled values indicate, the greatest preference is shown for tasks which are either very simple or very difficult.

A final important observation which should be made — not only in relation to Table 3.8, but to the theory of achievement motivation in general — concerns the T_r values for the *low* person. Since the resultant achievement motivation is negative in every instance (irrespective of the situation), it might be assumed that this person would never be sufficiently motivated to engage in achievement related activity. However, such an assumption would be unreasonable theoretically and practically.

The theoretical model presented to this point has been concerned with the factors influencing the level of *intrinsic motivation* brought to a particular situation. In short, whatever the situation, an individual with $M_s > M_{af}$ will have more intrinsic motivation than an individual with $M_{af} > M_s$.

Thus, the final factor which might be included in the model, the factor which leads the $M_{af} > M_s$ person and the $M_{af} = M_s$ person to engage in achievement activities, is the amount of *extrinsic motivation* present in the situation. Given a sufficient amount of "added incentives" a $M_{af} > M_s$ individual enters into the achievement situation. As a result, the final equation concerned with achievement theory is

$$\text{Achievement Behavior} = T_r + \text{Extrinsic Motivation} \qquad (16)$$

SPORT AND PHYSICAL ACTIVITY

The theory of achievement motivation has two dimensions which have particular relevance to sport and physical activity. One of these, which can be termed *risk taking behavior*, is summarized by the question "are there differences in preferences for motor skills of different difficulty among individuals who differ in the relative amount of M_s and M_{af} they possess?" The theoretical discussions presented above would, of course, predict that there should be.

A second dimension concerns the relationship of net resultant achievement motivation (T_r) to *performance effectiveness.* "Are there differences in performance which can be accounted for by differences in the internal dispositions of M_s and M_{af}?" According to the theoretical model, an $M_s > M_{af}$ individual possesses more innate motivation than an $M_{af} > M_s$ individual. Therefore, it should follow that if two individuals are of approximately equal ability, the $M_s > M_{af}$ person should show superior performance because of greater motivation.

Risk Taking Behavior. The predicted interaction between relative M_s/M_{af} and the preference shown for tasks of varying difficulty has been tested and generally supported in a large number of experiments (e.g., Atkinson and Litwin, 1960; Brody, 1963; de Charms and Carpenter, 1968; Hancock and Teevan, 1964; Isaacson, 1964; McClelland, 1958; Shaban and Jecker, 1969; Roberts, 1974; Veroff and Peele, 1969). Only a few studies have failed to show support (e.g., de Charms and Dave, 1965; Weiner, 1966).

One of the earliest in the positive category was reported by Atkinson and Litwin (1960). They permitted four groups of college males to select their own preferred distances (over a range from 1 to 15 feet) from which to attempt a ring toss. These four groups were analogous to the *high, intermediate* and *low* categorizations used in Table 3.8 with two intermediate categories being included (one in which $M_s > M_{af}$; the other in which $M_{af} > M_s$).

All groups showed the greatest preference for an intermediate distance (which is not completely in agreement with the predictions emanating from Table 3.8). However, the differences among the groups were consistent with theoretical predictions. The *high* group attempted a much greater percentage of shots from the intermediate distances than either the *intermediate* or *low* groups. In turn, the two *intermediate* groups showed a much greater preference for the intermediate distance than the *low* group.

Another set of results supporting the predictions was reported by Roberts (1974). A number of additional conditions were included. He noted that "previous research indicates that risk taking only occurs in the presence of other competing subjects" (Roberts, 1974). Therefore, five different social environments were incorporated into a research design. These conditions were: alone (A); with an audience of four passive spectators (P); in interpersonal comptition against two other individuals for a prize of $1.00 (CM); in a situation involving intragroup cooperation-intergroup competition where two groups of three individuals competed for a prize of $3.00 which was then shared equally among the winning team (CO-CM); and, in an intragroup competition-intergroup competition situation where one group of three individuals competed against another with the monetary prize being distributed on a sliding scale according to the relative contributions of the individuals (CM-CM). The task was a modified shuffleboard with eight lines (possible starting points) marked at increasing distances from the target. In a pretest session, all subjects were given 10 practice trials at each of the distances. These data were then used to empirically determine the .50 probability for success *for each subject*. As a result, specific behavior on any given trial (the degree of risk taken) could be assessed in terms of its deviation from this value.

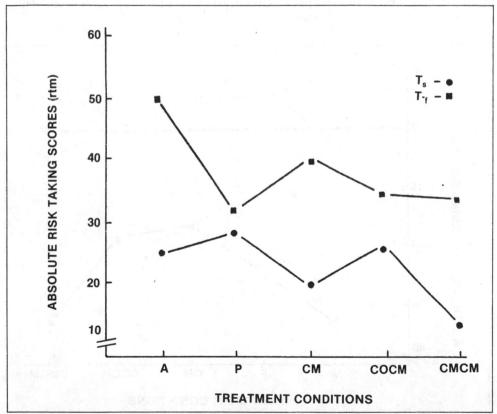

Figure 3.24. Absolute risk taking scores (From Roberts, 1974). Reproduced with permission of the publisher.

90

Figure 3.24 presents a summary of the results obtained when *absolute deviation* scores were utilized. In the case of these scores, the direction of deviation from $P_s = .50$ was ignored. That is, it was immaterial whether the level of risk selected was $P_s = .80$ or $P_s = .20$; the amount of absolute deviation was identical in both cases. "Therefore, a small total absolute risk taking score indicated that a subject preferred tasks of intermediate difficulty (tasks which had a probability of success of around .50) while a high score indicated a subject avoided tasks of intermediate difficulty preferring instead tasks that were either easy or difficult" (Roberts, 1974).

There were no differences among the five social conditions. However, the analysis did reveal that consistent with achievement motivation theory predictions, the subjects motivated to achieve success (T_s) showed a much greater preference for intermediate risk choices than subjects motivated to avoid failure (T_{af}).

Figure 3.25 shows the results obtained when *algebraic deviation* scores were utilized. In this type of assessment, the direction of deviation is taken into account. Consequently, "a large negative total risk taking score indicated extreme risk choices, a large positive score indicated conservative risk choices, whereas, a low positive or negative score indicated intermediate risk" (Roberts, 1974). Again, as the results, in Figure 3.25 show, the intermediate levels of risk were consistently elected by T_s individuals but consistently avoided by T_{af} individuals. Also, it is evident that the T_{af} subjects showed a preference for extreme risk choices — choices having a lower probability of success — rather than conservative ones.

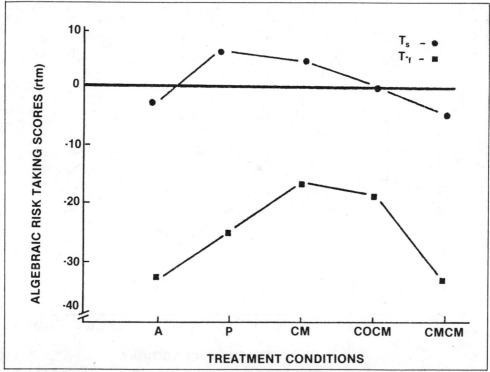

Figure 3.25. Algebraic risk taking scores (From Roberts, 1974). Reproduced with permission of the publisher.

A somewhat different approach was taken by Ostrow (1976) in a nonlaboratory study. He compared the goal setting behavior of $M_s > M_{af}$ and $M_{af} > M_s$ college males who were participating in a series of four handball contests. The participants level of aspiration and level of expectation were assessed objectively before and after each contest (i.e., assessed as the margin of points the participant expected and aspired to win or lose by). While Ostrow did find that $M_s > M_{af}$ participants set more realistic goals for themselves, this distinction was only present for the first contest. No differences were observed in the subsequent contests.

Performance. A number of studies have found that higher levels of n Ach are associated with superior performance (Atkinson, 1958; Atkinson and Raphelson, 1956; Block, 1962; Cox, 1962; McClelland, Atkinson, Clark and Lowell, 1953). However, research which has been carried out with motor skills has generally found that high n Ach individuals demonstrate superior performance to low n Ach individuals but *only in the early stages of performance.* (Healey and Landers, 1973; Ostrow, 1976; Roberts, 1972).

This was a finding in the Ostrow (1976) study with handball players which was presented above. Similarly, Roberts (1972) noted that performance differences between T_s and T_{af} subjects were present in the pretest session but not in the subsequent test session. Finally, Healey and Landers (1973) found that T_{af} individuals showed greater variability in performance than T_s individuals but in the initial trials only. No differences were found in the performance scores themselves.

This seemingly consistent but perplexing pattern of findings might be explained by drawing upon some generalizations advanced by Weiner (1972) on the basis of his analysis of the research literature. He observed that:

> . . . guided by the definition of achievement motivation, it is assumed . . . that individuals high in resultant achievement motivation expect to encounter little frustration and have a history of achievement success, while those low in resultant achievement motivation expect to experience failure and perceive that past achievement efforts have not resulted in goal attainment.

Given these differences between T_s and T_{af} individuals in expectation for success, it then might be expected that their responses to success and failure would differ markedly. And, this has apparently been the case as the evidence from a number of studies would seem to indicate. Weiner (1972) summarized the research results from previous studies with the following four generalizations:

1. Motivation is enhanced following failure among individuals high in resultant achievement motivation.
2. Motivation is inhibited following failure among individuals low in resultant achievement motivation . . . .
3. Motivation is decreased following success among individuals high in resultant achievement motivation.
4. Motivation is enhanced following success among individuals low in resultant motivation.

These generalizations are illustrated in Figure 3.26.

In motor skills learning, early success as manifested in performance improvements is virtually assured. (A typical learning curve was illustrated in Figure 3.3.) A motor skill learning curve can be described mathematically as a two-component exponential consisting of a fast early stage which is characterized by rapid, large improvements in performance. This is followed by a slower stage which is characterized by minimal im-

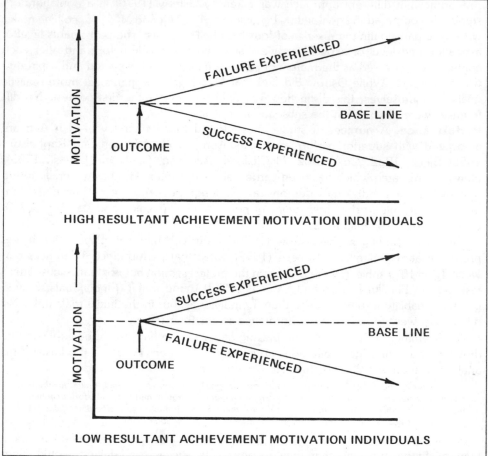

Figure 3.26. The motivational effect of success and failure outcomes on individuals high and low in resultant achievement motivation (Adapted from Weiner, 1972).

provements (Carron and Leavitt, 1968). Consequently, when T_s and T_{af} individuals are placed in a motor skill practice situation, some early success would be expected for both groups. And, the expected result of that success would be a decrease in motivation on the part of the T_s individuals and an increase on the part of the T_{af} individuals. Thus, any differences in performance attributable to the greater intrinsic motivation of the T_s individuals would also be expected to disappear as the groups became more similar in their level of motivation.

Ryan and Lakie (1965) have obtained results which suggest that competition is essential in order to obtain performance differences between individuals differing in achievement motivation. T_s and T_{af} subjects were initially tested alone on a ring peg task, given success-oriented feedback and then placed in a competitive situation against an experimental accomplice (ostensibly, an "expert" on the task). Consistent with their predictions, Ryan and Lakie found that T_{af} were superior to T_s individuals under the neutral (noncompetition) condition, but inferior under the competitive condition. It was observed that "the more anxious individual [T_{af}] appears to do well in a noncompetitive situation when he is not threatened or under pressure, but when placed in competition his anxiety or fear of failure tends to interfere with performance. In contrast, the competitive situation seems to motivate the individual with a high desire to succeed [T_s], energizing and improving his performance" (Ryan and Lakie, 1965). There is, of course, a parallel between this explanation and the emotional reactivity hypothesis advanced by Spence and Spence (1966) which proposes that a threatening or noxious stimulus is necessary in order to bring out the differences between high- and low-anxious individuals. In turn, a competitive situation may serve to magnify the difference between high and low n Ach individuals in their tendency to approach an achievement task.

SEX DIFFERENCES IN ACHIEVEMENT MOTIVATION

The theoretical model that was developed by Atkinson and McClelland to account for achievement-oriented behavior was intitially thought to apply equally to both males and females. However, subsequent investigations contributed to a conclusion that this was not the case. Harris (1978) charted the course of this development:

> . . . the greatest confusion in the understanding of achievement motivation has been that involving sex differences. The initial research efforts involved primarily data gathered from males even though comparisons of males and females responses were made. Inconsistent and contradictory findings have been reported and some investigators ceased to gather data from females because they did not get good, clean, predictable data . . . a number of investigators have suggested that males and females differ in need stimulating achievement behavior. It has been argued that females work for love and approval rather than mastery, that achievement motivation is bound to affiliative needs. These arguments stress quite different underlying mechanisms for equivalent achievement motivation in males and females.

The differences discussed by Harris were a principal factor behind Horner's (1968) efforts to rework the theory of achievement motivation in order to make it more applicable to women. Horner proposed that superimposed upon the schema already discussed, females also have a *motive to avoid success* (M_{-s}) — a disposition to feel anxiousness in non-feminine/masculine activities. This personality trait would presumably develop in a female during the process of socialization into her sex role and would be most highly aroused in highly competitive, achievement situations since these types of situations are traditionally viewed as "masculine" in nature. Thus, an achievement situation would not only evoke M_{af} in females, but also M_{-s}. In turn, both of these motives would detract from M_s. Conceptually, this would be presented as:

$$T_r = (M_s - M_{af} - M_{-s}) (P_s \times I_s) \tag{17}$$

However, to date, very few studies have been carried out to test Horner's formulations. The results from the few studies available have not been promising. At least part of the difficulty might lie in the projective test used by Horner to assess M_{-s}. Its validity and reliability are quite low.

Another approach, applicable to the study of achievement motivation in both sexes, has been developed by Helmreich and Spence (1977, cited in Harris, 1978). They constructed an inventory (Work and Family Orientation Questionnaire, WOFO) designed to assess four components of achievement motivation: *work orientation* (a desire to do one's best in whatever one undertakes); *mastery* (persistence in accomplishing tasks, of doing difficult things); *competitiveness* (enjoying the challenge of situations involving skill and competition); and, *personal unconcern* (not being concerned about what others might think).

A second inventory was also developed to classify individuals according to their perceived sex-role classification. The four factors include *androgynous* (possessing desirable human characteristics some of which are traditionally accorded to females, others to males); *masculine* (conforming to the traditional male-stereotype); *feminine* (conforming to the traditional female stereotype); and, *undifferentiated* (falling below the mean level for both male and female subjects).

Harris (1978) used these two inventories to examine the motivation of 240 female athletes. The results are summarized in Table 3.9. It is apparent that there are major differences in motivational orientation across the four categories of perceived sex-role classification. Particularly interesting is the difference in motivation between the female athletes with a perceived sex-role classification of femininity versus those who are androgynous and masculine. These findings support a conclusion that perceived sex-role is a determinant in the level of motivation toward achievement activities.

Table 3.9. Motivational orientation of 240 female athletes differentiated on the basis of their sex-role classification (From Harris, 1978).

SEX-ROLE CLASSIFICATION	N	MOTIVATIONAL COMPONENTS			
		MASTERY	WORK	COMPETITIVENESS	PERSONAL UNCONCERN
Androgynous	109	17.9	18.4	15.7	15.4
Masculine	58	25.7	25.0	23.7	24.2
Feminine	32	13.0	13.7	11.1	12.2
Undifferentiated	41	10.1	10.9	8.9	10.1

OVERVIEW

A number of other modifications have been suggested to the original theory of achievement motivation (e.g., Raynor, 1969, 1970; Weiner, 1965, 1972; Birney, Burdick and Teevan, 1969; Revelle and Michaels, 1976). The interested reader might wish to examine these; they are outside the scope of the present text.

Prior to closing this section on the theory of achievement motivation, it should be reiterated that attempts have been made to extend this theory into an amazing number of diverse areas. And, at the same time, serious criticisms have been leveled at the validity and reliability of the measures of M_s and M_{af} as well as at the general applicability of the theory in terms of its usefulness in accounting for motivated behavior in all achievement situations.

SPORT COMPETITION ANXIETY

In the introduction to this chapter, it was pointed out that only those major theories of psychological motivation which have had a significant impact upon sport and physical activity research would be discussed here. If that frame-of-reference was adhered to rigidly, there would be no basis for including Martens' (1977) theory of *sport competition anxiety*. Since it was only completely outlined recently, it has not yet been extensively examined beyond the initial validation studies carried out by Martens and his colleagues. As a result, it is difficult to adequately evaluate the effectiveness of the model as a predictor of behavior and performance in a sport context.

On the other hand, it does have the very real advantage of being specifically applicable to the context of sport and physical activity. One beneficial effect resulting from the ongoing debate related to the trait versus situationism versus interactionism perspectives of behavior (see Chapter 2) has been an increasing sensitivity to the need to understand the nature of the individual within a specific situation. This has been highlighted in sport research where it has become apparent that the incentives for participation, the antecedents of aggressiveness and/or the correlates of group cohesiveness — to illustrate only a few examples — cannot simply be extrapolated from the nonsport situation.

A similar point was emphasized by Martens (1977) in regard to the anxiety evidenced by sport competitors:

> . . . one person may become quite anxious when taking a math test, sitting in the dentist's chair, or delivering a speech but not become anxious when competing in a hockey game, performing at a piano recital, or taking a driver's examination. Thus, we can better predict behavior when we have more knowledge of the specific situation and how persons tend to respond to these types of situations . . . After reviewing some of the research using situation-specific A-trait instruments, Spielberger (1972b) concluded 'In general, situation specific trait anxiety measures are better predictors of elevations in A-state for a particular class of stress situations than are general A-trait measures.'

With this forming part of the underlying rationale, Martens proposed the concept of sport competition anxiety and provided a questionnaire to assess it — the *Sport Competition Anxiety Test (SCAT)*. He noted that "the competitive A-trait construct is a situation-specific construct especially developed to identify A-trait dispositions in competitive sport situations. Its development is based substantially on the evidence that situation-specific A-trait constructs are better predictors of behavior in the particular situation for which the construct was designed" (Martens, 1977).

THE MODEL

Competitive trait anxiety (A-trait) was defined by Martens (1977) as *"a tendency to perceive competitive situations as threatening and to respond to these situations with feelings of apprehension and tension."* Integral to the Martens theory of sport competition anxiety are an understanding of (1) the distinction between state anxiety (A-state) and trait anxiety (A-trait) as well as (2) the competitive process in sport and physical activity. The former was, of course, discussed previously in this Chapter in relation to Speilberger's work. Martens adapted and incorporated Spielberger's outline into his own model.

A-trait is a personality disposition which is acquired through experience. Individual differences in competitive A-trait are related to individual differences in the degree to which various competitive situations are perceived as threatening. On the other hand, A-state is the level of reaction which occurs to threatening stimuli (arising from internal and external sources). The two are considered to be intimately related since it is postulated that individuals possessing higher levels of A-trait will respond to threatening situations with more intense A-state reactions.

The model for the competitive process advanced by Martens includes four elements or components: the *objective competitive situation*, the *subjective competitive situation*, the *response*, and the *consequences* (see Figure 3.27).

The *objective competitive situation* represents the actual environmental demands

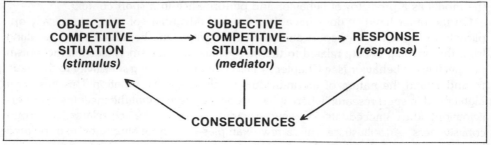

Figure 3.27. Martens' model of the competitive process (From Martens, 1977). Reproduced with permission of the publisher.

(both physical and social) for the person. These may or may not be potentially threatening and, therefore, may or may not influence the level of A-state. Factors within the objective competitive situation which could have an impact upon A-state level include the nature of the task, the ability of self relative to opponent, the incentives available, the presence of others, and so on.

The degree of threat contained within the objective competitive situation might be perceived quite differently by different individuals. As Martens (1977) noted, "most studies of the competitive process have assumed that the objective competitive situation is perceived identically by all individuals involved. Common sense suggests that this assumption is unfounded." Thus, the competitive process also includes a *subjective competitive situation* which is mediated by a number of intrapersonal factors. One of these is the individual's personality — specifically, the personality disposition of sport competition anxiety.

The output, the individual's *response* to the objective competitive situation (although it is largely a function of the subjective competitive situation) is the element that coaches and athletes are most concerned about. It can be considered from any or all of three perspectives: *behavioral responses* (e.g., Is performance effectiveness improved?); *physiological responses* (e.g., Is there a marked increase in heart rate, palmar sweating or other autonomic nervous system reactions?); and, *psychological responses* (e.g., What was the A-state reaction as assessed by the Spielberger STAI?).

The *consequences* of "engaging in the competitive process may be self-imposed or acquired from others, they may be tangible or nontangible, and they may be perceived as rewards or punishments . . . The long term consequences of competition have considerable influence on the subjective competitive situation, or how the person perceives future objective competitive situations . . . In large part, the accumulated consequences of participation in the competitive process are thought to determine the individual differences in competitive A-trait" (Martens, 1977).

Figure 3.28 illustrates the general model for the competitive process adapted to the specific study of competitive anxiety. Thus, competitive A-trait is considered by Martens to be an important mediator between the actual objective situation and the intensity of the A-state reaction. Individuals high in A-trait would perceive competitive situations as more threatening and this difference would be reflected in a higher A-state reaction. However, since competitive A-trait is a personality disposition which mediates A-state reactions for *competitive situations only*, it would also be predicted that individuals high and low in A-trait would not differ in their A-state reactions in noncompetitive situations. This general hypothesis is outlined in Figure 3.29.

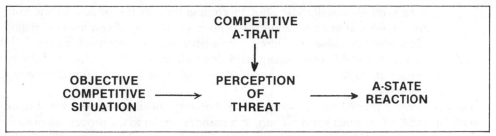

Figure 3.28. Competitive A-trait as a mediator between competitive stimulus and response (From Martens, 1977). Reproduced with permission of the publisher.

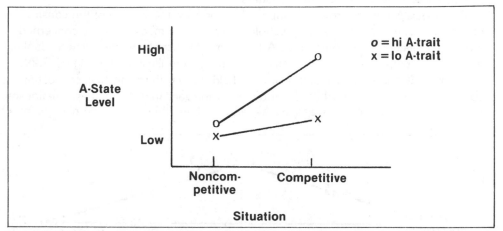

Figure 3.29. Basic prediction of differences in A-state for low and high competitive A-trait subjects in competitive and noncompetitive situations (From Martens, 1977). Reproduced with permission of the publisher.

SPORT COMPETITION ANXIETY AND BEHAVIOR AND PERFORMANCE

In his text, *Sport Competition Anxiety Test,* Martens (1977) reported the results of 11 studies carried out to test the validity of the competitive A-trait construct. Some of this research has also been published elsewhere (e.g., Martens and Gill, 1976; Martens, Gill and Scanlan, 1976; Scanlan, 1977).

In general, the experimental design used in the laboratory research comprised the following:

— a large number of children were initially tested with SCAT. Those individuals scoring at the upper and lower ends of the distribution (high competitive A-trait and low competitive A-trait respectively) were then selected as subjects. Thus, differences in competitive trait anxiety represented the independent variable of interest.[15]

— a preexperimental, basal measure of A-state (a measure secured in a relaxed, noncompetitive context) was obtained using Spielberger's STAI.

— the subjects were tested on a motor maze task and a number of A-state measures

15. Typically, other independent variables were also incorporated into the research design including sex, success-failure, and task type. However, the factor of interest here is competitive A-trait and only the results pertaining to it are discussed.

were secured — usually just prior to competition, in the middle of the competitive session, after completion of the competition and after a final debriefing.
— the dependent variable of interest (the response component of Figure 3.27)
varied across the different experiments depending upon the purpose of the experiment but, typically , behavioral, physiological and psychological measures
were assessed.

In general, the procedure used in the nonlaboratory (field) studies consisted of ad-
ministering SCAT to intact teams. Then, in a manner similar to the procedure outlined
above, a number of A-state measures were secured — basal, precompetition, mid-
competition and postcompetition. It was then possible, for example, to correlate the
A-trait measure with the A-state measures.

The results generally provided empirical support for the validity of the construct of
competitive A-trait insofar as the psychological response measures were concerned —
individual differences in competitive A-trait were significantly related to individual differences in competitive A-state (which is the prediction illustrated in Figure 3.29).

Figure 3.30 contains the results from one field study with female high school basketball players and their coaches. In addition to the fact that the highest relationship
($r = .64$) was outlined between SCAT and A-state, there are a number of other

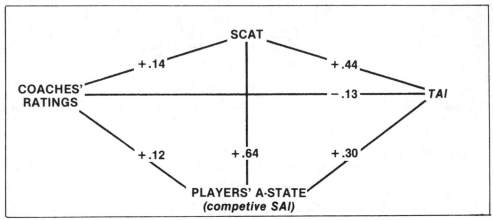

**Figure 3.30. Relationships among three measures of A-trait and players' competitive SAI
scores (From Martens, 1977). Reproduced with permission of the publisher.**

points of interest. For example, individual differences in the *general* trait of anxiety
(TAI) only correlated .30 with A-state indicating that a general measure of trait anxiety
is not as effective as a situation-specific one for predicting A-states. In addition, there
was a moderate relationship ($r = .44$) between competitive A-trait and the general
trait of anxiety indicating that the two measured similar (but not identical) constructs.
And, finally, the consistently low correlations between coaches' ratings and the
athletes' actual values indicates that the coaches were quite inaccurate in their perceptions of their athletes' dispositional level of trait anxiety (general and competitive) as
well as their athletes' level of state anxiety.)

In contrast to the promising pattern of results obtained with the psychological
measures, it was found that neither SCAT nor SCAT and A-state were able to reliably
predict motor performance effectiveness. That is, while differences in competitive
A-trait were found to be associated with differences in A-state, the differences in

A-state were not related to differences in performance. But, as Martens (1977) observed, "The failure of SCAT and A-state to predict motor performance . . . is not negative evidence of SCAT's validity. It is evidence that a simple measure of A-state is not an adequate predictor of motor performance."

SUMMARY

Motivation, which is thought to derive from the Latin word *movere*, to move, represents the energy or intensity underlying behavior. There are not only a number of different phenomena but numerous conceptual perspectives to account for the construct.

Drive theory is essentially a S-R interpretation for behavior in which a number of input variables (stimuli) are linked to output (response) variables via a series of intervening variables. In terms of sport and physical activity research, the most important intervening variables are *drive* (including *incentive motivation*) and *habit strength* which multiplicatively determine *excitatory potential*. Drive is the energizer for behavior while habit strength accounts for the direction that behavior takes.

Drive theory has been examined extensively in motor performance research with the drive component being manipulated through the use of personality variables (manifest anxiety) and/or external stressors (electric shock, the presence of an audience). However, the results have not been consistent with drive theory predictions — a pattern of findings which might reflect limitations in the theory itself or in the assessment of the intervening variables in a motor skills situation.

The optimal level theory, or inverted-U hypothesis as it is also called, is summarized by the proposal that a curvilinear relationship exists between the intensity of arousal and the effectiveness of performance. The optimal arousal level is also thought to be higher for simpler tasks. There has been some support for the inverted-U hypothesis but it is a difficult model to disprove — linear ascending and descending curves, for example, at best only fail to confirm the theory while measurement limitations restrict the possibility of predicting an optimal level a priori.

Attribution theory is viewed as a common sense or naive form of psychology since it is concerned with the theories that people use in everyday situations to account for behavior. The result of an action or outcome could be attributed to *environmental* and/or *personal factors*. In the bulk of the empirical analyses of attribution, the environmental factors focused on have been *luck* and *task difficulty* while *ability* and *effort* have been the personal factor utilized. The simplicity of the attribution model has been one of its predominant strengths. However, the model is better for postdictively explaining behavior than it is for predicting behavior a priori.

In the theory of achievement motivation, it is assumed that an individual possesses two personality dispositions which reflect individual differences in motivation toward achievement situations — the *motive for success* and the *motive to avoid failure*. In any achievement situation, these two motives interact multiplicatively with the *probability for success-failure* and the *incentive value* attached to success-failure to determine the individual's tendency to engage in achievement activities. Although the achievement motivation model has been used to predict achievement-oriented behavior in a wide cross section of situations, it has been repetitively criticized for its psychometric limitations.

In the model of sport competition anxiety, the situation specific personality trait of competitive anxiety is thought to be a mediator between the objective competitive situation and the intensity of the A-state reaction. Thus, individuals high in competitive A-trait view competitive situations as more threatening and respond with more intensity in their A-state reaction than do individuals low in competitive A-trait.

SECTION III
THE COACH

*Wars maybe fought with weapons but they are won by men.
It is the spirit of men who follow and of the man who leads
that gains the victory.*

George Patton

If the blind lead the blind, both shall fall into the ditch.

Matthew (15:14)

*When you're being run out of town, try to make it look like
you're leading a parade.*

Anonymous

*Some coaches pray for wisdom but I pray for 260-lb tackles.
They'll give me plenty of wisdom.*

Chuck Mills

THE NATURE AND DYNAMICS OF LEADERSHIP

4

Leadership may be considered from three related perspectives, each of which serves to define the construct. One of these is as an *interaction system;* this aspect of leadership is analyzed in the next chapter. A second perspective is as an *influence system* (Hollander and Julian, 1969). This perspective is in reference to the fact that there is an interactive exchange of influence in the process of leadership; the leader (the coach), the subordinates (the athletes, team), and the situation have a reciprocal impact upon each other. This is illustrated in Figure 4.1 (which is, of course, the behavioral model presented earlier in Chapter 1).

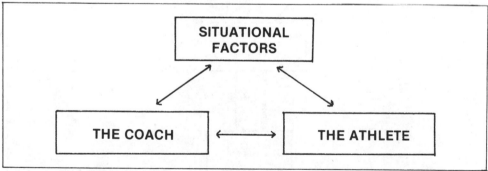

Figure 4.1. An influence system of leadership (From Carron and Chelladurai, 1978). Reproduced with permission of the publisher.

Hollander and Julian (1969), discussing the leadership subordinate aspect of the relationship, observed that:

> . . . the person in the role of leader who fulfills expectations and achieves group goals provides rewards for others which are reciprocated in the form of status, esteem, and heightened influence. Because leadership embodies a two-way influence relationship . . . the very sustenance of the rela-✓ tionship depends upon some yielding to influence on both sides.

The impact of the situation upon both the subordinate and leader must also be emphasized. It has been noted that a number of situational parameters including the

---

1. Some of the material in this chapter originally appeared in: P. Chelladurai and A. V. Carron, *Leadership,* Ottawa, Canadian Association for Health, Physical Education and Recreation Monographs, 1978.

nature of the task (e.g., Badin, 1974; Barrow, 1976; Hill and Hughes, 1974; Schriesheim and Murphy, 1976); the degree of pressure or stress present (e.g., Foder, 1976; Oaklander and Fleishman, 1964); the clarity of existing role expectations and standards (e.g., see House and Mitchell, 1974, Schreisheim, Murphy and Stogdill, 1974 for a literature review); and, physical and geographical aspects of the situation (e.g., Chelladurai and Carron, 1977) are interrelated with the leader-subordinate exchanges of influence.

In a third, somewhat related perspective which also serves to define the construct, leadership can be considered as a *power system*. That is, it is evident in most formal organizations that the leader plays a predominant part in the leader-subordinate relationship — leaders have a greater potential for exerting influence — as a result of their power which is inherent in their position.

French and Raven (1959) proposed a typology for the bases of power which was comprised of five categorizations: *reward* and *coercive* (both of which reflect the power which accrues to a leader as a result of control over the rewards available); *legitimate* (power which a leader has by virtue of rank or position); *expert* (power which results from expertise and knowledge of the task); and, *referent* (power accruing as a result of affection for the leader). Thus, a power system perspective of leadership reflects the fact that in leader-subordinate interactions, the leader has a stronger basis from which to exert influence than do subordinates (see Figure 4.2).

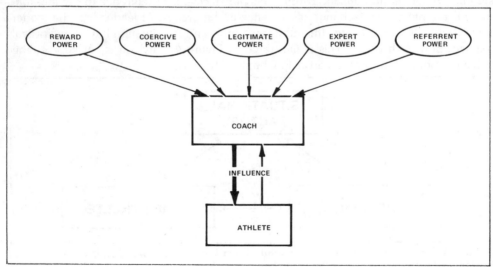

Figure 4.2. A power system of leadership. The heavy line reflects the greater power bases of the coach.

This would appear to be the case in the coach-athlete relationship. In sport and physical activity, two types of leaders are evident: *emergent leaders* and *prescribed leaders*. The former are most characteristic of the athlete dimension. Leaders emerge from within the team as leadership is either implicitly bestowed by the group upon one of its own members as a result of that individual's prowess, skill, competency and so on and/or explicitly bestowed via the process of nomination, selection, election, e.g., team captaincy. Thus, the bases of power for the athlete-leader are as a result of affection held, competency and skill exhibited, and/or specific formal group roles played. These are what French and Raven referred to respectively as referrent, expert and legitimate power bases.

Prescribed leadership, which is the focus of this chapter, is most characteristic of the coach dimension. The leader is appointed by an organization to lead/supervise/coordinate the task of a unit, team or group. As a result, that leader is in possession of not only legitimate and expert power (and possibly, although not necessarily, referrent power) but also reward and coercive power, the latter two by virtue of the control possessed over rewards available.

The nature of prescribed leadership leads to some unique concerns. It may be evident that emergent leaders have the tacit approval of the group. This is not necessarily the case with prescribed leaders. Their leadership accrues, initially at least, as a result of an organizational decision which may or may not have been influenced by input from those individuals who will be led. Thus, the prescribed leader is, in effect, a middleman between two units or forces: the larger organization and the group. And, as a result, the leader's two most difficult responsibilities, the responsibilities which are used to assess leader effectiveness, are insuring that (1) the organization's requirements — *task success* — are fulfilled; and, (2) the needs and aspirations of subordinates — *member satisfaction* — are achieved. It will become evident in this chapter that the major preoccupation in theories of leadership has been with the conflict between the organization's demands and the personal needs of members (Bennis, 1966).

The specific parameters which either contribute to or are associated with leader effectiveness have been a longstanding interest to theorists and researchers. Historically, the principal focus in the study of leadership has evolved from first, an emphasis on the examination of the *traits* of leaders (with particular reference to the characteristics possessed by successful leaders) to secondly, the examination of the actual *behaviors* of leaders in the leadership situation (with specific reference to those factors which contribute to performance effectiveness and individual satisfaction) and then, finally, to an analysis of the *situational parameters* influencing leadership (with specific reference to the interactive effects of those situations with the traits and behaviors of the leader). Each of these is discussed in turn in the present chapter.

LEADERSHIP CHARACTERISTICS

EARLY RESEARCH INTO LEADERSHIP

In the earliest research (which was largely carried out in management science), the interest in leadership centered around attempts to describe the personality characteristics of a leader. The rationale for this early work was that the progress of mankind is dependent upon the individual achievements of "great men." As a result, this approach has been traditionally referred to as the *Great Man Theory of Leadership*. The underlying assumption in this work was that effective leaders could be differentiated from nonleaders on the basis of the specific traits they possessed — as set of underlying predispositions contributed to behavioral consistency and consequently accounted for leadership ascendency and maintenance.

The assumption that effective leadership in management can be accounted for by a particular constellation of traits was subsequently challenged on the basis of both methodological (e.g., Cartwright and Zander, 1960) and conceptual considerations (e.g., Stogdill, 1959) and there is little current support for this view. The only underlying dispositional characteristic which has continued to receive support as a correlate of leadership is intelligence. However, as Mann (1959) and Campbell, Dunnette, Lawler and Weick (1970) reported in their comprehensive literature reviews, the median correlations between leader intelligence and task success are only in the range of .26 to .30. In short, leader intelligence only explains approximately 7 to 9 percent of the variability in task performance.[2]

These values are particularly low and might seem to provide a good basis for dismissing even intelligence as a "leadership trait." However, there has been some resistance. Recently, Fiedler and Leister (1977), in discussing the low correlational values, noted:

> . . . this is a curious finding. Intelligence is generally defined as the ability to cope with problems in a rational manner by planning, organizing, coordinating, and evaluating alternative modes of action through the use of innate cognitive abilities (Butcher, 1968). These functions are very similar, if not identical, to those which leaders and managers are expected to perform in organizational settings (e.g., Stogdill, 1974, p. 30). It seems logical, therefore, to assume a strong linkage between the leader's intelligence and task performance. The lack of success in identifying this linkage suggests that the intervening process in the chain between leader intellectual resources and task relevant behavior may not have been sufficiently well understood.

Fiedler and Leister then suggested that one reason for the low correlations might be that in previous research, group output was directly correlated with leader intelligence, a process which failed to take into account the fact that "the path between what is in the leader's head and what comes out in the form of task relevant behavior [is] strewn with numerous obstacles" (Fiedler and Leister, 1977).

They proposed a model for leadership intelligence-task performance which included some of these potential obstacles — four intervening variables, each of which, if unfavorable, could serve to detrimentally reduce the impact of a leader's intelligence upon group performance (see Figure 4.3). These variables are the leader's level of motivation (toward the accomplishment of the group task), the leader's degree of experience, the relationship between the leader and his supervisor and the relationship between the leader and the group.[3]

Fiedler and Leister did obtain some empirical support for this model in a study with army infantry squad leaders; the median correlations obtained between intelligence and performance when each of the four conditions was favorable was .335 (with a range from r = .07 to .40); and, only .145 (with a range of r = .01 to .34) when unfavorable. However, it should be emphasized that a correlation of .335 is still low, accounting for only 11 percent of the variability in leader intelligence and group performance. Thus, it must be concluded that even the most promising trait for leader effectiveness (in a management context) is not highly discriminatory.

CHARACTERISTICS OF THE COACH AS LEADER

Within sport and physical activity research, the question of leadership has received

2. The coefficient of determination (r²), when multiplied by 100 provides a percentage estimate of the common variance — the variance in one of the two parameters which can be accounted for/explained by the variance in the other parameter.
3. Fiedler and Leister (1977) emphasized that their model should not be considered completed. It was suggested that a number of other dimensions are likely involved including the type of task the group is engaged in, the role the leader plays and the style of leader behavior (i.e., autocratic vs. democratic).

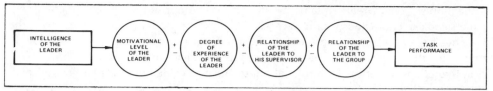

Figure 4.3. Parameters which modify the impact of leader intelligence upon task performance. (Adapted from Fiedler and Leister, 1977).

only minimal and peripheral attention. The focus does not appear to have been on determining what leadership factors contribute to performance success and athlete satisfaction, but rather, on providing a social psychological profile or description of coaches as a group of leaders. In this regard, the trait approach has been the predominant research strategy (as was pointed out in Chapter 2, this was also the case in the athlete dimension). As a result, a question which has arisen is "are coaches, as a group of leaders, characterized by an unique, extraordinary class of dispositions or traits?"

There do appear to be some traits which are characteristic of leaders in sport and physical activity if "trait" is considered in the more comprehensive context suggested by Guilford (1959), namely,

> "Trait" is . . . a very broad general term . . . A trait may be a characteristic indicated by behavior . . . or of physical make-up. The former is a behavior trait, the latter a somatic trait.

For example, Carter (1964, 1965) found a predominant mesomorphic component in male and female physical education teachers and a similar finding was reported for physical education students by a number of authors (e.g., Bale, 1969; Carter, 1964, 1965).

Further, Cratty (1967, 1968) has stated that physical size and athletic prowess are important factors in ascendency to leadership positions at particular age levels (see Figure 4.4).

There has also been some support for a conclusion that coaches are a unique group of individuals from a social psychological perspective. For example, Hendry (1973), after an extensive literature review, concluded that there is a *stereotype*[4] for "physical

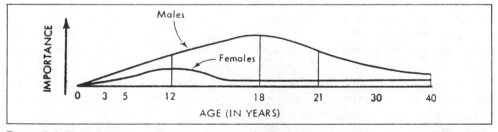

Figure 4.4. The interactive effects of physical prowess and age upon ascendency to leadership positions. Source: Bryant J. Cratty, SOCIAL DIMENSIONS OF PHYSICAL ACTIVITY, © 1967, p56. Reprinted by permission of Prentice-Hall, Inc., Englewood Cliffs, New Jersey.

4. In defining the concept of stereotype, Hendry (1973) stated:

> . . . given individual personality differences, there will be a degree of predictability in social behavior. Roles may give rise to stereotypes and stereotypes may be closely associated with roles. While roles are norms associated with differences of function among group-members, stereotypes are norms related to the group as a whole. So, stereotypes indicate variables which distinguish between groups: they are a simplification, categorized in terms of attitudes common to the groups that fall within the parameters, ignoring individual differences between them.

educationists" in Great Britain, a stereotype comprised of both physical and psychological characteristics. It has also been proposed by various authors that coaches are characterized by a definable set of traits; e.g., inflexibility and a low interest in the dependency needs of others (Ogilvie and Tutko, 1966, 1970), dominance, decisiveness, control, calmness, ability to hide emotions and organization (Hendry, 1974).

However, Sage (1975) in his paper *An occupational analysis of the college coach*, concluded after examining the available research literature that:

> . . . it is evident from this brief review of the personality and personal behaviors of coaches that the present research evidence is meager and that which has been done suffers from small and unrepresentative sampling. As if these limitations were not enough, the findings are equivocal.

In the discussion of the athlete's personality which was presented in Chapter 2, it was concluded that there is no basis at the present time for a conclusion that personality and athletic participation are related. A similar conclusion also appears warranted in regard to the relationship between coaching involvement and personality, and for much the same reasons.

LEADERSHIP, PERFORMANCE AND SATISFACTION

INTRODUCTION

On the basis of the available literature, it does appear that there are no general underlying psychological dispositions (traits) which account for ascendency to leadership positions — whether as coaches in athletics or managers in business. Possibly, this is not overly surprising since there is evidence which suggests that group leaders do not differ markedly from nonleaders. For example, McClintock (1963) observed that the behavior of leaders and active followers was highly similar — and both differed from inactive participants. Similarly, Nelson (1964) noted that accepted leaders and their subordinates evidenced a similar respect for authority in various forms and from different sources as well as a similar orientation toward group teamwork. A critical difference seems to lie between active and nonactive group participants.

However, it also should be emphasized that the trait has not been abandoned. In what might be categorized as one of two predominant research strategies in leadership analyses, specific *traits* are highlighted and emphasized (e.g., Fiedler's Contingency Theory and House's Path-Goal Model). A second research strategy has involved examining leader *behavior* to determine if there are consistent modes of response, characteristic types of adaptive and expressive behavior exhibited by those individuals involved in the process of exerting leadership. Behling and Schreisheim (1976) have classified various leadership theories into four categories according to whether the basic unit of reference has been the traits or the behaviors of the leader and whether these were viewed as being *universal* (general or all-encompassing across a number of situations) or *situational* in nature (see Table 4.1). This classification does provide an excellent frame of reference from which to examine the theories of leadership and their relevance to sport and physical activity.

A UNIVERSAL-BEHAVIORAL APPROACH TO LEADERSHIP

As the Great Man Theory of Leadership (with its preoccupation with the determina-

Table 4.1. A typology of leadership theories (From Chelladurai and Carron (1978) based on a scheme from Behling and Schriesheim, 1976).

	TRAITS	BEHAVIORS
UNIVERSAL	Early "Great Man" Theory	Ohio State and Michigan Studies
SITUATIONAL	Contingency Model of Leadership. (Fiedler, 1967)	Path-Goal Theory (House, 1971) Role-making Model (Graen and Cashman, 1975) Situational Theory (Hersey and Blanchard, 1969, 1977) Adaptive-Reactive Theory (Osborn and Hunt, 1975) Normative Model of Decision-making (Vroom and Yetton, 1973)

tion of those universal underlying traits associated with leadership) declined, the research emphasis shifted and attempts were made to determine those universal behaviors characteristic of the process of leadership. The ultimate objective of this work was to determine the relationship between specific behavior patterns of leaders and output criteria such as task performance and subordinate satisfaction. Foremost among these attempts were the projects that are generally referred to as the *Ohio State Studies* (e.g., Fleishman, 1957a, 1957b; Halpin and Winer, 1957; Hemphill and Coons, 1957) and the *University of Michigan Studies* (e.g., Bowers and Seashore, 1966; Cartwright and Zander, 1966; Katz, Maccoby, Gurrin and Floor, 1951; Katz, Maccoby and Morse, 1950).

In the Ohio State Study, nine dimensions of behavior that all leaders engage in with varying frequency were initially identified and assessed via a questionnaire (Hemphill and Coons, 1957). These were *initiation* (the introduction of new ideas and practices); *membership* (interaction with the group); *representation* (action on behalf of the group, in the group's interests); *integration* (the development of a group atmosphere); *organization* (the development of a structure for work); *domination* (permitting group involvement in decision making); *communication- up and down* (dissemination of information); *recognition* (approval/disapproval of the group members' behavior); and *production* (orientation toward achievement and productivity).

Subsequently, Halpin and Winer (1957) refined and modified the original questionnaire on the basis of their work with U.S. Air Force Bomber Crews. The result was that four factors were extracted from the nine dimensions: *consideration, initiating structure, production emphasis* and *sensitivity* or *social awareness*. The behavioral aspects of these are outlined in Table 4.2.

Since the factors *consideration* and *initiating structure* accounted for a relatively large percentage of the variance explained in leader behavior, namely 49.6 and 33.6 percent respectively versus 16.8 percent for production emphasis and sensitivity collectively, these latter two factors were dropped. Further, aspects of production emphasis were subsumed under initiating structure. The resulting questionnaire has been referred to as the *Leader Behavior Description Questionnaire, LBDQ.*

Table 4.2 Four leadership factors derived from the Leader Behavior Description Questionnaire (From Halpin and Winer, 1957).

FACTOR	DESCRIPTION
Consideration	Associated with behavior indicative of friendship, mutual trust, respect and warmth in the relationship between the leader and subordinates.
Initiating Structure	Associated with behaviors in which the leader organizes and defines the relationship between himself and his subordinates.
Production Emphasis	Associated with behaviors oriented towards motivating subordinates to greater activity.
Sensitivity (Social Awareness)	Associated with behavior indicative of the leader's sensitivity to and awareness of social relationships and pressures both inside and outside the group.

The identification of consideration and initiating structure as the two major behavioral dimensions in leadership must be viewed as a significant development in the research into leadership. In a general way these two represent *the* two important classes of behavior that leaders engage in in the process of leadership: viz., behavior which is interpersonal in orientation, which involves a recognition of the needs of the individual — *consideration;* and behavior which is production or goal oriented — *initiating structure.* Although a number of different terms or phrases have been used in leadership research to describe these two classes of behaviors, they have repeatedly appeared in similar or identical form in other theoretical approaches to leadership.

Even in the Ohio State Study, for example, Fleishman (1957a, 1957b) modified the *LBDQ* to obtain a questionnaire more applicable to an industrial setting — the *Supervisory Behavior Description Questionnaire (SBDQ)* — as well as a questionnaire which assesses leadership attitudes — the *Leader Opinion Questionnaire (LOQ).* In both instances the dimensions measured were conceptually identical to consideration and initiating structure.

While the Ohio State work was in progress, concurrent investigations were also underway at the University of Michigan Survey Research Center. The specific purpose of this work on leadership was to determine the " . . . principles which contribute both to the productivity of the group and the satisfaction that group members derive from their participation" (Likert, 1950). Thus, in a manner similar in orientation to the Ohio State researchers, the Michigan researchers were concerned with the identification of behaviors *universally* exhibited by leaders across all leadership situations. Also in similarity to the Ohio State study, no attempt was made to develop an empirical or theoretical linkage between a style of leadership and different situational contingencies. And, finally, the major contribution of both the Ohio State and Michigan studies has been in defining and describing the behaviors and roles displayed by leaders.

Table 4.3. Multidimensional scaling of commonly perceived coaching behaviors (From Danielson, Zelhart and Drake, 1975).

DIMENSION	DESCRIPTION
Competitive training	- Behavior concerned with motivation of athletes to train harder and better - Emphasis on winning via better training and performance - Little emphasis on behaviors involving coach-athlete relationship and individual and group participation in decision making
Initiation	- Behaviors involving an open approach to problem solving using new methods - Little emphasis on organization in the form of equipment provision - Little emphasis on criticism of performance
Interpersonal team operation	- Coordination of team members in an attempt to facilitate cooperation at possible expense of protocol - Behaviors concerned with getting members to interact so that the team functions efficiently - Little emphasis on criticism of performance
Social	- Socially oriented behavior outside the athletic situation - Little emphasis on consistency of performance, organization, or team morale
Representation	- Behavior concerned with representing the team favorably in contacts with outsiders
Organized communication	- Behaviors concerned with either organization or communication with no concern for interpersonal support - Little emphasis on either criticism or reward
Recognition	- Behaviors concerned with feedback and reinforcement of both performance and team participation in decision making - Little emphasis on winning, socialization, or team interaction
General excitement	- Arousing behaviors involving disorganized approach to team operation - Little emphasis on recognition or team integration

The Ohio State scales (i.e., *LBDQ, SBDQ, LOQ*), measuring the two dimensions of behavior (consideration and initiating structure) have been the most frequently used by researchers. However, a number of issues may be raised pertaining to these questionnaires and their two scales.

One issue which is directly applicable to the study of leadership in sport and physical activity is whether leader behaviors should be considered as universal. Thus, as an example, is it possible to classify all behaviors that coaches as leaders engage in under the categorizations of *consideration* and *initiating structure*? Since the answer is obviously no, it is also obvious that there is a need to examine the dimensions of leader behavior which are appropriate to the specific context.

The importance of identifying relevant dimensions of leader behavior in the athletic context was exemplified in the research of Danielson, Zelhart and Drake (1975) and Chelladurai and Saleh (1978). Danielson *et al* modified 140 of the 150 original *LBDQ* items and administered the resulting questionnaire to 160 hockey players, ages 12 to 18 years. The respondents were required to indicate whether the behavior described was characteristic of their coach. Eight dimensions of leader behavior were extracted from the hockey situation: *competitive training, initiation, interpersonal team operation, social, representation, organized communication, recognition* and *general excitement*. The behavioral correlates of each of these are outlined in Table 4.3.

Danielson *et al* noted that the "commonly perceived behaviors in hockey coaching are mainly of a communicative nature with surprisingly little emphasis on domination." The authors also pointed out that this finding contradicts Hendry's

Table 4.4. Leader behavior dimentions in sport (Adapted from Chelladurai and Saleh, 1978)

DIMENSION	DESCRIPTION
Training Behavior	Behavior aimed at improving the performance level of the athletes by emphasizing and facilitating hard and strenuous training, clarifying the relationships among the members.
Autocratic Behavior	Tendency of the coach to set himself, (herself) apart from the athletes, and to make all decisions by himself (herself).
Democratic Behavior	Behavior of the coach which allow greater participation by the athletes in deciding on group goals, practice methods, and game tactics and strategies.
Social Support Behavior	Behavior of the coach indicating his (her) concern for individual athletes and their welfare, and for positive group atmosphere.
Rewarding Behavior	Behavior of the coach which provide reinforcement for an athlete by recognizing and rewarding good performance.

(1972) contention that coaching behavior is characterized by dominance, aggression and authoritarianism.

In a somewhat similar study in which male and female undergraduate students were tested, Chelladurai and Saleh (1978) examined the relationship between the leader behavior preferred (using items drawn and modified from the *LBDQ, SBDQ, LOQ, LBDQ XII*) and the type of sport involvement preferred. Thus, the subjects indicated a preferred sport but were not necessarily participants in the sport at the time of testing. When the results were analyzed, five different dimensions of preferred leadership behavior were identified: *training behavior, autocratic behavior, democratic behavior, social support behavior,* and *rewarding behavior.* The behavioral correlates for these are outlined in Table 4.4.

There do appear to be some direct parallels between the Danielson *et. al.* study and the Chelladurai and Saleh findings. For example, the Chelladurai and Saleh behavioral dimensions of training, social support and rewarding are directly analogous to the Danielson *et al* dimensions of competitive training, social and recognition respectively. The remaining two factors (autocratic and democratic behavior) in the Chelladurai and Selah study reflect decision style preferred.

A SITUATIONAL-TRAIT APPROACH TO LEADERSHIP

A theoretical approach to leadership which emphasizes the traits of the leader as well as the nature of the situation is Fiedler's *Contingency Theory of Leadership.* A major postulate of this theory is that "leadership effectiveness depends upon the leader's style of interacting with his group members and the favourableness of the group-task situation" (Fiedler and Chemers, 1974).

The leader's style of interacting is measured in a unique fashion. The questionnaire, *The Least Preferred Co-worker Scale (LPC),* assesses the esteem which a leader has for a least preferred co-worker. The 16 to 20 items (depending on the form used) are bipolar adjectives such as friendly-unfriendly, pleasant-unpleasant, efficient-inefficient and these anchor an eight-point continuum. The underlying rationale for the *LPC* according to Fiedler (1967) is that:

> . . . the high-LPC individual (who perceives his least preferred coworker in a relatively favorable manner . . . derives his major satisfaction from successful interpersonal relationships, while the low-LPC person (who describes his LPC in very unfavorable terms) derives his major satisfaction from task performance.

Thus, the leader's style of interacting is considered to vary along a single dispositional dimension: task versus person oriented. And, the *LPC* reflects the degree to which this is present. Further, the orientation of the leader is viewed as a stable personality characteristic (i.e., a trait). In short, a leader would tend to be task oriented or person oriented in all circumstances.

As indicated above, the relative effectiveness of person versus task orientation is thought to depend upon the favorableness of the group-task situation. In turn, the group-task favorableness is viewed as being a product of three subfactors: the *leader-member relations,* the *task structure,* and the *power position of the leader.* Leader-member relations refer to the quality of the personal relationship between the leader and subordinates. Thus, if subordinates like the leader, it will be easier for that leader to exert influence. According to Fiedler, this is the subfactor which is most important in the determination of situational favorableness.

In regard to the second situational factor, the task itself, it was proposed that there are differences among tasks in the degree of structure present; differences in the degree to which the goals of tasks are clearly specified and the procedures for goal achievement are not ambiguous. A postulate of the Contingency Theory is that the more structured the task performed by the group, the easier it is for a leader to exert influence.

The third and final factor within situational favorableness, the power position of the leader, is determined by the leader's control over rewards and sanctions, the degree of authority over group members and the level of support provided by the organization. The more powerful the leader's position, the more favorable is the situation.

The specific interaction proposed by Fiedler for the leader's style of interacting with subordinates and the degree of situational favorableness is illustrated in Figure 4.5. It is apparent that Fiedler rank ordered situational favorableness into eight segments varying from a situation in which leader-member relationships are good/task structure is high/leader power position is strong to a situation in which leader-member relations are poor/the task is unstructured/the leader-power position is weak (these are presented across the horizontal axis of Figure 4.5).

It is also apparent that Fiedler considered a task oriented leader (low LPC) to be most effective in situations both very high and very low in favorableness. On the other

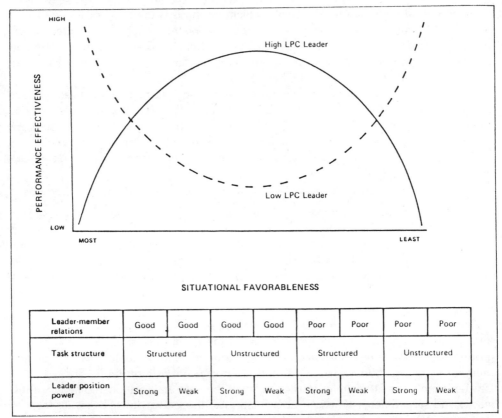

Leader-member relations	Good	Good	Good	Good	Poor	Poor	Poor	Poor
Task structure	Structured		Unstructured		Structured		Unstructured	
Leader position power	Strong	Weak	Strong	Weak	Strong	Weak	Strong	Weak

Figure 4.5. Fiedler's (1967) Contingency Model of Leadership (From Chelladurai and Carron, 1978). Reproduced with permission of the publisher.

hand, a person (relations) oriented leader (high *LPC*) was considered to be most effective in moderately favorable situations.

Thus, the main tenets of the Contingency Theory are that: group-work situations differ in their degree of favorableness; individual leaders vary along a continuum from task to person orientation; and any individual can be an effective leader provided his/her leadership style coincides with a situation of appropriate favorableness.

Although Fiedler's theory had its origins in his studies of basketball teams (Fiedler, 1954), very few researchers have attempted to test the model in the athletic context. Further, even in those studies which have utilized the *Least Preferred Co-worker Scale,* there has not been any support for the theory.

For example, Inciong (1974) examined 43 high school basketball teams (43 head coaches, 27 assistant coaches, 535 players). Leadership style was assessed with the *LPC*; one of the components of situational favorableness, leader-member relations, was measured using Fiedler's (1967) *Group Atmosphere Questionnaire;* and the team's won-loss record was used as a measure of performance effectiveness. Consistent with Fiedler's theory, Inciong hypothesized that the *LPC* score would be positively correlated with performance effectiveness in moderately favorable situations and negatively correlated in very favorable and unfavorable situations. While the correlations were in the direction predicted, they were nonsignificant leading Inciong to conclude that the *LPC* is unrelated to team success in high school basketball.

Danielson (1976) also examined the Contingency Theory in his study of 40 minor hockey league coaches. The *LPC* was used to measure leadership style. The coach's power position was assumed to be high and equal among all coaches (since the players were relatively homogeneous with respect to age and therefore hockey level; the mean age being 14.82 years). A *Team Atmosphere Scale* (a modification of Fiedler's *Group Atmosphere Scale*) was used to assess leader-member relations. Since the task (hockey) was identical across different teams, an indirect measure, the Coach-Director subscale of the *Learning Environment Inventory* (Anderson, 1973), was used to measure the goal clarity dimension of task structure.

The results did not support Fiedler's theory. On the basis of his findings, Danielson (1976) concluded that:

> . . . leadership in hockey situations appears to be more effective when the leader is oriented toward personal relations between himself and his team than when he is oriented primarily toward the completion of the group task (i.e., winning). Hockey is a social situation and may therefore require a different style of leadership than that required in industrial or business settings.

Bird (1977), in a study using female intercollegiate volleyball teams from two levels of competition (a total of 71 players and 8 coaches), hypothesized that winning teams would have (1) greater team cohesion (i.e., better leader-member relations) and (2) task oriented coaches. The coaches style of leadership was assessed using the *LPC* scale. Insofar as the three situational factors were concerned, the *Group Atmosphere Scale* was used to measure leader-member relations (cohesion) while Fiedler's (1967) *Measure of Position Power* was used for assessing the leader's power position. Bird assumed that the task structure was high since "the goal of the team is obvious — winning and team members usually perform rather specialized roles such as setters and hitters" (Bird, 1977).

Although Bird's first hypothesis was confirmed, the second received only partial support; viz., perception of the coach's leadership style in successful teams varied according to level of competition. As Bird noted:

116

. . . in the more highly skilled division winning coaches were viewed as more socioemotional, while losing teams saw leadership to be task-oriented. The converse was true in the less skilled division.

The research applications of Fiedler's theory to the athletic context do not appear to have provided for the specific contingencies specified by the theory, particularly in reference to those parameters comprising situational favorableness. For example, Inciong (1974) incorporated only one aspect of the determinants of situational favorableness. Also, and somewhat related, in both the Inciong and Danielson studies, teams from the same sport and level of competition were used (the latter factor was varied by Bird in her study). Thus, the situation was highly similar for all leaders tested. Fiedler's construct of situational favorableness assumes variance in the dimension and requires complex measurements. In the absence of differences in the situational parameters, Fiedler's model cannot be adequately tested.

A SITUATIONAL-BEHAVIORAL APPROACH TO LEADERSHIP

A number of different theorists have attempted to account for the differences which exist in carrying out the process of leadership by centering upon the specific behaviors of the leader across different situations. The major theories representative of this approach include the *Path-Goal Theory* (House, 1971), the *Situational Theory* (Hersey and Blanchard, 1969) and the *Normative Model of Decision Making* (Vroom and Yetton, 1973).

The Path-Goal Theory. The path-goal theory originally proposed by House (1971) provided an interesting contrast with Fiedler's work. As was noted previously, the focus in the contingency theory is on the leader's motivational orientation — task versus interpersonal — and the favorableness of the situation. In contrast, in House's theory, the emphasis is on the needs and goals of subordinates and their situation.

A basic assumption in the path-goal view is that subordinates (the individual workers) are directly oriented toward those rewards offered by the organization and its environments.[5] As the subordinate moves along the organizational path toward his goal (the rewards), the strategic function of the leader is "to provide . . . the coaching, guidance, support and rewards necessary for effective and satisfying performance that would otherwise be lacking in the environment" (House and Dessler, 1974). This is illustrated schematically in Figure 4.6. Thus, the path-goal view of leadership has as a basis, the expectancy theory of motivation.[6]

One major proposition of the path-goal theory is that *the leader's function is a supplemental one.* The behavioral/motivational function of a leader is directed toward clarifying the relationship between the behavior of subordinates and their goals. The nature of this responsibility was outlined by House and Dessler (1974) who stated that "the motivational function of the leader consists of increasing personal pay-offs to subordinates for work-goal attainment, and making the path to these pay-offs easier to travel by clarifying it, reducing road blocks and pitfalls, and increasing the opportunities for personal satisfaction en route."

5. Although the validity of this assumption seems questionable in its applicability to all workers in all situations, it does seem to have reasonable generalisability in the voluntary membership situations characteristic of athletics.
6. As an example of expectancy theory in its simplest form: the athlete has an expectation that effort will lead to a more effective performance. In turn, that effective performance is expected to lead to rewards.

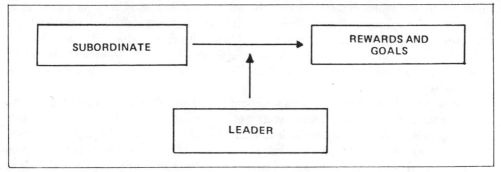

Figure 4.6. A path-goal theory of leadership (From Chelladurai and Carron, 1978). Reproduced with permission of the publisher.

A second major proposition of the path-goal theory is that *the optimal leader behavior which will lead to effective accomplishment of this motivational function is a product of the situation in which the leader operates.* In this context, House and Dessler (1974) proposed two classes of situational variables which would have an influence on the optimal behavior of a leader: (1) the characteristics of the subordinate and (2) the environmental demands and pressures that subordinates must cope with in order to successfully carry out their task and satisfy their needs.

The specific characteristics of the subordinate that were considered were *personality* and *ability*. As examples of the potential role of personality, House and Dessler suggested that subordinates with a high need for affiliation would prefer interpersonally oriented leaders whereas subordinates with a high need for achievement would show a greater preference for a task oriented leader. In other words, as these two types of subordinates proceed within the organization toward their respective goals, the types of coaching, guiding, supporting and rewarding behaviors required or desired from the leader could be expected to differ markedly.

The second class of situational variable (the environmental demands and pressures that subordinates must cope with) also was subdivided by House and Dessler into three broad categories: the *task;* the *formal authority system of the organizations;* and the *primary work group.*

While these three situational variables are all emphasized within the path-goal model, the nature and importance of the task does seem to have particular relevance for athletics. In path-goal theory, tasks are characterized according to their level of routineness/variability, dependence/interdependence and inherent satisfaction/nonsatisfaction. Thus, since the leader's role is supplemental, and since the primary function of the leader is to coach, guide, support and reward, then, the specific form and nature of leader behavior must vary, by necessity, according to whether the subordinates are engaged in tasks which are or are not routine, independent and/or satisfying. In short, according to the path-goal theory, different task requirements dictate differentiated patterns of behavior from a leader.

As indicated above, this seems to have direct relevance for the athletic context since sport tasks do vary in their level of routineness (e.g., the practice session for a gymnastic or figure skating program versus practice sessions for a sport such as basketball, hockey, etc.); dependence/interdependence (e.g., most team sports can be differentiated from individual sports on this basis); and, satisfaction.

In an early paper, House (1971) advanced a number of hypotheses which were an attempt to delineate the relationship between task demands and specific leader behaviors. For example, it was proposed that leader behavior which was highly directive and task/goal/production oriented (initiating structure behavior) would have a different impact upon subordinates depending upon whether the task was satisfying or unsatisfying to those subordinate and whether the task role demands were clear or ambiguous.

It was also proposed that if the subordinate's tasks were varied and interdependent and if group norms for performance were not developed (e.g., a situation which exists in a team sport such as basketball) leader behavior which was task/goal/production oriented and which involved close supervision would serve to clarify the path-goal relationship. That is, these leader behaviors would result in increased coordination, satisfaction and performance on the part of subordinates.

The final hypothesis advanced by House which has a direct relevance for athletics was that in those situations where tasks were varied, interdependent and ambiguous, interpersonally oriented behavior on the part of the leader would result in social support, friendliness, increased cohesiveness and team effort among group members.

The path-goal model was tested directly in a study with physical education students by Chelladurai and Seleh (1978). In the initial phase of that study, five dimensions of leader behavior were derived through factor analysis of 99 items (drawn from the LBDQ, SBDQ, LOQ, and LBDQ XII). This aspect of the study was discussed earlier and an outline and description of the five dimensions (training behavior, autocratic behavior, democratic behavior, social support and reward) is presented in Table 4.4.

The purpose of the second phase was to examine the leader behavior preferred by the subjects and its relationship to the type of sport preferred. The subjects were asked to choose a sport for participation under the restrictive condition that they would be limited to only one choice. The sports chosen were then classified by Chelladurai and Saleh on the basis of variability (an open task such as badminton was distinguished from a closed task such as a sprint in track) and dependence (individual sports were distinguished from team sports). Thus, four conditions were formed: independent/open; independent/closed; interdependent/open; and interdependent/closed.

Insofar as the task attribute of dependence was concerned, the path-goal theory was supported. Individuals with a preference for interdependent sports also indicated a preference for increased training behavior — behavior from the leader which is aimed at 1) improving performance by emphasizing and facilitating hard and strenuous training and 2) clarifying the relationships among team members.

However, the results in regard to the task attribute of variability were in a direction contrary to that predicted by the path-goal theory. The individuals who preferred closed sports showed a greater preference for training behavior than individuals who expressed a preference for open sports. Chelladurai and Saleh suggested that for closed sports, the leader's training behavior (which according to path-goal theory is behaviorally analogous to interference) might be viewed as motivating. Since practice sessions for a closed sport such as distance swimming are repetitious and monotonous, the training behavior of a coach would be essential for sustained performance.

There were no other differences related to the task variable. However, the authors did note sex differences in preferred leader behavior. While males expressed a preference for more autocratic and socially supportive behavior, females preferred a coach who was more democratic and who did not provide as much social support. These findings are consistent with McMurray's (1958) suggestion that the leader who is an "autocrat" could be expected to be "benevolent," but they are in contrast to the traditional view that democratic behavior and social support behavior are correlated.

The Situational Theory of Leadership. Another theory which focuses upon the appropriate behaviors for leaders in specific situations is the Situational Leadership Theory of Hersey and Blanchard (1969, 1977). The major tenets of the theory (which was originally referred to as the Life Cycle Theory of Leadership) are illustrated in Figure 4.7.

Hersey and Blanchard (1977) postulated that:

. . . . as the level of maturity of their followers continues to increase in terms of accomplishing a specific task, leaders should begin to reduce their task behavior and increase relationship behavior until the individual or group reaches a moderate level of maturity. As the individual or group begins

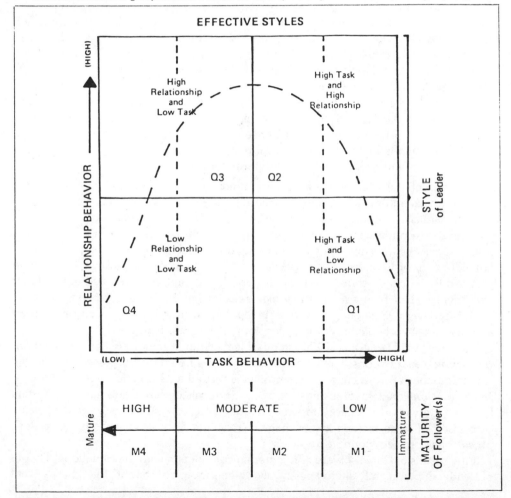

Figure 4.7. A Situational Leadership Theory. Source: Paul Hersey and Ken H. Blanchard, MANAGEMENT OF ORGANIZATIONAL BEHAVIOR (3rd Edition), ©1977, p.167. Reprinted by permission of Prentice-Hall, Inc., Englewood Cliffs, New Jersey

to move into an above average level of maturity it becomes appropriate for leaders to decrease not only task behavior but also relationship behavior.

The term task behavior and relationship behavior correspond to the two traditional dimensions of leader behavior which have repeatedly arisen in the discussion of other theories — namely, initiating structure and consideration.

The theory centers almost entirely upon the maturity of the subordinate or group. Maturity was defined as "the capacity to set high but attainable goals (achievement motivation), willingness and ability to take responsibility, and education and/or experience of an individual or group" (Hersey and Blanchard, 1977). Thus, both the personality and the ability of the individual were combined to determine the level of maturity.[7] Hersey and Blanchard also emphasized that the variables which comprise maturity should only be considered insofar as they relate to the specific task being performed.

Although the Situational Theory of Leadership has not been empirically tested, Hersey and Blanchard did provide an example using the parent-child relationship which does illustrate the interrelationship of the various parameters. It was proposed that parental behavior — the leader style — should vary in a curvilinear manner in relation to the maturity level of the child (or the individual or group). This is illustrated in Figure 4.7. When the individual is immature, the leader style should consist of high task behavior and low relationship behavior. This is represented by the lower right quadrant, Q1, of Figure 4.7. As the child increases in maturity, the parent exhibits both high task behavior and high relationship behavior (the upper right quadrant of Figure 4.7, Q2). As maturity further increases, the task behavior of parents is lowered while relationship behavior is high (Q3). Finally, when the child is fully mature both the relationship and task behavior of the parent are reduced to a minimal level.

Even though the operationalization of maturity is extremely difficult for athletics, it is possible to extend the Hersey and Blanchard theory to this context. If it can be assumed that "athletic maturity" progressively increases from the elementary school level through the secondary school level to university and professional levels, then there are rather specific leadership styles recommended for each of these through the Situational Theory of Leadership. Specifically, it would be consistent with this theory to propose that a coach should be high task and less relationship oriented at the junior high level (Q1 of Figure 4.7); show high relationship and low task behavior at the university level (Q3, Figure 4.7); and finally demonstrate both reduced relationship and task oriented behavior at the professional level (Q4, Figure 4.7).

However, the Danielson (1976) study of leadership in minor hockey provided findings which are not consistent with this proposal. He noted that increased relationship oriented behavior from coaches was positively related to team effectiveness across all levels of situational favorableness (it may be recalled that Danielson was testing Fiedler's Contingency Theory in which situational favorableness is viewed as being comprised of three factors: leader-member relations, task structure and the leader's power position; see Figure 4.5).

If the results of Danielson are considered in conjunction with the Situational Theory of Leadership, a slightly altered perspective seems more appropriate for athletics. That

---

7. As Chelladurai (1978) has noted, the rationale for combining personality which is relatively stable and ability which is transient might be questioned. The path-goal theory of leadership treats these two characteristics as separate and distinct (House, 1971).

is, by transposing the two axes, a curvilinear relationship between leadership style and subordinate maturity is retained but the ordered pattern represented in each of the four quadrants is changed. Figure 4.8 provides an illustration of this modification. Thus, when the individual matures through the various stages from elementary to professional sports the most appropriate leadership style should vary from low task/high relationship (Q1) to high task/high relationship (Q2), to high task/low relationship (Q3), and finally, to a low task/low relationship (Q4).

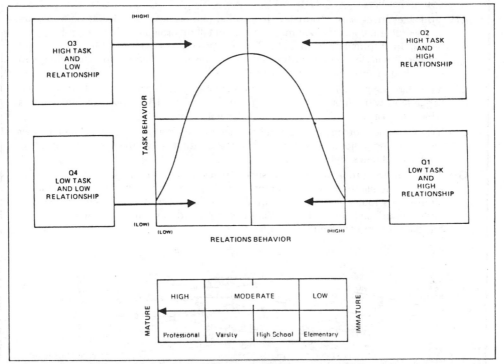

Figure 4.8. A model for situational leadership for athletics. (From Chelladurai and Carron, 1978). Reproduced with permission of the publisher.

The Normative Model of Decision-Making. The final approach dealing with situation-specific behavior of leaders, involves the development of a normative model of decision making. This approach is concerned with only one component of the leader's behavior; namely, the degree to which a leader allows participation by subordinates in decision making. A fundamental premise is that the most appropriate method with which to arrive at a decision will vary depending upon the nature of the situation.

Vroom and Yetton (1973) broadly classified decision methods as (1) *autocratic,* where the leader alone makes the decision; (2) *consultative,* where the leader still makes the decision but after gaining information through consultation with subordinates either individually or collectively; and (3) *group decisions,* where the group including the leader jointly make the decision and the leader then implements this group decision.

The authors then outlined eight problem attributes which collectively serve to determine the appropriateness of a specific decision process. These were outlined in the form of a set of questions or guidelines. A flow chart was also developed which included eight factors or attributes which must be considered in order for a leader to rationally select a decision style for the particular situation (see Figure 4.9).

In order to test the proposition that these eight attributes should determine the leader's decision style (and the level of participation by members in decision making),

AI You solve the problem or make the decision yourself using information available to you at that time.

AII You obtain necessary information from subordinate(s) and then decide on a solution to the problem yourself. You may or may not tell subordinates what the problem is in getting the information from them. The role played by your subordinates in making the decision is clearly one of providing the necessary information to you, rather than generating or evaluating alternative solutions.

CI You share the problem with relevant subordinates individually, getting their ideas and suggestions without bringing them together as a group. Then you make the decision which may or may not reflect your subordinates' influence.

CII You share the problem with your subordinates as a group, collectively obtaining their ideas and suggestions. Then, you make the decision which may or may not reflect your subordinates' influence.

GII You share the problem with your subordinates as a group. Together you generate and evaluate alternatives and attempt to reach agreement (consensus) on a solution. Your role is much like that of chairman. You do not try to influence the group to adopt "your" solution and are willing to accept and implement any solution which has the support of the entire group.

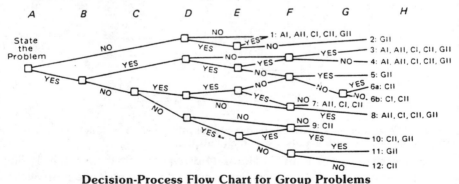

Decision-Process Flow Chart for Group Problems

A. Is there a quality requirement such that one solution is likely to be more rational than another?

B. Do I have sufficient info to make a high quality decision?

C. Is the problem structured?

D. Is acceptance of decision by subordinates critical to effective implementation?

E. If I were to make the decision by myself, is it reasonably certain that it would be accepted by my subordinates?

F. Do subordinates share the organizational goals to be attained in solving this problem?

G. Is conflict among subordinates likely in preferred solutions? (This question is irrelevant to individual problems.)

H. Do subordinates have sufficient info to make a high quality decision?

Figure 4.9. A normative model of decision making (From Vroom and Yetton, 1973). Reproduced with permission of the publisher.

Vroom and Yetton developed a set of 30 problems in which different problem attributes were systematically varied. A total of 551 managers were asked to indicate what decision style they would use in each of these 30 problems. The results indicated that the problem attributes accounted for 29.2 percent of the variance while individual differences accounted for 8.2 percent of the variance in the decision styles adopted. As Vroom and Yetton noted " . . . for that population the amount of influence of situational factors in determining choice of leadership methods is roughly four times the influence of individual differences."

A normative model of decision making also seems applicable to athletic situations and Chelladurai and Haggerty (1978) have adopted the Vroom and Yetton model to the athletic context. Three types of decision styles were proposed including *autocratic* (the coach makes the decision solely); *participative* (the group including the coach as a member arrive at the decision); and *delegative* (the coach allows one or more members of the group to make the decision).

The problem attributes viewed by the authors as relevant to an athletic situations were *time pressure, decision quality required, information location, problem complexity, group acceptance, power,* and *group integration.* (The interaction of each of these with the three decision styles is outlined in Figure 4.10).

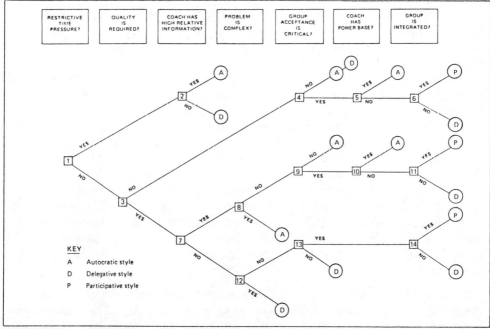

Figure 4.10. A normative model for decision making in athletics (From Chelladurai and Haggerty, 1978). Reproduced with permission of the publisher.

Time pressure refers to the degree to which there might be restrictions in the time available to consult with team members. Thus, football, with its intermittent action can be contrasted with ice hockey. Similarly, there is less time pressure for decisions made in a practice environment versus a game situation.

The factor of level of decision quality required is a function of the importance attached to the outcomes. Thus, if a team captain is only a nominal designation with no significant responsibilities attached to it, the coach may attach very little importance to the decision outcome and use a delegative style.

In relationship to the third factor, it was proposed that there are two sets of information relevant to the coaching context: the general knowledge and expertise in the sport and information concerning actual and potential performance capabilities. Thus, the third factor, information location, refers to the fact that the coach must draw on the most appropriate information source in arriving at a decision on game strategies, selection of personnel, etc.

The fourth factor, problem complexity, is an acknowledgment that as the situation increases in complexity, the best individual is likely to make a better decision than the group. This view has been supported by the work of Kelley and Thibault (1969) in a problem solving experiment. An appropriate sport analogy might be the quarterback calling the offensive plays (autocratic) versus the offensive unit as a whole (participative) arriving at the decision.

A fifth factor, group acceptance, refers to the extent to which acceptance of the decision by subordinates is critical for ultimate performance effectiveness. Thus, a coach might autocratically decide to introduce a full court press in basketball but if the group is convinced it will be ineffective, performance would suffer.

Power, the sixth factor, was viewed by Chelladurai and Haggerty as conceptually similar to Vroom and Yetton's concept of "prior probability of acceptance by subordinates." Power was included in the model because " . . . if a coach actually has power, it is likely that team members would accept the decision" (Chelladurai and Haggerty, 1978).

The final concept included in the model, group integration, encompassed the quality of interpersonal relations among team members and the relative homogeneity of the team in terms of tenure and ability.

A Model for Leadership Effectiveness in Athletics. The major impetus behind the development of theoretical models for the examination of leadership has come from management science research. This is unfortunate since the dynamics of leadership and its impact upon the performance and satisfaction of "subordinates" is as pertinent and critical an issue for sport and physical activity as it is for business and industry. As indicated previously, the principal research concern in sport and physical activity has been in the area of description — providing a social psychological profile of coaches as a group. One exception has been the *Multidimensional Model of Leadership* proposed by Chelladurai (1978). A schematic overview of this model is presented in Figure 4.11.

In this multidimensional model, the *satisfaction* and *performance* of the athlete are viewed as being the product of three types or categories of leader behavior: *prescribed leader behavior;* the *leader behavior preferred* by the athlete or team; and the *actual behavior*. In turn, antecedents for these three types of behavior are viewed as comprising three categories: the characteristics of the *situation;* the characteristics of the *leader;* and the characteristics of the *members* (athletes, team).

The prescribed leader behavior is behavior dictated by factors within the organizational system itself. These factors set the limits or boundaries for behaviors considered appropriate for a leader. The preferred leader behavior is a product of both the characteristics of the situation (discussed above) and the characteristics of the

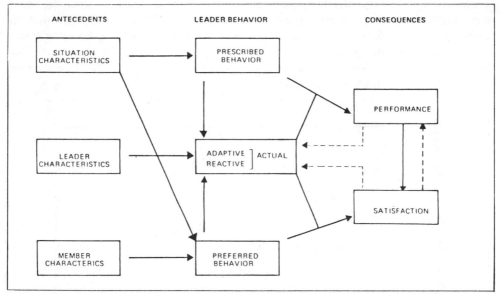

Figure 4.11. A multidimensional Model of Leadership (From Chelladurai, 1978). Reproduced with permission of the author.

members/athletes/team. The inclusion of situational variables as a factor influencing the subordinates preference for particular leader behaviors is an acknowledgment by Chelladurai that both coaches and athletes are socialized into the behavioral prescriptions for the athletic situation.

The third category of behavior, the actual leader behavior was considered to be affected indirectly by characteristics of the leader (personality and ability) and somewhat more directly by those behaviors preferred by subordinates as well as by those behaviors prescribed through the dictates of the situation. The impact of these latter two categories is consistent with the viewpoint held by Osborn and Hunt (1975) that total leader behavior is comprised of *adaptive* behavior (representing those adaptations by the leader to the prescriptions of the situation) and *reactive* behavior (representing those behaviors which are discretionary, reflecting individually oriented behaviors).

Since the adaptive behaviors are required or prescribed, they would be homogeneous across all members. On the other hand, the reactive behaviors would be quite heterogeneous since they are in response to the needs and desires of the individual subordinates.

As the extension to the above, the environment for a coach can be considered more or less favorable depending upon the degree to which it is possible for the coach to engage in adaptive versus reactive behavior (see Figure 4.12). That is, sport organizations differ in the extent to which situational variables such as the group norms present, the size of the team, the level of organization required etc., control the behavior of the coach. For example, the greater the clarity of the organizational goals, the more bureaucratic the structure, the more organized the task, and the more detailed the group norms, the greater would be the extent to which the coach's behavior would be largely prescribed.

If the coach's behavior is largely prescribed as a result of these situational parameters, then the leadership process is easier — *more favorable* — since the coach can simply follow these prescriptions. This would also be aided by the fact that the same situational factors also influence the athlete's preference. On the other hand, where there is greater proportion of discretionary (reactive) behavior required, the environment would be *less favorable* for the coach since the athletes would have varied and sometimes conflicting preferences.

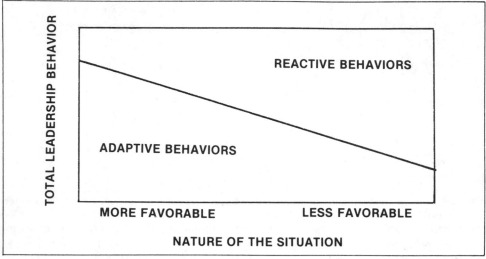

Figure 4.12. Leader behavior as a function of the nature of the situation (From Chelladurai, 1978). Reproduced with permission of the author.

However, while the situational factors affect the coach's behavior, the coach's own personality and ability are the major determinants of the coach's actual behavior. This is illustrated in Figure 4.11. In this regard the major personality traits highlighted are *task* and *interpersonal relations* orientation.

The focus of this model is on individual or group *satisfaction* and *performance*. What effect does the coach's behavior have upon the athlete's satisfaction — the degree to which the individual is satisfied with the leadership given? Further, what effect does the coach's behavior have upon the athlete's performance — output of the athlete or team relative to the output of competitors or to a previous performance standard? To date, these questions cannot be answered for the sport context.

SITUATIONAL FACTORS MEDIATING LEADERSHIP

It may be apparent from the preceding section that in current views of leadership, it is generally accepted that *there are no inherent traits or dispositions within an individual which contribute to ascendancy and maintenance of leadership*. Instead, it is believed that the specific requirements of different situations dictate the particular leadership qualities which will be most effective. Fleishman (1953) pointed this out over one-quarter of a century ago when he stated that "leadership is to a great extent situational and what is effective in one situation may be ineffective in another." This view was, of course, emphasized in the Contingency Theory of Leadership where Fiedler rank-ordered various situations according to their favorableness.

There are also other situational factors, which, while not incorporated into any of the various theories, do have a major impact upon ascendancy and maintenance of leadership roles within a group. Two of these, *geographical location* and *degree of stress present,* have a very direct relevance for sport and physical activity.

PHYSICAL AND GEOGRAPHICAL FACTORS

It has been repeatedly demonstrated in laboratory and nonlaboratory research that *individuals occupying the most central position within a group are most frequently chosen as leaders* (e.g., Bass and Klubeck, 1952; Danzig and Galanter, 1955; Grusky, 1963; Hearn, 1957; Kipnis, 1957; Leavitt, 1951). A large number of reasons have been advanced in an attempt to account for this finding.

One possible reason may be that individuals in central positions are most frequently the focal point for group *interaction and communication*[8] — communication within the group tends to filter through central positions and, therefore, those individuals occupying such positions assume a pre-eminent status within the group. The now classic work of Bavelas and his associates (e.g., Bavelas, 1948, 1950, 1951; Leavitt, 1951) is frequently cited to illustrate this point.

In Leavitt's (1951) work, for example, five-person groups were used to examine the relative effectiveness of *chain, wheel, Y* and *circle* communication networks (these are illustrated in Figure 4.13). Communication within each structure was restricted to immediate neighbors (i.e., only those positions directly adjacent). In the case of the wheel, for example, all communication was channelled through the hub position. A problem solving task was assigned to the groups — to determine the one symbol from among a group of symbols that was held in common by all group members. Thus, in order to achieve task success, it was necessary to channel the information into one position. The common symbol was then selected and the information relayed back to all group members.

In terms of group success, the most effective structure (as reflected in performance time, number of errors and number of messages required to complete the task) in decreasing rank order were the wheel, Y, chain and circle. Of more importance insofar as the issue of leadership is concerned, the individual occupying the most central position in the structure usually evolved into the group decision maker and was most frequently selected as the most influential group member.

A second, related reason could be the factor of *visibility* — the greater degree to which a central position is seen by all other positions results in greater status being ascribed to it. As Steinzor (1955) noted:

> . . . *if a person happens to be in a spatial position which increases the chances of his being more completely observed, the stimulus values of his ideas and statements increase by virtue of that very factor of his greater physical and expressive impact on others.*

In this regard, for example, Strodtbeck and Hook (1961) found that the foreman of a jury was most frequently selected from one of the two persons seated at the ends of a table. It was also noted that proprietors and managers tended to choose seats at the

---

8. The topic of group communication is discussed in greater detail in Chapter 6.

128

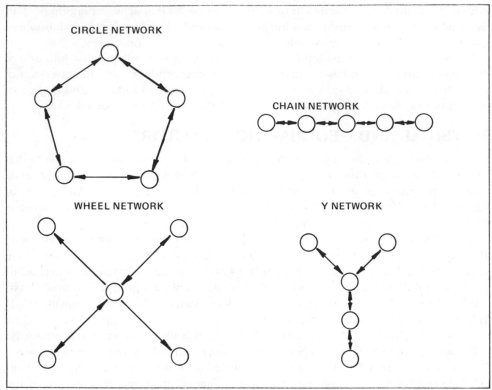

Figure 4.13. The chain, circle, Y and wheel communication networks (Adapted from Leavitt, 1951).

end positions of a table rather than in other position.

The use of visible space to reflect leadership would seem to be cultural in nature. Hall (1959) pointed this out in the observation that "space (or territoriality) meshes very subtly with the rest of culture in many different ways. Status, for example, is indicated by the distance one sits from the head of the table on formal occasions."

The cultural trait of visibility permeates all social groups. For example, the head of a household sits at the far end of a table, the king on his throne. Adams and Biddle (1970) noted that "the teacher's spiritual and temporal home appears to be the center front of the room." Further, Sommer's (1961) study relating to group geography indicated that it was common for the group members to seek arrangements in which the leader could be faced. Sommer proposed that:

> . . . perhaps our results mean, then, that communicating with all members of the group is not the primary ingredient of the leader's role. Perhaps being seen by his followers rather than being able to converse with them is a more fundamental aspect of the leader in this culture.

However, it has also been suggested (e.g., Chelladurai and Carron, 1977; Hopkins, 1964) that being visible and being in a central physical location are not as important as having *observability* — a knowledge of ongoing events. In contrasting observability and geographic centrality, Chelladurai and Carron (1977) suggested that:

> . . . observability or knowledge of the ongoing situation is the more important criterion; geographic or structural centrality is neither a necessary nor a sufficient condition for observability. Physical prox-

imity to the center of action does not necessarily warrant authority or rank, if it does not afford greater knowledge or observability to the occupant.

An example which might illustrate this point is that both the football center and quarterback are geographically central. However, the former lacks the overall perspective, the awareness of the total situation which is a characteristic possessed by the quarterback. Therefore, the center also has considerably less status, prestige and leadership within the team.

Chelladurai and Carron pointed out that in most athletic situations, a leadership role is held by individuals who are located at the rear of the action zone which is comprised of most of their teammates and opponents. Thus, the quarterback, the catcher in baseball and the playmaking guard in basketball may seem to be central because most of the play originates or revolves around them. But, they are actually on the perimeter of the main body of players (opponents and teammates).

A number of authors (e.g., Ball, 1973; Grusky, 1963; Loy, 1970; Loy and McElvogue, 1970; Sage, Loy and Ingham, 1970) have analyzed the general formal structure and specific spatial location of various positions in sport in order to assess whether these are related to differential status, prestige, leadership and rewards for the participant. The results of this research seem quite straightforward — namely, that there are systematic differences in parameters such as leadership, and so on, across the different playing positions of various sports. However, the underlying rationale proposed to account for these differences does vary.

For example, Grusky (1963), in a study of baseball, developed a model based upon three interdependent factors: *spatial location, the nature of the task* and the *frequency of interaction*. He theorized that "all else being equal, the more central one's spatial location: (1) the greater the likelihood dependent or coordinative tasks will be performed, and (2) the greater the rate of interaction with occupants of other positions." Grusky then categorized the different baseball positions according to whether they were high or low interactors and found that high interactors (i.e., catchers and infielders) were more likely to be recruited as managers than low interactors (i.e., outfielders and pitchers). Other investigators (e.g., Loy, 1970) have also obtained results which supported Grusky's model.

Loy and McElvogue (1970) proposed the general concept of *physical centrality* as the basis of distinguishing among playing positions. As Ball (1973) has explained "from a structural standpoint it [centrality] is best operationalized, at least in the case of fixed-position team sports taken-as-formal-organizations (for example, football or baseball), by spatial location."

The centrality framework was used by Loy and McElvogue to determine whether racial discrimination existed in baseball and football. Different palying positions were initially classified as central or noncentral. For instance, in baseball, the infielders and catchers were classified as central while outfielders were classified as noncentral; in football, the quarterback, center and guards on offense and linebackers on defense were viewed as central positions while the tackles, ends, flankers and running backs on offense and tackles, ends, backs and safeties on defense were noncentral. Their findings indicated that racial discrimination in the form of stacking existed in the ‑ noncentral positions.

Ball (1973) proposed an alternate model to that of physical centrality. He classified

130

the playing positions in football as *primary* or *supporting*, the distinction between them being that:

> . . . the primary positions *are those within the organization charged with the basic achievement and realization of the organization's goals.* Supporting positions, *on the other hand, are defined as those responsible for assisting the primary positions in their efforts toward goal achievement, but are not ordinarily directly involved in such accomplishments.*

The positions classified as primary were quarterbacks, running backs, flankers, receivers and ends on offense; tackles, ends and linebackers on defense. The center, guards and tackles on offense; backs and safeties on defense represented the supporting positions. Using this classification schema, Ball found that in the Canadian Football League, imports (i.e., American players) were more likely to occupy primary rather than supporting positions.

More recently, Chelladurai and Carron (1977) proposed a model consisting of two dimensions which were referred to as *propinquity* and *task*. The first dimension, propinquity, consisted of the combined attributes of (1) *observability*, the extent to which a position affords a knowledge of ongoing action — including the locations and movements of other positions — relevant to the accomplishment of the task; and (2) *visibility*, the degree to which a position is seen and watched by other positions on the playing field including the opponents.

The second dimension, the task, was incorporated to reflect the nature of the task imposed interactions which are characteristic of various sport positions. While some positions are highly interdependent, involving a great deal of task-imposed interaction, others are quite independent (e.g., contrast the goaltender in hockey with the forwards).

Chelladurai and Carron then classified the various positions of baseball and the offensive and defensive positions of football according to these dimensions. The result is

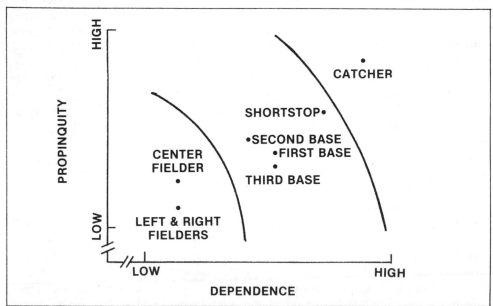

Figure 4.14. Categorizations of baseball positions on the basis of the interaction of propinquity and task dependence (From Chelladurai and Carron, 1977). Reproduced with permission of the publisher.

illustrated in Figures 4.14, 4.15 and 4.16 respectively. The data reported in previous studies of baseball (Grusky, 1963; Loy and Sage, 1968; Sage, Loy and Ingham, 1970) were reanalyzed. It was found that the achievement of leadership, status and rewards was highly related to the degree of task dependence and propinquity present

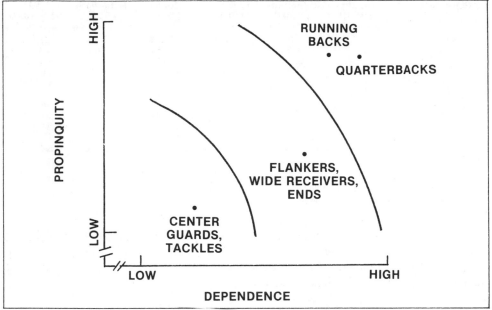

Figure 4.15. Categorization of football offensive positions on the basis of the interaction of propinquity and task dependence (From Chelladurai and Carron, 1977).   Reproduced with permission of the publisher.

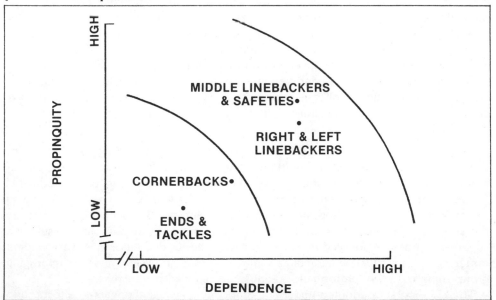

Figure 4.16. Categorization of football defensive positions on the basis of the interaction of propinquity and task dependence (From Chelladurai and Carron, 1977).   Reproduced with permission of the publisher.

TABLE 4.5. The Recruitment of Manager/Coaches and Selection of Team Captains and Most Valuable Players on the Basis of Playing Position (From Chelladurai and Carron, 1977). Reproduced with permission of the publisher.

Categories	Grusky (1963)[1]	Sage, Loy & Ingham (1970)[2]	Loy & Sage (1968)[3]	Sage, Loy & Ingham (1970)[4]	Sage, Loy & Ingham (1970)[5]	Average from All Studies
I Catchers	26.2%	27.0%	27.3%	15.5%	12.9%	21.8%
II Infielders	12.2%	11.0%	16.7%	13.3%	10.4%	12.7%
(First Base)	(11.2)	(12.6)	(0.0)	(9.9)	(8.9)	(8.5)
(Second Base)	(10.3)	(8.6)	(20.0)	(13.8)	(9.8)	(12.5)
(Shortstop)	(14.0)	(17.1)	(40.0)	(14.6)	(11.8)	(19.5)
(Third Base)	(13.1)	(5.8)	(6.7)	(14.8)	(11.1)	(10.3)
III Outfielders	5.3%	1.8%	2.2%	6.4%	6.4%	4.4%
(Left Field)	-	(1.0)	(0.0)	(6.1)	(4.9)	(3.0)
(Center Field)	-	(4.5)	(6.7)	(10.5)	(11.5)	(8.3)
(Right Field)	-	(0.0)	(0.0)	(2.5)	(2.9)	(1.4)

[1]Recruitment of professional baseball managers.
[2]Recruitment of collegiate coaches.
[3]Selection of Interscholastic team captains.
[4]Selection of intercollegiate team captains.
[5]Selection of most valuable players.

in the position. Specifically, positions which varied from high propinquity/high task dependence to low propinquity/low task dependence also systematically varied in the degree to which they produced managers and coaches, team captains and most valuable players. This is outlined in Table 4.5.

STRESS

It appears that the *degree of stress present in the situation has an effect upon (1) the decision style adopted by leaders (not only utilized by leaders but found acceptable by subordinates) and (2) the type of leader behavior which is prevalent.* This stress could arise from an external source such as competition or threat to the group or an internal source such as group conflict or performance incompetence.

Insofar as decision style is concerned, a model was developed by Korten (1962) in which it was proposed that under conditions of stress, a group seeks out or becomes receptive to authoritarian styles of leadership. It was also proposed that in the absence of group stress a more democratic style of leadership emerges. This is illustrated in Figure 4.17.

This model has received support from a number of authors (e.g., Foder, 1976; Lowin and Craig, 1968; Rosenbaum and Rosenbaum, 1971). Foder (1976), for example, manipulated group stress in a laboratory experiment involving industrial foremen and supervisors by having one member of the work group make disparaging remarks about the supervisor and the experimental task. This behavior was seen by the supervisor as producing a negative effect upon group morale. As a result, the supervisors not only adopted more authoritarian modes of control than were evident under the nonstressful condition but also gave the total group (not just the disparaging group member) lower performance ratings and reduced pay increases.

The decision style adopted under stressful conditions also appears to affect group performance. Rosenbaum and Rosenbaum (1971) found that when the competitive nature of the group task was emphasized (i.e., the stress situation), performance was

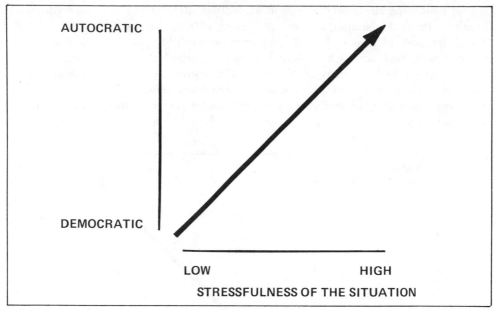

Figure 4.17. The interaction of leadership style with level of stress present.

enhanced under the authoritarian decision style. Conversely, under the low stress conditions (i.e., the competitive pressure was minimized), group performance was optimal under a democratic style of leadership.

It is assumed that the source of the stress is irrelevant — authoritarian decision styles are preferred by subordinates irrespective of whether the source of the threat/stress is internal or external — but, intuitively, this doesn't seem probable. This can be readily illustrated by drawing upon Fiedler's Contingency Theory of Leadership. It will be recalled that Fiedler rank ordered situations according to their degree of favorableness for the leader. If the source of the stress is internal (e.g., dissension), the implication is that leader-member relations (which is one of the components contributing to situational favorableness in Fiedler's theory) are poor which, in turn, implies that the situation is unfavorable. According to the Korten model illustrated in Figure 4.17, the leader would tend to be autocratic. Similarly, according to Fiedler, the autocratic, task oriented leader would be most effective.

On the other hand, if the source of the stress/threat is external, the group (including the leader) becomes more cohesive (Lott and Lott, 1965). Thus, the leader-member relations are good; consequently, the situation is favorable for the leader to adopt an autocratic decision style. In short, a fundamental difference between internal versus external sources of stress is that, in the latter case, members would tolerate or even welcome their leader's autocratic behavior while in the former case it would be resented and resisted.

Figure 4.18 illustrates the impact of situation stressfulness upon leader behavior. It was pointed out in earlier sections of this chapter that task and interpersonal oriented behavior (called initiating structure and consideration in the Ohio State studies) are viewed as being the two general classes of behavior leaders engage in during the process of leadership. In a similar fashion to decision style, it has also been observed (Fiedler, 1967; Fleishman, Harris and Burtt, 1955; Lowin and Craig, 1968; Oaklander and Fleishman, 1964; Schreisheim and Murphy, 1976) that group pressure and stress acts as a moderator between leader behavior and group performance and satisfaction. In relatively relaxed, nonstressful situations, consideration behavior on the part of the leader enhances subordinate satisfaction and performance but under highly stressful conditions, initiating structure behavior from a leader is more beneficial.

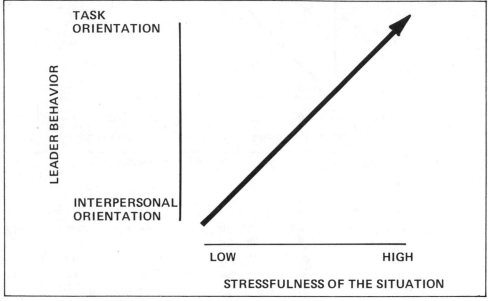

Figure 4.18. The interaction of leadership behavior with level of stress present.

Since competition is stressful and sport and physical activity are characterized by competition, there does appear to be a direct relevance for the athletic context. That is, Sage (1975), in discussing the popular stereotype of coaches, observed that "in recent years American collegiate athletic coaches have been characterized as being highly authoritarian, dogmatic, and manipulative." As Sage also pointed out, this stereotype is emphasized in the writing of a number of authors (e.g., Scott, 1969, 1971). However, the causal factor is usually assumed to be dispositional in nature — a coach possesses the underlying traits of dominance, aggressiveness or authoritariansim, for example. The corollary of this assumption, of course, is that since the disposition is present, the coach would be authoritarian, dogmatic, manipulative, etc. in a wide cross-section of situations — not simply in athletics. On the basis of the available research literature on the personality of coaches, it can be concluded that this is not the case. But, what is not clear at this point is whether coaches in their leadership role exhibit those same typical decision styles and/or behaviors under stress conditions that are characteristic of leaders in general. If there was an answer to this question it might shed some light on the coaching stereotype.

SUMMARY

Leadership may be considered (and defined) from three component aspects: *interaction* (see Chapter 5), *influence* and *power*. An influence perspective of leadership reflects the fact that the leader, subordinate and situation have an interactive impact upon each other in terms of influencing the process of leadership. Also, however, from a power perspective, the leader has an unique base which derives from (1) control over the rewards which can be made available to subordinates (called *coercive* and *reward* bases of power); (2) status or rank within the organization (called a *legitimate* basis of power); (3) expertise or knowledge of the task (called an *expert* basis of power); and possibly, affection (called a *referrent* basis of power). As a result, the leader plays a predominant part in the leader-subordinate relationship — leaders have a greater potential for exerting influence.

The earliest research (which was carried out in management science) into the leadership issue involved attempts to describe the personality characteristics of leaders in terms of the specific traits possessed (this approach is now referred to as the Great Man Theory of Leadership). The research and conclusions derived from this work have been subsequently challenged on methodological and conceptual grounds. The only underlying disposition or trait which still receives some support as a correlate of leadership effectiveness is *intelligence*. However, even leader intelligence is not very promising since it only accounts for 7 to 11 percent of the variance in group performance.

In sport and physical activity, leadership *per se* has received only minimal and peripheral attention. The research emphasis has not been directed toward determining what leadership factors contribute to performance success and athlete satisfaction but, rather, toward providing a social psychological profile of coaches. On the basis of the research evidence available it can be concluded that with the possible exception of some physical factors there is no unique profile of traits which distinguish coaches from the general population.

Modern theories of leadership, with their predominant interest in the factors contributing to performance effectiveness and individual satisfaction, can be distinguished according to whether the basic unit of analysis was the *traits* or *behaviors* of leaders and whether these were viewed as being *universal* or *situational* in nature.

Illustrative of an universal-behavioral approach is the Ohio State Study. The various questionnaires developed under the auspices of this study (e.g., *Leader Behavior Description Questionnaire*, *Leader Opinion Questionnaire*, *Supervisory Behavior Description Questionnaire*) assess two major behavior dimensions which are considered to be characteristic of leaders during the process of leadership: *consideration* and *initiating structure*. The former is goal, production or performance oriented behavior while the latter is interpersonally oriented behavior.

The Contingency Theory of Leadership proposed by Fiedler is an example of a situational-trait approach to the study of leadership. Leadership effectiveness is viewed as the product of the leader's style of interacting with subordinates and the favorableness of the situation. Style of interacting, the trait, was classified as either task or interpersonal relations oriented while situational faborableness was comprised of three factors; the leader-member relations, the structure of the task and the power position of the leader.

A number of current leadership theories have advocated a situational-behavioral approach. In the Path-Goal Theory proposed by House and his associates, the leader's involvement is supplemental — to assist the subordinate toward the achievement of organizational goals. The extent to which the leader is able to do this is a product of two classes of situational variables: (1) the characteristics of the subordinate (consisting of personality and ability); and (2) the environmental pressures and demands present in the situation (consisting of the demands of the task, the formal authority system of the organization and the nature of the primary work group).

In the Hersey and Blanchard Situational Theory of Leadership, it was proposed that the relative extent to which a leader engages in task versus relationship behavior depends upon the degree of maturity of the subordinates (maturity being a function of personality and ability).

The Normative Models of Decision Making (Chelladurai and Haggerty; Vroom and Yetton) are concerned with the situational conditions which predispose the leader to engage in autocratic, democratic or consultive decision making.

In the Multidimensional Model of Leadership (Chelladurai), satisfaction and performance of the subordinate are viewed as being the product of a complex interaction of actual, prescribed and preferred leader behavior.

There are also a number of general situational factors which influence ascendancy to or maintenance of leadership. One of these is geographical location within the group — individuals occupying central positions are most frequently chosen to fulfill leadership roles within the group. A second situational factor is the degree of stress present in the situation — both the decision style utilized (not only utilized by leaders but found acceptable by subordinates) and the type of behavior which is prevalent are moderated by the degree of stress present.

COACH-ATHLETE INTERACTION

5

Since social psychology, as a science, is oriented toward the analysis of social influence processes, it is not surprising that the issue of leadership—the subject under discussion in the previous chapter—should be included in an examination of the coaching dimension. As pointed out, leadership can be viewed as an *influence system* with the coach, as leader, and the athlete, as subordinate, having a reciprocal influence upon each other's behavior.

However, also from a social psychological perspective, another way in which the coaching dimension might be approached—a way which is related to the influence system approach—is as a *social interaction system*. "The essence of any interpersonal relationship is *interaction*" (Thibaut and Kelley, 1966).

As Hollander (1971) defined it, "social interaction refers essentially to a *reciprocal relationship* between two or more individuals whose behavior is *mutually dependent*. It may be thought of as a communication process that leads to influence upon the actions and outlooks of individuals." A similar point was made by Thibaut and Kelley (1966) — "by interaction it is meant that [the individuals] emit behavior in each other's presence, they create products for each other, or they communicate with each other. In every case we would identify as an instance of interaction, there is at least the possibility that the actions of each person affect the other."

Viewed from this perspective, the coaching dimension can be readily characterized as a social interaction system. The very process of coaching involves social interaction between the coach and athlete. Further, the coach-athlete relationship is highly reciprocal with the behavior of the two being mutually dependent.

This feature of interaction has been referred to in discussions of the coaching dimension. For example, Singer (1972) observed that "many grueling hours with meaningful interactions between coach and athlete serve as the basis for athletic achievement." In a slightly different vein, Hendry (1974) suggested that "one difficulty of personality studies of athletic populations is that they have not been very fruitful in predicting actual behavior. Perhaps this is because the personality patterns of the participants have not been considered within a social context. Clearly the influence of coaches' and athletes' personalities is important to their social interactions and to the outcome of these interactions on acquisition of skills and competitive performance."

And, a similar suggestion was made by Carron and Chelladurai (1978). In terms of the Lewinian formula outlined previously—B = f (P, E)—there are two systems involved in the coach-athlete interpersonal relationship. One of these can be referred to as the *personality system*. It is comprised of the coach's personality, personal preferences, need dispositions, and so on *and* the athlete's personality, personal preferences, need dispositions, etc. The second can be called the *situational system*. Factors contributing to it and having an impact upon coach-athlete interpersonal behavior include the nature of the *task demands*, the *normative standards* and *role expectations* prevalent, the extent to which a highly organized *formal structure* exists, the *level of technology* within the team/group situation, the *size* of the team and the *organizational setting*. Figure 5.1 contains an overview of this social interaction model.

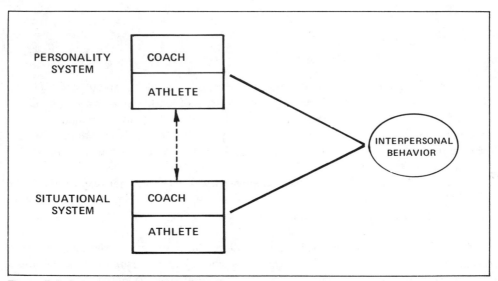

Figure 5.1. Interaction as a product of environmental and personal factors.

This schema presented in Figure 5.1 is, of course, simply another form of the model presented in Figure 4.1 of the previous chapter. It is also a prototype of one presented by Getzels and Guba (1957). They proposed that social behavior is a product of the interaction of an *ideographic* dimension and a *nomothetic* dimension. An overview of their model is illustrated in Figure 5.2.

The nomothetic dimension refers to the prescribed or established modes or standards for behavior present within a social situation. As Shakespeare said:

...All the world's a stage, And all the men and women merely players: They have their exits and their entrances; And one man in his time plays many parts, ...
[W. Shakespeare, *As You Like It*, Act II, Scene 7]

Thus, a social system contains countless "institutions," one of which we can describe as "sport and physical activity." The principals within that institution—the coaches and athletes—enact specific roles which are associated with a general style of social behavior. Each person also has membership in a number of other social institutions in-

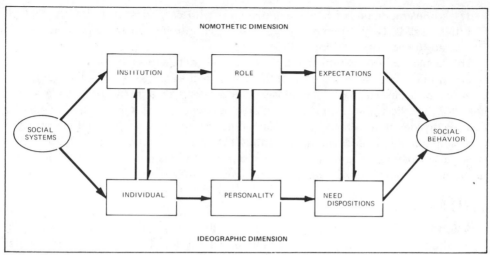

Figure 5.2. Interaction as a product of the nomothetic and ideographic dimensions (Adapted from Getzels and Guba, 1957).

cluding the family, profession, church, social group, etc. In turn, each of these includes an implicit, specific standard for conduct and behavior.

Also the individuals within any institution vary markedly in their attitudes, personality, need dispositions, and so on—the ideographic dimension. And, these wide individual differences interact with the normative standards to influence behavior.

A number of different models which might be used to analyze coach-athletic interaction in the context of sport and physical activity have been discussed in the literature (Carron and Chelladurai, 1978; Hendry, 1974). Although some of these have not been directly examined in the context of sport, they are presented here in overview.

A COMPLEMENTARITY MODEL

What are the antecedents for interpersonal attraction? Aronson (1973) has suggested that several emerge from an examination of the research. These factors include:

(1) *propinquity* —individuals who are in closer proximity have a greater chance of being liked (Festinger, Schachter and Back, 1950; Kendall, 1960; Newcomb, 1961; Gullahorn, 1952),

(2) *similarity in values and beliefs* —individuals who are in agreement on fundamental issues are attracted to each other (Richardson, 1940; Precker, 1952; Schachter, 1951; Newcomb, 1961; Byrne, 1969),

(3) *similarity in personality traits* —individuals who are alike are attracted to each other (Shapiro, 1953; Secord and Backman, 1964),

(4) *high ability* —competent people are better liked than incompetent ones (Stotland and Hilmer, 1962; Iverson, 1964),

(5) *pleasant or agreeable characteristics or behavior* —individuals who are "nice" or who do "nice" things are better liked (Bonney, 1944; Lemann and Solomon, 1952; Jackson, 1959),

(6) *being liked* —affection is reciprocated (Backman and Secord, 1959), and

(7) *complementarity of needs* —individuals who can reciprocally satisfy each others needs (e.g., dominance-submission, nurturance-dependency) are attracted to each other (Winch, 1958).

This last factor—the complementarity of needs—differs from the other six in at least one important way. Whereas each of the first six factors suggests that either *sameness* or *more of* a particular positive quality, characteristic or attribute provides a strong basis for attraction, the complementarity factor suggests that a meshing of needs is a critical consideration. Although Aronson did not make reference to it in that context, a complementarity of needs approach formed the basis for Schutz's (1966) theory of individual orientations to interpersonal relationships and his questionnaire, *Fundamental Interpersonal Relations Orientation-Behavior (FIRO -B)*.

THE MODEL

A fundamental axiom in Schutz's theory is that *people need people*. That is, in much the same way that people have biological needs which must be satisfied in order to sustain the healthy individual, it is also necessary to satisfy specific interpersonal (social) needs. These interpersonal needs are fulfilled through the establishment and maintenance of relationships with other people. According to Schutz, interpersonal needs exist within three broad dimensions of behavior: *inclusion, control* and *affection*.

Inclusion is behavior relating toward association, communication and companionship with others. It is a reflection of the extent to which a relationship exists—without inclusion behavior, there is no interpersonal relationship. Control is behavior associated with the decision making process between people; it is directed toward power, authority, dominance, influence and control. Finally, affection behavior, which refers to the personal-emotional feelings between two people, is directed toward love and affection.

Table 5.1. Dimensions of the Fundamental Interpersonal Relations Orientation Theory. (From Schutz, 1966). Reproduced with permission of the publisher.

	INCLUSION (1)	CONTROL (C)	AFFECTION (A)
Expressed (E)	I make efforts to include other people in my activities and to get them to include me in theirs. I try to belong, to join social groups, to be with people as much as possible.	I try to exert control and influence over things. I take charge of things and tell other people what to do.	I make efforts to become close to people. I express friendly and affectionate feelings and try to be personal and intimate.
Wanted (W)	I want other people to include me in their activities and to invite me to belong, even if I do not make an effort to be included.	I want others to control and influence me. I want other people to tell me what to do.	I want others to express friendly and affectionate feelings toward me and to try to become close to me.

Another integral aspect of Schutz's model is his postulation that each of these three interpersonal dimensions is manifested in two ways: as the behavior that an individual exhibits or *expresses* towards others; and, as the behavior that the individual desires or *wants* from others. A simplified version of this model as well as a definitional statement for each of the six separate dimensions is presented in Table 5.1.

OVERVIEW

Two important considerations should be noted. One of these is that it is possible for an individual to adopt any one of four positions (in terms of interpersonal behavior) within each of the need areas of inclusion, control and affection: *receiver only, originator only, high interchanger* or *low interchanger*. This is presented in schematic form in the four quadrants of Figure 5.3.

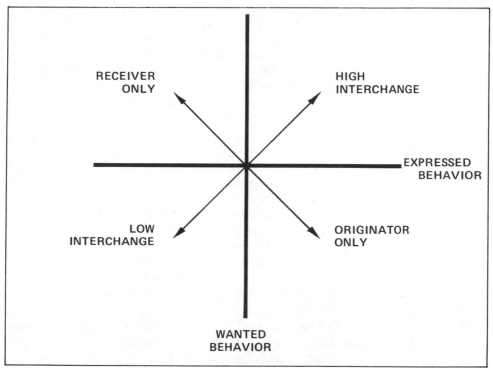

Figure 5.3. General schema for describing interpersonal behavior (Adapted from Schutz, 1966).

Thus, a *receiver only* would be an individual who wants affection (or control or inclusion) but does not express it to others. On the other hand, an *originator only* would express affection behavior (or control or inclusion) but not want it from others. A *high interchanger* would both want and express a great deal of affection (or, again, control or inclusion) while a *low interchanger* would neither want nor express it.

A second consideration which should be highlighted in overview is the interpersonal nature of these needs. An individual has a need to both express and receive affection and to express and receive both control and inclusion (with the uniqueness of individual behavior being a product of the individual differences in these dimensions). In order to achieve compatibility in an interpersonal relationship, an equilibrium between the self and others is necessary.

COMPLEMENTARITY AND BEHAVIOR[1]

The Personality System. Carron and Bennett (1977) used Schutz's model to examine the factors contributing to effective interpersonal interaction between coaches and athletes. Specifically, the upper portion of Figure 5.1 was examined. Two categories of coach-athlete dyads were examined: *compatible* and *incompatible*. The former was comprised of coaches and those athletes identified as satisfying a gestalt definition of most coachable and least disruptive in the athletic situation—in short, those athletes who were furthest removed from being "problem athletes." The incompatible category consisted of coaches and those athletes that the coach felt caused the greatest problem in the athletic environment.

While it was hypothesized that the important areas would be affection and control (since these two are the most frequently mentioned in critical assessments of the coaching dimension), interestingly, the results indicated that the predominant factor contributing to incompatibility was inclusion behavior. It was observed that: "...the interpersonal relationship within incompatible coach-athlete dyads was characterized by relatively detached, withdrawn, isolated behavior on the part of *both* the coach and athlete" (Carron and Bennett, 1977).

There is a question of why neither control nor affection were major sources of incompatibility in the Carron and Bennett study. One possibility lies in the differences among the three behavioral dimensions. That is, inclusion compatibility is a measure of the degree to which a relationship actually exists. Only after the relationship is established is compatibility in the areas of dominance and power (i.e., control) and the giving and receiving of affection an issue. Since those athletes judged compatible had been participants with the coach for a longer period of time (2.68 years versus 1.85 for the incompatible), it was proposed that either "there is attrition of athletes judged incompatible (they quit or are cut) or ... with longer opportunities for interpersonal contact, the coach no longer classifies them as 'least compatible' ... if attrition is a factor this could account for the question of why control and affection were not discriminating factors" (Carron and Bennett, 1977).

When Pease, Locke and Burlingame (1971) analyzed the reasons why individuals quit or are cut from teams, they did find support for the view that player-coach incompatibility (assessed using Schutz's FIRO-B scale) is a "factor in the athlete's decision to quit the squad. In the interpersonal need area of control and, to a degree, the interpersonal need area of affection, a relatively smaller number of compatible and a larger number of incompatible athletes quit their respective squads."

The Situational System. In any social situation, including athletics, social norms and role expectations are operative. This was amply illustrated by the quote from Shakespeare. As a result, all groups or institutions are characterized by social behaviors which are normative in nature and, in turn, participants within those groups enact specific roles. Thus, the general form and content of behavior is dictated to a large extent by the standards emanating from these existing norms and the expecta-

---

1. The discussion in this section was presented originally in Carron and Chelladurai (1978).

tions of others concerning acceptable behavior.

This point was emphasized by Argyle who noted that in order for compatible interaction to be possible, it is essential that the "two people must agree on the role-relations between them ... they must agree on the definition of the situation, and be prepared to play socially defined parts in it." It may well be that failure to achieve consensus in role definition (role conflict on the part of either the coach or athlete) is a contributing factor to incompatibility in the coach-athlete relationship.

Carron (1978), using the Schutz model, examined the characteristic role behaviors within an athletic situation for coaches and athletes (as determined in both instances by both coaches and athletes). There were three major issues in the study: (1) whether coaches and athletes were in agreement on the role behaviors for both coaches and athletes; (2) whether the role behavior of coaches was comprised of those characteristics suggested in critical essays (i.e., authoritarianism, detachment, lack of affection); and (3) whether the role behavior of coaches, when compared to athletes, might contribute naturally to conflict/incompatibility.

The results revealed that both coaches and athletes were in complete agreement in regard to both the role behaviors considered characteristic of coaches and the role behaviors considered charcteristic of athletes. This is illustrated in Figure 5.4.

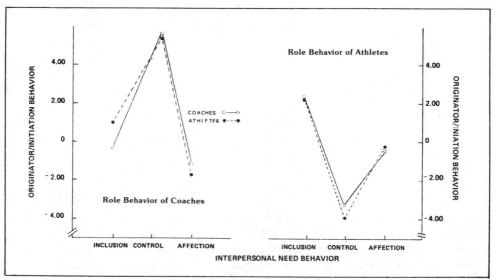

Figure 5.4. Role behaviors of coaches and athletes as perceived by coaches and athletes (From Carron, 1978).

Further, the results also supported a conclusion that the role behavior of coaches in an athletic situation does include those behaviors suggested in previous writings. This is also illustrated in Figure 5.4. The dependent variable in this figure—*originator/initiation behavior*—is a measure derived from the original subscales of FIRO-B by subtracting the wanted behavior from the expressed behavior, or

$$\begin{matrix} \text{Originator/Initiation} = \text{Expressed -} & \text{Wanted} \\ \text{Behavior} & \text{Behavior} & \text{Behavior} \end{matrix} \qquad (1)$$

It reflects the preferred behavioral mode of an individual—whether there is a preference for initiating or being the recipient of behavior. Thus, for example, a positive score in the control dimension indicates a behavioral tendency toward exerting authority, power and influence; while a lower, negative score indicates a behavioral tendency toward being the recipient of authority.

As Figure 5.4 shows, coaches were perceived as dominating the athletic environment by initiating a high degree of control; athletes, on the other hand, were perceived by coaches and athletes as recipients. Coaches were also perceived as being relatively passive in regard to initiating interactions (i.e., inclusion behavior) and developing warm, personal friendships (i.e., affection behavior); they were considered to be more of a recipient than a giver in each of these two areas.

And finally, the characteristic role behaviors of coaches in the areas of inclusion and affection were concluded by Carron to be possible sources of incompatibility since the preferred behavioral mode for both groups were perceived to be that of recipient. In short, with neither coaches nor athletes initiating either affection or inclusion behavior, the athletic environment would be characterized as aloof, detached, etc. Control behavior did not appear to be a potentially troublesome area since there was complete agreement between the coaches and athletes that coaches are the initiators of control behavior, the athletes the recipients.

By way of overview, it should be reiterated that the normative expectations which are present in a social situation do have a significant impact upon behavior. Also, the specific social situation has a major effect upon those personal characteristics or personality traits which are likely to appear (Argyle, 1969). So, for example, even the most extroverted, uninhibited doctor will exhibit behaviors which are within a very restricted range during consultation with a patient. A similar situation applies for the coach facing 50 athletes at the first practice sessions of a season. However, as an examination of Figure 5.1 or the Lewinian formula shows and common sense suggests, it is not reasonable to assume that the behavior demonstrated by doctors or coaches is solely a product of the norms or roles operative. Also, in Chapter 2 it was pointed out that Endler and Hunt (1968) and more recently, Fisher, Horsfall and Morris (1977) using an athletic situation, have provided strong support for an interactionist interpretation for behavior. That is, they found that the greatest amount of variance was not explained by the person alone or the situation alone but, rather, through their interaction. Therefore, what Carron's findings might reveal is the underlying basis for the persistence of a strong stereotype for the coach as an individual "more interested in power and manipulation and less interested in humanistic approaches" (Ogilvie, 1971) when personality research has failed to yield a consistent profile.

COMPLEMENTARITY AND PERFORMANCE

Although complementarity, as Schutz developed his model, involves a congruence between the needs of the two persons in the interpersonal relationship, it also must be considered in terms of the congruence between three factors comprising the situational demands and the two persons interacting (i.e., their particular characteristics, needs, etc.). One situational factor which is particularly important insofar as complementarity and performance is concerned is the *task*. Chelladurai (1978), in his multidimensional model for leadership in athletics (see Chapter 4) pointed out that the tasks of athletes from different teams differ along a number of dimensions and these differences impose certain constraints and/or demands upon the behavior of coaches and athletes. For example, it has been observed that the behavior of a leader (coach) in an interdependent task situation[2] is comprised of more structuring and coordinating functions than is the case in independent task situations (Chelladurai and Saleh, 1978; House, 1971; House and Dessler, 1974). This is illustrated in Figure 5.5.

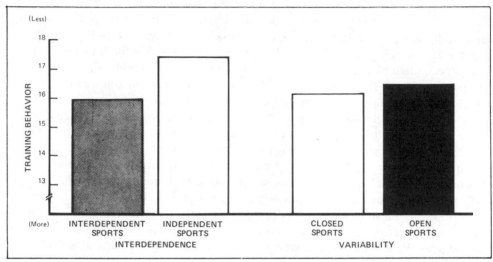

Figure 5.5. Training behavior as a function of the interdependence and the variability present in the sport (Based on data from Chelladurai and Saleh, 1978).

Similarly, the extent to which there is variability[3] within the sport task also influences the degree to which the coach engages in structuring behavior (see Figure 5.5). Chelladurai and Saleh found that individuals who preferred closed sports also showed a preference for more training behavior (i.e., a behavior of the coach which stresses working to full capacity as well as maintaining orderly and uniform methods of training) from their coach than those who preferred open sports. A possible explanation for this difference is that closed sports are characterized by routineness and monotony and the coach's training behavior provides the necessary stimulation and change from this routine.

Thus, any discussion of interpersonal behavior and its relationship to performance effectiveness in athletics should consider the three variable of *coach*, *athlete* and *task*.

2. Dependence is the extent to which the successful performance of a task depends upon the interaction of members of the team or unit. The distinction between team and individual sports is based on this dimension. Dependence versus independence is discussed in relation to cohesiveness and performance success (see Table 8.4).
3. Variability refers to the degree of environmental changes and the extent to which the performer must respond to these changes. A low variability task is characterized by a *closed* form of behavior where the skills are executed in an environment where the stimuli are relatively stable, static and unchanging. On the other hand, high variability would require an *open* form of behavior where skills are used to respond to objects that move in space and require spatial/temporal adjustment on the part of the performer (Robb, 1972). This distinction is illustrated by the difference between the high jumper and basketball rebounder. The high jumper, whose environment is stable and predictable, initiates his own movement—the skill may be categorized as *closed*. On the other hand, the basketball rebounder also exhibits jumping ability but the stimuli in his environment are unstable and unpredictable and his movements are paced externally by the location and velocity of the ball and other players. In this sense, the skill may be categorized as *open*.

However, the characteristic approach has been to examine the interrelationship of two of the three. For example in the Chelladurai and Saleh study presented above, the focus was on the differences among athletes from different sports in their preference for leader behavior. Also, Carron (1978) and Carron and Bennett (1977) examined the coach and athlete variables only.

An exception is an interesting study by Liddell and Slocum (1976) which incorporated all three dimensions with a view to determining the effect of compatibility upon performance. The task/apparatus was the wheel network (see Figure 4.13 in Chapter 4) in which a control/leadership position is centered in the hub while subordinate/secondary positions occupy the peripheral, spoke positions. Communication was permitted only through the hub. Thus, as Liddell and Slocum stated: "(1) the wheel network requires high interchange and differentiation of control, (2) the central position in the wheel network requires high expressed control and low received control, and (3) the peripheral positions in the wheel network require low expressed control and high received control" (Liddell and Slocum, 1976).

The subjects were selected on the basis of their extreme scores on the control dimension of Schutz's FIRO-B and assigned to one of three conditions. In the *compatible* condition, an individual with a high expressed-low wanted control need occupied the hub position while the peripheral positions were staffed with individuals with a low expressed-high wanted control need. Thus, the leader and the subordinates had behavioral preferences which were compatible with one another and with the task demands.

In the *incompatible* condition, an individual with a low expressed-high-wanted control need occupied the hub while individuals with high expressed-low wanted control were in the periphery. Again, the leader and members were compatible with each other but in this condition, their behavioral needs were incompatible with the task demands. The third condition used involved a *random* assignment to the different positions.

The results, which are summarized in Figure 5.6, supported the hypothesis that compatible groups would solve problems faster and make fewer errors than either incompatible or random groups. The random groups were, in turn, more effective than the incompatible groups.

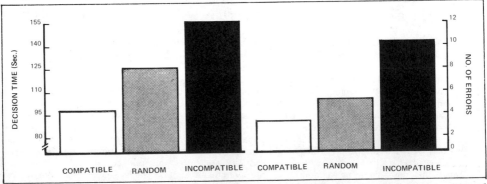

Figure 5.6. Performance as a function of the degree of compatibility present between personal dispositions and the demands of the task (Based on data from Liddell and Slocum, 1976).

The Liddell and Slocum study is not unique in its finding that higher compatibility results in more effective outcomes. This finding has been reported in such diverse settings as group therapy (Sapolsky, 1965); student teacher interactions and resultant student learning (Hutcheson, 1963); and, experimental problem solving situations (Reddy and Barnes, 1972; Schutz, 1958, 1966).

However, studies concerned with work productivity or problem solving behavior in nonlaboratory situations have presented conflicting results. For example, Carron and Garvie (1978) examined the relationship between coach-athlete compatibility and the performance of Olympic and FISU Games' wrestlers. Again, Schutz's FIRO-B measures were used to assess compatibility while the performance measure used was a relative assessment—the athlete and the coach independently provided their estimate of the athlete's performance relative to what was expected prior to competition. The results of the multiple regression analysis revealed that the FIRO-B measures contributed only minimally to the accounted for variance.

As other examples, Hill (1975) and Underwood and Krafft (1975) found that incompatibility among individuals, not compatibility, led to increased effectiveness in performance. Hill suggested that a moderate amount of tension (rather than interpersonal harmony) contributes to productivity since individual competitive impulses arising from the incompatibility are channeled into task performance.

Hill also proposed that the discrepancy in the findings between laboratory and nonlaboratory research might be due to the degree of interdependence inherent in the task. That is, in highly interdependent, face-to-face task situations, compatibility would be a prerequisite for successful performance but, for the reasons outlined above, in independent tasks incompatibility would be desirable. Although Landers and Luschen (1974) were not testing the effects of coach-athlete compatibility (but rather, the issue of cohesion—athlete-athlete compatibility), their results do provide some support for this suggestion. Landers and Luschen found that bowling teams that were the most successful showed the lowest levels of cohesiveness. This work generally as well as the manner in which it might relate to the nature of the task is discussed in Chapter 8.

A SOCIAL SKILLS MODEL

One approach used in the analysis of human *motor* performance has been to treat the performer as an information processing model (e.g., Crossman, 1964; Fitts and Posner, 1967; Marteniuk, 1976; Welford, 1958; Whiting, 1975) that senses, attends to, processes and stores, and transmits information. That is, there is an input of information which is "translated" and acted upon. Marteniuk (1976) illustrated this process for motor skill performance—see Figure 5.7. He also pointed out by way of explanation that:

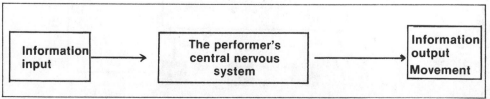

Figure 5.7. A simplified information processing model. (Adapted from Marteniuk, 1976)

...The performer's central nervous system is likened to a communication channel through which information from the environment must be processed. Thus one can conceive of the performer as a communication system, receiving information from the environment (information input) and acting upon it in such a way that what results is a message (information output) that is sent to the muscles so that movement can occur. If the channel or central nervous system has been efficient and accurate in processing the information input, what should result is a movement that is coordinated to the demands of the environment.

It may be evident that with minimal or no adaptations, Marteniuk's description is equally applicable to the situation in which an individual is involved in the process of social interaction. This point was made by Argyle and Kendon (Argyle, 1967, 1969; Argyle and Kendon, 1967) who drew very direct parallels between social skill performance and motor skill performance. They proposed that the social encounters between individuals might be viewed as social performances which, in the same fashion as motor performances, may or may not be skilled. For a social context, *skill* was defined as:

...an organized, coordinated activity in relation to an object or a situation, which involves a whole chain of sensory, central and motor mechanisms. One of its main characteristics is that the performance, or stream of action, is continuously under the control of sensory input. This input derives in part from the object or situation at which the performance may be said to be directed, and it controls the performance in the sense that the outcomes of actions are continuously matched against some criterion of achievement or degree of approach to a goal, and the performance is nicely adapted to its occasion [Argyle, 1969].

Using this rationale as a basis, they presented an information processing model adapted from motor skills research—the general outline of which is presented in Figure 5.8.

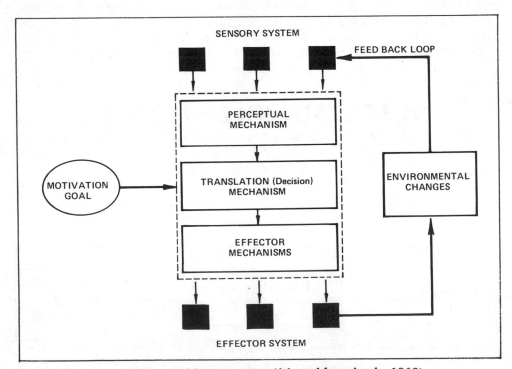

Figure 5.8. A social skills model for interaction (Adapted from Argyle, 1969).

THE MODEL

Argyle (1969), in his presentation of the social skills model of interaction, pointed out that in a manner similar to the information processing model developed to account for motor performance, a distinction must be made between the *perceptual input*, the *central translation processes* and the *output*, or *performance*. Also, just as a motor skill has an underlying *goal* and there is *feedback* concerning performance effectiveness, so too does a social performance. These components were included as an examination of Figure 5.8 shows and, therefore, are discussed in turn.

Motivation, Goal. In the coach-athlete context, for example, the motivation or goal of the social performance could be a desire on the part of the coach, as the *social operator*, to convey knowledge, establish team coordination and cooperation, produce a happy emotional state or change an attitude, behavior or belief in the athlete. And, since a basic objective in sport and physical activity is the accomplishment of some sport task, presumably each of these goals would be related, in turn, to the more basic goal of effective task achievement. Thus, in much the same fashion as is characteristic of a motor skill such as a basketball jump shot, a series of subtasks-subgoals are linked in an overall strategy for performance.

However, social interaction can also occur for reasons other than task achievement—for purely social, interpersonal reasons such as the satisfaction of the inclusion, control and affection needs discussed by Schutz (1966) for example. Argyle did note that the performer-social operator acts as an information processor in those situations as well. In those cases, the goal is a basic social motivation. But, again, the general process would be identical with subtasks-subgoals being linked in an overall strategy. As an example, the coach's goal in interaction with an athlete might be to "develop a good friendship."

The Perceptual Mechanisms. The function of the perceptual mechanism is to organize and classify input information from the sensory system (i.e., sight, sound, kinesthesis, etc.) and convey a series of perceptual responses to the translation (decision) mechanism. In turn, the translation (decision) mechanism uses these perceptual responses to determine an immediate course of action. The perceptual responses are also stored in memory for use in prediction in subsequent social situations.

Selective attention is as necessary a component of social performance as it is for motor performance. During the execution of a motor skill, the individual is bombarded with sensory information—kinesthetic, visual and auditory—and only a small proportion of that can and must be attended to for effective performance.

A similar situation exists with respect to social performance situations. For example, Crossman (1964) postulated that an individual is only able to retain one-hundredth of the information presented in a speech. And, of course, the information received in a social situation is not solely auditory—an equally significant proportion is visual.

Clore and Byrne (1974) highlighted this latter point when they distinguished between two major classes of stimuli which are utilized in impression or attitude formation in interpersonal relationships. *Affect* are the stimuli associated with pleasant and unpleasant experiences with the person while *information* are the stimuli relating to positive or negative information about the person. These two represent the major aspects in the attractiveness of one individual for another.

In light of the excessive amount of information available, the social operator must perceive, organize and classify the input information from others. According to Argyle (1969), "one of the main processes involved in person perception is the assignment of people to categories and the application of relevant stereotypes." This is usually effected by making inferences from physical cues such as hair coloring or wrinkles (as an inference for age), accent and clothes (as an inference for social class), facial features (for race), and so on. Allport (1961, cited in Argyle, 1969), summarizing the stereotypic inferences made by Americans, listed the following:

1) ascribing attributes of unfriendliness, hostility, lack of humor to dark skinned people,
2) ascribing favorable attributes to people of blond, fair complexion,
3) seeing faces with wrinkles at the eye corners as friendly, humorous, easygoing,
4) seeing older men as more distinguished, responsible and refined,
5) seeing older women as motherly,
6) ascribing greater intelligence, dependability, industry to individuals wearing glasses,
7) seeing smiling faces as more intelligent,
8) perceiving women with thicker than average lips as sexy and those with thin lips as asexual,
9) perceiving bowed lips as indicating conceit, demandingness and even immorality,
10) attributing to any Negro face the stereotypes of easygoingness, religiosity and superstition,
11) attributing more favorable traits to faces that are average in size of nose, hairgrooming etc. versus faces that deviate from the average e.g., large nose, exceptionally long or short hair, etc.

Stereotyping is not confined solely to attributes of physical appearance. It may also be done on the basis of occupation. Hendry (1973) has discussed the stereotype for coaches and physical educators in Great Britain and noted that it consists of both physical and psychological parameters (see Chapter 4 again).

Further, in sport and physical activity another stereotyping can also exist—in the appraisal of motor performance. Preperformance expectations of a performer's ability for example, do influence the allegedly objective evaluation of the subsequent performance. In one experiment which clearly demonstrated this point, Hatfield and Landers (1978) had three groups of physical education majors rate stabilometer performance. One group was given a positive bias/expectancy for performance when they were informed that they would be observing superior performers. A second group was given a negative bias/expectancy when they were told that the performers to be observed were inferior; the third group was given no expectancy. In reality, the performers were experimental accomplices who had highly similar or nearly identical abilities. Nonetheless, when a comparison was made of the observers' evaluations, those observers who began the appraisal process with a positive bias assessed greater time-on-balance and fewer performance errors than the negative bias group. Their expectations clearly influenced the way they rated the performance.

There may also be a sex bias or stereotype operative when motor performance is evaluated. For example, Brawley, Landers, Miller and Kearns (1979) had observers of both sexes judge the performance of a male and female on a muscular endurance task. Although the actual performance of the two participants was held constant, all observers gave the males a higher estimate in preperformance and postperformance times.

A final set of experiments which also clearly shows how preperformance expectations/biases/stereotypes can have an effect upon motor performance appraisal was reported by Scheer, Ansorge and their colleagues (Scheer and Ansorge, 1975, 1979; Ansorge, Scheer, Laub and Howard, 1978). In a gymnastic competition, those athletes on a team with lesser ability usually compete first. Thus, gymnastics coaches usually rank-order their gymnasts from poorest to best and then use these rankings to determine the order of appearance. But, judges are also familiar with this protocol and, thus, it might be suspected that they "would have the natural expectation that scores would improve as a function of the within-team order of competition" (Scheer and Ansorge, 1979). And, this was demonstrated to be the case. When the performances of gymnasts were recorded on videotape and the same gymnasts were shown early and then later in the order, the scores awarded for a particular routine, were significantly higher when the gymnasts appeared later in the order.

Two final factors relating to social interaction and perception are that the perception may not be *accurate* or *reciprocated*. For example, Percival (1971) surveyed athletes and coaches and had them rate the coaches' professional behavior and competencies. An overview of some of his findings is presented in Figures 5.9 and 5.10.

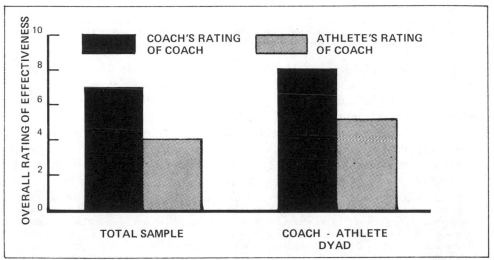

Figure 5.9. Athletes' and coaches' assessment of the coaches' overall professional behavior and competency (Adapted from Percival, 1971).

When the overall results from the total sample surveyed were examined, it was noted that while coaches assigned themselves an average rating of 7, the athletes assessed the coaches at 4 out of a possible 10 (Figure 5.9).

The athletes and coaches also provided an assessment of the coaches within four separate categories: personality, technique and methods, knowledge, and mechanics (Figure 5.10). Again, the coaches perceived themselves much more favorably than did their athletes. The largest discrepancy was for "personality"where 72% of the coaches considered themselves to have a positive personality whereas only 49% of the athletes rated the coaches favorably.

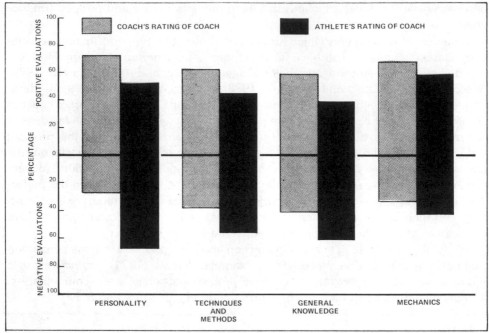

Figure 5.10. Athletes' and coaches' assessment of the coaches' personality, technique method, knowledge and mechanics (Adapted from Percival, 1971).

The Translation (Decision) Mechanism and the Output. The function of the translation mechanism is to arrive at a plan-for-action, e.g., "shoot the ball," "smile," "say hello." This plan-for-action comprises a specific series of responses from the repertiore of possible alternatives previously learned. Just as is the case for motor skills, the elements of a social performance may become more or less automatic with frequent experience. Thus, for example, the coach who has taught a particular technique for a number of years does so effectively and efficiently without hesitation or awkwardness. This point was emphasized by Argyle (1969) who stated that:

> ...social interaction...depends on the existence of a learnt store of central translation processes. In the course of socialisation people learn which social techniques will elicit affiliative or other responses from those they encounter. Research has shown how these can be improved upon in many cases. For example, to get another person to talk more, the best techniques are (1) to talk less, (2) to ask open-ended questions, (3) to talk about things he is interested in, and (4) to reward anything he does say.

The specific plan-for-action, in turn, leads to the output or response. A social response may be considered as a hierarchy of elements with the smaller, lower level units being more habitual and automatic than the larger, higher level units. Thus, as indicated above, the social performance for coaches could be expected to be more *polished* in those areas in which they have had more previous experience.

Feedback. An important component of the social skills model is the feedback loop. Feedback provides information for corrective action and is an integral aspect of social performance in the same fashion as it is for motor performance. Facial cues, body posture and voice tone are particularly important in social situations. Argyle, Lalljee and Cook (1968, cited in Argyle, 1969) reported that an interaction requires feedback from the other's face in order to gauge emotional reactions whereas feedback from the

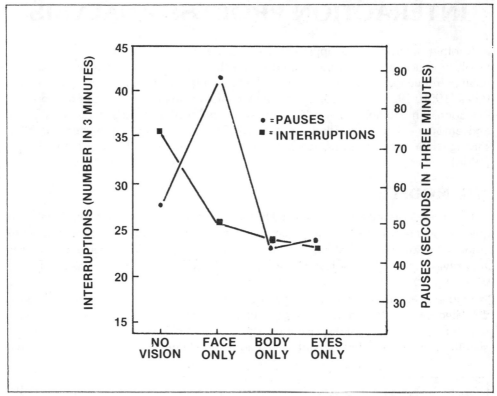

**Figure 5.11. Effect of visibility on meshing (From Argyle, 1969).   Reproduced with permis-
sion of the publisher.**

other's eyes are required for channel control (i.e., when to nod agreement, continue
talking etc.). The Argyle, Lalljee and Cook findings are reproduced in Figure 5.11.

OVERVIEW

A distinctive feature of the social skills model is that each individual in the encounter
is viewed as a "manipulator" who is oriented toward the attainment of personal goals.
As Argyle (1969) pointed out this is "probably how psychopaths deal with people, but
this doesn't quite fit the social behavior and experiences of normal people." Thus, he
suggested that the social skills model could also be extended in two ways to make it
less psychopathic. As one instance, the interactor's goal might be to provide positive
experiences for the other individual. This could quite easily be the case in coaching
and teaching. Therefore, the motive or goal behind this type of interaction would not
be Machiavellian but, rather, to provide the athlete or student with more personal skills
or a more positive and enjoyable environment.

Secondly, one primary objective in social interaction is *self-presentation*. In order to
insure that this occurs, the interactor must attend to the needs of the other individual.
This second viewpoint has some very direct parallels with the *social exchange theory*
of interaction advocated by Homans (1961) and Thibaut and Kelley (1959). This approach to interaction is outlined in a subsequent section of this chapter.

INTERACTION PROCESS ANALYSIS

Another methodological approach which has been used to study social interaction involves concentrating on the *output* only—the characteristic behaviors (and their relative frequency) which are evidenced by individuals interacting in group situations. Bales (1950, 1955, 1966) coined the phrase *interaction process analysis* to represent this approach. He noted that it "is an observational method for the study of the social and emotional behavior of individuals in small groups—their approach to problem solving, their roles and status structure, and the changes in these over time" (Bales, (1966).

THE MODEL

The model was initially presented by Bales and Strodtbeck (1951) to analyze the sequential stages or phases in the process of problem solving within small groups (and, in fact, is presented within that context in the next chapter). The original model was later revised; the 12 revised categories are presented along the vertical axis of Figure 5.12.

Figure 5.12 summarizes the relative frequency of interaction (as reflected in these 12 categories) for 24 different groups (four of each group size from two to size seven) which met on four separate occasions. Bales (1966) observed that for these groups, slightly over half (i.e., 56%) of the interactions were in regard to problem solving while

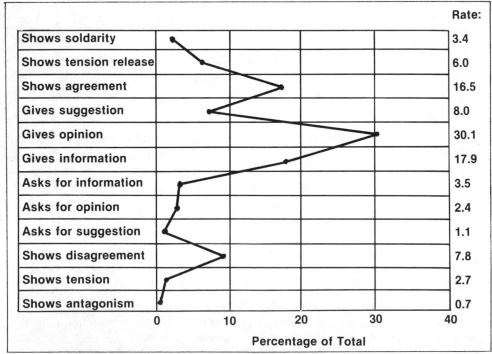

Figure 5.12. Types of interaction in groups and their relative frequency (From Bales, 1955). Reproduced with permission of the publisher.

the remaining 44% were distributed among positive and negative reactions and questions. As a result, Bales (1966) stated that the process of interaction "tends to be two-sided, with reactions serving as a more or less constant feedback on the acceptability of the problem-solving attempts."

INTERACTION AND THE DEVELOPMENT OF TASK ROLES AND SOCIAL ROLES

Bales (1966) has also used interaction process analysis to examine the nature of role development in task-oriented, problem solving situations. On the basis of previous factor analytic studies, three underlying, independent (i.e., uncorrelated) dimensions of group behavior were identified: *activity*, which is behavior of the individual relating to efforts to stand out from others and achieve personal goals; *task ability*, which is behavior oriented toward the achievement of group goals; and, *likeability*, which is behavior oriented toward the establishment and maintenance of socially satisfying relationships.

Table 5.2. Task and social roles which evolve during the process of group interaction in problem solving situations (Adapted from Bales, 1971).

| Role Type | DIMENSIONS | | | Overview |
	Activity	Task Ability	Likeability	
Group Leader	High	High	High	This type conforms to the traditional "great man" view of leadership. They are quite rare.
Task Specialist	High	High	Low	This type is relatively prevalent and may combine effectively with the social specialist.
Social Specialist	Low	Low	High	This type is relatively prevalent and may combine effectively with the task specialist.
Underactive Deviant	Low	Low	Low	This type is relatively rare in group situations.
Overactive Deviant	High	Low	Low	This type is quite prevalent; they are the type described in leadership literature as showing *dominance* rather than *leadership*.

Using these three dimensions as a basis, Bales observed that five distinctive types of roles can appear during the process of group interaction: *group leader* (or "great man"), *task specialist, social specialist, overactive deviant* and *underactive deviant.* Each of these roles differs in the degree to which the factors of activity, task ability and likeability are evident during interaction (see Table 5.2).

The group leader who is high on all three factors and the underactive deviant who is low on all three factors are rare. An individual high on activity and task ability but low on likeability (categorized as the task specialist) and the opposite profile—an individual high on likeability but lower on activity and task ability (a social specialist)—are more prevalent. Finally, an individual high on activity but relatively low on task ability and likeability is the overactive deviant—a type quite prevalent in task performing groups.

SPORT AND PHYSICAL ACTIVITY

While interaction process analysis has been used extensively in educational settings (with different behavioral categories than those used by Bales) over the past 20 years (e.g., see Dunkin and Biddle, 1974; Flanders, 1970; Rosenshine and Furst, 1973), its implementation in the context of sport and physical activity has been relatively recent. In the mid 1970s, a variety of different descriptive systems were devised by Anderson (1975), Cheffers, Amidon, and Rodgers (1974), Fishman (1974), Laubach (1975), and Morgenegg (1978). These have been used to describe physical education classes in terms of *student behavior* (Costello and Laubach, 1978), general *teacher behavior* (Anderson and Barrette, 1978), the pattern of *augmented feedback* utilized by teachers (Fishman and Tobey, 1978), *communication patterns* of students and teachers (Morgenegg, 1978), and *student-teacher interaction* (Cheffers and Mancini, 1978).

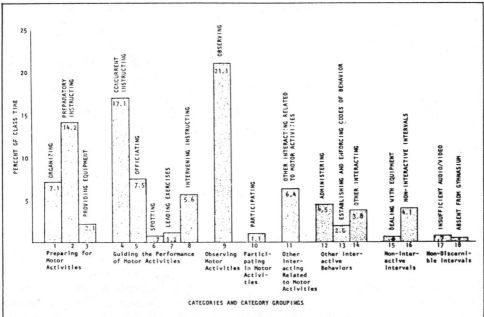

Figure 5.13. Teacher time devoted to groups of functions (From Anderson and Barrette, 1978). Reproduced with permission of the publisher.

Hurwitz (1978), after reviewing this comprehensive body of research, suggested that three major themes emerge. The first is related to the *pace* at which things occur in the gymnasium, the second with the *general model of teaching* utilized by the teachers, and the third with the *patterns of variability* observed in the behaviors of both teachers and students.

The pace theme is highlighted by Anderson and Barrette's (1978) analysis of teacher behaviors. Their results are illustrated in Figure 5.13. It was noted that the teachers devoted over 94% of their total class time to performing interactive functions (categories 1-14 in Figure 5.13). Also:

> . . . the duration and frequency data clearly indicated that the gymnasium is a very busy, highly in-
> teractive educational setting. The teachers . . . averaged over six separate teacher behaviors . . . per
> minute, averaging approximately 200 distinctive behavior shifts for each class period. The duration
> of these behavior units ranged from a fraction of a second to several minutes, with an average 9.9
> seconds in length. Even such functions as Organizing, Preparatory Instructing, Leading Exercise,
> Observing, Administering and Other Interacting, which one might think would occur for relatively
> longer periods, in fact did not. The notion that teachers spend large blocks of interrupted time in
> Preparing, Guiding, and Observing Motor Activities in well ordered and well defined chronological
> blocks is simply not supported by the data. Whether planned or as a result of the circumstances of in-
> teraction endemic to teaching motor activities, teachers engaged in numerous and varying teacher
> behaviors of relatively short duration.

The second theme which emerged from the various studies listed above was that a *traditional teaching model* was predominant in the physical education classes observed. Figure 5.14 contains the results obtained by Cheffers and Mancini (1978) with male and female teachers in elementary and secondary schools. The categories used represent the verbal and nonverbal behavior of students as well as a nonpersonal category (reflecting confusion and silence).

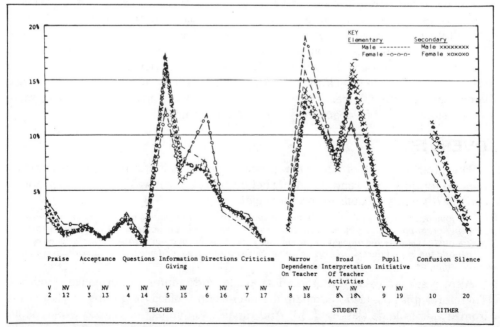

Figure 5.14. Student-teacher interaction (From Cheffers and Mancini, 1978). Reproduced with permission of the publisher.

The most important positive finding obtained was that in contrast to Flanders (1970) who found that the ratio of teacher contributions to student contributions was 2:1 for classroom situations, students contributed substantially more in physical education settings, the ratio being approximately 3:2 (These student contributions tended to be more nonverbal in nature.)

Despite the evidence of a relatively large amount of student involvement, the pattern of student-teacher interaction clearly indicated an emphasis on the traditional approach to education—the predominant teaching behaviors were lecture, information giving and a giving of directions to the students. Further, there was relatively little praise, acceptance of student's feelings and ideas or constructive criticism on the part of the teachers.

On the basis of these results, Cheffers and Mancini (1978) suggested that:

> ...a number of serious questions arise which may not be considered entirely positive...
> In an era which consistently emphasizes humanism in educational processes, why do physical educators overwhelmingly adopt direct, traditional teaching behaviors such as lecture, demonstration, and direction giving?...
> If today we insist that education be geared toward developing student initiative and responsible independence, why are these behaviors in such scant evidence in the sample lessons?
> If knowledge of results and positive feedback are necessary for student learning, why is constructive criticism and praise not a feature of the sample?

The third theme or pattern of findings discussed by Hurwitz was the many instances of *variability* observed in the student and teacher behaviors. In some cases, only minimal variability was observed. For example, the overall behaviors of students and teachers at the elementary level were highly similar to the overall behaviors of students and teachers at the secondary level. Also, only minimal differences in teaching behaviors were noted between male and female teachers.

On the other hand, in other cases, large amounts of variability were evidenced; e.g., (1) the frequency and duration of specific teaching functions varied from class to class; (2) students in dual sports received more feedback than students in team sports; (3) students in small classes spent more time awaiting and less time practicing than students in large classes; (4) teachers who were more experienced or who had smaller classes gave more feedback than teachers who were less experienced or who had large classes; and (5) teachers who were more skilled in an activity gave more demonstrations and feedback than those who were unskilled.

OVERVIEW

The principal value of interaction process analysis is that it provides an empirical method for quantifying and describing behavior. This point was highlighted by Anderson (1978) when he outlined his rationale:

> ...I joined with a group of physical educators who were intent on finding out more about what was going on in physical education classes. Convinced that our current sources of knowledge were inadequate, we were determined to extend that knowledge beyond our own subjective impressions, beyond the limited number of settings we normally encountered, and beyond the idealized program descriptions we found in the literature.

Also, a second value is that the data available do represent normative standards. Therefore, it is possible to compare the interaction profiles for groups varying in size from dyads to large classes of 30. And, finally, the impact of various experimental conditions (such as external threat, cohesiveness, success or failure, and so on) can be examined for intact groups with the results being compared against these norms.

INTERACTION AS A SOCIAL EXCHANGE

Social exchange models of human interaction were originally developed independently in sociology by Blau (1964) and Homans (1961) and in social psychology by Thibaut and Kelley (1959). In their essential form, these models view social behavior in a manner analogous to an economic transaction. Thus, just as there are profits and costs associated with an economic exchange, there are also rewards and costs associated with a social exchange—in order to obtain psychological rewards, the individuals involved in the interaction must incur psychological costs. Further, in any social interaction, an attempt is made by both principals to maximize their personal rewards while minimizing personal costs. Consequently, the "profit" in a relationship, viewed from the individual's perspective, is the total reward minus the total cost. As a result, one activity, behavior or situation may be chosen at the expense of another if it is potentially more rewarding (i.e., profitable) or less costly (i.e., expensive).

Blau (1964) provided an excellent overview of the social exchange rationale when he stated that:

> ...mutual attraction prompts people to establish an association, and the rewards they provide each other in the course of their social interaction, unless their expectations are disappointed, maintain their mutual attraction and the continuing association.
>
> Processes of social attraction, therefore, lead to processes of social exchange. The nature of the exchange in an association experienced as intrinsically rewarding...differs from that between associates primarily concerned with extrinsic benefits...but exchanges do occur in either case...Whether reference is to instrumental services or to such intangibles as social approval, the benefits each suppies to the other are rewards that serve as inducements to continue to supply benefits, and the integrative bonds created in the process fortify the social relationship.

It might be apparent from this sketch that the underlying rationale is basically quite simple with the variable of *reinforcement* being a major factor influencing continued social interaction. In fact, reinforcement theory had a significant part in the origins of social exchange. Homans (1961), for example, introduced his work by drawing upon the behavioristic tenets of B. F. Skinner—human behavior is motivated by the desire to obtain or increase satisfaction and avoid or reduce dissatisfaction.

This is clearly illustrated in a social encounter presented by Peter Gent in his book, *North Dallas Forty:* *

> ...The trick would be to get her to leave with me. It was obvious she wasn't one of Beaudreau's regulars, someone who might ultimately end up on loan to his favorite defensive tackle. She seemed too much in control, too confident. If there was a relationship, she controlled it and more than likely she was sitting alone now because she preferred it.
>
> When I got back to her, I noticed the party had picked up intensity. Those who weren't drunk or outrageously stoned had already been driven off. The terror was escaping each individual's personal limits to flood the room with energy.
>
> "It looks like the direction is set," I said, handing her a perfectly poured Pepsi. "Now to await the obscenities."
>
> "Thanks." She took the Pepsi, then looked quizzically at me. "You mean it gets worse?"
>
> "I don't know if I'd call it worse. It definitely gets different."
>
> "Far out." She smiled and leaned back, relaxing.
>
> "Yeah," I said, "Say, I'm sorry, but I don't know your name."
>
> She extended a thin white hand. "I'm Charlotte Caulder. Charlotte Ann Caulder."
>
> "Charlotte Ann Caulder, it's very nice to meet you." As I gripped her soft, warm fingers, a chill went through me. I find good-looking women almost uncontrollably exciting. "I'm Phillip Elliott. Phillip J. Elliott."

* From *North Dallas Forty* by Peter Gent. Used with permission of William Morrow and Company, Inc.

"What's the J. for ?"

"Jurisprudence. I'm very together."

I looked into her brown eyes. The lines at the corners pulled slightly when she realized I was staring, trying to penetrate. The smile faded and she looked away.

"Let's go someplace other than here," I said, keeping my eyes on her face.

"No. I'm here with someone."

"I know. But you don't have to leave with him just because you came with him."

She raised her eyes to meet mine. They were set, angry. "I don't have to leave with you either. Just because you're here and have shiny eyes."

"I'm a lot more fun and fully skilled in the art of acupuncture," I said, figuring retreat now would bring disaster, if it hadn't already arrived.

"I'll bet you are," she sneered.

In a few short seconds I had made a fool of myself. I started again. "I'm sorry, I fail miserably at small talk. If you're interested, we could try and have a conversation."

"It's worth a try." Her face and voice betrayed little enthusiasm.

"Great," I said, and was immediately lost in her eyes again. I could think of nothing to say. The silence was awkward. Her eyes kept getting larger.

"You have fantastic eyes." It was all I could think to say.

"Tinted contact lenses." She frowned and cocked a look up at me. "Your style is pretty lame."

"I don't get much practice."

"Ah." She held up one finger. "A man of status much sought after by the ladies, I assume."

I nodded. "Who knows? Someday I may be a bubble-gum card."

"You can read to me from it. But till then what have you got to recommend you?"

"Well," I paused and thought a moment, "I graduated summa cum laude from a land-grant college and have never to my knowledge fathered any syphilitic children. I have all my own teeth, except for these front ones. They're always the first to go. I have never beaten up a woman even though my first wife tried to murder me in my sleep — on two separate occasions. How about you?"

Charlotte smiled up at me.

"Well, I'm self-sufficient and only have two fillings in my whole head. In my early teens I considered silicone but now seldom think of it. I consider no sex act repulsive although there are several I would classify as sick. I'm from California and own a Mercedes Benz."

"Mother!!" I cried, reaching for her. She knocked my hands away.

"I also find professional football players boring egomaniacs."

I stepped back sheepishly. Then all hell broke loose in the front of the apartment.

In the encounter, Elliott continually attempts to provide what Blau (1964) referred to in the earlier quote as the *rewards which serve as inducements to continue the relationship*. It is apparent that Caulder didn't perceive the rewards in that social exchange in a positive manner and, thus, there was a strong likelihood that the relationship would be terminated.

THE MODEL

The general features of Thibaut and Kelley's (1959) social exchange model are illustrated in Figure 5.15. It is postulated that each individual brings a large repertoire of possible behaviors to the social situation and any of these could appear in interaction with the other individual. The *behavior sequence* or *set*, the basic unit of analysis in the model, is the series of behaviors between the interacting parties. These have as their objective, an immediate *goal* or *end state*. The behavioral sequence might be instrumental or simply oriented toward obtaining enjoyment and satisfaction from the relationship. As an example, the coach and athlete could interact during a practice session with the objective being either a more skillful performance from the athlete or simply a noninstrumental objective such as affiliation. In either case, the total series or organized sequence of behavior would represent a set.

The specific set or behavior sequence which appears at any given time is a product of *internal factors* (e.g., needs or drive states, etc.), *external factors* (e.g., incentives, problems to be solved, task demands, situational requirements, etc.), and *previous*

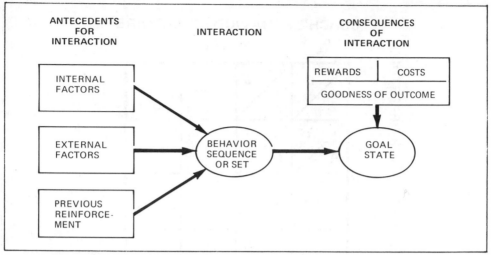

Figure 5.15. The Thibaut and Kelley social exchange model for human interaction.

reinforcement associated with a particular set. Thus, from their large repertoire of potential behavior, each individual selectively utilizes a particular series or set of behaviors in the interaction.

Thibaut and Kelley (1966) observed that the selectivity which is present is a function of the relative rewards and costs for the individual. They stated that:

> ...Although there are several different ways of accounting for this selectivity, we assume that in part it indicates that different interactions in different relationships have different consequences for the individual. Some relationships are more satisfactory than others, and the same is true for some interactions within a given relationship. The selectivity observed in interaction reflects the tendency for more satisfactory interactions to recur and for less satisfactory ones to disappear.

The factor effecting whether a given interaction is more or less satisfactory is the *goodness of outcome* which is the difference between the *rewards* received versus the *costs* incurred. In order to determine the goodness of outcome, the individual evaluates the satisfactoriness of the outcome against the alternatives available. Thibaut and Kelley introduced the concept of a *comparison level for alternatives* for this purpose. It represents the lowest level of positive outcome that is equal to what the individual could secure from some alternate (and available) behavior or social relationship (The availability feature is important. An individual may maintain an apparently unsatisfactory relationship if there are no alternatives possible. For example, athletes may continue with the same unsatisfactory coach if transfer to another team is not possible.) The factors influencing goodness of outcome may be expressed as follows:

$$\text{Goodness of Outcome} = \text{Rewards} - (\text{Punishment} + \text{Comparison Level for Alternatives}) \qquad (2)$$

Since two individuals engaged in an interaction have a wide choice of possible behaviors (with every combination having a different pay-off for each person), their interaction can be represented as a pay-off matrix—a matrix containing the possible rewards for each individual. This matrix is scaled according to the overall goodness of possible outcomes. An example is presented in Figure 5.16.

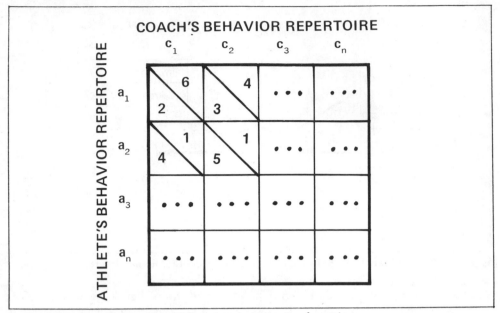

Figure 5.16. A goodness of possible outcomes behavioral matrix.

The coach's behavior sets are presented along the horizontal axis, the athlete's along the vertical axis. The relative goodness of outcome for each of the behavior sets is presented in each cell with the coach's presented in the upper section and the athlete's in the lower section. The optimum behavior from the coachs' viewpoint would be represented by the cell 6-2 while that for the athlete would be the cell 1-5.

It should be noted that the matrix presentation concept was never intended by Thibaut and Kelley to be anything more than an effective illustrative device for presenting the essential features of social exchange—to illustrate diagramatically why some sets of behavior are eliminated in social exchange. The matrix approach cannot be considered definitive or comprehensive in terms of the behaviors of the interactors.

OVERVIEW

Four additional points should be made by way of overview. The first is that in order to preserve a relationship which is on the whole rewarding, the two interactors must learn to either (1) eliminate any cells which are highly unrewarding (incompatible) to the other person or (2) synchronize their behavior in order to insure that mutually beneficial pairs of behavior sets are simultaneously aroused. As an example of the first instance, the coach who is quite aloof and withdrawn may be forced to become sociable and outgoing in order to maintain a minimum relationship with the athletes. To illustrate the second, the athlete who likes to kibitz would chance endangering the relationship with the coach if this behavior was exhibited when the coach wanted to discuss pregame strategy.

Secondly, the role relationships between the two individuals must be superimposed on the social exchange model presented here. Thus, synchronization can also occur via the rules for behavior implicit in the social roles of the interactors. "A main contribution of role to the achievement of set-compatibility is that roles frequently suggest (when they do not clearly specify) a synchronized order of interaction" (Thibaut and Kelley, 1966). The cues which serve to activate a set of appropriate role behaviors in the coach would also trigger the corresponding role behaviors in the athlete.

Thirdly, Thibaut and Kelley have distinguished between *behavior control* and *fate control*. The model of social exchange presented to this point has been oriented toward a behavior control point of view—a coach and an athlete influence each other's behavior by conducting themselves in a manner which is mutually reinforcing. There is, in effect, a *norm of reciprocity* so that a coach, by varying personal behavior, makes it desirable for the athlete to change as well.

However, in the context of organized sport, a coach also has fate control over the athlete since the coach can affect the athlete's behavior (and the outcome of the coach-athlete interaction) regardless of what the athlete does. Thus, athletes operating under understanding or insensitive, outgoing or introverted coaches will comply with the coach's behavioral prescriptions because of the coach's control over the situation.

The final point evolves directly from this. In the previous chapter it was pointed out that the bases for social power can be classified under five dimensions: *reward, coercion, legitimacy, expertness* and *reference* (French and Raven, 1959). While reward and coercion are most directly analogous to the factors contributing to goodness of outcome (cf. Formula 2 again), all five sources of power can be viewed as *commodities* which can be exchanged in the social relationship for a particular mode of behavior or performance. The leader, the individual possessing fate control, has a major control over these commodities and, therefore, has a major control over the social behavior which is shown.

In summary, the appeal of the social exchange theory lies in its general applicability to a wide cross section of social situations. Literally any social behavior can be explained in terms of an exchange model. But, and this is an important qualifier, the model can only be utilized postdictively—it has no predictive power.[4] Thus, it is not possible to determine the coach or athlete's behavioral repertoire, the relative rewards or the costs associated with each of these and, consequently, it is not possible to predict how the coach and athlete will behave in specific instances. However, after-the-fact, the specific behavior may be readily understood and explained from a social exchange perspective.

SOCIAL EXCHANGE AND BEHAVIOR AND PERFORMANCE

Given the above qualification, it is not surprising that the social exchange model has not been tested directly. Indirect evidence is available from studies on the effects of reward and reinforcement on behavior and performance. But as Collins and Raven (1969) observed *"who would be surprised to find that a person is more likely to conform to the demands of another if he is promised a reward or threatened with punishment for noncompliance?"* [emphasis is added].

One study which clearly shows the influence of reward upon involvement in problem solving activity was reported by Banta and Nelson (1964). Forty-eight dyads

---

4. This is, of course, not a suggestion that the effects of reinforcement cannot be predicted. The principle of reinforcement has been well documented in psychology—behavior which is rewarded is strengthened while behavior which is not reinforced weakens or extinguishes. The theory of social exchange implies more than reward or reinforcement effects—it involves the concepts of both rewards and costs with the social behavior that accrues being the result of a trade-off between the two.

engaged in a problem solving discussion were supervised by the experimenter (who, as the authority or reference source to the correct solution, might be viewed as possessing legitimacy and expertness in the French and Raven schema). One of the pair was arbitrarily singled out and her opinions were consistently reinforced or rewarded. The impact of this differential rewarding is outlined in Figure 5.17.

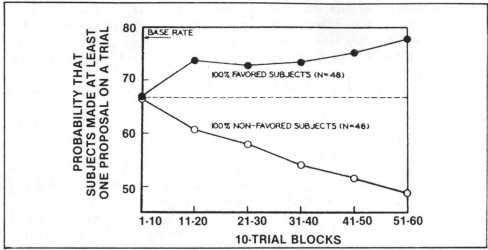

Figure 5.17. Rate of participation as a function of the reinforcement of opinions expressed (From Banta and Nelson, 1964). Reproduced with permission of the publisher.

The nonrewarded subject showed a systematic decline in the rate at which proposals were made during the discussion while the favored or rewarded subject showed an increase.

Similar results were obtained by Pepinsky, Hemphill and Shevitz (1958) and Bavelas, Hastorf, Gross and Kite (1965) in a series of experiments. Bavelas *et al.* found that when signs of approval were introduced, members of a group who had previously been silent during the group's discussions showed marked increases in their participation. Pepinsky *et al.* examined four man production groups which were composed of two actual subjects and two confederates. In a positive feedback condition the confederates reacted favorably to any attempts by the true subjects to lead while in the negative feedback condition, their reaction was unfavorable and discouraging. Not surprisingly, a large significant difference was obtained in leadership activity between the individuals in the positive feedback versus those in the negative feedback condition.

Conformity behavior can also be interpreted in terms of a social exchange model (conformity is discussed in the subsequent chapter). If the individual's behavior is not consistent with the normative standards prevalent, the rewards and costs of conformity are evaluated and a decision for conformity or anticonformity is reached.

SOCIAL REINFORCEMENT AND MOTOR PERFORMANCE

Insofar as motor performance tasks are concerned, research has focused on the effects of *social reinforcement* upon both performance and learning. Social reinforcement is viewed as comprising those positive and negative evaluative comments or reactions which are evident to the performer either through visual or verbal cues — praise, favorable gestures, smiles, frowns, reproof, criticism (Harney and Parker, 1972; Wankel, 1975).

The findings from the available research have not fallen into the same apparently unequivocal pattern typified by the Banta and Nelson, Bavelas *et al.* and Pepinsky *et al.* results—*social reinforcement does not consistently result in a modification/improvement in motor skill performance.* It would appear that a number of factors mediate the impact that social reinforcement has on the performance and acquisition of motor tasks.

One of the mediating factors which has been suggested is the *nature of the task* (Harney and Parker, 1972; Martens, 1970, 1971, 1972). For example, Stevenson (1961) and Stevenson and Allen (1964) found that social reinforcement improved performance when a speed of movement task was utilized. And these are not isolated findings. On the basis of an extensive review of the literature, Stevenson (1965) concluded that social reinforcement generally leads to an improvement in performance when children are practicing on a *simple* or *quantitative* motor task.

However, a number of authors have found that with more *complex* or *qualitative* motor tasks, social reinforcement does not have the same beneficial effect (Martens, 1970, 1971, 1972; Roberts and Martens, 1970). For example, Roberts and Martens (1970) reported no differences in the performance of male subjects practicing on a coincident timing task under positive, negative and nonreactive-control social reinforcement conditions. Similarly, Martens (1970), using a ball roll-up accuracy task, found no performance differences among children under positive, negative, combined positive-negative social reinforcement conditions and nonreactive-control and conversation control (i.e., involved task irrelevant conversation) conditions.

On the basis of these results, two additional factors were advanced as possible mediators between social reinforcement and motor task performance: (1) the *rate* at which the social reinforcement is administered (Harney and Parker, 1972); and (2) the *ability* level of the subjects (Martens, 1970; Martens, Burwitz and Newell, 1972; Wankel, 1975).

In regard to the *rate of reinforcement*, Harney and Parker (1972) postulated that social reinforcement "administered periodically throughout performance may not ...[be] ... of such frequency or intensity as to sufficiently arouse subjects and thereby affect qualitative motor performance." This proposal was supported when it was tested by Harney and Parker using grade six males and females on a ball roll-up task under positive, negative and conversation control social reinforcement conditions (which were administered "enthusiastically" after every performance trial). The results are presented in Figure 5.18.

When the results from the males and females were combined, the positive and negative social reinforcement conditions did not differ from each other but both were superior to the conversation control condition. However, a significant interaction was also noted between sex and social reinforcement—the males in the conversation control condition were inferior to those in the positive and negative social reinforcement conditions while the females did not show any differences across these three conditions (this is also illustrated in Figure 5.18).

Insofar as the factor of *ability level* is concerned, Martens (1970) reasoned that an

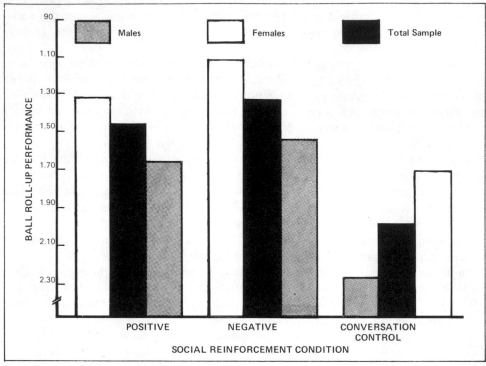

Figure 5.18. Male and female performance on a motor task as a function of social reinforcement (Based on data from Harney and Parker, 1972).

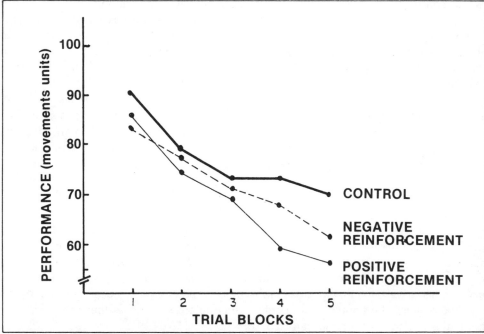

Figure 5.19. Motor task performance with practice as a function of social reinforcement (From Wankel, 1975). Reproduced with permission of the publisher.

individual might be unable to modify performance despite the introduction of social reinforcement if the task-to-be-performed was exceedingly complex or difficult. In short, if the task is not well learned and/or the individual possesses a very low degree of ability, the introduction of criticism, praise, encouragement or reproof is ir-relevant—even with the best of intentions, the performer is incapable of performing any better. In a subsequent study, Martens (1972) directly tested this ability level ex-planation but failed to find support for it.

However, Wankel (1975) did find some support for this proposal when he tested grade seven and eight boys on a stabilometer task under control and positive and negative social reinforcement conditions. In Figure 5.19, the effects of these three conditions over five blocks of practice are illustrated.

In blocks one to three (a block consisted of five 20-second trials), no differences were noted between the three conditions whereas in blocks four and five, the positive reinforcement condition was superior to the control condition (with the negative rein-forcement condition being intermediate and neither significantly better than the control nor significantly worse than the positive reinforcement condition). Thus, early in prac-tice, the social reinforcement had no apparent impact upon performance. With repeated practice and the acquisition of skill, a difference appeared.

IMITATIVE BEHAVIOR AND MOTOR PERFORMANCE AND LEARNING

According to Landers (1975), the study of *imitative behavior* "is concerned with the causal relationship between the model's exhibition of novel responses and the observer's subsequent attempts to perform them in substantially identical form." An analysis of imitative behavior (or *modeling* or *observational learning* as it has also been called) has a very direct application to both the specific issue of reinforcement effects and to the general issue of social exchange theory. The studies which have been discussed to date clearly emphasize the link between reinforcement and behavior. However, consistent with a social exchange interpretation, an observer (O) may also modify behavior in order to match or approximate the behavior of a model (M) even when there is no apparent, direct, contingent reinforcement for this modification.

Landers and Landers (1973) clearly outlined the interrelationship of imitative behavior to a social exchange view of behavior when they noted that:

> ...In observation learning, it is necessary for M to exhibit novel responses which O has not yet learned to make and which O must later reproduce in substantially identical form (Bandura, 1969). It has been commonly assumed that the reinforcement of either O or M is a necessary component of im-itative behavior. This has led to a proliferation of research investigating observational learning as af-fected by contingent reinforcement, vicarious reinforcement, and various incentive conditions. An often overlooked area of research, however, has been the examination of the effects of the reponse of M per se, which in turn causes or influences O's response. In research of this latter type, the effects of a nonreinforced M on a nonreinforced O are examined. The motivation for O to imitate a consis-tent pattern of responses by M in the absence of contingent or vicarious reinforcement may stem from unseen or eventual rewards (Kelley, Thibaut, Radloff and Mundy, 1962). In many human behaviors, particularly the learning by children of highly salient motor skills, child O's may be par-ticularly motivated to achieve success and eventual rewards which may be bestowed by peers and adults. The nonreinforced imitative behavior of O to M's motor behavior may therefore serve in subsequently inhibiting or enhancing O's motivation to match M's responses.

It was also pointed out by Landers and Landers that if imitative behavior is to occur in the absence of direct rewards to the observer, the characteristics of the model are an important factor. Therefore, characteristics such as the *relative importance* of the model (including age, influence, status, power, social status), the model's *ability or level of skill* (i.e., competent models are more likely to be observed and imitated than incompetent models), and whether the model is *present* or *absent* following the observation (thereby influencing the observer's motivation to adopt the behavioral mode) are particularly important. These factors were incorporated into an experimental design by Landers and Landers. In their study, young girls first observed a teacher or a peer model who were either skilled or unskilled and then practiced on a ladder climb task with the model either present or absent. When the results for all the groups that had observed a model were compared with those of a control group *(who practiced with no task demonstration)*, it was revealed that the control group was significantly inferior (see Figure 5.20). "The facilitative effects of exposure to M is illustrated by examining the performance means over all blocks of trials. Controls did not achieve, until Block 3, the level of performance that all other groups performed in their first block" (Landers and Landers, 1973).

An interaction was also obtained between the type of model observed (teacher versus peer) and the ability level of the model (skillful versus unskillful). This is presented in Figure 5.21. Performance was significantly more effective after observation of a skillful teacher than an unskilled teacher or skillful peer. Also, however, the performance of those observing an unskilled peer was significantly better than those observ-

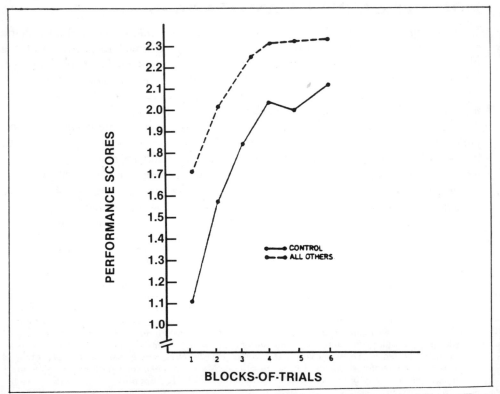

Figure 5.20. Control versus all other groups' performance as a function of blocks (From Landers and Landers, 1973). Reproduced with permission of the publisher.

ing an unskilled teacher. The rationale proposed by Landers and Landers to account for the results of Figure 5.21 was that the smaller discrepancy between the observers and their unskilled peer model versus that between those observers of a skillful peer model produced a strong competitive motivation to do well. In short, the performance standard was readily attainable. Further, in the case of those individuals who observed the performance of the unskilled teacher, imitative responses interfered or hindered effective overall performance.

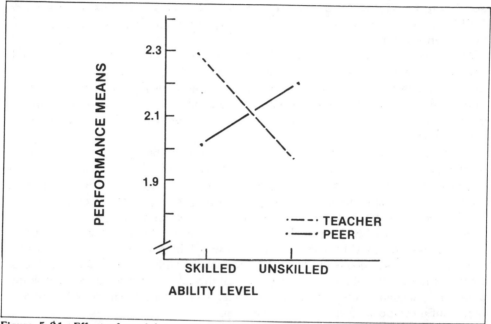

Figure 5.21. Effect of model type X model's ability on performance (From Landers and Landers, 1973). Reproduced with permission of the publisher.

Observation and imitation are particularly suited for the acquisition of social behavior, tasks involving all or none (one trial) learning, or tasks which are verbal, cognitive or simple. However, Landers (1975) and Martens, Burwitz and Zuckerman (1976) have pointed out that observing and then imitating a motor skill does not necessarily result in effective acquisition.

Landers (1975) felt that this inability to reproduce a modeled motor performance could be a result of three factors: insufficient cueing on the part of the model; inadequate coding on the part of the observer/performer; and inability on the part of the observer/performer to carry out the task. Thus, if the modeled performance is incorrect or not clearly presented or the performer misunderstands or mininterprets the model's performance or the performer simply does not have the requisite skills, learning by observation will be ineffective.

A similar point was made by Martens, Burwitz and Zuckerman (1976) when they reasoned that in order to determine whether learning by observation and imitation will be effective, it is necessary to determine "whether the observer can distinguish between the relevant and irrelevant cues presented in a rapidly performed series of complex actions, or whether he has the motor capability to perform the modeled behavior, or indeed whether he has the inclination to imitate the model." Consistent with this viewpoint, they felt that observation can facilitate acquisition in two ways: by providing *information* relative to the appropriate, relevant response (s); and by increasing the *motivation* of the performer to carry out the task.

In a series of four experiments, Martens *et al.* compared a control and three modeling conditions on the acquisition of two motor tasks. The modeling conditions included a *correct model* (CM), an *incorrect* model (IM) and a *learning sequence model* (LSM). In the latter case, the model being observed showed progressive improvements over practice trials.

Martens *et al.* found that when the task was simple, the observation of a correct model (i.e., the CM and LSM conditions) resulted in superior performance scores in the initial, earliest trials. However, this superiority was quickly overcome with subsequent practice. When the task was more difficult and required a very specific strategy in order to achieve an optimal performance level, the modeling effects were more pronounced and permanent.

It was also concluded that the principle factor contributing to performance improvements through observation was the conveyance of *information* relating to the cognitive components of the skill. Figure 5.22 illustrates the results from one of the Martens *et al.* experiments in which this aspect of information conveyance is highlighted. The experimental protocol consisted of three stages (1) a film was presented of a model performing the task (10 trials on a ball roll up task); (2) a second film was presented in which a model initiated the task performance, the film was interrupted while the subjects estimated the performance result and then, the actual result was shown (ten estimations were required); (3) the subjects practiced on the task (ten trials). This sequence was then repeated. Thus, both of the estimations in Figure 5,22 represent a composite from 10 individual trials.

The results revealed a significant interaction with the correct model and learning sequence model conditions both being significantly superior to the control condition on the first test estimate. No differences were present among the four conditions on the second test estimate. "These results are evidence that the CM and LSM conditions conveyed information ... before any actual practice on the task. After practicing, additional modeling had no effect on performance estimation" (Martens *et al.* 1976).

Feltz and Landers (1977) also directly analyzed the informational and motivational effects of a model's demonstration upon motor performance in a ladder climb task. Four groups were compared: an *informational cues only* group (who observed a model demonstrating the task); an *informational/motivational cues group* (who observed a model demonstrating the task and were given verbal knowledge of results of the model's performance); a *motivational cues only group* (who were given verbal knowledge of results of the model's performance but no demonstration); and a *no cue group* (who were not given a demonstration or knowledge of results).

It was observed that motivation—in the form of the knowledge of results provided—did not influence performance. However, individuals who received information via a demonstration—whether knowledge of results was provided or not—performed significantly better than individuals not receiving the demonstration. On the basis of their results Feltz and Landers concluded that the conveyance of information

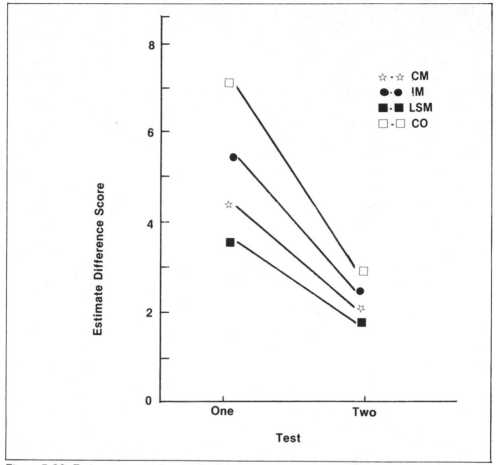

Figure 5.22. Estimate scores for the modeling X test interaction (From Martens, Burwitz and Zuckerman, 1976). Reproduced with permission of the publisher.

was the primary component of a model's performance insofar as its subsequent impact upon an observer's performance.

SUMMARY

The coaching dimension can be viewed as an *interaction system* in which the coach-athlete interpersonal relationship is characterized by reciprocity and mutual dependence. The nature of the interpersonal relationship is dependent upon both ideographic factors (personality characteristics and personal needs, motives and so on of the coach-athlete) and nomothetic factors (normative considerations and role expectations influencing both the coach and athlete).

A number of different models have been proposed to examine social interaction. A *complementarity model*—Fundamental Interpersonal Relations Orientation—was proposed by Schutz (1966). This model has as a basis the axiom that *people need people*. That is, all individuals have interpersonal or social needs which are manifested in the giving and receiving of inclusion, control and affection behavior. An important aspect of this model is the emphasis on the interpersonal nature of these needs. Each individual has the need to both express and receive inclusion, control and affection with the uniqueness of individual behavior being a product of the individual differences in these dimensions. In order to achieve compatibility in an interpersonal relationship, an equilibrium between the self and others is necessary.

In the *social skills model* which was advanced by Argyle (1969), the individual is treated as an information processor who senses, attends to, processes, stores and acts upon input information. In the social skills model, the social performance is viewed as having an underlying motive or goal. The individual, as a social operator during the interaction, senses, organizes and classifies input information obtained via the perceptual mechanism. This is transmitted to the translation (decision) mechanism where a plan-for-action is established and initiated. At the same time, ongoing feedback via visual, kinesthetic and auditory cues provide continuous information for corrective action.

In *interaction process analysis* (Bales, 1951, 1955, 1966), the focus is on the actual output of the interaction—behavior itself. Thus, the relative frequency of behaviors which reflect solidarity, tension release, agreement, antagonism, tension, disagreement and the giving and asking for of opinions, suggestions and information are charted. On the basis of factor analysis, three dimensions of group behavior have been identified from these twelve original categories: task ability, activity and likeability. Further, the role behavior of any individual within an interaction can be categorized into five types according to the extent to which each of these dimensions is present: group leader, task specialist, social specialist, overactive deviant and underactive deviant.

Interaction has also been considered as a *social exchange model* (Blau, 1964; Homans, 1961; Kelley and Thibaut, 1959). In this model social behavior is viewed in a manner analogous to an economic transaction. That is, from a personal perspective, a social interaction will yield "rewards" to an individual. However, in order to maintain the relationship, it is also necessary to provide rewards to the other person and thus, there are "costs" involved. Consequently, both individuals in the interaction attempt to maximize their personal rewards while minimizing personal costs. As a result, the "profit" in a relationship is the total reward minus the total cost.

SECTION IV
THE TEAM

Independence? That's middle class blasphemy. We are dependent on one another, every soul of us on earth.
George Bernard Shaw

Many hands make light work.
John Heywood

Many hands make like work.
Anonymous

THE GROUP 6

The nature of groups and the dynamics of group involvement are fundamental issues in sociology and social psychology. Luthans (1973) pointed out, for example, in a discussion of the role of the group in sociology that "the group is the unit of analysis most closely associated with modern sociology." He then also noted that "the main reason for this is that it is such a common social unit." In fact, to be more precise, it has been *small groups* which have most intrigued the sociologist, not only because they are the most prevalent type of group within our culture but also because they are the easiest to control experimentally and to study empirically (Davis, 1969).

Mills (1967) outlined yet another reason for the emphasis which has been placed upon the analysis of small groups by social scientists:

> . . . not only are they micro-systems, they are essentially microcosms of larger societies. They present, in miniature, societal features, such as a division of labor, a code of ethics, a government, media of exchange, prestige rankings, ideologies, myths and religious practices. Through careful examination of these micro-systems, theoretical models can be constructed and then applied to less accessible societies for further test and modification. Small group research is thus a means of developing effective ways of thinking about social systems in general.

In social psychology, this interest in the group has been broadened in order to encompass the *dynamics of group involvement* — the nature of group development and group life. The rationale underlying the study of group dynamics was well summarized by Cartwright and Zander (1968):

> . . . whether one wishes to understand or to improve human behavior, it is necessary to know a great deal about the nature of groups. Neither a coherent view of man nor an advanced social technology is possible without dependable answers to a host of questions concerning the operation of groups, how individuals relate to groups, and how groups relate to larger society.

In turn, this view on the importance of understanding group dynamics probably could be very readily extended to sport and physical activity. That is, to paraphrase Cartwright and Zander — *if we wish to understand behavior in sport and physical activity, it is necessary to know a great deal about the nature of sport groups*. The basis for this suggestion is that a fundamental distinguishing characteristic of sport is its organizational structure. The individual athlete practices and competes within the context of a larger social system comprising an organization, a group or team. In turn, this social structure has both a direct and an indirect influence upon the athlete's behavior

175

and performance effectiveness. Consequently, it might be expected that the team per se and the dynamics of team involvement would be topics which have received careful scrutiny within the social psychology of sport and physical activity. Unfortunately, with only a few exceptions,[1] this has not been the case. As a result, any insight into teams and team dynamics must be derived by extrapolating from conceptual systems developed in sociology and social psychology.

THE NATURE OF THE GROUP

DEFINITIONS

A number of different definitions have been presented for the social psychological construct of *group*. While these definitions often reflect the specific underlying orientation and research interests of their authors, they also serve to delimit the group and highlight its essential features. Thus, it might be beneficial to initially present a representative sample of some of these definitions.

In his classic book, *The Human Group*, Homans (1950) described a group as:

> . . . a number of persons who communicate with one another often over a span of time, and who are few enough so that each person is able to communicate with all the others, not at secondhand, through other people, but face-to-face.

Subsequently, in the same text, Homans elaborated upon this description:

> . . . a group is defined by the interaction of its members. If we say that individuals A, B, C, D, E, . . . form a group, this will mean that at least the following circumstances hold. Within a given period of time A interacts more with B, C, D, E, . . . than he does with M, N, L, O, P, . . . whom we choose to consider outsiders or members of other groups. B also interacts more often with A, C, D, E, . . . than he does with outsiders . . . It is possible just by counting interactions to map out a group quantitatively distinct from others.

A similar perspective was advanced by both Merton (1957) and Schein (1965) who each listed three criteria which they felt serves to define the group. In Merton's view:

> . . . one objective criterion of a group [is] . . . 'frequency of interaction.' A second . . . is that the interacting persons define themselves as 'members', i.e., that they have patterned expectations of forms of interaction which are morally binding on them and other 'members' but not on those regarded as 'outside' the group. The correlative and third criterion is that the persons in interaction be defined by others as 'belonging to the group', these others including fellow-members and non-members.

Schein (1965) who was specifically concerned with the psychological characteristics of groups within organizations proposed that:

> . . . a psychological group is any number of people who (1) interact with one another, (2) are psychologically aware of one another, and (3) perceive themselves to be a group. The size of the group is thus limited by the possibilities of mutual interaction and mutual awareness. Mere aggregates of people do not fit this definition because they do not interact and do not perceive themselves to be a group even if they are aware of each other as, for instance, a crowd on a street corner watching some event.

In a definition which has particular relevance to sport and physical activity, Newcomb (1951) highlighted the normative nature of the interaction and communication which occurs within groups:

---

1. Two notable exceptions are the topic of group cohesiveness and its relationship to performance effectiveness and the topic of group structure — particularly the influence of *centrality* (i.e., being in a central position in terms of the group's interaction and communication network). Cohesiveness is analyzed in depth in Chapter 8 while aspects of group structure are discussed in Chapter 5 as well as in a subsequent section in this chapter.

> . . . for social psychological purposes, at least, the distinctive thing about a group is that its members share norms about something. The range covered by shared norms may be great or small, but at the very least they include whatever it is that is distinctive about the common interests of the group members — whether it be politics or poker. They also include, necessarily, norms concerning the roles of group members — roles which are interlocking, being defined in reciprocal terms. . . . These distinctive features of a group — shared norms and interlocking roles — presuppose a more than transitory relationship of interaction and communication.

The factor of interdependence among group members was emphasized by both Lewin (1948) and Cartwright and Zander (1968). For example, Lewin stated:

> . . . it is not similarity or dissimilarity that decides whether two individuals belong to the same or different groups, but social interaction or other types of interdependence. A group is best defined as a dynamic whole based on interdependence rather than on similarity.

In a similar vein, Cartwright and Zander proposed that:

> . . . a group is a collection of individuals who have relations to one another that make them interdependent to some significant degree. As so defined, the term group refers to a class of social entities having in common the property of interdependence among the constituent members.

A final perspective, one which also has a very direct application to the context of sport and physical activity, was advanced by Deutsch (1949) in preview to his analysis of competitive versus cooperative situations. The former were considered to be inherent in those situations characterized by the presence of *contriently interdependent* goals—goal achievement by one individual reduces the reward potential of other performers. On the other hand, the cooperative situations were considered to be chacterized by *promotively interdependent goals*—the progress of one individual toward goal achievement also enhances the progress of other individuals toward goal achievement. Within this framework, Deutsch stated that:

> . . . a sociological group exists (has unity) to the extent that the individuals composing it are pursuing promotively interdependent goals. A psychological group exists (has unity) to the extent that individuals composing it perceive themselves as pursuing promotively interdependent goals.

Thus, it follows from the above that the principal properties which serve to define a sport group — and, in turn, to distinguish it from a crowd of individuals or a random collection of people — are the following (which are present in the group in varying degrees depending upon the type of sport): *a collective identity, a sense of shared purpose or objectives, structured patterns of interaction, structured modes of communication, personal and/or task interdependence,* and *interpersonal attraction.*

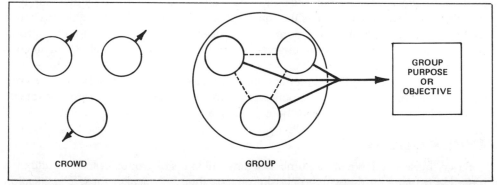

Figure 6.1. A group versus a collection of individuals which is not a group. The broken lines represent group processes such as interaction, personal and task interdependence and communication. The circle represents a collective identity or unity which is characteristic of groups while the sense of shared purpose and objectives in groups contrasts with the independent behavior of separate individuals.

An illustration which serves to highlight the distinction between a collection of individuals that is not a group and one which is, is presented in Figure 6.1. The broken lines between individuals within the group or "team" represent interaction, interpersonal attraction, interdependence and communication while the encirclement of the individuals represents the unity, the collective totality or collective identity which is characteristic of sport groups. And finally, the shared purpose which is present in sport groups can be contrasted with the independent behavior of those individuals who are not members of a sport group.

THE INDIVIDUAL VERSUS THE GROUP AS THE UNIT OF ANALYSIS

A longstanding issue relating to the nature of groups concerns their reality as a unit of analysis. That is, the group has been considered conceptually from two different general perspectives. In one, the group is viewed as an entity or unit which is distinguishable from the individuals who compose it. This perspective does recognize that each group member brings individual needs, aspirations, motives and abilities to a group and these have an influence upon the total membership and its output. However, it is also emphasized that the needs, aspirations, motives and abilities of the group cannot be arrived at through the process of a simple summation of the individual properties. *The group exists in its own right and must be analyzed as a totality.*

In the second perspective, *the group is conceived of as the additive product of its collective membership.* Thus, if the individual members within a group are overly aggressive, friendly, well-behaved and so on, the collective entity would reflect these facets. From this perspective, a group is considered to be the sum of its parts and, therefore, the individual members are the important unit for analysis.

Rather than endorse one of these viewpoints at the expense of the other, Cattell (1948, 1953) contended that the group — in a manner analogous to individual personality — might be described at various levels which he called *panels*. These panels were *population, structure* and *syntality*. Description of the group at the population level focuses on the psychological characteristics of the individual group members — their personality, neeeds, motives, attributes, etc. Analysis of the group at the structural level involves an examination of the pattern of interaction within the goup while syntality "defines for the group precisely what personality does for the individual. It is, therefore, that which determines the [group's] reactions when the stimulus situation is defined" (Cattell, 1953). Thus, *population* concerns the individual within the group situation, *structure* concerns the member-to-member interactions while *syntality* concerns the group as a whole.

While research into group dynamics utilizes all three of these "panels," from a conceptual point of view at least, the perspective which emphasizes the group as a totality — Cattell's syntality — has been the one most actively endorsed.

TYPES OF GROUPS

Since there are such a large number of different kinds of groups in society, attempts have been made by theorists to classify or type them. Typically, these classification schemes have as their basis the presence or absence of one or two significant properties. In fact, usually *the* single most important property is selected and a dichotomy established on the basis of whether that property is present or not. The most frequently used properties in this regard (Cartwright and Zander, 1968) include: *size* (the number of group members); the extent to which there is *physical interaction* among members of the group; the *level of intimacy* within the group; the degree to which there is a *sense of group solidarity;* the *locus of control* for the group's activities; and the nature of the group's *organizational structure* (including whether it has a set of formalized rules which govern relationships among group members and whether the interpersonal behavior among group members is basically normative in style). As a result, the current literature on groups includes references to and descriptions of various group types such as *formal-informal; membership-reference; primary-secondary; in-group-out-group; small group-large group;* and so on. Each type is considered to have different essential features and a different impact upon its members. A number of examples might serve to illustrate this point.

One distinction frequently made (e.g., Schien, 1965) is between *formal* and *informal* groups. The former are groups set up in order to fulfill certain objectives and carry out specific tasks. They may be of two kinds depending upon their duration: *permanent* or *temporary*. A players' committee set up to develop an award system for a school's athletic program would be one example of a temporary formal group while the actual athletic teams themselves would be examples of permanent formal groups. Informal groups, on the other hand arise within formal groups or in a collection of individuals in response to a specific need of its membership — often an interpersonal need. A clique which exists within a team would be one example of an informal group.

Another group dichotomy which has been frequently utilized is *primary* versus *secondary*. The primary group was originally defined in 1909 by Charles Cooley in his book *Social Organization:* "by primary groups I mean those characterized by intimate face-to-face association and cooperation. They are primary in several senses but chiefly in that they are fundamental in forming the social nature and ideals of the individual" (Cooley, 1911; originally published in 1909). Two of the more prevalent groups in society are the family and peers and, therefore, not unexpectedly, primary groups have been extensively analyzed.

A distinction has also been made by Kolsa (1969) between *membership* versus *reference groups* and *in-groups* versus *out-groups* in a discussion of business and organizational behavior. Groups to which the individual actually belongs were labeled membership groups while those which the individual identifies with or would like to join were called reference groups. It was further proposed that "the in-group represents a clustering of individuals holding prevailing values in society or, at least, having a dominant place in social functioning . . . The out-groups are the conglomerates looked upon as subordinate or marginal in the culture" (Kolsa, 1969).

The list of group-types presented here is by no means a comprehensive summary of the population of group types which have been discussed and/or examined in the literature. One might wonder how so many (often only marginally different) group types could emerge. The most obvious explanation is that the various classification systems evolved as researchers and theorists attempted to delimit and operationalize their own specific area of interest. Further, and somewhat related to this point, since groups have been generally dichotomized according to their essential characteristics and the impact they have upon their membership, it is not surprising that such diverse disciplines as counseling psychology, management science and sport and physical activity have focused upon such fundamentally different groups. Thus, in sport and physical activity, for example, the focus has been on task performing small groups (Donnelly, Carron and Chelladurai, 1978) while in counseling psychology it has been on the group as a means of therapy and personal education (Nichols, 1976). As a consequence, a classification of groups according to type or property and an emphasis on the dynamics of these specific types has been inevitable.

Cartwright and Zander (1968) have cautioned against the possibility that numerous exclusive theories of group dynamics could develop on the basis of these selected properties, e.g., a theory for small groups (i.e., dyads versus triads), a theory for physically interacting groups, and so on. It was pointed out that:

> . . . the identification of group dynamics with the study of any one [type of group] . . . or a limited number of them, would seem to us to be unfortunate. Our reluctance to restrict the field in this way does not arise from any desire to minimize the importance of such things as group size, opportunity for physical interaction, degree of intimacy, and the rest as determinants of what happens in groups. In fact, it is because of the importance of these features that they should not be used to define the boundaries of a field of inquiry. Such important variables should be the center of attention. . . . Thus, it should not be assumed without good evidence that one set of laws applies to informal groups while another applies to formal ones, or that a single theoretical system cannot encompass face-to-face groups and organizations. Similarly, it should not be taken for granted that a special field of knowledge is required for groups having some particular objective.

In short, until we have a better understanding of athletic teams as groups, we should consider them within the framework initiated in sociology and social psychology.

GROUP DEVELOPMENT

LIMITATIONS IN THE THEORETICAL ANALYSIS OF GROUP DEVELOPMENT

Possibly as an extension of the fact that traditionally there has been a tendency toward the classification of different group-types, there has also been a large number of explanations advanced to account for the way in which groups develop. In fact, Hill and Gruner (1973) noted that there have been over 100 distinct theories of group development presented in the literature. This proliferation of theories hasn't been due to complexities in the process of group development as much as to practical difficulties in empirically testing the validity of many of the theories. One problem of analysis, for example, has been that if the group is examined in a laboratory setting, the duration of its existence is generally too brief to chart all stages in the developmental process. A second problem, on the other hand, is that if a nonlaboratory intact group is examined in a field study situation, it is difficult to ascertain the precise stage of development it is at at the time of test. And finally, a third consideration is that many theories have either not been presented in testable terms or, if testable, the amount of data required to do so is prohibitive.

THE GROUP AS A UNIT

Tuckman (1965) did review a large number of studies of group development and upon this basis, proposed that in terms of both group structure and task productivity, the development sequence in groups follows four stages which he called *forming, storming, norming,* and *performing.* This schema is outlined in Table 6.1. It was proposed that while the duration of each of the four stages might vary for different groups, the sequential nature of the stages is inevitable in the process of group development.

Table 6.1. The developmental sequence for group structure and task activity in groups (Adapted from Tuckman, 1965).

Developmental Stage	Behavioral Characteristics Relating to Group Structure	Behavioral Characteristics Relating to Task Activity
Forming	Orientation problems are predominant; there is testing to identify the boundaries for interpersonal behavior; dependency relationships are established with the leader, other group members, or existing normative standards.	Primary concerns are with orientation; group members determine what the task is, what methods are acceptable, how the task may be carried out.
Storming	Conflict and polarization occur around interpersonal issues; rebellion against the leader and resistance to control by the group.	Resistance develops to group influence and the task requirements.
Norming	Resistance is overcome; cohesion and group solidarity evolve; group roles are stabilized.	Task cooperation among group members is present; free exchange of information.
Performing	Structural issues are resolved; interpersonal relations are stabilized; interpersonal structure becomes the tool of task activity.	Group energy is channeled into the task; constructive effort toward task solution.

A slightly different sequential schema was set out by Schutz (1966). The three dimensions of Schutz's theory — inclusion (I), control (C) and affection (A) — were discussed in detail in the previous chapter. In regard to group development, it was proposed that "every time people form themselves into groups, including two-person groups, the three interpersonal problem areas are dealt with in the same order" (Schutz, 1966), namely;

$$\text{Inclusion} \text{\textemdash\textemdash} \text{Control} \text{\textemdash\textemdash} \text{Affection} \qquad (1)$$

Thus, the inclusion phase occurs during the formation of the group as individual members determine how much contact, interaction and communication they wish to have. In the control phase, which follows when inclusion problems have been sufficiently resolved, the issues of degree of involvement in decision making, influence, authority and the procedures for resolving the group task are predominant. Finally, when the problems in the control area are satisfactorily resolved, the group members become emotionally integrated.

It was emphasized that these are not distinct phases — rather, they are the problem areas which are *emphasized* at certain stages during a group's growth. That is, "all three problem areas are always present but not always of equal salience" (Schutz, 1966). Also, it was noted that after the group has gone through these three phases, it could possibly begin another cycle or cycles:

$$\text{I} \text{\textemdash} \text{C} \text{\textemdash} \text{A} \text{\textemdash} \text{I} \text{\textemdash} \text{C} \text{\textemdash} \text{A} \dots \qquad (2)$$

And, this sequence could be repeated until there is a break-up of the group with the termination of the group following an opposite sequence to its development; or

$$I \ C \ A \ I \ C \ A. \ldots . \ A \ C \ I \qquad (3)$$

In commenting upon this sequence, Schutz (1966) observed that:

> . . . in the process of resolution there seems to be a particular sequence in which [the three dimensions] . . . are dealt with. The personal positive and negative feelings are dealt with first . . . Next, discussion focuses on the leader and on the reasons for compliance or rebellion to his wishes. Later come discussions about the possibilities of continuing the group and about how committed each member really was; finally, about the fact that they are all going into different groups and will no longer be members of the present one. This sequence reverses the formation sequence by first decathecting (withdrawing investment from) the affectional ties, then the control problems, and finally the inclusion phenomena.

A developmental model for the phases or stages which are present in the problem solving process (i.e., the analysis and planning) for groups working toward the goal of a group decision was developed by Bales and Strodtbeck (1951). They hypothesized that in their interaction, all problem solving groups move through three phases — qualitatively distinct subperiods within a continuous period of group interaction when the group moves from initiation to completion of a problem and arrives at a group decision. In these phases, the relative emphasis in group interaction shifts from problems of *orientation* to problems of *evaluation*, to problems of *control*. Also, during their transition through these phases, there is a concurrent increase in the relative frequencies of both *negative reactions* and *positive reactions* by group members.

A schematic overview of the operationalized components of the Bales and Strodtbeck model is presented in Figure 6.2. Within the 12 categories presented, Categories

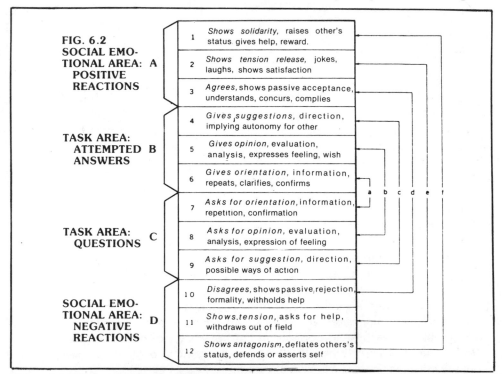

Figure 6.2. Phases or stages in the problem solving process within groups (From Bales and Strodtbeck, 1951). Reproduced with permission of the publisher.

6 and 7 were assumed to deal with problems of orientation; Categories 5 and 8 with problems of evaluation; Categories 4 and 9 with problems of control; Categories 10, 11 and 12 with negative reactions; and Categories 1, 2, and 3 with positive reactions.

THE INDIVIDUAL WITHIN THE GROUP

While each of the above conceptual models deals with the development of the group as a unit, an individual member's assimilation into a group — either a forming group or in one which is already established — is not considered markedly different. For example, Mills (1967) listed four sequential stages in the assimilation of members into a group; (1) the individual's concern is with the *basic individual needs or motives* which led to an attraction to the group, (2) there is *conformity to group norms*, (3) the individual's concern is with *social interaction* within the group and the pursuit of *group goals,* and (4) there is involvement in the *leadership* of the group and the direction that the group should take.

It would seem then that all of the models presented here bear some relationship to each other. In the early stages of group development, the principal concern is with acclimatizing/acceptance/orientation issues. Subsequently, these give way to issues relating to the establishment of control/leadership/influence and close personal ties are established. Finally, the most effective production of the group is then carried out.

THE REPLACEMENT PROCESS IN SPORT ORGANIZATIONS

The process of group development per se is not an issue of any concern with sport groups since, "in comparison with other types of formal organizations, sport teams are exceptionally stable" (Loy, Theberge, Kjeldsen and Donnelly, 1975). Interscholastic, intercollegiate, professional, and amateur youth sport teams, for example, continue to function year-after-year. However, there is a regular turnover in the team's composition as a result of graduation, resignation, retirement, promotion, transfer, dismissal, and so on. Thus, a major problem evolves around the assimilation of new players.

John Loy and his students have carried out a series of studies using the records from various sport organizations (e.g., the National and American Baseball Leagues) in order to determine what parameters are associated with this assimilation — *the correlates of the replacement process.* Loy, Theberge, Kjeldsen and Donnelly (1975) subsequently reviewed this work as well as previous studies by Ball (1974), Eitzen and Yetman (1972), Grusky (1963), McPherson (1973), and Rose (1970) in an attempt to determine if there was a consistent pattern of findings among the different studies.

It was noted that the amount of stability (or, conversely, the amount of turnover) associated with different playing positions is not random — there are systematic differences. Ball, for example, found that the degree of stability in football varied across the different offensive position: tackles (76%), guards (75%), centers (74%), running backs (67%), flankers and wide receivers (56%), tight ends (55%), and quarterbacks (38%). Differences in stability were also reported across playing positions in baseball (Theberge, 1973) and hockey (McPherson, 1973). However, there was no apparent underlying reason which could link these findings into a coherent picture causing Loy *et al.* to conclude that "the nature of replacement rates by position appears to be sport specific and adequate theoretical explanations. . .are largely lacking."

There are a number of potential problems associated with the replacement of members in terms of the effect upon performance effectiveness. For example, new members require time to adjust to the general environment, learn a new team system, become familiar with any idiosyncrasies of their teammates, establish rapport and cohesiveness, and so on. Consequently, Loy *et al.* reasoned that organizational effectiveness is related to member replacement rates; teams that experience large turnovers will be less successful than teams with smaller turnovers.

Strong support was observed for this hypothesis in studies of professional baseball, basketball, football, and high school gymnastics. Professional hockey was the sole exception. Schwartz (1973, cited in Loy *et al.*, 1975), for example, examined the records of professional basketball, baseball, and football teams for the period 1960 to 1969 and found correlations of -.47, -.51, and -.54 respectively between winning percentages and personnel succession rates. Similarly, Theberge (1973, cited in Loy *et al.*) analyzed major league baseball records for the period 1951 to 1960 and found correlations of -.54, .55, and .57 between personnel succession and percentage of games won, personnel succession and league standing, and personnel succession and games behind, respectively.

Thus, it is apparent that too large a turnover in personnel is detrimental to team performance. On the other hand, no turnover whatsoever could be equally damaging since the players would "all grow old together." Instead of a gradual process of assimilation, the organization would be faced with wholesale changes. Obviously, a compromise or "middle road" is necessary.

Marin (1969, cited in Loy *et al.*, 1975) did examine the relationship between length of member tenure and team effectiveness using the records from the National Football League between 1955 to 1959 (see Table 6.2). He found that while experienced teams were not always winning teams, losing teams were generally more inexperienced.

Donnelly (1975, cited in Loy *et al.*, 1975) analyzed the relationship between the half-life of six major league baseball teams (i.e., the length of time required for a group

Table 6.2. Interrelationship between team performance and player experience (Adapted from Loy, Theberge, Kjeldsen and Donnelly, 1975, based on data from Marin, 1969).

TEAM EXPERIENCE	TEAM PERFORMANCE	
	Winning Record (%)	Losing Record (%)
MATURE TEAMS (2¼ years or more average playing experience per athlete)	92.9%	7.1%
YOUNG TEAMS (less than 2¼ years of average playing experience per athlete)	75.9%	24.1%

of individuals to be reduced via replacement to one half of its original complement) and the mean games behind. The results, which are presented in Table 6.3, indicate that there is an inverted-U relationship between the length of member tenure and team effectiveness. Since similar findings were also observed for the length of a coach's tenure and team effectiveness, Loy *et al.* concluded:

> . . . the relationship between organizational effectiveness and personnel replacement rates in sport organizations is markedly influenced by the longevity of tenure of managers and by the length of service and experience of members. Moreover, although findings are far from firm, recent research suggests that longevity of service by managers and members of sport organizations is related to performance in an inverted-U manner. This inverted-U hypothesis implies that neither very new nor very old coaches are as effective as coaches with middle-levels of tenure; and the hypothesis also suggests that teams with few experienced players and teams with large numbers of very old players are not as effective as teams having players with moderate levels of playing experience.

Table 6.3. A comparison of organizational half-life* and organizational effectiveness (Adapted from Loy, Theberge, Kjeldsen and Donnelly, 1975, based on data from Donnelly, 1975).

DURATION TO HALF-LIFE (yrs.)	N	AVERAGE NO. OF GAMES BEHIND FIRST PLACE
2	175	28.38
3	126	19.33
4	60	13.79
5	20	11.33
6	9	13.38
7	4	13.70

*Duration of time required for a group of individuals to be reduced via replacement to one-half of its original complement.

GROUP STRUCTURE AND COMMUNICATION

STRUCTURE, COMMUNICATION AND PERFORMANCE

Interest in the process of communication has been closely interrelated with the growth in interest in group structure and group dynamics in general. Bavelas (1950) clearly outlined the basis for this:

> . . . imposed patterns of communication may determine certain aspects of group processes. This raises the question of how a fixed communication pattern may affect the work life of a group. Do certain patterns have structural properties which may limit the group performance? May it be that among several communication patterns — all logically adequate for the successful completion of a specified task — one will result in significantly better performance than another? What effects might pattern, as such, have upon the emergence of leadership, the disruption of organization, and the degree of resistance to group disruption?

Bavelas and his associates (Bavelas, 1948, 1950, 1957; Leavitt, 1951; Leavitt and Knight, 1963) were responsible for most of the earliest significant contributions to the study of communication processes in groups. For example, in his paper "A mathematical model for group stuctures" which was published in 1948, Bavelas included a comprehensive mathematical theory for group stucture. Then, two years later he presented the outline for a laboratory procedure to examine group communication, a procedure which is still the predominant methodological strategy used today[2] (Bavelas, 1950).

The original communication networks developed were the five-person Chain, Circle, Y, and Wheel. These were illustrated in Figure 4.13 in Chapter 4. In later research, variations were introduced in terms of both the number of individuals incorporated into the group communication network (i.e., three-, four- and five-person networks) and the type of networks examined.

Although the Bavelas (1948) work outlined a number of theoretical issues in group communication, subsequent research has tended to center almost exclusively on the parameters of *centrality* and *distance*. Leavitt (1951) defined these as follows:

> . . . one way in which communication patterns vary can be described by the sum of neighbors that each individual member has, neighbors being defined as individuals to whom a member has communication access. So too, the concept of centrality, as defined by Bavelas, is of value in describing differences within and between structures. The most central position in the pattern is the position closest to all other positions. Distance is measured by the number of communicative links which must be utilized to get, by the shortest route, from one position to another.

The task used by Leavitt (1951) consisted of having group members; first, communicate to establish which symbol was held in common by all five individuals; and secondly, to communicate to insure that all individuals possessed this information. The group members were seated around a table separated by vertical partitions. Communication, via written messages, was achieved through slots which were opened or closed by the experimenter. Each of the five group members were given a list of five symbols from a set of six (circle, square, diamond, triangle, asterisk, and plus sign) with one of the symbols being held in common by all individuals. In their attempts to determine the common symbol, individuals could only communicate with immediately adjacent neighbors.

In terms of the dependent variables examined — the amount of time required, the number of messages relayed, the number of errors made, the leadership nominations among group members, and the level of satisfaction with performance in the group — the results were generally quite consistent. The extent to which the group was effective conformed to the degree to which its communication network was centralized — the rank order for both effectiveness and degree of centralization being Wheel, Y, Chain and Circle. Thus, the groups in the Wheel network, the most centralized communication network, performed quickest, sent the fewest messages, had a clearly established leader but found their group experience the least satisfying.

On the other hand, the groups in the Circle network, the most decentralized communication network, were slowest, sent a larger number of messages, had no definable leader, but were more satisfied with their group experience.

While these results seem unequivocal, subsequent research has not clearly fallen into a consistent pattern. In fact, when Glanzer and Glaser (1961) carried out a comprehensive review of those studies which have used the various communication networks, they observed that *"the area has been worked not only exhaustively, but to exhaustion. After a promising start, the approach has led to many conflicting results that resist any neat order"* [emphasis added].

In sport and physical activity, the question of group structure and its impact upon

2. The technique was used by Leavitt in a dissertation and subsequently published in an article in 1951 (see Leavitt, 1951).

group communication and problem solving, performance does not seem to be overly critical for at least two reasons. First, in most team sports, the group structure is relatively fixed and constant across teams. Thus, in baseball, for example, a team's defensive posture varies minimally across all teams at all levels of competition (with the notable exception of those rare instances when a team adopts an unusual defense to take advantage of idiosyncratic batting tendencies of an opposition player). Therefore, whether structure is a benefit or a hindrance to performance effectiveness, it is at least constant across teams.[3] Secondly, the nature of the task or problem is also relatively fixed and constant — score points, prevent scoring, etc. Therefore, in the athletic event itself, the predominant type of interaction is physical and this is usually of a highly normative type. So, as noted above, structure and communication per se are not important factors in athletic performance.

STRUCTURE, COMMUNICATION AND BEHAVIOR

Another dimension of the issue of structure and communication which does pertain more directly to sport and physical activity concerns their relationship to group behavior. For example, those athletes who, by virtue of the group structure and the demands of the specific sport, are in a position which permits (1) greater involvement in task interaction, (2) greater visibility to teammates and opponents and (3) greater knowledge of ongoing events, also have greater opportunities to obtain organizational rewards (Chelladurai and Carron, 1977). These rewards include such things as most valuable player awards, captaincy nominations and the opportunity to ascend to coaching and managerial positions within the organization.[4]

A second aspect of the interrelationship of structure, communication and interaction is that in permanent formal working groups (of which athletic teams are one example), structure and the differentiation of function which exists either contributes to the emergence or serves to maintain a *normative* pattern of interaction and communication within teams. This is illustrated in George Plimpton's account of his experiences with the Boston Bruins of the National Hockey League:

> . . . Don Cherry, the Bruin coach, did not lift my spirits by telling me that he never really thought of goalies as being hockey players anyway. Goalies were another species, he felt, pointing out that when hockey coaches were asked about their rosters they always said they were carrying so many hockey players and x number of goalies.
> My roommate, Jim Pettie, himself a goaltender, said I should be proud to be considered apart from the rest of the players. 'Cherry is right,' he said. 'Welcome to the union.' He went on to say that Gerry Cheevers, the first-string Bruin goalie, never shook hands with opposing players in the lineup ceremonies at the end of a playoff series, never, never — it was a contradiction to shake hands with someone who had been firing a puck at you — but that he would skate past these people to shake the hand of the opposing goalie. They were both in the same union. Why, if a rival goalie got in a slump, Cheevers would try to help him out of it. Goalies stick together. They look after each other.

A third aspect is that the structure also contributes to the emergence of normative patterns of interaction and communication *between teams*. Again, this is well illustrated in an anecdote by Plimpton:

> . . . the Bruins were not popular in Philadelphia at all. We wheeled around in our half of the ice, the Flyers in theirs. There was no communication between the two teams; indeed, the players seemed to put their heads down as they approached the center line, sailing by within feet of each other without so much as a glance. Pettie had told me, 'In hockey you don't talk to the other guy, ever. You don't pick him up when he falls down, like in football. You'll never see anything like the conversations

3. Another exception would be sports like football and soccer where adaptations in offensive and defensive structure are an integral component of game strategy.
4. See Chapter 4 for a comprehensive outline of these issues.

baseball players have at first base, the guys chatting and passing the time of day with each other.' He told me about a pregame warmup in one of the Soviet-NHL series, in which our teammate Wayne Cashman had spotted a Russian player coming across the center line to chase a puck; Cashman had intercepted the Russian and checked him violently into the boards. 'Well, the guy was in the wrong place.' Pettie said when I expressed my astonishment. 'He should have known better.'

A final aspect of structure and its interrelationship to interaction and communication is the Sommer (1971) observation that *certain arrangements of people are more suited to certain group activities than others*. A general overview of his results are illustrated in Figures 6.3 and 6.4. Sommer found that when individuals are in a conversing situation, a seating arrangement emphasizing both physical proximity and visual contact is preferred. In a competitive situation, preference was shown for a face-to-face arrangement because this perspective stimulated competition. Although a variety of arrangements were endorsed for coacting pairs, individuals in a cooperative context, indicated a strong preference for being side-by-side.

GROUP CONFORMITY

THE NATURE OF CONFORMITY

Interwoven with the process of group interaction, communication and social influence is the phenomenon of *group conformity*. Formal groups with their associated structure, intragroup interaction, communication and task and/or interpersonal interdependence develop expectations for conformity to specific behavioral prescriptions (i.e., norms). Thus, as Hollander (1971) pointed out, "conformity is seen as something which undercuts individuality." But, as he also noted, it "is not a single thing, but rather a social phenomenon which can be defined in many ways." From an examination of the experimental work which has been carried out, this seems apparent — conformity has been defined in a number of ways. For example, terms such as social influence, compliance, control, dominance, status, power, dependence, nonconformity, and anticonformity have been used in discussions of conformity behavior.

THE ANALYSIS OF CONFORMING BEHAVIOR

Sherif (1935) and Asch (1951) were responsible for developing and popularizing a laboratory technique used to study conformity. Essentially, the experimental paradigm involved bringing an individual into the laboratory for a study in "visual perception." The subject, seated at a table in a group (with all other subjects being confederates of the experimenter), was required to indicate which line on a screen was matched with three unequal reference line. On selected trials, the group (i.e., the experimenter's confederates) responded in a clearly incorrect fashion thus placing social pressure on the subject to show conformity. Asch did find that there was a general convergence toward the group standard although one-quarter of the subjects responded independently.

The approach used by Milgram (1965) has also been frequently discussed in terms of the phenomenon of social influence and conformity. His experimental paradigm involved an *experimenter*, a *teacher*, who was actually the naive subject, and a *learner*, who was actually an accomplice of the experimenter. These two were supposedly participating in a learning experiment designed to test the effect of punishment on learn-

PERCENTAGE OF Ss CHOOSING THIS ARRANGEMENT				
Seating arrangement	Condition 1 (conversing)	Condition 2 (cooperating)	Condition 3 (co-acting)	Condition 4 (competing)
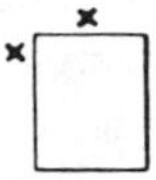	42	19	3	7
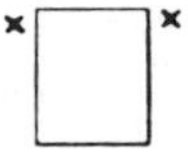	46	25	32	41
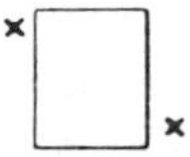	1	5	43	20
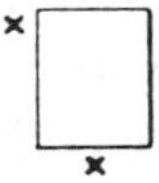	0	0	3	5
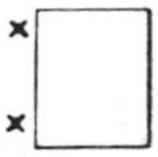	11	51	7	8
	0	0	13	18
TOTAL	100	100	100	99

Figure 6.3. Seating preferences at rectangular tables. Source: Robert Sommer, PERSONAL SPACE: The Behavioral Basis of Design, ©1969, pp62, 63. Reprinted by permission of Prentice-Hall, Inc., Englewood Cliffs, New Jersey.

PERCENTAGE OF Ss CHOOSING THIS ARRANGEMENT				
Seating arrangement	Condition 1 (conversing)	Condition 2 (cooperating)	Condition 3 (co-acting)	Condition 4 (competing)
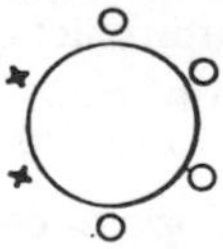	63	83	13	12
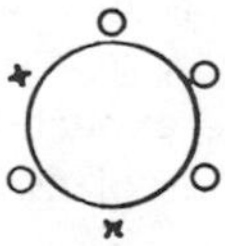	17	7	36	25
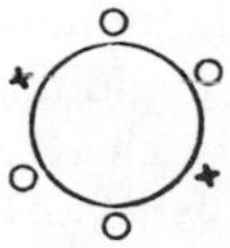	20	10	51	63
TOTAL	100	100	100	100

Figure 6.4. Seating preferences at circular tables. Source: Robert Sommer, PERSONAL SPACE: The Behavioral Basis of Design, ©1969, pp62, 63. Reprinted by permission of Prentice-Hall, Inc., Englewood Cliffs, New Jersey.

ing. The teacher was informed that the conditions of the experiment would require him to give increasing levels of what was purported to be an extremely painful electric shock whenever mistakes were made by the learner. The teacher administered the shock upon the instructions of the experimenter. After receiving a shock of 45 volts (to establish authenticity), the teacher was given responsibility for a shock generator with an apparent potential of delivery voltage levels clearly marked as varying from 15 to 450 volts (and labeled with descriptions varying from "slight shock" to "danger: severe shock"). Milgram (1965) found that almost two-thirds of the subjects complied with the experimental conditions:

> . . . with numbing regularity good people were seen to knuckle under the demands of authority and perform actions that were callous and severe. Men who are in everyday life responsible and decent were seduced by the trappings of authority, by the control of their perceptions, and by the uncritical acceptance of the experimenter's definition of the situation, into performing harsh acts."

While there have been a number of criticisms of Milgram's work, most of these are not directly related to the topic of conformity per se and, therefore, are not discussed here. However, a criticism which can be leveled from the point of view of conformity vs. nonconformity, is that the extremely high exprimenter status created in the experimental paradigm produced a situation heavily biased against nonconformity.

SITUATIONAL FACTORS AND CONFORMITY

Research which has examined conformity as a function of situational demands and constraints has revealed some relatively persistent trends. *Conformity is a function of the relative perceived status of the principals involved.* If individuals have less relative status, power, prestige, competence, influence, etc. than the reference source (the experimenter, the coach, the group, a teammate), their behavior is characterized by movement conformity — a shifting toward the position held by that reference. On the other hand, if subjects have greater relative status, etc. than their reference, their behavior is characterized by independence or nonconformity (Croner and Willis, 1961; Berkowitz and Macauley, 1961; Hollander, 1961, 1964; Kelley and Thibaut, 1969; Wiggins, Dill and Schwartz, 1965). Thus, in sport and physical activity, rookies and newcomers to a team quickly learn and typically adopt the prevalent attitudes and behavioral modes of the veterans and team leaders. Similarly, coaches, because of their greater relative status, competence and power, have a major impact upon the attitudes, etc. of their players — not only in the athletic dimension itself, but in non-athletic situations as well.

A dimension of conformity which is interrelated with status, competence and power within the group is what Hollander (1958, 1964, 1971) has referred to as *idiosyncrasy credit.* By virtue of greater status or competence as well as by virtue of perceived previous conformity and behavior consistent with the normative expectations of the group, the individual accumulates *credits* — positive impressions of that individual held by others in the group, organization or social situation. As a result of a credit balance obtained, the individual is later permitted greater latitude for nonconformity. "A basic feature of the idiosyncrasy credit model is the view that conformity and non-conformity are *not* invariably defined relative to a fixed norm to which everyone in the group is expected to comply equally . . . Rather, nonconforming behavior is seen to be variously defined by the group for any given actor depending upon how that actor is perceived. Conformity is thus considered to be person-specific and functionally related to status" (Hollander and Willis, 1971). This is evident in athletics. Well established veterans will be implicitly or explicitly permitted greater deviations from expected or "normal" behavior than will newcomers or less competent athletes.

The number of individuals exerting the social influence (i.e., the size of the opposition) effects conformity. While the results have been varied, a curvilinear relationship has been suggested between opposition size and conforming behavior: progressive increases in the number of individuals in opposition from one to three persons leads to an increase in conformity but further opposition increases do not have any additional effects upon conformity (Asch, 1956; Rosenberg, 1961).[5] The lack of additional impact upon conforming behavior as a result of increased opposition sizes has been attributed to a decline in credibility; the subjects either suspect collusion among the opposition (Asch, 1956; Gerard, Wilhelmy and Conolley, 1968) or perceive the opposition as interdependent, e.g., "leader" and "followers" (Gerard and Greenbaum, 1962).

However, increased opposition numbers per se may not be the critical factor in terms of increased conformity effects. Wilder (1977) found that when the size of the opposition was categorized as a single entity (i.e., a group of six persons), it was less influential in terms of producing conformity, than when it was categorized as multiple units (i.e., two groups of three persons or three groups of two persons). Thus, the common behavior exhibited by separate entities may be regarded as more informative and credible than when that behavior is shown by persons in a single entity. Thus, a coach who is under criticism for a particular decision would be more inclined to reevaluate and possibly change that decision if the opposition was seen as a number of quite different groups (parents, administrators, media, athletes) rather then a single entity (athletes). Wilder (1977) felt that "an implication of these findings is that the more dissimilar communicators are, the more influential they should be. The more dissimilar they are to one another, the more difficult it is for an observer to categorize them into a group and regard them as a single entity rather than as several individuals."

The presence of supportive partners or coactors (social support) reduces the effect of social influence upon conformity (Allen, 1975; Allen and Levine, 1971; Asch, 1951; Hollander and Willis, 1964; Kelley and Thibaut, 1969; Milgram, 1965; Wilder, 1977). It has been suggested that the presence of social support serves to reduce the credibility and resultant influence of the majority (Allen and Levine, 1971). A hockey player who is opposed to a violent style of play is more inclined to maintain that attitude if other athletes are considered to be in agreement. Results from the research conducted by Milgram (1965), which was outlined earlier, bears this out. These results are illustrated in Figure 6.5.

The extent to which input or situational demands are ambiguous and the task is difficult influences conformity (Nordholm, 1975; Sistrunk and McDavid, 1971; Weiner, 1958). As Blake and Mouton (1961) summarized:

 . . . *conformity behavior increases when it is necessary for the individual to rely more heavily on the responses of others in making his own adjustment. Attitudes are more easily shifted than are reactions to factual or logical items, probably because attitudes are more social in character. Increasing the difficulty of items, reducing external cues which provide objective information, and increasing the*

---

5. It should be noted that Gerard, Wilhelmy and Conolley (1968) found a linear relationship between conformity and size (varied from two to eight persons); Milgram, Bickman and Berkowitz (1969) obtained both a curvilinear and a linear relationship depending upon which conformity measure they used (with oppositions of 1, 3, 5 or 15 persons); and Goldberg (1954) and Kidd (1958) found no changes with increased size.

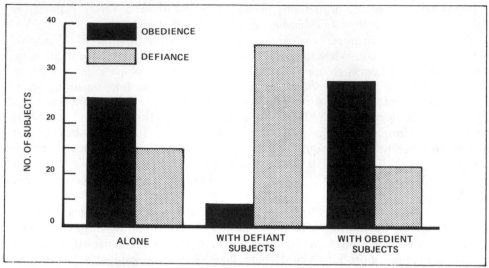

Figure 6.5. Conforming behavior exhibited alone, in the company of defiant cohorts and in the company of compliant cohorts. (Adapted from Milgram, 1965).

strength of command in the direction of the compliant behavior all serve to increase the effectiveness of conformity pressures in shifting a person's response.

Kelley and Thibaut (1969) approached this same issue from a slightly different orientation; namely, that of cooperative problem solving groups in which, "in general, information will be freely given and freely accepted, with resistance to acceptance occurring only if doubts arise about the validity or credibility of the information received." In these situations in which there is a strong predisposition toward group solidarity and uniformity, "it seems plain that the factors affecting receptivity to information will be restricted to variables which affect post-communication stability of attribution: . . . (1) the verifiability of a proposed solution, (2) the multiplicity of alternative solutions proffered, and (3) the expertness of the source" (Kelley and Thibaut, 1969).

PERSONALITY FACTORS AND CONFORMITY

Are there specific personality characteristics which predispose an individual toward conforming behavior? Some of the traits which, intuitively at least, might be expected to show a strong relationship include, dominance, self-esteem and personal adjustment. A comprehensive summary of available research was presented by Mann in 1959. A summary of his findings is presented in Table 6.4. The findings for adjustment, extroversion and dominance are mixed; some studies showed a positive effect while others showed either a negative or no effect. Mann did point out that there is evidence supporting a conclusion that conservatism and conformity are related. However, not only was conformity assessed in a number of different ways in the studies Mann reviewed but this was also the case for the various personality dimensions. Thus, Mann (1959) also noted that "no single measure of the conservatism dimension emerges as an especially potent predictor of conformity in all conditions; in fact, there is a suggestion that it is important to control for a number of conditions if the relationship is to hold at all." It seems probable that the determinants of conforming behavior are similar to the determinants of the other specific behaviors examined in

Table 6.4. The percentage of significant relationships reported in 27 studies containing 102 comparisons on the relationship of various personality dimensions to conformity behavior From: Mann, R. D. A review of the relationship between personality and performance in small groups. *Psychological Bulletin*, 1959, 56, 241-270. Copyright, 1959 by the American Psychological Association. Reprinted by permission.

Personality Factors and the Number of Studies of Each	No. of Findings	% Yielding Sig. Positive Relationship	% Yielding Sig. Negative Relationship	% Yielding Neither
Adjustment				
Self-ratings -2	(18)	73% (13)	5% (1)	22% (4)
Sociometric ratings & personality inventories -8	(30)	7% (2)	14% (4)	79% (24)
Extroversion:				
Self-ratings -2	(16)	62% (10)	6% (1)	32% (5)
Projective techniques & personality invent- ories - 5	(10)	0% (0)	10% (1)	90% (9)
Dominance	(8)	0% (0)	25% (2)	75% (6)
Conservatism	(20)	80% (16)	0% (0)	20% (4)

personality research; namely, conformity is best understood in terms of the interaction of the person and the situation (see Chapters 2 and 4).

SUMMARY

The nature of groups, particularly small groups, and the dynamics of group involvement have been fundamental concerns in sociology and social psychology. From a sociological perspective, groups are essentially microcosms of the larger society and, therefore, theoretical models may be developed and applied to less accessible organizations or cultures. From a social psychological perspective, both generally and in the specific context of sport and physical activity, a considerable proportion of individual behavior occurs within groups. Thus, in order to gain an understanding of the antecedents and consequences of behavior it is imperative to focus on the group.

A number of definitions have been proposed for the group, many of which reflect the specific orientation and research interests of their authors. The principal properties which serve to define a sport group and, in turn, to distinguish it from a crowd of individuals or a random collection of people include the following (which may be present in varying degrees depending on the type of team): a collective identity, a sense of shared purpose or objectives, structured patterns of interaction, structured modes of communication, personal and/or task interdependence, and interpersonal attraction. While the group is a composite of individuals, it also does exist in its own right as a unit of analysis.

Sport groups tend to be relatively stable and, thus, the process of group development is not as critical as the processes associated with the assimilation of new team members. A number of correlates of this replacement process have been identified. For example, the amount of personnel turnover varies from one position to another across different sports. Also, teams that experience a large turnover in playing personnel are less successful than teams with a smaller turnover. Further, it appears that an inverted-U relationship exists between both the length of coaches' tenure and team effectiveness and player experience and team effectiveness. That is, optimal team effectiveness is present in those organizations that have had coaches and players with middle levels of tenure — teams with very old or very new coaches and/or very experienced or very inexperienced playing personnel are less successful.

It is difficult for practical reasons to adequately chart the course of group development. There is some consensus that groups do go through developmental stages or sequences but the exact nature and duration of these stages is unclear. As an overview, it would appear that the principal concern in the earliest stage is with acclimatization. This is followed by the establishment of control and leadership and, then, the effective work of the group can begin. With continued group involvement, social-personal relationships may evolve.

An integral aspect of group structure has been its effects upon communication and performance. Although the early research showed a clear relationship between the communication network factors of *centrality* and *distance* and various performance and satisfaction criteria, later research has been equivocal.

Specific spatial aspects of group structure and communication are interrelated with (1) organizational status and rank, (2) the attainment of rewards and (3) activities of a competitive vs. cooperative vs. coacting vs. conversing situation.

An aspect of group life interwoven with group communication and interaction is conformity. The situational factors which influence conforming behavior include the relative perceived status of the principals involved; the number of individuals both in opposition and in support; and the extent to which the situational demands are ambiguous and the task is difficult. With the possible exception of conservatism, personality per se does not appear to influence conformity.

DYNAMICS OF TASK PERFORMING GROUPS 7

The term *dynamics* has a connotation of activity, force, energy and change. Thus, it was no accident that Kurt Lewin originally introduced the term to represent those processes underlying the changes associated with group involvement. Lewin placed particular emphasis on two processes or categories of forces: *cohesiveness* and *locomotion*. The former is considered to be particularly important because it represents a property which contributes to the development and maintenance of the group and group unity and solidarity. The latter is the group's *raison d'etre*, the reason or purpose behind the group's existence. Group cohesiveness is the exclusive focus of the next chapter while the processes relating to group locomotion are discussed here.

The specific topics examined under the rubric of group locomotion include group motivation and aspiration; attributions to causality for performance outcomes; a comparison of the individual versus the group in terms of performance effectiveness and selected behavioral dimensions; and a comparison of the process of cooperation versus the process of competition.

GROUP-ORIENTED MOTIVATION AND ASPIRATION[1]

Probably the most comprehensive contributions to our present understanding of group aspiration and motivation derives from the work of Alvin Zander (see, for example, Zander, 1971) and his associates at the University of Michigan. Moreover, there does appear to be some very direct implications for sport and physical activity from this research. Not only were some of the tasks used of a physical performance nature but, more importantly, the group situations examined were characterized by conditions closely related to those which are prevalent in an athletic team. For example, the

---

1. The source for the material in this section is Alvin Zander's (1971) text *Motives and goals in groups*. Since the topic of group aspiration and motivation is only one of many aspects of group life, it is necessarily presented in overview here. Consequently, much of Zander's model has either been presented briefly or not included. The reader wishing a more comprehensive discussion should refer to the Zander text.

operational premises for his research were that:

(1) the group exists for doing work,

(2) all member's interdependently carry out the group's task,

(3) any group member may perceive that he has more or less responsibility for the success of the group,

(4) the group performs its task on repeated occasions,

(5) a group member knows the score for the unit as a whole but does not know his own personal score,

(6) one out of a number of possible group scores may be earned on any occasion (trial),

(7) these scores each occupy some point on an objective scale of difficulty from easier to harder,

(8) the difficulty of attaining a given score can be described in terms of the probability of group success, and

(9) the subjective probability of group success may be different from the objective probability.

Only the direct relationship of the fifth point to sport and physical activity might be questionable. On the one hand, there are even instances in sport where members of the team are either unaware of their own score or where individual performances are not specifically evaluated. Rowing would be the best example. However, in the majority of team sports, individual athletes are either implicitly or explicitly informed of their relative contribution to the team product.

Two additional points which concern the nine conditions also should be brought out to place Zander's work in its proper perspective. The first is related to his view of the group. Zander emphasized that the group and the individual should be considered separate (albeit related) units of analysis. That is, the individual group member does have personal aspirations, motives and goals and these do have an influence upon the group. But, in addition, Zander emphasized that the welfare of the group as a totality is also considered by group members during group decisions — "members often suppress any inclination to put their own needs first . . . They concentrate instead on what the total group should do . . . what is 'good for the group' " (Zander, 1971). An overview of Zander's general perspective is outlined schematically in Figure 7.1.

A second point which evolves directly from the first is that in a manner completely analogous to an individual in an achievement situation, the group-as-a-unit has a performance goal, an aspiration level for that goal and group-oriented motives. These

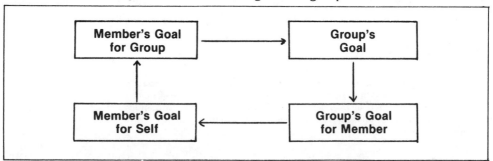

Figure 7.1. Relations among individual and group goals (From Zander, 1971). Reproduced with permission of the publisher.

considerations, then, form the basis for Zander's model for group aspiration and motivation.

THE ACHIEVEMENT MOTIVE IN GROUPS

The Historical Basis. The model for achievement motivation in groups developed and tested by Zander and his associates is highly similar to the model for achievement motivation in individuals. Zander pointed out, however, that his research:

> . . . was not initiated with that similarity in mind and had progressed through several of the experiments . . . before it became evident that the findings in many ways resembled those that Atkinson and Feather had reported. When this similarity became evident, it was convenient to speak informally about a need for group achievement. Later, after becoming more familiar with the work of Atkinson and Feather, it was decided to use their concepts more explicitly and to seek further similarities and dissimilarities in theory and results.

Thus, the theory which follows shall be familiar to anyone who is familiar with the material in Chapter 3.

Theoretical Formulations. It was proposed that when groups are in achievement situations, two dispositions, tendencies or inclinations are aroused toward the given activity: the *tendency to achieve group success* (Tgs) and the *tendency to avoid group failure* (Tgaf). The former is a disposition of the group to approach a task with interest and an intention of performing well. The latter is an inclination to have the group resist engaging in the activity because it could lead to failure. The difference between the two of them is the *resultant tendency to action* (Rg). This can be presented as

$$Rg = Tgs - Tgaf \tag{1}$$

In turn, three factors contribute in a multiplicative manner to Tgs, the tendency to achieve group success. These are the *desire to achieve group success* (Dgs), the *perceived probability of group success* (Pgs) and the *incentive value of group success* (Igs), or

$$Tgs = Dgs \times Pgs \times Igs \tag{2}$$

The desire for group success (Dgs) is a group-oriented motive, the basis of which is the group members' disposition to derive pride and satisfaction with the group if it is successful in accomplishing its task. If we are members of a team, we want that team to be successful so that we can feel proud of our association. When the group engages in performance over repeated instances, it encounters success and failure in varying degrees. As a result, prior to any given performance, group members have an estimate or judgment of the probability (which can be expressed as a numerical value which varies from 0 to 1.00) that the group will attain a given score or outcome. This judgment, which is referred to as the perceived probability of group success (Pgs), is smaller for a difficult objective and larger for an easy objective. The incentive value for group success (Igs), the third factor which contributes to the tendency to achieve group success (Tgs), is the anticipation a group member has for the degree of satisfaction which will develop if the group attains a given score. The degree of incentive is inversely related to the probability for success — that is, incentive (satisfaction) is greater when the task is more difficult and the probability for success is lower. A team (and the individuals within that team) will derive greater satisfaction from a victory over a strong opponent than from a victory over a weak opponent.

Also, three factors contribute to the tendency to avoid group failure (Tgaf): the *desire to avoid group failure* (Dgaf), the *perceived probability of group failure* (Pgf) and the *incentive value of group failure* (Igf), or

$$Tgaf = Dgaf \times Pgf \times Igf \tag{3}$$

The desire to avoid group failure (Dgaf) is the group-oriented motive which derives from the disposition on the part of group members' to experience embarrassment or dissatisfaction with the group if it fails at its task. In turn, the perceived probability of group failure (Pgf) is the judgment of the group members regarding the probability that the group will experience failure in the pursuit of its goal. This judgement is larger for a difficult objective and smaller for an easy one. Finally, the incentive value of group failure (Igf) is the anticipation of the degree of dissatisfaction that will develop in the group following failure. As was the case above, the degree of incentive is inversely related to the probability of failure — dissatisfaction is less after failure to achieve a harder objective than after failure to achieve an easier one. Thus, the team which loses to an opponent they were expected to handle easily will be more dissatisfied than the team that loses to an opponent that was a strong pregame favorite. These parameters are summarized in Table 7.1.

GROUP ASPIRATION

Implicit in the model outlined in Table 7.1 (indeed, in any theory of achievement motivation) is the concept of *aspiration level*. When individuals or groups are placed in achievement situations they develop expectations for the performance outcome (i.e., a standard of excellence). These expectations are reevaluated upward or downward with subsequent experiences and concommitant success and/or failures in the group task. Thus, "the group level of aspiration may be defined as the score members expect their group will attain in the future" (Zander, 1971). Coaches coming into a situation where the team has been a consistent loser realize the need to reorient the team's "attitude" — the team must be convinced that success is at least possible.

The group aspiration level is based upon the two general factors of *probability* and *incentive*. That is, with repeated experience on a group task, the group members become aware of the chances of obtaining a given objective. Therefore, as was pointed out in the previous section, for a given group objective, there is a *perceived probability of group success* (Pgs) and a *perceived probability of group failure* (Pgf). One is the inverse of the other; as Pgs increases, Pgf decreases. Further, the relative level of each is directly related to the difficulty of obtaining the given objective. This, of course, is almost self-evident. The chances for success are directly associated with the strength of the opposition — a weak opponent means that the chances for success are great but a very strong opponent means the chances are small.

It was also noted in the previous section, that the expectation that group members have for a future outcome leads to the anticipation of a future degree of satisfaction: the *incentive value of group success* (Igs) is the degree of satisfaction anticipated from success while the *incentive value of failure* (Igf) is the degree of dissatisfaction anticipated from failure. If the group achieves a difficult objective rather than an easy one, the anticipated level of satisfaction is greater. Thus, the level of incentive (Igs) is inversely related to the perceived probability for success (Pgs). Similarly, the anticipated level of dissatisfaction is greater if the group fails at an easy task rather than a difficult one and, as a result, the level of incentive (Igf) is inversely related to the perceived probability of group failure (Pgf).

Table 7.1 The basis for group achievement motivation (Adapted from Zander, 1971).

FACTOR	DESCRIPTION	SYMBOLIC REPRESENTATION
Desire for group Success	A group member's disposition to derive satisfaction from the group if it is successful in accomplishing its task.	Dgs
Desire to avoid Group Failure	A group member's disposition to experience embarassment and dissatisfaction with the group if it is un-successful in accomplishing its task.	Dgaf
Perceived probabil-ity of Group Success	The estimate or judgement by group members (in terms of a probability between 0 and 1.00) that the group will attain a given score.	Pgs
Perceived probabil-ity of Group Failure	The estimate or judgement by group members (in terms of a probability between 0 and 1.00) that the group will experience failure in the pursuit of its goal.	Pgf
Incentive Value of Group Success	The anticipation a group member has for the satisfaction which will develop if the group attains a given score.	Igs
Incentive Value of Group Failure	The anticipation a group member has for the dissatisfaction which will develop if the group fails to attain a given score.	Igf
Tendency to Achieve Group Success	The disposition, tendency or inclin-ation of the group to approach a task with the intention of performing well.	Tgs = Dgs x Pgs x Igs
Tendency to Avoid Group Failure	The disposition, tendency or inclin-ation of the group to resist engaging in an activity because it could lead to failure.	Tgaf = Dgaf x Pgf x Igf
Resultant Tendency to Action by the Group	The dispositional tendency or inclin-ation of the group to engage in the group task. It is determined by the strength of the members' tendency to approach the task minus the strength of their tendency to avoid it.	Rg = Tgs - Tgaf

These four factors interact to produce a group aspiration level, "one that best resolves the conflict between the attractiveness of success, repulsiveness of failure, and the perceived probabilities of success and failure. It is set at a location that will provide as much satisfaction as is reasonably possible" (Zander, 1971). This can be presented symbolically as follows:

$$\text{Group Aspiration Level} = (\text{Pgs} \times \text{Igs}) - (\text{Pgf} \times \text{Igf}) \qquad (4)$$

The effect of success and failure upon group level of aspiration has been examined in a number of experiments with a variety of group tasks (Zander and Forward, 1968; Zander, Forward and Albert, 1969; Zander and Medow, 1963, 1965; Zander, Medow and Efron, 1965; Zander and Newcomb, 1967; Zander and Wulff, 1966). The results indicate that the effects that success or failure have upon the aspiration that members have for a group follow a consistent pattern. That is, success leads to an increase in group aspiration, failure to a decrease. Further, the amount of absolute change is greater with success. This is illustrated in Figure 7.2.

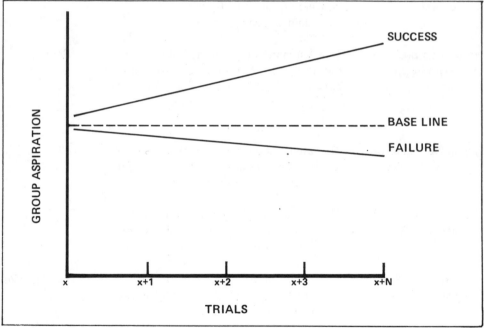

Figure 7.2. A schematic illustration of the relationship of group success and failure to group level of aspiration. (Adapted from Zander, 1971).

THE INDIVIDUAL VERSUS THE GROUP

Since the group is a composite of individuals and since the model for achievement motivation in groups proposed by Zander was patterned after the model for achievement motivation in individuals developed by McClelland and Atkinson, the two approaches are highly similar and to some extent interrelated. However, the differences between the two approaches and their interrelationship bear close scrutiny.

One distinction between the two models lies in the *conceptual basis* for the group-oriented versus individual-oriented achievement motives. It may be recalled from the discussion in Chapter 3 that the two individual motives — the *motive for success* (M_s)

and the *motive to avoid failure* (M_{af}) — are considered to be stable and enduring personality traits. Therefore, it could be predicted that the behavioral effect of M_s and M_{af} would be consistent over time and generalizable across different achievement situations. An individual who has a high motive for success and a minimal motive to avoid failure will bring a relatively consistent motivational disposition to all achievement situations — athletics, academics, bridge games, etc.

On the other hand, the two group-oriented motives — the *desire to achieve group success* (Dgs) and the *desire to avoid group failure* (Dgaf) — are assumed to be "dispositions which are unique to the one group under consideration at the moment, and are not necessarily relevant to the member's relationship with any other group" (Zander, 1971). Thus, the totality of individuals which is a basketball team might have a particular level of Dgs. Even though the team members also might be members of another group — a social group — the Dgs in that group would not necessarily be similar.

A second factor is that the individual achievement motive and the group-oriented motive are considered *separate* and *independent* factors. An individual working within a group may be interested in personal achievement, the achievement of the group or both (Forward, 1969; Zander and Forward, 1968). As Zander (1971) stated "person-oriented and group-oriented motives may supplement one another in an additive manner, increasing the strength of the total tendency to approach or avoid, or . . . the two types of motives may act in contrasting directions, each weakening the effect of the other." In short, even if we knew the level of achievement motivation present in each of the members of a basketball team, we still couldn't be sure what motive was present in the group as a totality.

Finally, there is a close *similarity in individual and group aspiration:* (1) the factors accounting for a member's aspiration for the group are the same as those which influence the individual's aspiration (the factors of incentive for success/failure and probability of success/failure); (2) the aspiration group members privately set for the group tend to conform to the group's aspiration; and (3) the effects of success versus failure within groups versus individuals has an identical effect upon aspiration — *succeed, raise; fail, lower*. This, of course, was illustrated in Figure 7.2.

GROUP ATTRIBUTIONS FOR PERFORMANCE OUTCOMES

Another important aspect of achievement situations which is characteristic of both groups and individuals is that an attempt is made either implicitly or explicitly to account for the outcome; to explain *why* the event occurred. In Chapter 3 it was noted that causality for outcomes is usually attributed to either of two generic classes of determinants: (1) the *person dimension*, including individual ability, effort, motivation and intention and (2) the *environment dimension*, including the nature of the task, luck, and so on (see Figure 3.16). Also, it was pointed out that there has been a considerable amount of research which suggests that individuals show a rather consistent tendency to attribute their task successes to the personal dimension while failures are attributed to the environmental dimension.

PROBLEM SOLVING GROUPS AND ATTRIBUTION

Not surprisingly, the examination of causal attribution has also been extended to the area of group dynamics. As Schlenker, Soraci and McCarthy (1976) pointed out:

> . . . egocentric perceptions are equally prevalent in group settings. Most group actions take place in an interdependent atmosphere where some type of consensus is required prior to a group commit-ment to action. The other group members serve as an environmental factor whose influence on the eventual group product can be perceptually maximized or minimized to decrease or increase, respec-tively, an individual's feelings of having contributed to the outcome. If a group succeeds and pro-duces a desirable outcome, a person can maximize the degree to which he feels he contributed to the success by enhancing feelings of personal responsibility, both absolutely and relative to the respon-sibility attributed to other group members. If the group fails, a person can decrease feelings of having contributed to the fiasco by minimizing personal responsibility, both absolutely and relative to the responsibility attributed to the others.

A relatively persistent pattern of results have emerged from the research on causal attributions to group outcomes. This pattern which is illustrated schematically in Figure 7.3 is consistent with the Schlenker, Soraci and McCarthy proposition: namely, that *individuals who are members of successful groups have a greater tendency to assume responsibility for group performance than do individuals who are in unsuccessful groups* (Forsythe and Schlenker, 1977; Medow and Zander, 1965; Mynatt and Sher-man, 1975; Schlenker, 1975; Schlenker and Miller, 1977; Schlenker, Soraci and Mc-Carthy, 1976; Wolosin, Sherman and Till, 1973); and also, that *individuals who are members of a successful group tend to view their own relative contribution as being greater than that of the "average" group member whereas individuals who are members of an unsuccessful group tend to view their own relative contribution as be-ing less than that of the "average" group member* (Schlenker, 1975; Wolosin, Sher-man and Till, 1973). Some of the research leading to these conclusions does provide insight into the dynamics of group involvement.

Mynatt and Sherman (1975) contrasted the attributions of individuals operating alone versus in group situations characterized by a "negative consequence." They hypothesized that in such situations a *diffusion of responsibility* occurs among group members — group members in failure situations feel less personally responsible than

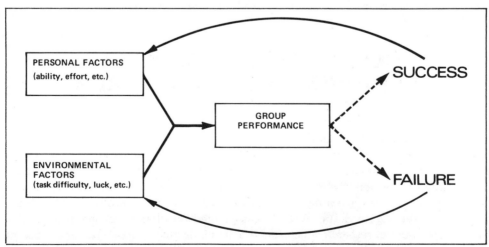

Figure 7.3. The impact of group success and group failure upon the attributions made to causality.

do individuals acting alone. For example, a losing wrestler has no possibility for diffusion of responsibility (unless the coach is considered to be partly responsible because of poor strategy) whereas the members of a losing basketball team do.

This hypothesis was examined in an experiment in which subjects, either alone or in a group of three, gave advice to another individual (who was actually a confederate of the experimenter) engaged in a concept solving problem. In turn, this advice was observed to lead to success or failure. It was found that there were no differences in acceptance of responsibility between the groups and the individuals when the outcome was successful. That is, causality for the success was personalized — there was no diffusion of responsibility. However, when the outcome was unsuccessful, major differences were noted. That is, the group members were accurate in their judgment of the extent to which their advice was taken; felt that while they had had an influence on the decision process, performance was poor nonetheless; and denied responsibility for the outcome. Mynatt and Sherman categorized this as a *The outcome was pretty bad but I'm not responsible* position. On the other hand, the sole individuals, while not denying responsibility, underestimated the extent to which their advice was taken; thought that they had had less influence; and rated the outcome more positively. This position was categorized by the authors as *I'm responsible, but what happened wasn't so bad. Furthermore, he took my advice only half the time.*

Through a series of experiments, Schlenker and his associates (Forsythe and Schlenker, 1977; Schlenker, 1975; Schlenker and Miller, 1977; Schlenker, Soraci and McCarthy, 1976) have attempted to determine the factors which mediate the attributions to causality by group members.

Schlenker and Miller (1977), in a comparison of the self-serving bias explanation and the information processing explanation, proposed that if members of a group attribute causality according to the latter model, then those individuals in a majority position — those individuals who provide problem solutions which are consistently in agreement with the solution ultimately utilized by the group — should assume greater personal responsibility for the group product, regardless of outcome. When this hypothesis was examined with 4-man problem solving groups, it was found that under successful conditions, the majority subjects did assume greater responsibility than the minority subjects. However, this was not the case, when the group output led to failure. The majority subjects exhibited defensive, self-protective biases and they rated both their responsibility and performances as equal to that of the minority subjects. Thus, the results strongly supported a self-serving bias explanation for causal attributions.

Schlenker, Soraci and McCarthy (1976) incorporated the personality dimension of self-esteem into another analysis of causal attributions to group performance. They reasoned that "egocentric perceptions presumably occur in order to protect or enhance one's self-evaluation. Self esteem therefore should affect the type of egocentric perception an individual will employ. Persons with high self-esteem are accustomed to personal success, prefer to receive favorable feedback about themselves, and tend to reject negative feedback; low self-esteem persons generally have a history of personal failure, more willingly accept negative information about themselves, and sometimes reject positive information" (Schlenker, Soraci and McCarthy, 1976). When high and low self-esteem individuals were compared in terms of their perceptions of personal and environmental responsibility following group success and failure, no differences were found. However, after success, high self-esteem individuals reported that their problem solving and decision making behavior was relatively uninfluenced by other group members while low self-esteem individuals reported being highly influenced. Conversely, after failure, the reverse was the case.

THE ATHLETIC TEAM

A number of studies have also analyzed the causal attributions adapted to account for team success and failure in sport and physical activity (Iso-Ahola, 1975, 1976, 1977a, 1977b; Roberts, 1975; Spink, 1977, 1978). The results obtained have been in general agreement with the findings from research with problem solving groups. That is, *athletes exhibit egocentric perceptions in their assignment of responsibility for team success and failure. There is a tendency to assume personal responsibility for successful outcomes but to avoid responsibility for negative outcomes.*

However, an important qualifying note is necessary in regard to the role assigned to *effort* in athletic performance outcomes. It will be recalled that effort, along with ability is considered to be an internal or personal factor while the nature of the task assignment (i.e., its difficulty), luck, and officiating are considered to be external or environmental factors. Further, the typical pattern of findings in both achievement (athletic) and interpersonal (social) situations has been that positive outcomes are attributed to personal factors; negative outcome to environmental factors. In short, and as indicated above, the perception of responsibility is characteristically egocentric. However, Iso-Ahola (1977b) observed that:

> . . . effort has a different attributional meaning in the case of experiencing success and failure: When individuals succeed they interpret their outcome internally so that the main cause for success is effort which is enhanced by interpretation of the presence of personal abilities. When individuals fail, they interpret their outcome externally so that one of the main causes for failure is lack of effort which is seen to be tied to external environmental stimuli.

The basis for this observation was a study with Little League baseball teams. Iso-Ahola (1977b) reported that team success was attributed to the personal factors of ability and effort while team failure was attributed to the factors of task difficulty *and* effort. In yet another result which was consistent with this general finding, when the data were factor analyzed, under the win conditions, effort loaded highly with personal factors but under the loss conditions, it loaded highly with the environmental factors.

Roberts (1975), in a study which also used Little League baseball players, compared the attributions made to team and self in success and failure situations. The only attribution which showed differences between the team and self as a result of the type of outcome was effort (see Figure 7.4). While the individual athletes felt that their level of effort was identical under the win and loss conditions, they perceived that their team as a unit expended less effort in losing situations as compared to winning situations.

Similar results were reported by Iso-Ahola (1977a) — again with Little League baseball players (see Figure 7.5). The judgments of self ability and self effort remained unchanged from a win to a loss situation. (In fact, it was also observed that a previous history of team failure also did not result in a lowering of perceived self ability and self effort.) However, the perception of team ability and team effort both decreased from a win to a loss situation.

Iso-Ahola (1976) also had college students evaluate and then provide feedback of a positive versus negative nature for 20 hypothetical achievement situations. These

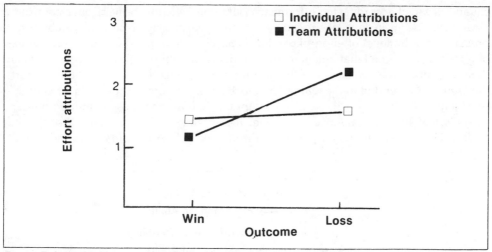

Figure 7.4. Attributions made to team versus individual effort under win and loss conditions (From Roberts, 1975). Reproduced with permission of the author.

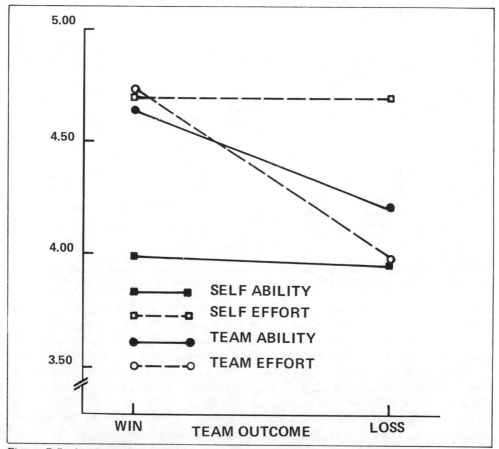

Figure 7.5. Attributions made to team ability and effort and individual ability and effort (Adapted from Iso-Ahola, 1977a).

situations varied according to performance outcome (five possibilities from clear win to clear loss), the ability level possessed by the team (yes, ability present or no, ability not present) and the level of effort expended (yes, effort expended or no, effort not expended). It was noted that outcome and the degree of effort expended were the main determinants in the evaluation of the group's performance (see Figure 7.6). In short, the "rewards extended to the team members decreased from success to failure but appreciably more so among those who did not try than among those who tried harder. Appraisal of success was noticeably lower if the team did not try hard" (Iso-Ahola, 1976). This is consistent with the Weiner and Kukla (1970) findings with individuals (see Figure 3.23).

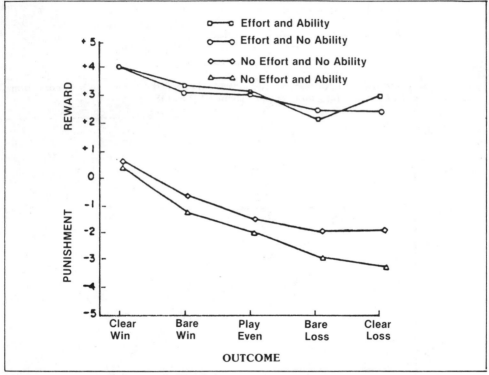

Figure 7.6. Rewards extended to teams under win versus loss conditions as a function of ability and effort (From Iso-Ahola, 1976). Reproduced with permission of the publisher.

A final perspective, unrelated to the above but related to the process of attribution in athletics, is what Cialdini and his associates (1976) referred to as *basking in reflected glory*. A major feature of the phenomenon of basking in reflected glory — one which distinguishes it from the phenomenon under examination in causal attribution studies — is that while the individual may identify with positive outcomes and disassociate from negative outcomes, there has not been any direct involvement with the outcome. The sport fan is the most obvious example.

In a series of experiments, the tendency for college students to identify with their intercollegiate football teams (as assessed by wearing school-identifying apparel and using the pronoun *we* when discussing the team) was examined. It was observed that the tendency to bask in reflected glory was significantly increased when the team was victorious. In short, there was an increased tendency to personalize and identify with the success of groups to which the individual did not directly belong.

THE GROUP VERSUS THE INDIVIDUAL

A contrast which has been emphasized repeatedly has been performance and behavior in the group versus as an individual alone. For example, in this chapter, the distinction between group versus individual achievement motives and aspirations was discussed as well as the differences in attributions for causality. Further, in the previous chapter, it was pointed out that from a conceptual viewpoint, the group has been treated as a composite of individual members as well as a totality which has its own frame of reference. In this section, the contrast is extended to encompass the differences between groups versus individuals in *performance* and *behavior*.

PERFORMANCE

In sport and physical activity, the question of whether individuals or groups are more effective in terms of an *absolute* standard of performance is largely irrelevant. The rules of competition govern not only whether an individual must compete alone or in a group but also the size, general structure and organization of that group. A swimming relay team provides a useful illustration. The number of athletes on a team, their preperformance alignment, starting cue and specific swimming strokes are all carefully spelled out. The question of whether a sole individual should be assigned to the task in order to insure maximum efficiency and performance effectiveness simply does not arise.

However, what is of importance in terms of performance on motor tasks, is whether the group product or output is as effective as it should be *relative* to the resources available — the resources being the collective talents, skills and abilities of the individual group members. Given that there will be an increase in resources available with any increase in group size, can the group effectively *coordinate* these resources to achieve the maximum outcome possible? The answer to this question seems to lie somewhere between "not necessarily" and "probably not."

As Steiner (1972) pointed out with the use of an analogy:

> . . . an increase in group size may augment potential productivity without creating a corresponding increase in actual productivity. Too many cooks may spoil the broth because they get in one another's way or because each insists on adding his own favorite seasoning. This can happen even if, collectively, many cooks know more about brewing broth than do few cooks. Although superior resources often permit large groups to have a higher level of potential productivity than smaller groups, size also tends to complicate the procedures by which resources must be used if maximum efficiency is to be attained . . .
>
> If only one person is available to perform a task, organizational problems are likely to be comparatively simple. The individual must decide what he should do when, but questions concerning who should do what, or who should act when, have already been answered . . .
>
> When two persons work collectively on a task, all of the decisions required of a single person remain pertinent, and others are added . . . When a monad becomes a dyad, the number of different ways a task can conceivably be attacked increases dramatically . . . even if the dyad succeeds in selecting the best possible organizational pattern, it may experience grave difficulties in establishing and maintaining the kinds of interpersonal coordination that are required.

In short, a major problem which exists when a group develops or when the size of a group is increased, is coordinating the individual activities effectively. The most *dramatic way of illustrating this problem is to consider the potential* interaction (and this interaction could be either social or task related although the principal concern here is with the latter) or coordination links between pairs of group members in groups of increasing size (see Figure 7.7). For example, a dyad contains one coordination link between the two individuals; a triad, three links among each of the possible pairs while a 10-person group has 45 possible coordination links (this is calculated using the formula $(n^2 - n)/2$). Thus, while a 10-person group has approximately three times the available resources to draw upon when compared to a triad, it also has nine times as many coordination links to maintain.

Steiner (1972), in his text *Group process and productivity*, proposed a schema to account for the differences between actual group performance and potential group performance. He contended that group productivity[2] is a function of three interdependent classes of variables: the *task demands, group resources* and *group process*. The latter, the group process, reflects the manner in which the group carries out the task. It "consists of the individual or collective actions of the people who have been assigned the task" (Steiner, 1972). If a volleyball team possesses a poorly integrated and coor-

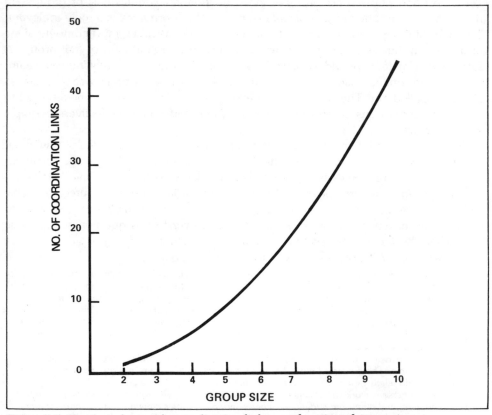

Figure 7.7. Number of possible coordination links as a function of group size.

2.   Steiner was actually concerned with the general factors underlying group and individual performance. However, the emphasis here is on the group and consequently the discussion is oriented in that direction.

dinated offense and defense, for example, its group process could be termed ineffective.

The group resources include those knowledges, skills, abilities, or tools that each individual brings to the group. Thus, a hockey team with three outstanding goal scorers might be considered to possess good group resources.

Finally, the task demands comprise those prescriptions or requirements for performance which are either imposed by the task itself or are present through the rules which dictate how the task must be performed. The task demands would vary from one situation to another. The task demands for a swimming relay team, for example, are considerably different than for a lawn bowling squad.

Steiner did provide a classified schema for group and individual tasks. It would be beneficial to provide a selected, cursory overview of this classification scheme since it will be helpful in terms of understanding some of the predictions made in regard to group size and group productivity.

One of the distinctions which was made between task-types was *sequential versus simultaneous*. In the former, the individual group members carry out the task in a prescribed order, one-after-another, whereas in the latter, the performance of all group members occurs at the same time. An example of the former task would be a swimming relay team while a rowing team would be an example of the latter.

A second distinction made was between *unitary* versus *divisible* tasks. In unitary tasks, all group members perform a similar or identical skill (i.e., the rowing team example again applies) but in divisible tasks there is a division of labor as group members perform different subtasks (e.g., baseball, football).

A third distinction made was *maximizing* versus *optimizing* tasks with the goal of the former being to carry out the task as rapidly as possible or by doing as much of the task as possible. Any sports requiring objectively assessed speed or strength scores (e.g., weightlifting, sprinting) would be illustrative of maximizing tasks. Optimizing tasks, on the other hand, involve accuracy and precision — qualitative dimensions which cannot be easily assessed, e.g., figure skating, gymnastics.

A final distinction which is pertinent here is the method for arriving at a group score. In *additive tasks*, the individual member's contributions are summed in order to obtain one "group" score, e.g., the successive times for the members of a relay team are implicitly summed to get a single team value. In *compensatory tasks* the average of the group members contributions are taken to determine the group value. Examples which illustrate this latter approach are synchronized swimming and the pairs events in figure skating — the total artistic impression created by the team contributes to the overall group score.

Steiner argued that given a knowledge of the task demands and the member resources, it should be possible to obtain an estimate of the potential performance of the group. Further, any discrepancy between the potential productivity of the group and its actual productivity must be due to losses resulting from faulty group processes. This can be presented as follows:

$$Actual\ Productivity = Potential\ Productivity - Losses\ Due\ to\ Faulty\ Processes \quad (5)$$

It is possible to determine with reasonable precision what the potential productivity of a group is in tasks such as rowing or tug-of-war — tasks which are *simultaneous, unitary, maximizing* and *additive*. That is, all individuals are engaged in the identical task at the same time (these tasks are unitary and simultaneous), the tasks are objectively assessed (i.e., maximizing) and the individual members contribute their collective efforts to one group score (the task is additive). As a consequence, if the ten members of a tug-of-war team can each pull 50 kg., on the average, then the potential productivity for the group should be 500 kg. What effect does an increase in group size (with the concommitant increase in the number of coordination links) have upon group productivity in a tug-of-war task?

In a study by Ringlemann (cited in Steiner, 1972), using the tug-of-war task, it was noted that, on the average, a single individual could exert 63 kg. of tension. Consequently, the potential productivity dimension of Formula 5 would be estimated for groups of two, three, and eight members at 126 kg., 189 kg. and 504 kg. respectively. The actual values obtained in Ringlemann's study are presented in Table 7.2.

Table 7.2. The potential and actual productivity for the rope pulling groups in Ringlemann's study (From Steiner, 1972). Reproduced with permission of the publisher.

Number of Participants	Number of Coordination Links	Potential Productivity	Actual Productivity	Process Losses
1	-	63	63	-
2	1	126	118	8
3	3	189	160	29
8	28	504	248	256

It is apparent that the *absolute performance* of the group increased from 63 kg. to 248 kg. with increases in group size from one to eight persons. However, the relative performance for each individual showed a progressive decline. If it can be assumed that a "group-of-one" performed at 100% efficiency, then individuals in dyads performed at 93% of their potential, the individuals in triads at 85% and the individuals in 8-person groups at 49% of their potential. If these results are considered in terms of Formula 5 then the differences between actual and potential performance must be attributed to "faulty group processes." In this regard Steiner (1972) observed "the discrepancies between the potential and actual productions of these groups form an interesting progression; they are very nearly proportional to the number of links along which coordination was needed — one, three and 28."

Two possible factors (Ingham, Levinger, Graves and Peckham, 1974) in the faulty group process might be *poor coordination* (for example, the individuals could pull maximally at different times, there would be differences in foot slippage, hand slippage etc.) and/or *decreased motivation* (for example, there could be a diminished effort as a result of the lack of direct personal appraisal since individual performance is hidden in a group effort).

Ingham, Levinger, Graves and Peckham replicated the Ringlemann study using a tightly controlled experimental procedure. The apparatus (see Figure 7.8) was designed to reduce hand and foot slippage, provide a constant pulling angle on the rope and reduce measurement error. Also, fatigue and learning effects as well as any effects accruing from possible advantages at any one pulling station were eliminated through

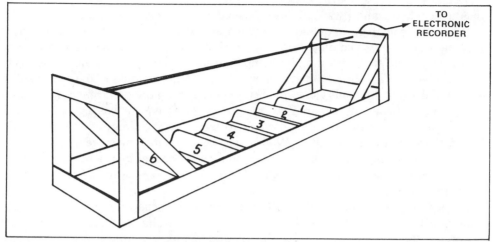

TO
ELECTRONIC
RECORDER

Figure 7.8. Rope pulling apparatus (Adapted from Ingham, Levinger, Graves and Peckham, 1974).

the experimental design. (Ringlemann may also have controlled for these factors, as Ingham *et al.* noted, but the available accounts of his work are sketchy.)

Ingham *et al.* did obtain results similar to Ringlemann for groups up to a size of three persons. That is, the dyads showed a decline in efficiency (using the average for a single individual as the base, or 100%) to 91% while the triads were at 82%. However, contrary to the findings of Ringlemann and the theoretical formulations of Steiner, further increases in group size did not lead to corresponding linear decreases in group efficiency. There was a general leveling off effect so that groups of six pulled at an average of 78%. This is illustrated in Figure 7.9.

A second study was also carried out by Ingham *et al.* in an effort to determine whether the process losses resulting from increased group size were largely a product of poor coordination or reduced motivation. In order to separate these two, coordination was eliminated as a factor. This was done by testing only one subject at any one time — the other members of the group were confederates of the experimenter. Thus, motivation losses resulting from perceived group size were free to vary but coordination losses resulting from an actual increased number of group members (and coordination links) were eliminated.

The results were almost identical to the initial findings; there was a decline in efficiency to a group size of three followed by a leveling effect. Thus, Ingham *et al.* concluded that the differences between actual and potential performance were not due to a decrease in coordination resulting from an increase in the number of coordination links but rather to a reduction in motivation.

There have been a number of other studies which have deomonstrated that an elemental feature of group performance is difficulty in coordinating responses. In one series of experiments (Comrey, 1953; Comrey and Deskin, 1954a, 1954b) in which the Purdue pegboard task was used to compare the performance of individuals working alone versus in a pair, it was observed that the pairs assembled more pegs than did their most proficient number (i.e., absolute performance was better). However, this absolute standard was considerably less than twice the number an "average" individual could assemble (i.e., in short, relative performance was poorer).

When the pairs were required to proceed alternately (so that the most proficient member of the pair could only utilize his speed 50% of the time), group performance was highly correlated with the less competent individual's performance.. (McCurdy and Lambert (1952) also reported a similar result.) In tasks requiring less coordination or where the task demands were modified to permit the more proficient individuals in the pair to contribute more than 50%, the group's performance was highly correlated with the more proficient individual's score (Comrey, 1953; Comrey and Staats, 1955; Wiest, Porter and Ghiselli, 1961). While it was observed that the more homogeneous the two individuals were in terms of individual performance, the more effective they were as a team, the measures of individual performance were generally not very good predictors of team coordination.

Steiner (1972) did propose a conceptual model depicting the interaction of the various parameters which are influenced by group size: the *potential productivity* of the group, the *group process losses*, the *total actual group productivity* and the *mean actual production per member*. This is presented in Figure 7.10. It was suggested that with increases in group size, both the potential productivity of the group and the losses due to faulty group processes will increase — the former at a decelerating rate, the latter at an accelerating rate (see Figure 7.10a). In turn, and as a consequence of the relationship of these two factors, both the total actual productivity of the group and the mean actual production per group member should decrease (see Figure 7.10b). If total actual group productivity is the objective then, the optimal group size should be approximately four or five members.

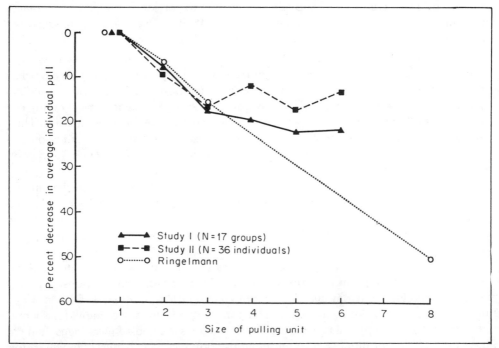

Figure 7.9. Rope pulling scores as a function of group size (From Ingham, Levinger, Graves and Peckham, 1974). Reproduced with permission of the publisher.

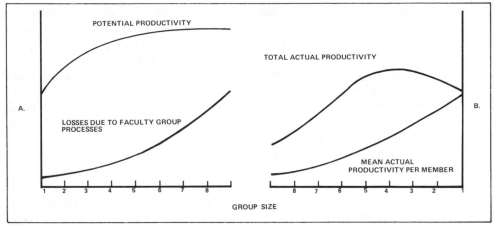

POTENTIAL PRODUCTIVITY

TOTAL ACTUAL PRODUCTIVITY

A.

LOSSES DUE TO FACULTY GROUP PROCESSES

B.

MEAN ACTUAL PRODUCTIVITY PER MEMBER

GROUP SIZE

Figure 7.10. Conceptual model illustrating the interrelationship of increasing group size with potential productivity and mean actual production per member (Adapted from Steiner, 1972).

BEHAVIOR

The Risky Shift Phenomenon. A phenomenon which dramatically illustrates the differences which are present in decision-making behavior when an individual is alone versus when the individual is in a group has been referred to as the *risky-shift* phenomenon (Kogan and Wallach, 1964; Wallach and Kogan, 1965; Wallach, Kogan and Bem, 1962, 1964). This phenomenon derives its name from the shift which occurs in the level of risk which individuals find acceptable or are prepared to tolerate when they arrive at a decision as a member of a group versus when they act alone.

In the experimental paradigm originally used to examine risky-shift, 12 real life dilemmas were presented to the subjects for consideration. One of these, for example, used a sport situation:

> . . . Mr. D is the captain of College X's football team. College X is playing its traditional rival, College Y, in the final game of the season. The game is in its final seconds, and Mr. D's team, College X, is behind in the score. College X has time to run one more play. Mr. D, the captain, must decide whether it would be best to settle for a tie score with a play which would be almost certain to work or, on the other hand, should he try a more complicated and risky play which could bring victory if it succeeded, but defeat if not.
>
> Imagine that you are advising Mr. D. Listed below are several probabilities or odds that the risky play will work.
>
> Please check the *lowest* probability that you would consider acceptable for the risky play to be attempted [Kogan and Wallach, 1964].

Another of the situations presented used a competitive situation in a chess tournament:

> . . . Mr. G, a competent chess player, is participating in a national chess tournament. In an early match he draws the top-favored player in the tournament as his opponent. Mr. G has been given a relatively low ranking in view of his performance in previous tournaments. During the course of his play with the top-favored man, Mr. G notes the possibility of a deceptive though risky maneuver which might bring him a quick victory. At the same time, if the attempted maneuver should fail, Mr. G would be left in an exposed position and defeat would almost certainly follow.
>
> Imagine that you are advising Mr. G. Listed below are several probabilities or odds that Mr. G's deceptive play would succeed.
>
> Please check the *lowest* probability that you would consider acceptable for the risky play in question to be attempted [Kogan and Wallach, 1964].

The remaining 10 situations were similar in type. Essentially, a central character is confronted with a choice which is both attractive and yet, risky. The subjects, in the role of advisor, must select the minimum level of probability for success which they would require in order to advise the central character to choose the riskier but more attractive alternative. The choice is made on a scale containing different probability levels — the riskiest being a 1 out of 10 chance for success, the most conservative being a 9 out of 10 probability of success. After initially responding to the problem alone, the subjects are brought into a group where the cases are discussed and a group decision is reached.

Characteristically, with few exceptions, the group consensus involves a shift to a higher level of risk for the central character than is acceptable to the average group member prior to the discussion. This is accomplished both by an upward displacement in the modal response (the most frequent response elicited from individuals in the group) and a reduction in group variability. In short, individuals in the group situation exhibit very close agreement on a higher level of acceptable risk.

One of the explanations advanced to account for this phenomenon is that a *diffusion of responsibility* occurs (Wallach and Kogan, 1965) — an individual feels less personal responsibility for a potential failure as a member of a group than when acting alone. Parenthetically, it might also be noted that this explanation has also been proffered to account for bystander intervention effects; namely, individuals are more likely to lend assistance in emergency situations (e.g., when people are in distress or have had an accident) than are members of a group (Darley and Latane, 1968; Latane and Darley, 1968; Latane and Rodin, 1969; Schwartz and Clausen, 1970).

In Schwartz's (1968) view, a *norm of social responsibility* is present in emergency situations. This norm becomes diffused among the members of a group and thus, its resultant force is diminished. Insofar as the risky shift phenomenon is concerned, the diffusion of responsibility is considered to reflect blame avoidance rather than a decrease in a perceived norm of responsibility (Wallach and Kogan, 1965). Nonetheless, the effects are thought to be similar with sole individuals exhibiting more responsibility than members of a group. In a sport situation, the decision arrived at by a sole coach would be much more conservative than a decision arrived at by the coach in consultation with other coaches or the athletes.

Another explanation proposed by Brown (1965) for the risky-shift lies in a *cultural value for risk* explanation. That is, within our culture, value is attached to moderate risk taking, to being venturesome. Thus, a sole individual, while initially conservative, arrives through the process of group discussion to a position considered to be moderately risky.

Levinger and Schneider (1969) tested and provided support for the value of risk hypothesis by asking students to indicate (1) their own choice, (2) how they felt their fellow students would choose, and (3) the position they most admired. The results are presented in Figure 7.11. The position admired most was the riskiest. In turn, the subjects selected a personal level of risk which was perceived to be greater than that held by other members of the group. (In a subsequent investigation Wallach and Wing (1970) also reported similar results.) In short, these findings suggest that there is a predilection toward riskier alternatives among all individuals within the group with the group discussion serving the function of eliminating a *pluralistic ignorance*.

Some other related explanations have been proposed for the risky-shift and these

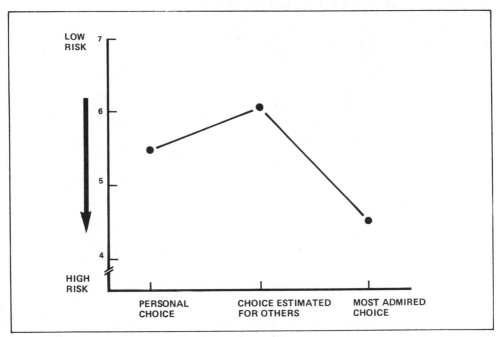

Figure 7.11 Level of risk chosen personally, level of risk most admired, and level attributed to others (Based on data from Levinger and Schneider, 1969).

are tied into a *distribution of information* explanation — factors in the group discussion contribute to a shift in position. One possibility is that individuals who are more oriented toward risky alternatives are more influential within the group discussion. When retrospective assessments have been made on the group discussion by group members, a strong relationship has been reported between the amount of influence exerted on the group and the level of risk present in initial judgments (Brown, 1965; Marquis, 1962; Wallach, Kogan and Bem, 1962; Wallach, Kogan and Burt, 1965).

Another explanation consistent with the distribution of information interpretation was advanced by Brown (1965) who argued that the "rhetoric of risk" contains more potent language possibilities which can be more intensely delivered than is possible within the "rhetoric of caution." Consequently, in a group discussion, individuals advocating a risky alternative have an innate advantage over individuals advocating a conservative option.

A football game serves a useful example. Two options exist for the offensive team faced with a short yardage situation on fourth down at midfield — gamble and pass/run or punt. The former can be strongly advocated by assistant coaches who can support their arguments with phrases like "play attacking football," "maintain our momentum," "be aggressive," and so on. The beleaguered head coach must defend the punt option with phrases like "play it safe," "avoid the gamble," "too early in the game," and so on. Clearly, the rhetoric of risk can be more intensely delivered than the rhetoric of caution.

COOPERATION VERSUS COMPETITION

THE NATURE OF COOPERATION AND COMPETITION

Definitions. A significant impetus for research into the processes of competition and cooperation was Morton Deutsch's conceptual model which was originally published in 1949 (Deutsch, 1949a, 1949b).[3] In that work, he defined a *cooperative social situation* as one in which the gains by one individual contribute to a gain by all individuals in the situation — the rewards are shared equally, independent of personal contributions. Conversely, in a *competitive social situation*, the gain by one individual reduces the gain which can be obtained by any other group member — the rewards are dependent upon the level of contribution made and are, therefore, unequally shared.

Depending upon the way in which the rewards are distributed, a competitive situation can also be referred to as a *zero sum* condition — the presence of a winner (+) in a wrestling match is balanced off by the presence of a loser (− .) In turn, cooperative situations can be referred to as *non-zero sum* since the full complement of individuals are rewarded.

Cooperation-Competition Between and Among Groups. Theoretically, at least, in task performing groups, it is possible to have cooperation and competition both *within* a group (intragroup cooperation and intragroup competition) and *between* different groups (intergroup cooperation and intergroup competition). These dimensions are illustrated in Figure 7.12. These four conditions have been created in laboratory studies but there is some question whether a completely cooperative condition is possible in a natural, nonlaboratory context like sport. Collins and Raven (1969), drawing upon the work of Schelling (1958) would argue that it is possible:

> . . . for many groups, the 'rules of the game' strongly encourage the group to work jointly against a common antagonist such as the environment or another group. It is greatly to the advantage of the five members of a basketball team, for instance, to avoid fragmentation into competing individuals or subgroups. Schelling (1958) would refer to the basketball team as an example of pure coordination . . . . [on the other hand], pure conflict or zero-sum games . . . would be illustrated in a five-man poker game, where the rules of the game strongly encourage individual competitive activity among the group members.

Conversely, a contrasting viewpoint, which also used a basketball team to illustrate the point, was made by Deutsch (1968):

> . . . the members of a basketball team may be cooperatively interrelated with respect to winning the game but competitive with respect to being the 'star' of the team.

The Sport Team. The sport team would seem to be characterized by three possible processes only: intragroup cooperation, intragroup competition and intergroup competition. This point was made by Carron and Chelladurai (1979) who suggested that athletic teams bear some resemblance to the *coalitions* which have been identified in *game theory*.

A coalition situation, as viewed and defined by Gamson (1964), can be "defined by mixed-motive, *n*-person games. In such games there is an element of conflict since there exists no outcome which maximizes the payoff to everybody. There is an ele-

3. Although Deutsch originally published his work in 1949, I did not consult that work but rather, the condensation of his two articles which appears in Cartwright and Zander's (1968) text *Group dynamics: Research and theory.*

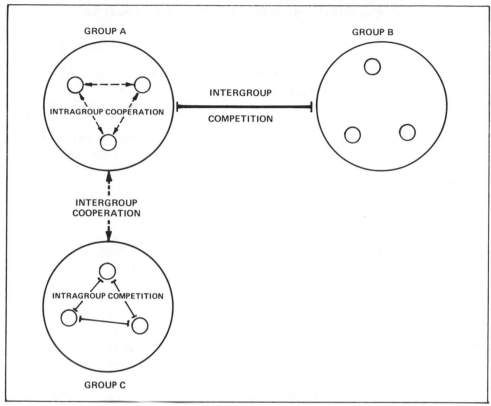

Figure 7.12. Intergroup and intragroup cooperation and competition.

ment of coordination, since there exists for at least two of the players the possibility that they can do better by coordinating their resources than by acting alone." When the individuals combine their resources to maximize personal rewards, the combine is referred to as a coalition.

The parallel with athletics seems apparent. Both cooperation (coordinative group effort) and competition coexist in a coalition. The cooperation results from the mutual recognition of a common task, problem or objective of the group while competition arises as members of the group strive for personal rewards. This situation is present within sport teams such as the basketball example cited previously. Every member of the team strives for excellence in terms of personal performance. However, that excellence can only be maximized through effective cooperation with other team members who have resources which are necessary in order for the group to be successful. As a consequence, the individual performer must combine and coordinate personal resources with other team members in order to insure a successful outcome.

There are also important distinctions between coalitions, coalition research, game theory and team performance in sport and physical activity. First, theoretical models advanced to account for *how* and *why* coalitions develop in group situations have emphasized either of two rational explanations: the *minimum resources* interpretation and the *maximum power* interpretation (Caplow, 1956, 1959; Gamson, 1961, 1964). Fundamental to the formation of coalitions generally are the suppositions that:

— individuals bring different resources (strengths, abilities, power, etc.) to the situation,

— relative control, power and/or rewards are distributed according to the amount of resources possessed,

— within the performance situation, subgroups (coalitions) are formed which maximize the opportunity for personal power and control, and

— this is effected through the process of bargaining among the weaker and stronger members.

In the minimum resources model, it is proposed that the high resource and low resource individuals strive to form coalitions which contain the minimum number of resources necessary in order to achieve control within the total group. As Caplow (1959) pointed out in a discussion of coalition formation within a triad, "the 'chooser' . . . seeks the maximum advantage or minimum disadvantage of strength relative to his coalition partner."

A slightly different perspective is adopted in the maximum power model — it is proposed that an attempt is made to maximize the strength of the coalition relative to the excluded member. Thus, the two individuals with greater resources attempt to form a subgroup which excludes the weakest individual(s).

There are two categories of factors which lead to a suggestion that neither of these models can adequately account for the effective "team" play which occurs in sport and physical activity. For example, if two of three stonger players attempted to maximize personal rewards through coalition formation within a basketball team (i.e., development of a subgroup which excludes the other participants), the total team coordination necessary for success would be absent. What is necessary then is a coalition of the most effective five athletes from the total squad of 10 to 12 — in short, a coalition of *maximum resources* (Carron and Chelladurai, 1979). This may not occur in all situations — cliques do exist — but it must occur if the team is to be successful.

A second point, one which was made by Vinacke (1969) in his review of game theory research, is that the great majority of studies using game models have used only two persons. Vinacke argued that the dyad is grossly inadequate as a model for several reasons. One of these is that, as Simmel (1965) pointed out, there is a considerable difference between research findings for dyads and larger groups. The dyad represents a unique group type when contrasted with any groups of larger size. If the dyad is subdivided, the group is eliminated. And, coalition research with three persons reverts to a dyad who are in coalition versus the remaining single individual.

A second reason advanced by Vinacke is that the opportunity for personality variables to have an impact upon the social situation is limited in dyads whereas they can operate in a less constrained fashion in larger groups. "There may be, of course, some upper limit, but certain phenomena attributable to personality may appear more clearly in triads, tetrads, or pentads than in dyads" (Vinacke, 1969).

A final reason suggested was that the parameters relating to social interaction should be more pronounced within larger groups than in dyads. This can be clearly illustrated by considering group structure (e.g., communication and interaction) or group dynamics (e.g., cohesiveness, pressures toward conformity). The impact of these factors are not as readily apparent in dyads.

The interest in group competition and cooperation has been oriented in two directions: their effect upon performance and upon behavior. Although these two are closely related, it might be easier to independently analyze the work which has been done in these two separate perspectives.

GROUP PERFORMANCE

Deutsch (1949a, 1949b), in the classic work which has already been introduced briefly, tested college students on puzzle problems and human relations problems over a five week session (i.e., a 50 minute session per week). The *cooperative condition* created for the experiment actually involved intragroup cooperation-intergroup competition — a single group solution was required, the group product was placed in competition with the solutions from four other groups and all of the successful group members shared equally in the group reward. The *competitive condition* involved intragroup competition only — each individual in the group was placed in direct competition with the other four group members.

A number of dependent measures were utilized to assess performance and an overview of Deutsch's findings is presented in Table 7.3. The overwhelming superiority of the cooperative condition is clearly evident. Deutsch (1968), commenting on his findings, stated that:

> . . . to the extent that the results have any generality, greater group or organizational productivity may be expected when the members or subunits are cooperative rather than competitive in their interrelationships. The communication of ideas, coordination of efforts, friendliness and pride in one's group which are basic to group harmony and effectiveness appear to be disrupted when members see themselves to be competing for mutually exclusive goals. Further, there is some indication that competitiveness produces greater personal insecurity through expectations of hostility from others than does cooperation.

On the other hand, Julian and Perry (1967) found that while the cooperative condition in their study resulted in the highest amount of satisfaction among the performers, it yielded the most inferior performance. Using a laboratory exercise in psychology as the task, they compared three conditions: *pure cooperation* (it involved intragroup cooperation only; students received a grade based on the group product); *group competition* (it involved intragroup cooperation-intergroup competition in a condition similar to that used by Deutsch); and *individual competition* (it involved intragroup competition only; students received a grade based on their individual product in a condition similar to the other Deutsch condition). When the quantity and quality of the work assignments were assessed by a rater unfamiliar with the subject's experimental condition, the pure cooperation condition was inferior to both group competition and individual competition.

Miller and Hamblin (1963) and more recently, Goldman, Stockbauer and McAuliffe (1977) have emphasized the importance of taking the *task interdependence required* into account in any comparison of the effects of cooperation and competition upon performance. That is, if groups are engaged in intergroup competition, then the task demands will dictate whether a high level of intragroup cooperation is essential or not. (This is also discussed in Chapter 8.) Miller and Hamblin found that on tasks requiring a great deal of mutual dependence — cooperative interaction among group members, a condition which was referred to as *high means interdependence* — intragroup cooperation was positively related to performance. On the other hand, when the tasks could be readily completed by a sole individual — little cooperative interaction was required among the participants, a condition referred to as *low means interdependence* — intragroup cooperation was negatively related to performance.

Table 7.3. Differences between cooperative and competitive groups engaged in problem solving tasks (Adapted from Deutsch, 1968).

Variable	Results
Group Organization:	
Coordination of Effort Within the Group	Coop > Comp
Diversity in Number of Contributions per Member	Coop > Comp
Specialization in Group Functions (e.g., "mediator")	no difference
Specialization in Individual Function (e.g., "aggressor")	Comp > Coop
Specialization in Task Function (subdivision of tasks)	Coop > Comp
Motivation/Pressure Toward Conformity:	
Achievement Pressure	Coop > Comp
Amount of Interest or Involvement	no difference
Communication:	
Attentiveness to Fellow Members	Coop > Comp
Mutual Comprehension of Communication	Coop > Comp
Common Appraisal of Communication	Coop > Comp
Orientation and Ordliness:	Coop > Comp
Productivity:	
Productivity of Signs in Puzzle Problem	Coop > Comp
Productivity of Signs in Human Relations Problem	Comp > Coop
Productivity per Unit of Time	Coop > Comp
Quality of Product and Discussions	Coop > Comp
Amount of Learning	no difference
Interpersonal Relations:	
Friendliness During Discussions	Coop > Comp
Favorable Evaluation of the Group & Its Product	Coop > Comp
Perception of Favorable Effects Upon Fellow Members	Coop > Comp
Incorporation of the Attitudes of the Generalized Other	Coop > Comp

In a similar study but one with a more complex design, Goldman, Stockbauer and McAuliffe (1977) examined the effects of two levels of intergroup relationship (competition and cooperation), two levels of intragroup relationship (competition and cooperation) and two levels of task means interdependence (high and low). Thus, all four of the cooperative/competitive conditions contained in Figure 7.12 were included in the research design. The task was to solve anagram puzzles and the extent to which cooperation was actually mandatory (i.e., the degree of means interdependence) was manipulated.

The results are presented in Figure 7.13. Performance was more effective under intergroup cooperation than under intergroup competition (Figure 7.13a). When the nature of the task was taken into account (Figure 7.13b), the findings revealed that intragroup cooperation was superior on the high means interdependence task while intragroup competition was superior on the low means interdependence task. However, this relationship was present only when there was intergroup cooperation and not when there was intergroup competition.

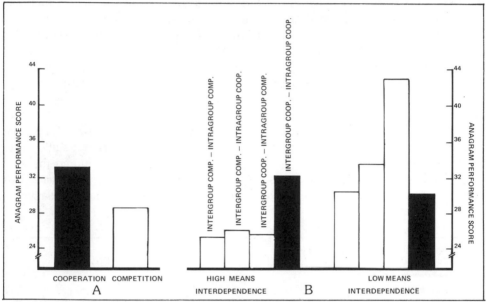

Figure 7.13. Performance effectiveness under cooperative versus competitive conditions (Based on data from Goldman, Stockbauer and McAuliffe, 1977).

Thus, these findings are similar to those reported by Miller and Hamblin — intragroup cooperation was positively related to performance effectiveness when the task demands required a coordinated group effort but were negatively related when the individual group members could carry out the task independently. However, Goldman *et al.* felt that their results "suggest an added refinement. If intragroup and intergroup reward structures are functioning simultaneously, then Miller and Hamblin's findings will only occur when there is intergroup cooperation, but not when there is intergroup competition" (Goldman, Stockbauer and McAuliffe, 1977).

BEHAVIOR

A frequently cited research project relating to the impact of cooperation versus competition upon the behavioral dimension is the *Robbers Cave Experiment* carried out by Muzafer Sherif and his associates (Sherif, Harvey, White, Hood and Sherif, 1961). The project was carried out at a boys' camp. In the original selection of subjects and in their eventual assignment to one of two groups, care was taken to insure that there were no idiosyncratic aspects within the samples which could lead to alternate explanations for the findings. Thus, the boys were highly homogeneous in terms of age, race, religion and socioeconomic status. In addition, there were no pronounced differences in physical appearance, no previous friendship ties and the two camp groups were matched as closely as possible on size and ability. Sherif *et al.* then charted group formation within each of the two camp settings, brought the two groups together "under conditions designed to produce competition, hostility and social distances between them. Later, they met under conditions designed . . . for the reduction of hostility and derogatory stereotypes" (Sherif, 1970).

The consequences of intragroup competition both generally and under winning and losing conditions are presented in overview in Figure 7.14. The results dramatically show that a highly competitive situation serves to produce intragroup harmony and solidarity but to lead to an increase in the social distance between the competing groups. In fact, Sherif (1970) observed that the intergroup competition was responsible for improving intragroup cooperation. These findings are not unique; they have been replicated consistently in a number of experiments. In fact, the pattern of findings is so consistent that a laboratory experiment has been developed around them (Blake and Mouton, 1961).

The reduction of intergroup conflict and hostility was also charted. It was found that casual contacts between the groups in pleasant environments were not sufficient to reduce the hostility; nor was a single emergency situation which required the joint cooperation of the two groups. It was only after a series of cooperative activities was introduced (which required *superordinate goals* and which produced a cumulative ef-

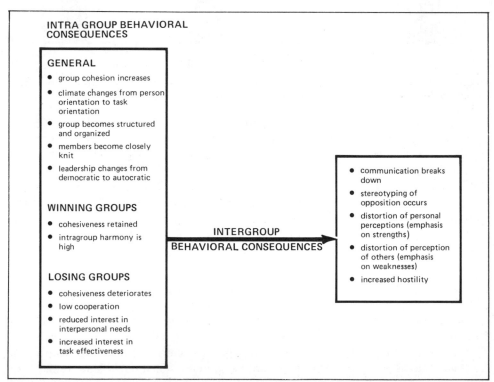

Figure 7.14. The consequences of intragroup cooperation and intergroup competition (Adapted from Sherif *et al.*, 1961).

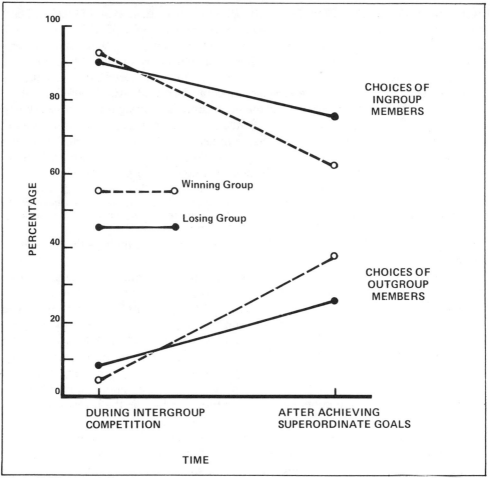

Figure 7.15. Friendship choices before and after the reduction of intergroup hostility (Adapted from Sherif, 1970).

fect) that there was a reduction in the intergroup hostility. This was also accompanied by a decrease in intragroup solidarity.

Figure 7.15 illustrates the friendship choices which were made for ingroup and outgroup members when the hostility was at its peak versus after the program of superordinate goals was implemented. It is evident that there was a considerable increase in the choice of individuals in the outgroup (with a parallel decrease in the choice of friends from within the group) after the program of cooperation was initiated.

Competition: Theraputic or Detrimental? From the research evidence available, it seems evident that the behavioral consequences of competition are considerably different when viewed from an intergroup versus an intragroup perspective. For example, in the first instance, the group becomes cohesive, friendship choices increase — there is a great deal of intragroup goodwill. However, the intergroup relations show a different trend entirely; friendship ties decrease and interpersonal relationships deteriorate.

In a series of experiments by Myers (1962) and Julian, Bishop and Fiedler (1966), the process of competition was analyzed to determine if it held any *theraputic potential*. Myers did find that a group rifle shooting competition, even when the outcome was unsuccessful, resulted in improved personal adjustment of the participants.

In another study, Julian, Bishop and Fiedler (1966) compared army squads in a *competitive training situation* (i.e., intersquad competition was strongly emphasized in all phases of the training program — in the actual training, during routine tasks, during recreation activities etc.) and a *control situation* (no special instructions were given to the trainees). The authors found that the competitive condition led to improved work relations within the group, to higher self-esteem, lower anxiety and a greater satisfaction with the squad. They summarized their study by stating the following:

> . . . we are inclined to feel . . . that the improvement of the interpersonal relationship was causal to the improvement in adjustment . . . the importance of this experiment is probably in the demonstration that task groups under field conditions can be engineered by appropriate environmental manipulation to contribute to the individual group member's adjustment.

In short, they argued on the basis of their results and previous findings that intergroup competition was a potential theraputic tool.

On the other hand, on the basis of their experiment, Dunn and Goldman (1966) have been extremely critical of any tendency to induce competition because of its known positive intragroup consequences. In their study, psychology students involved in a laboratory exercise (i.e., discuss and submit a report on a human relations problem) were assigned to one of four conditions: *group merit* (involved intragroup cooperation where one grade was assigned to the unit for the group product); *individual competition* (involved intragroup competition only); *group competition* (involved a intragroup cooperation-intergroup competition condition); and *individual merit* (involved intragroup cooperation with grades assigned on the basis of individual merit).

They found that it was not competition per se which led to lower satisfaction and the rejection of outgroup members but rather, the fact that individuals work for independent rewards. Dunn and Goldman concluded that:

> . . . the results . . . show the needlessness of including intergroup competition in developing both mutual satisfaction or greater acceptance among members of a group.
> There exists the tendency to include intergroup competition as part of a 'cooperation' treatment, perhaps under the assumption that this induces cohesiveness or 'good ingroup feelings' . . . The present study points to the possibility that this rivalry may not only be unnecessary but may do social harm through the intergroup tensions that it arouses [Dunn and Goldman, 1966].

In short, the view endorsed was that competition was potentially harmful and should not be encouraged. This has also been a position explicitly or implicitly advocated by a number of authors interested in the impact of sport and physical activity upon children. While this literature does not relate directly to a discussion of the *group* per se (and, therefore, might have been more appropriately discussed in an earlier section), it is presented in the following sections.

COMPETITION IN SPORT AND PHYSICAL ACTIVITY

The most comprehensive discussion of the behavioral effects of competition and cooperation in the context of sport and physical activity has been provided by Orlick and his associates (Hyland and Orlick, 1975; McNally and Orlick, 1975; Orlick, 1974, 1975, 1976; Orlick and Botterill, 1975; Orlick, Partington, Scott and Glassford,

1975). Two of the most significant criticisms leveled have been the *emphasis on eliticism* and the *reward system* operative in sport. Orlick (1976), commenting on the former, argued that:

> . . . setting limits on the kind and number of kids allowed to be involved . . . is an all too common occurrence in communities and schools across the nation . . . we may have 100 boys try out for a basketball team, or 100 girls try out for a gymnastics team — but in each case, only about ten or fifteen make the team. Instead of cutting children, we should be personally encouraging them to come out for sport and making it a meaningful place for them.
>
> We should field as many teams as there are interested kids to fill them. It is ridiculous to promote participation on the one hand, and then to cut interested individuals from the team, or in any way limit their participation. This type of action provides the rejected child with massive negative reinforcement and counters our basic reason for existing . . . It is comparable to a doctor refusing to treat his sickest patients to insure that his win-loss record looks good.

The second factor, the reward system, is highly related to the issue of eliticism. Intergroup competition in sport is generally a zero-zum situation — there is a winner and a loser. However, Orlick (1976) pointed out that even in intergroup situations, the reward system benefits only a minority of the participants:

> . . . the reward structure which now exists in organized sport does not appear to be consistent with what is in the best interest of the majority of children. There appears to be an over-emphasis on winning at the expense of fun involvement. This gives rise to an elitist atmosphere wherein many youngsters eliminate themselves before they start, while others begin to withdraw at seven and eight years of age.
>
> In many cases, organized sport (team or individual) appears to operate as an extremely efficient screening process for the elimination of children.

Consistent with this view of athletics as an "extremely efficient screening process for the elimination of children" has been an interest in the *athletic drop out*. What are the principal reasons expressed by the athletes themselves for dropping out and what is their resultant attitude toward sport, physical activity and/or physical education?

The Sport Drop Out. Orlick (1974) attempted to ascertain why individuals who were once active in sport and physical activity elected to withdraw and quit competing. He interviewed 60 athletic drop outs who were between the ages of 7 and 19 years. When the stated reasons were analyzed, it was noted that 50% of the older former competitors listed dissatisfaction with some aspect of the competitiveness dimension while another 17% cited their former coach as the primary causal agent. On the other hand, at the elementary school level, 60% listed the lack of successful or rewarding experiences while 40% cited the lack of playing time.

The relationship between withdrawal and attitude seems straightforward. Triandis (1971), in a discussion on attitude change, pointed out that an individual's attitude toward an activity, person or object is related to the nature of previous associative experiences — to the degree that the individual has had pleasant or unpleasant experiences with the activity, person or object, there will be a positive or negative associative attitude. If this is the case, it might be expected that those individuals who have not had successful or rewarding experiences (and consequently chose to withdraw) would have negative attitudes toward sport and physical activity. This question has been examined directly by Fisher and Driscoll (1975) and Hare (1976), and, indirectly, by Freischlag (1973), Hyland and Orlick (1975) and Vincent (1967).

Fisher and Driscoll (1975) administered Kenyon's (1968) *Attitude Toward Physical Activity Inventory*[4] to three groups of high school students: *varsity athletes; non-*

4. This inventory contains seven subscales which assess the individual's attitude toward physical activity (1) as a social experience, (2) for health and fitness, (3) as the pursuit of vertigo, (4) as an asthetic experience, (5) as a catharsis, (6) as an ascetic experience, and (7) as a game of chance.

athletes (had never participated on an organized team and were not involved at that time in any recreational or sport pursuit); and *one-time athletes* (had participated in varsity athletics but were dismissed either for lack of ability or disciplinary reasons). A marked difference in attitude was observed among the three groups. This is illustrated in Figure 7.16. There is an apparent similarity between the profiles of the non-athletes and the one-time athletes.

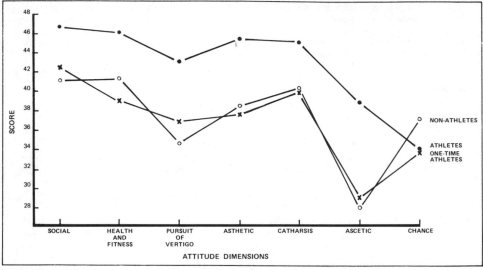

Figure 7.16. Attitudes toward physical activity as a function of the degree of involvement in varsity athletics (Based on data from Fisher and Driscoll, 1975).

A similar experiment was carried out by Hare (1976). He surveyed four groups of college males who differed in their degree of participation in minor hockey. One group had never participated, a second had participated but withdrew from hockey prior to the age of 12 years, a third had participated but withdrew between the ages of 12 and 16 years while the fourth were still participating. These groups were contrasted on their attitudes toward physical activity (using a modified version of the Kenyon inventory), their attitude toward various aspects of hockey (the coaching, level of aggression in the game, etc.) and their current level of participation in physical activity. No group differences were reported for any of these measures. Thus, Hare concluded that any possible negative effects associated with withdrawal from sport must dissipate with the passage of time.

Both Vincent (1967) and Freischlag (1973) have reported a relationship between successful experiences and positive attitudes toward physical education. In an explanation consistent with Triandis's postulations, Freischlag pointed out that there is a *law of effect* operative whereby a person will repeat those experiences which are successful and, therefore, which are perceived as pleasant. Conversely, an individual will withdraw from unpleasant, unrewarding or unsuccessful experiences.

Hyland and Orlick (1975) tested a grade nine sample of students comprised equally of individuals who either had elected not to participate in physical education or had registered for physical education. When this total sample listed all the reasons why students might elect to enroll in physical education, *enjoyment* was cited by 63% and *ability* by 40%. Conversely, in response to the question of why students would not elect physical education, *inability* was mentioned by 54% and *dislike* by 52% of the sample.[5] The authors concluded that "to insure that more children elect to participate in and benefit from physical education, it should above all be enjoyable" (Orlick and Hyland, 1975).

Possibly, not surprisingly, a reference to the potentially low enjoyment value in sport and physical activity resulting from the strong emphasis on competitiveness and success has been a recurring theme in Orlick's writing. For example, he has stated that there is a negative relationship between the emphasis on winning/performance outcomes and the degree of enjoyment experience. However, the issue of what factors contribute to children's enjoyment in competitive sport may not be that easily answered. Certainly situational factors and individual difference factors would also seem to play an important role.

A study of Baytor (1978) supports this viewpoint. Minor hockey league players were tested in a complex factorial design which included two age levels (7 and 11 years) in two hockey leagues (a highly competitive all-star league and a recreational house league) experiencing two different performance outcomes (top of the league and bottom of the league). Two inventories were developed to assess the level of enjoyment in a variety of different hockey situations (these were similar in principle to Endler and Hunt's (1966) S-R Inventory of Anxiousness) and the proportions of variance accounted for by the situational factors, individual difference factors and their interactions were determined. It was noted that situational factors accounted for the largest proportion of variance in children's enjoyment of competitive sports (see Figure

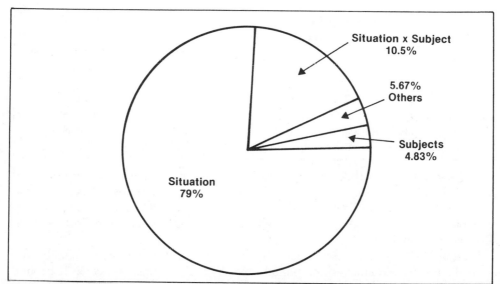

Figure 7.17. The proportion of variance accounting for children's enjoyment in competitive sport (From Baytor, 1978). Reproduced with permission of the author.

5.   The Hyland and Orlick study was also concerned with perception of ability, body image and self-esteem. While the differences between participants and nonparticipants were analyzed for these variables, there was no breakdown of the data for the analysis of reasons for electing versus not electing physical education.

7.17). Neither the organizational emphasis placed on winning (the houseleague versus all-star), nor the age of the participants nor the final team standing were major factors contributing to children's enjoyment of sport.

Athletic Involvement, Status and Self-Esteem. While the impact of athletic involvement upon status and self-esteem is only indirectly related to the issue of competition per se, it is of sufficient importance to be mentioned here. On the basis of his famous study which was carried out in the late 1950s, Coleman (1961) concluded that athletic prowess is the single most important factor contributing to status among adolescents. More recently, Eitzen (1976) replicated these findings (see Table 7.4). Thus, as a result of the prestige ascribed to achievement in athletics, it might be expected that self-esteem is also related to involvement in sport and physical activity. And, there is some evidence to suggest that this is the case.

Table 7.4. Relative ranking of various criteria for status (Adapted from Eitzen, 1976).

| | CRITERIA FOR STATUS | AVERAGE RANKING | |
		Coleman (1961)	Eitzen (1976)
RANKING TO BE POPULAR WITH BOYS	Be an athlete	2.2	2.06
	Be in the leading crowd	2.6	2.10
	Leader in activities	2.9	2.82
	High grades, honor roll	3.5	3.73
	Come from right family	4.5	3.98
	CRITERIA FOR STATUS	**AVERAGE RANKING**	
		Coleman (1961)	**Eitzen (1976)**
RANKING TO BE POPULAR WITH GIRLS	Be an athlete	2.2	1.94
	Be in the leading crowd	2.5	2.12
	Have a nice car	3.2	2.81
	High grades, honor roll	4.0	3.87
	Come from the right family	4.2	3.89

In the Hyland and Orlick (1975) study cited earlier, individuals who elected to participate in physical education scored higher on self-esteem (as assessed by the Rosenberg Self-Esteem Test) and personal perception of ability and personal perception of body image (both were assessed through adaptations of the Thomas Self-Concept-Values Test).

Purdon (1978) administered Coopersmith's Self-Esteem Inventory to 300 children — male and female athletes and nonathletes aged 10, 13 and 16 years. She found that the athletes had higher levels of self-esteem than the nonathletes and that there was an interaction between age and athletic status. That is, differences were noted between the athletes and nonathletes at ages 10 and 13 years but no differences were noted at age 16 years. These results are illustrated in Figure 7.18. No differences were observed in self-esteem between the male versus female athletes and between the males versus female nonathletes.

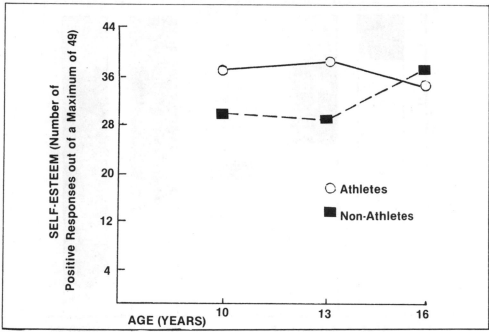

Figure 7.18. Self esteem and athletic involvement. (From Purdon, 1978) Reproduced with permission of the author.

Individuals not involved in sport can pursue other hobbies or activities (e.g., music, reading, etc.) and these could serve as a substitute for sport. Purdon was also interested in comparing the nonathletic subjects' perception of their nonathletic activity involvement with the athletic subjects' perception of their sport involvement. In this regard, the athletes indicated a greater degree of enjoyment experienced and a higher self-perception for level of talent than the nonathletes. On the basis of her results, Purdon (1978) suggested that "athletics are a source for those experiences which serve to enhance self-esteem."

The Cultural Basis for Competition. The origins of competitive behavior do appear to have a strong link with the culture. For example, Madsen and Shapiro (1970) and Shapiro and Madsen (1969) reported that American children competed even when it was not to their advantage to do so. Conversely, Mexican and Israeli Kibbutz children readily accepted a cooperative plan which was mutually more beneficial than competition.

In another experiment, McNally and Orlick (1975) changed the scoring system for the game of broomball in order to deemphasize competition and emphasize a more cooperative approach. This game was then introduced to both Northern Indian children (ages 7 and 8 years living 100 miles south of the Artic Circle) and a sample of children from central Canada. When the game was evaluated by the children, the Northern sample showed a much more positive response than did the Southern sample; this is illustrated in Figure 7.19. There was also a considerable difference between the two sexes and this is also evident in that illustration.

A similar pattern was also observed between the Northern and Southern children when they were asked "how much fun was it to play using these new rules compared

230

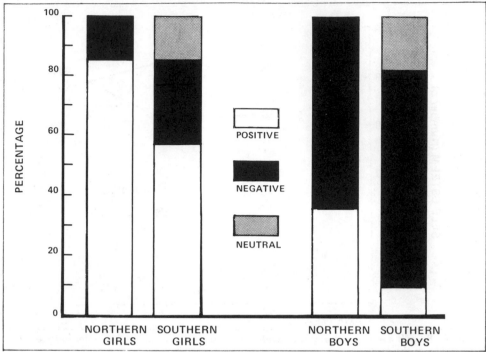

Figure 7.19. Evaluation of cooperative game experience by Northern and Southern Canadian children (Based on data from McNally and Orlick, 1975).

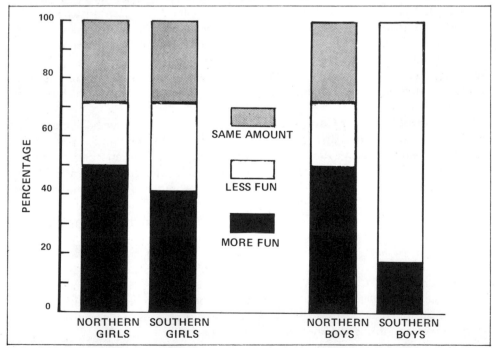

Figure 7.20. Level of enjoyment in a cooperative game by Northern and Southern Canadian children (Based on data from McNally and Orlick, 1975).

to regular rules?" These results are presented in Figure 7.20. The authors reported two other findings which are suggestive of a learning explanation for competitiveness: namely, the younger the group, the more willing they were to accept the cooperative games; and, cooperative games became more acceptable with repeated exposure.

SUMMARY

The present chapter was concerned with selected aspects of group dynamics — analyses of (1) group oriented motivation and aspiration, (2) the nature of the attributions made to causality under positive and negative group outcomes, (3) the distinctiveness of the behavior and performance of an individual working alone versus in a group, and (4) the contrast between the competitive versus cooperative process.

According to Zander (1971), there are two group based dispositions in achievement situations: the tendency to achieve group success and the tendency to avoid group failure. The former is the result of three factors: the desire to achieve group success, the perceived probability of group success and the incentive value of group success. In turn, the tendency to avoid group failure is also a result of three factors which are similar in type but different in orientation: the desire to avoid group failure, the perceived probability of group failure and the incentive value of group failure.

Further, the two incentive values (the incentive values of group success and group failure) and the two perceived probabilities (the perceived probability of group success and of group failure) interact to produce a group level of aspiration. In a manner similar to individuals in achievement situations, groups increase their aspiration level with successful experiences and decrease it with failure experiences — the amount of absolute change being greater with success.

A relatively consistent pattern emerges when members of problem solving groups retrospectively assign responsibility for group success or failure. Individuals who are members of successful groups have a greater tendency to assume responsibility for group performance than do members of unsuccessful groups. In a similar vein, individuals who are members of a successful group tend to view their own relative contribution as being greater than that of the "average" group member whereas members of unsuccessful groups tend to view their own relative contribution as being less than that of the "average" group member.

In athletic teams, a similar pattern of results has emerged. However, the factor of *effort* appears to play an exceptional role. That is, there is some evidence which indicates that effort has a different attributional meaning depending upon whether the team was successful or not. When the team is successful, effort (both team and individual) is viewed as a major contributing factor. However, when the team is unsuccessful, individual team members have a tendency to rate their own effort as high but the team effort as low.

In sport and physical activity, the question of whether the group is more or less efficient than a solitary individual on an absolute scale is irrelevant since the rules of sport competition dictate how a task must be carried out. What is of concern is the relative effectiveness of group performance. Steiner (1972) has developed a theoretical model to examine this issue, the foundation of which is the contention that group productivity is a product of three classes of factors: the task demands, the group resources and the group processes.

One significant behavioral correlate of group participation is the risky-shift phenomenon. The risky-shift phenomenon derives its name from the upward shift which occurs in the level of risk which individuals find acceptable when arriving at a decision as a member of a group versus when they are alone.

Cooperation and competition are integral aspects of group life. Theoretically at least, in task performing groups, it is possible to have both intragroup cooperation and competition and intergroup cooperation and competition. Team situations in sport appear to be characterized by three of these: intergroup competition, intragroup cooperation and some degree of intragroup competition. Since this is the case, it might be useful to view a sport team as a special type of coalition — a coalition of maximum resources.

Although the earliest research suggested that cooperation is most effective in terms of performance effectiveness, it has been noted more recently that the nature of the task is an important mediating variable. If the task can be carried out independently by the group members, intragroup competition can be more effective than intragroup cooperation.

It has been observed from a behavioral perspective that intragroup cooperation-intergroup competition serves to produce intragroup harmony and solidarity but to lead to social distance between the competing groups. In sport and physical activity, the strong orientation toward competitiveness, with its concommitant emphasis on eliticism and a reward system which benefits only a few successful performers, has been criticized. The orientation toward competitiveness appears to have a cultural origin.

GROUP COHESION [1] 8

It might be apparent from the previous chapters that a group is not simply a crowd of people — a group is characterized by purposive interaction in goal directed and/or interpersonal behavior. As Carron and Chelladurai (1979) stated "an elemental and critical characteristic of the group/team which distinguishes it from being simply a casual collection of individuals is the degree of attraction, commitment and/or involvement of the individual members to the collective whole. This attraction, commitment and/or involvement is referred to as cohesiveness."

A traditional assumption in sport and physical activity has been that cohesiveness — and this includes any of the number of synonyms frequently substituted for cohesion such as togetherness, team spirit, team unity, satisfaction, and teamwork — is directly linked with team success. Zander (1974) illustrated this viewpoint, observing that "in spite of the individual athletes who make headlines when they strike off for themselves, team spirit is the rule rather than the exception. In fact, both amateurs and professionals generally feel that a team can't become a winner without it."

This viewpoint would suggest that a linear relationship exists between cohesiveness ✓ and performance success; those teams with the greatest amount of cohesion are the most successful. Unfortunately, the issue is not so straightforward — a fact also both implicitly and explicitly acknowledged by Zander (1971, 1974) in his other discussions on group dynamics. The complexity of the performance-cohesiveness relationship has been highlighted in both practical situations and theoretical analyses. For example, there have been numerous examples in sport of teams which have apparently had only minimal levels of team unity, togetherness, and so on, but which have been highly successful. The incredible performance, despite internal conflict, of the German rowing eights team is among the best known. In discussing their accomplishment, Lenk ✓ (1969) noted that:

> . . . several times conflict almost led to the destruction of the team. By means of sport, within this eight, no performance detriment as a result of the tensions within the group was noticeable. But there should have occurred a performance decrement in comparison with the initial situation (the compatibility and conflictlessness among members from different clubs), as the training regimen and

1. The material in this chapter has been adapted from recent discussions on group cohesion in athletics by Carron and Chelladurai (1978) and Donnelly, Carron and Chelladurai (1979).

the technical control of workouts remained on the same level. At best there could have been only a small performance increase. Actually, the performance did increase and paralleled the sharpness of the conflict during the two years in which the eight existed. Performance was systematically measured using their very frequent training sessions over eight by 560 meters in racing tempo. The team became unbeaten Olympic champions. A sport team, therefore, is able to achieve in spite of strong internal conflicts, the highest of performances.

The complexity of cohesion and its relationship to performance is also illustrated from a conceptual or theoretical point of view. Cohesion is still not very well understood. There is only minimal disagreement concerning what cohesiveness is in the abstract — the term itself conveys a binding, sticking together or unitedness of the total. However, there is considerable debate on how that abstract should be operationalized, measured, assessed. An additional factor which also illustrates the complexity is that cohesion may be examined empirically as either an independent or dependent variable. An example of the former instance is contained within the question: "Do team differences in level of cohesiveness contribute to differences in performance success?" And, an example of the latter instance is the question: "Do team differences in performance success contribute to differences in cohesiveness?" The question of which is the strongest relationship — cohesion leading to performance success or performance success leading to cohesiveness — is yet another issue. This circular nature of the cohesion-performance interaction makes it difficult to pinpoint cause-effect relationships.

THE NATURE OF COHESIVENESS

DEFINITIONS

Since cohesion can be thought of as the degree of commitment and involvement by individual members to the group, it is, therefore, "the adhesive property of groups — the force that binds group members together. There can be no such thing as a non-cohesive group; it is a contradiction in terms. If a group exists, it is to some extent cohesive" (Donnelly, Carron and Chelladurai, 1978). That is, there may be low or minimal levels of togetherness/unity, but there cannot be "zero cohesiveness" since the group would cease to exist.

As the adhesive property of groups, cohesion may be considered from two perspectives: as the impetus underlying participation or involvement within the group — the factors drawing members to the group (see Figure 8.1a); and, as the impetus underlying the maintenance of the group — the factors preventing group dissolution (see Figure 8.1b). In his discussions on the group and group dynamics, Lewin (1941) emphasized the former viewpoint. He referred to two general categories of forces which influence group participation/involvement: those which attract individuals to the group; and those which cause members to leave the group. The former were incorporated under the term group cohesiveness.

Later, in a field study, Festinger, Schachter and Back (1950) supported Lewin's viewpoint with their proposal that cohesiveness can be defined as *the total field of forces causing members to remain in the group*. Thus, they supported the model contained within Figure 8.1a. The Festinger, Schachter and Back study might be considered *the* significant pioneer work in the area of cohesion if only because of the continued endorsement that their definition has received. But, there have also been criticisms of this definition and a number of limitations have been highlighted.

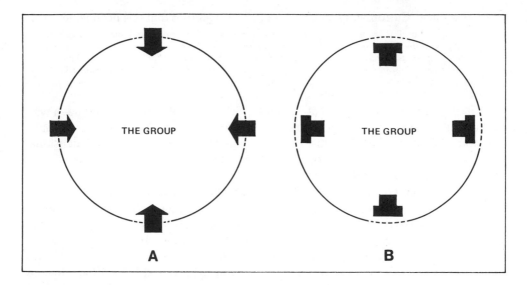

Figure 8.1. Schematic illustrations of conceptual views of cohesiveness: (a) Cohesion as the forces which attract and cause members to remain in the group; and, (b) Cohesion as resistance to disruptive forces.

One criticism has been that this definition *focuses on the individual as the unit of reference rather than on the group*. In this regard, Gross and Martin (1952) argued that it is conceptually more logical to consider cohesion as *resistance by the group to disruptive forces* (i.e., the model presented in Figure 8.1b) since:

> . . . the conception of 'attractiveness' or total field of forces results in an emphasis on individual perceptions and minimizes the importance of the relational bonds between and among group members. The attractiveness concept raises the question: 'How attractive is the group to each member?' In contrast, the resistance conception raises the question: 'How strong or weak a disruptive force will be required before the group begins to fall apart?' In short, the emphasis is on the strength of relational bonds between and among group members under varying conditions of crises.

A second limitation in the Festinger, Schachter and Back definition has been its *generality and the resultant difficulty in converting "the total field of forces" into operational terms*. For example, the word "total" is so all-encompassing that for practical purposes it has no utility. Further, the concept of a "force" is also too vague to be practically useful.

Hagstrom and Selvin (1965) did attempt to delineate these specific forces when they factor analyzed 19 possible measures of cohesiveness. Two dimensions were obtained: *social satisfaction* and *sociometric cohesion*. The former reflected satisfaction with the group and the group's influence upon behavior; the latter, personal friendship with other group members. However, the direct relevance of these findings for the specific context of sport and physical activity is questionable. Certainly, it seems obvious that athletes join and remain on athletic teams for reasons other than simply social satisfaction and sociometric cohesion.

For example, it has been customary (e.g.,Homans, 1951) to broadly categorize the forces which attract individuals to a group under the terms *task* and *social* with the former reflecting an orientation toward group goals, group performance, and the task itself; and, the latter, an orientation toward personal relationships. In addition to these two there is undoubtedly a third type of force prevalent in athletic groups; namely a *normative force.* Carron and Chelladurai (1979) suggested that this normative force:

> . . . includes cultural, functional and practical considerations. For example, there are strong cultural expectations for the athlete to stick with the team; there is a social stigma to the act of quitting. In addition, eligibility and/or transfer rules, geographical restraints, contractual obligations (in the case of many amateur and professional sports) prevent the athlete from leaving the team if he/she wishes to compete. The effect of this category of forces is to contain (restrain) the individual within the group, independent of the group's properties.

Finally, a third criticism leveled at Festinger, Schachter and Back has not been with their definition *per se* but rather the *restricted manner in which they operationalized cohesion* within their study. That is, while they made reference to a multidimensional construct (i.e., the total field of forces), cohesiveness was only indexed through the single aspect of *interpersonal attraction.*

Despite the inadequacies of interpersonal attraction as either *a* measure or *the* measure of cohesiveness (both Escovar and Sim, 1974, and Carron and Chelladurai, 1979, have discussed various limitations of cohesion as attractiveness and these are summarized in the next section), a number of researchers have focused on it to the exclusion of other measures. In many instances, attraction has become synonomous with cohesion in definitional statements. For example, Lott and Lott (1965) defined cohesion as "that group property which is inferred from the number and strength of mutual positive attitudes among the members of a group."

In a similar vein, Bonner (1959) stated that "if we analyze group cohesiveness . . . in terms of a group's attractiveness for its members, we are confronted by the obvious fact that without at least a minimal attraction of members to each other a group cannot exist at all." Also, Shaw (1974) noted that "by far the most powerful determinant of attraction of the group is the attraction of one person to another. When a given individual is attracted to the members of a group, then he is likely to find the group attractive and to desire membership in the group." And finally, Cartwright (1968), in his comprehensive review, stated that:

> . . . the resultant force acting on a member to remain in a group has at least two types of components: (a) forces that derive from the group's attractiveness and (b) forces whose source is the attractiveness of alternate memberships. Most investigators have equated the term cohesiveness with 'attraction to the group.'

Thus, as might be expected, the various operational measures of cohesiveness have generally reflected a cohesion-as-attraction orientation.

OPERATIONAL MEASURES OF COHESIVENESS

Cartwright (1968) presented five traditional approaches to the measurement of cohesion. And, as indicated above, each has involved some assessment of attraction. The first, *interpersonal attraction among members* is essentially a reflection of the level of friendship within the group. Thus, it is assumed that the stronger the bonds of friendship among and between group members, the more cohesive that group.

A second approach has been to assess *the attractiveness of the group as a whole.* That is, the group and its attractiveness to members rather than friendships among individuals is the primary focus. However, there is also some evidence that these two parameters are highly related. Jackson (1959, cited in Cartwright, 1968), using two scales — one to measure the benefit the respondent received from the group and the other to assess the level attraction to individual group members — reported a correlation of .61 between them.

✓ Estimating the *expressed desire to remain in the group* has been another approach used. Schachter (1951), attempting to determine the extent to which a group was cohesive, asked:

1. Do you want to remain a member of this group?
2. How often do you think this group should meet?
3. If enough members decide not to stay so that it seems this group might discontinue, would you like the chance to persuade others to stay?

The first question is, of course, a very direct measure of the expressed desire to remain in the group.[2]

In a fourth general approach, the degree of *closeness or identification with the group* is analyzed. For example, Indik (1965) asked members of work groups "How strong a sense of belonging do you feel you have to the people you work with?" and noted that this index correlated .41 and − .30 with measures assessing the ease of communication within the group and absenteeism respectively.

A fifth approach has been to use a *composite index* based upon all of the above. ✓ This appears to have been the general strategy adopted by Martens, Landers and Loy (1972) in the development of the *Sports Cohesiveness Questionnaire*. This questionnaire (or component aspects of it) has had frequent use in sport and physical activity research (e.g., Arnold and Straub, 1972; Ball and Carron, 1976; Carron and Ball, 1977; Landers and Luschen, 1974; Martens and Peterson, 1971; Peterson and Martens, 1972). The specific items are listed in Table 8.1.

The *Sports Cohesiveness Questionnaire* contains seven individual measures: interpersonal attraction; personal power or influence; value of membership; sense of belonging; enjoyment; teamwork; and closeness. These can be classified within three ✓ general categories: measures of *individual to individual* relationships (interpersonal attraction and personal power or influence); measures of the *individual to group relationships* (sense of belonging, value of membership, and enjoyment); and the *group as a unit* (teamwork and closeness). Each of these, with the possible exception of teamwork, measures attraction — either attraction between and among group members or the attractiveness of the group itself.

LIMITATIONS IN THE TRADITIONAL VIEW OF COHESIVENESS

Escovar and Sim (1974) have strongly criticized the use of attraction as a measure of cohesiveness and four major reasons were advanced. The first proposal was that *operational measures of cohesion based upon attraction underrepresent the concept.* In short, there are other forces at work which serve to maintain the individual within the group. These might include among others: *task forces* (the individuals orientation toward group goals); *personal forces* (the expectation of personal payoffs or rewards which would accrue through the group's endeavors); and *normative forces* (the

2.   Landers (Personal Communication, 1979) has endorsed Schachter's third question as a potentially valid method of assessing cohesiveness in the context of sport and physical activity. He observed that "this is what Escovar and Sim concluded was the essence of group cohesion. Some of Lenk's work with socio-drama shows that when oarsmen are asked under simulated stress to give up various values, group loyalty is the last to be given up. One way of measuring this would be to go to school districts that have experienced budget cuts and assess the desire on the part of group members to maintain the group's integrity."

Table 8.1. Cohesion items from the Martens, Landers and Loy (1972) *Sports Cohesiveness Questionnaire.*

ITEM	QUESTION
INTERPERSONAL ATTRACTION	On what type of friendship basis are you with each member of your team
PERSONAL POWER OR INFLUENCE	For many reasons some of the members of a team are more influential than others. How much influence do you believe each of the other members of your team have with the coach and other teammates?
VALUE OF MEMBERSHIP	Compared to other groups that you belong to, how much do you value your membership on this team?
SENSE OF BELONGING	How strong a sense of belonging do you believe you have to this team?
ENJOYMENT	How much do you like competing with this particular team?
TEAMWORK	How good do you think the teamwork is on your team?
CLOSENESS	How closely knit do you think your team is?

cultural, functional and practical reasons why individuals must maintain group membership).

A second reason listed by Escovar and Sim was that *operational definitions of cohesion based upon attraction fail to consider cohesion in situations of negative affect.* That is, the group can be maintained even when there is no interpersonal attraction, when there are extreme levels of hostility among group members (with one example from sport being the previously mentioned German rowing eights studied by Lenk, 1969). There are obviously other significant forces operative which serve to bind the group together.

Escovar and Sim also pointed out that *operational definitions of cohesion based on attraction have often not been supported empirically.* There is correlational evidence (e.g., Carron and Ball, 1977; Eisman, 1959; Gross and Martin, 1952; Rumuz-Nienhuis and Van Bergen, 1960) which suggests that attraction is not a unitary concept and is not the only force binding members to the group.

Carron and Ball (1977) provided some indirect evidence for this view in an athletic context. Twelve intercollegiate ice hockey teams were tested with the *Sports Cohesiveness Questionnaire* in early, mid and post season and the stability of individual differences in the seven measures were examined (see Table 8.2). From one immediate test period to the next, i.e., early season to midseason and midseason to post season, all seven individual measures evidenced a relatively high stability. However, when the early season cohesion measures were correlated with the post

Table 8.2. Intercorrelations for cohesion measures secured in early, mid- and postseason (From Carron and Ball, 1977). Reproduced with permission of the publisher.

COHESION PARAMETER	EARLY SEASON COHESION WITH MIDSEASON COHESION	MIDSEASON COHESION WITH POSTSEASON COHESION	EARLY SEASON COHESION WITH POSTSEASON COHESION
FRIENDSHIP	.784**	.749**	.736**
INFLUENCE	.691**	.728**	.817**
ENJOYMENT	.559 *	.774**	.293
BELONGING	.641 *	.756**	.338
TEAMWORK	.610 *	.849**	.269
CLOSENESS	.756**	.775**	.294
VALUE OF MEMBERSHIP	.621 *	.647**	.554 *
COMPOSITE	.750**	.821**	.372

* p < .05
** p < .01
Note. Composite cohesion is an average of the seven individual measures.

season measures (the values in the third column), only three (friendship, power-influence and value of membership) were of sufficient magnitude to be statistically significant.

In short, individual differences which were present in early season in the two individual to individual measures and the one individual to team measure was not greatly influenced by a season of competition (and the resulting different levels of success of the various teams). Individual differences in these three attraction measures were established early in the season and they remained stable. On the other hand, over the course of that season, individual differences in the degree of enjoyment, sense of belonging, closeness and teamwork changed markedly; there was no stability in these attraction measures. Presumably the different levels of success and failure experienced throughout the season produced marked changes in these measures.

The final reason advanced by Escovar and Sim was that *attraction is not a necessary condition for group formation* Groups may be formed for a number of reasons other than that of attraction. In turn, these other forces and not interpersonal attraction would represent the primary reasons why the group would not be dissolved.

If cohesion, as it relates to performance effectiveness, is the focus (and not merely cohesion as a factor which contributes to the stability of a social group or cohesion as a contributor to the satisfaction of group members), then there is yet another reason why interpersonal attraction as *a* measure or *the* measure of cohesiveness is subject to question (Carron and Chelladurai, 1979). That is, interpersonal attraction as the cohesive force would be associated with the development of cliques within a team which, in turn, would result in less effective performance in those sports which require team coordination.

This has been illustrated in a study with basketball teams. Klein and Christiansen (1969) observed that athletes who liked each other tended to pass to each other to a greater extent than to less-liked teammates. They concluded that "the sociometric structure of the team has an immediate influence upon the communication pathways during the game situation and consequently an indirect influence upon success."

A similar finding was reported by Yaffe (1974) for soccer teams — "players who were friendly with one another passed the ball to each other significantly more than to those with whom they were not friendly, or did not like, or did not know — such as new signings."

Thus, not only does interpersonal attraction seem to (1) underrepresent the concept of cohesion, (2) fail to account for cohesiveness under conditions of negative affect, (3) lack empirical support, and (4) fail to account for group formation, but (5) it also does not account for the improved coordination evident in a team. If "teamwork" is to remain a synonym for cohesiveness, then interpersonal attraction does not seem to be the factor which accounts for improved team play and performance success.

THE ANTECEDENTS OF COHESIVENESS

One general approach used to gain insight into cohesiveness and how it develops has been to determine the underlying *motivational basis or orientation* for group membership and participation. In this regard, one perspective involves focusing on the individual group members' orientation while in a second, the orientation of the group-as-a-unit is the focus.

A second general approach to understanding cohesiveness has been to examine the *process of group formation*. The underlying rationale for this is that "Since a group cannot exist without some degree of cohesion, the process of group formation may also be seen as the formation of cohesion. Thus, the various conditions that lead to group formation are also key determinants of group cohesion" (Donnelly, Carron and Chelladurai, 1978). Each of these approaches is discussed in the sections which follow.

ORIENTATION TOWARD THE GROUP AND GROUP PARTICIPATION

Individual Orientation. A number of authors have emphasized a need to distinguish among the various motives, needs and activities of members within the group. The underlying rationale is that since motives provide both an impetus (force) and focus (direction) to behavior, it should be possible to determine the principle group goals (i.e., the direction) and the relative degree to which these are important (i.e., the force) from an examination of the type and intensity of individual members' orientations. This view was supported by Dunteman and Bass (1963) who suggested that behavior in interpersonal situations is a reflection of inherent personal needs and the types of satisfactions sought. In fact, Bass, Dunteman, Frye, Vidulich and Wambach (1963) have stated that the group is "merely the theatre in which certain generalized needs can be satisfied."

In a related fashion, Homans (1951) differentiated between a *primary system* of activity which is oriented toward the completion of the group task and a *secondary system* which is comprised of the social interactions effected for interpersonal reasons.

A slightly broader perspective was offered by Bass (1963) who suggested that an individual's orientation toward group membership and participation is comprised of three factors: *self, task* and *affiliation (interaction) motivation*. With a self-motive, concern is oriented toward the achievement of direct personal rewards or satisfactions from the group and its activities. The task motive consists of an orientation toward the effective completion of the group task. With an affiliation motivation, the individual is oriented toward the establishment or maintenance of happy harmonious relationships within the group.

Some assessment of the task orientation within the group does seem critical. As Strauss and Sayles (1960) have suggested, cohesion enhances performance/productivity only if the group is motivated toward performance/productivity. A team might be highly cohesive but not perform successfully or to an optimal level if individual members were participating to fulfill an affiliative as opposed to task oriented motive. A number of investigators examining the effect of cohesion upon performance in sport have also incorporated prototype measures of the task and affiliation motives outlined by Bass (e.g., Arnold and Straub, 1972; Ball and Carron, 1976).

Five reasons why individuals join groups were listed by Shaw (1974): namely, *interpersonal attraction* (the individual is attracted to individuals who are in the group and rewarding interaction is anticipated from group membership); *group goals* (the group's goals are perceived as worthwhile and congruent with the individual's goals; the individual views group membership as an opportunity to facilitate the attainment of these goals); *social interaction* (the opportunity to interact with others is enhanced through group membership); the *group activities* (the activities engaged in by the group serve as a source of attraction); and the *instrumental effects of group membership* (the individual joins the group to obtain secondary goals — payoffs or rewards which are not an obvious, inherent function of the group's activities).

It has been suggested (Carron and Chelladurai, 1979) that the varied needs individuals bring to the group result in the development of both task and socially oriented forces to remain in the group.[3] If the affiliative forces are predominant, clique development occurs and the result is performance decrement. On the other hand, if task forces are predominant, the result is the development of a coalition of maximum resources among the group members (see Chapter 7). That is, if the primary orientation of group members is toward the group goals and task performance and/or personal goals and rewards (a task and self motivation respectively), then the maximum payoff or reward can only be achieved through cooperation and a coordination of the best talents and skills available. Individual group members effect this cooperation and coordination through the development of coalitions. It is these coalitions which are the cohesive force underlying effective performance.

3. There are also the normative forces discussed earlier. However, it could be assumed that their effects are relatively constant across teams at the same level of competition. Therefore, they are not an important factor insofar as their contribution to performance effectiveness is concerned.

Group Orientation. It was pointed out previously, that an alternative to viewing the group as a sum of its individual parts — the sum of the individuals' needs, motives, skills etc. — is to view it as an interdependent entity. Shaw (1974) aptly summarized this view when he noted that a group is "different from the sum of its parts. An individual behaves differently in a group situation because he is experiencing a different set of stimuli." These stimuli are specific to the group context — they do not exist in nongroup situations.

Thus, an alternate strategy to focusing on the individuals' orientation is to emphasize the group's orientation. This was the perspective adopted by Alvin Zander — the foundation of his approach was outlined in the previous chapter (see Table 7.1).

The two motives postulated for task performing groups were the *desire for group success* and the *desire to avoid group failure*. The former is, of course, the group members' disposition to experience, pride and satisfaction in the group if it is successful in accomplishing its task; it contributes to the tendency to approach a task with interest and the intention of performing well. Similarly, the latter is the group members' disposition to experience embarrassment and dissatisfaction with the group if it is unsuccessful and fails in accomplishing its task; it contributes to an inclination to have the group resist engaging in the task.

Direct relationships were proposed by Zander between the desire for group success, group cohesiveness and the group's performance success. That is, it was hypothesized that groups with a stronger desire for group success would perform better than groups with a weaker desire for group success. Also, it was proposed that this desire for group success is more strongly aroused in a strong group than in a weak group where "a *strong* group is one of high unity (members are aware it is a group) and high cohesiveness (members are attracted to the group); a *weak* group is one of low unity and low cohesiveness" (Zander, 1971). To date, there have not been any studies carried out in a sport context which have utilized the 'group orientation' approach and examined the question of the effects of group cohesiveness upon performance.

THE PROCESS OF GROUP FORMATION[4]

Groups may be formed for a wide variety of reasons and, as suggested earlier, this gives some insight into their cohesiveness — the forces attracting and binding individuals to the group. Cartwright and Zander (1968) outlined three general ways in which groups are formed: *deliberately, spontaneously* and, as a result of *ascription or external designation*.

Groups may be deliberately formed in the belief that objectives can be achieved and purposes accomplished more efficiently in a group then they could by one or more individuals working alone. Cartwright and Zander identified six general types of deliberately formed groups: work groups; problem solving groups; social action groups; mediating groups; legislative groups; and client groups. The specific description for each is presented in Table 8.3.

Examples of all of these types of deliberately formed groups may be found in sport and such groups tend to achieve varying degrees of success. The success of deliberate-

4.   The material in this section has been taken directly from Donnelly, Carron and Chelladurai, (1978).

Table 8.3. Types of deliberately-formed groups (Adapted from Cartwright and Zander, 1968).

GROUP	DESCRIPTION
WORK GROUPS	The objective in forming a work group is to perform some task more efficiently through the pooling and coordination of the behavior and resources of a collection of individuals.
PROBLEM-SOLVING GROUPS	The underlying rationale for the formation of a problem-solving group is the belief that the solution to a problem will be attained more efficiently, inappropriate strategies discarded more quickly and appropriate strategies adopted more readily when a collection of people work together than when the problem is assigned to a single individual or several groups working independently.
SOCIAL-ACTION GROUPS	Social-action groups are formed in order to exert pressure and influence in an attempt to have an impact upon the course of events in society.
MEDIATING GROUPS	Mediating groups are created for the purpose of coordinating the activities of other groups, distributing the resources among them, or reconciling conflicting interests.
LEGISLATIVE GROUPS	Behavior is governed in society by rules, regulations, laws, or policies set up by the decisions of groups whose basic purpose is to formulate such legislation.
CLIENT GROUPS	The purpose of client groups is to "improve" the members of the group in some way. The creation of client groups by a social agency rests on the assumption that the performance of such services is more effective or efficient if the "clients" are treated as groups rather than individuals.

ly formed groups will depend in part on the degree and type of cohesion that is generated within the group. A group may be disbanded before its purpose is achieved if it suffers from a lack of cohesion or if its purpose proves too difficult to achieve. Other groups may disband once the task is achieved because they were instrumentally cohesive — once the task is completed the group lacks purpose and ceases to be cohesive. Groups that achieve a high degree of interpersonal cohesion may continue to exist once their instrumental purpose is achieved or deliberately prolong the task in order to remain together as long as possible.

Spontaneously formed groups may be quite different in nature from deliberately formed groups. They exist because they primarily serve the needs of members rather than the needs of some external agency. Membership is voluntary and may be short-lived (as is the case of individuals who come together for pick-up basketball games) or longlasting (as is the case of some friendship groups). Cartwright and Zander (1968) noted that:

> . . . since the formation is based on voluntary interpersonal choices, the group's composition is deter-mined by processes of mutual consent — each member wants to be in the relationship and each is accepted, or at least is not rejected, by the others. Such groups are often quite informal, with shifting boundaries and few explicit goals or tasks, but they may develop a stable structure, take on certain tasks, and even acquire recognized legal status, as illustrated by a family established through mar-riage as the result of courtship.

Cliques, juvenile gangs and subcultures associated with new sports, activities or in-terests are all examples of spontaneously formed groups.

A number of factors may contribute to the spontaneous formation of groups. The most basic condition is *geographical* or *physical proximity* since people need some degree of interpersonal contact in order for groups to develop. Festinger, Schachter and Back (1950) provided a particularly striking example of this process in their study of friendship groups in a housing project.

Another condition for spontaneous group formation is the *assumed similarity bet-ween individuals*. Heider (1958) proposed that individuals will be attracted to each other if they believe that they are similar, particularly in terms of their attitudes and values. Newcomb (1961) found empirical support for this proposition and found that the greater the similarities, the stronger the attraction, especially if the values and at-titudes are believed to be important.

Thibaut and Kelley (1959) have suggested that people join or form groups only after weighing the advantages and costs that may result from the membership. The groups that occur are then judged sufficiently appealing because of *mutual advantages*. Festinger's (1954) social comparison theory suggests that people tend to form groups in order to *confirm and obtain support for their view of social reality* — that groups function in order to relieve uncertainty. Two major themes in the theoretical work on the formation of subcultures are also relevant here. The first views subcultures as resulting from specific environmental conditions or problems with the subculture emerging as a response to the situation. Schachter (1959) provided support for this view when he found that people in stressful situations showed a desire to affiliate with others in the same situation. The second theme views subcultures as resulting from in-teraction or differential association. People who are thrust together because of their particular life circumstances will tend to form groups or subcultures.

Groups that are formed as a result of ascription or external designation are, in a sense, an example of the self-fulfilling prophecy. Since certain people are generally considered to be similar on the basis of some obvious characteristic such as a handicap or skin color, they may come together to form groups, although there are usually addi-tional factors associated with their group formation. In other cases, the externally designated group may only exist in the public mind and not in actuality. Such characteristics as age, sex, or occupation may form the basis for this type of group.

CONSEQUENCES OF THE COHESION-PERFORMANCE RELATIONSHIP

PERFORMANCE

The results of studies which have examined the effect of cohesion upon performance have not been consistent. For example, using the *Sports Cohesiveness Questionnaire* (see Table 8.1 again), Ball and Carron (1976) found that successful intercollegiate ice hockey teams were more cohesive as indicated through the teamwork, closeness and enjoyment measures. Martens and Peterson (1971) reported that successful intramural basketball teams showed greater cohesiveness in terms of the teamwork, closeness and value of membership measures. Similarly, Arnold and Straub (1972) found that intercollegiate basketball teams that were successful had greater cohesiveness as reflected in the teamwork and closeness measures. Vos and Brinkman (1967) and Bird (1977a, 1977b) with volleyball teams, Klein and Christiansen (1969) with basketball teams, and Landers and Crum (1971) with baseball teams also reported positive effects for performance and cohesion.

On the other hand, a number of authors have reported a negative relationship. Lenk's (1969) report on the German rowing team is one example, McGrath's (1962) research with rifle teams another, and a study with intramural bowling teams reported by Landers and Luschen (1974) yet another; unsuccessful bowling teams showed significantly greater interpersonal attraction than did successful teams.

One factor which has been forwarded to reconcile these divergent findings is the parameter — *task structure and demands*. Landers and Luschen (1974) provided an overview of the general rationale when they observed that:

> . . . investigators have restricted their investigations to teams within a given sport, but have at times stated their conclusions as if to encompass different types of competitive team sports. To do this is to overlook the task structure of differing sports as well as processes whereby members' adapt in patterned ways to differing task-imposed demands. Without the elucidation of important task requirements among differing team sports, the generality of findings as well as the perusal of scientific explanations is greatly curtailed.

The task dimension proposed by Landers and Luschen in their study was *coacting* versus *interacting* with the critical difference between them being the *rate of interaction* among team members. That is, in interacting teams, the total group effort is a product of teamwork — a combining of the various specialized skills of individual team members through interdependent action — in short, a condition sometimes referred to as *high means-interdependence* (Thomas, 1957) is present. On the other hand, in the coacting situation, the group product is achieved via a simple summation of individual group members' efforts — a condition of *low means-interdependence*.

Historically, the underlying dynamics which have been studied in conjunction with task means-interdependence have been intergroup and intragroup competition and cooperation.

In their review of the early research concerned with task structure, competition and cooperation, Miller and Hamblin (1963) observed that performance was more effective for intragroup cooperation (as opposed to intragroup competition) in all of the experiments in which high means-interdependent tasks were utilized. However, when low means interdependent tasks were utilized, performance was better in 14 out of 18 studies for intragroup competition (as opposed to intragroup cooperation). These results (which were also discussed under the category of competition versus competition in the last chapter; are in the same direction as the findings for the sport cohesion research outlined above. In short, if the nature of the task is taken into account, the apparent discrepancy which exists in published research on the cohesion-performance question disappears.

A task model which outlines the specific instances in which cohesiveness should contribute to performance effectiveness (in the context of sport and physical activity) was presented by Carron and Chelladurai (1979). Their model was developed and presented through a series of sequential propositions.

The first proposition, which concerned the degree to which group members *must* engage in coordinative activity, stated that *a distinction must be made between the group members' social interactions and those interactions necessitated by the demands of the task*. That is, in any group activity, there are interpersonal interactions of a performance nature and interpersonal interactions of a social nature. It was emphasized that insofar as the interactive effects of task dimension/cohesiveness/performance are concerned, interdependence should be viewed as an interaction required by the dictates of the task (e.g., to solve a problem, exchange task relevant information, carry out an assignment). The principal concern in cohesiveness research is with task interdependence.

The second proposition was that *specific sports should be differentiated on the basis of the degree of performance interdependence required from participants*. That is, the degree of interdependence required in different sports can be determined by referring to the rules of the sport. Insofar as the rules provide for a recognition and rewarding of individual performance and permit overt competition between individuals from the same group/team, individuals must be viewed as engaging in independent tasks. The *ad hoc* groupings of individual participants into "teams" (e.g., rifle shooting, wrestling, track and field, bowling) do not possess a qualifying characteristic of inherent required interaction among group members. Consequently, the question of cohesion and its relationship to performance success is irrelevant.

The third proposition was that *task interdependence in sport may be classified into four types: independence; coactive dependence; reactive-proactive dependence; and interactive dependence*. The definition and examples for each of these is outlined in Table 8.4.

The fourth proposition was that *the type of coordination required for successful performance is a function of the degree of task interdependence*. Thompson (1967) proposed that there are three general types of coordination procedures which can be utilized in a group situation: *standardization, planning* and *mutual adjustment*. A definition for each of these is presented in Table 8.5. It was proposed by Carron and Chelladurai that the tasks of individual team members in interactively dependent sports must be coordinated through mutual adjustment and planning with the most prevalent mode for effecting coordination being the former.

In proactive-reactive dependent tasks, coordination can be again achieved through mutual adjustment and planning but the most frequently utilized mode is planning. For example, a quarterback and pass receiver may practice specific pass routes prior to

Table 8.4. A schema for task interdependence in sport and physical activity (Adapted from Carron and Chelladurai, 1979).

CATEGORY	DEFINITION	EXAMPLES
INDEPENDENCE	Coordinative action between individuals is not required for performance success; there is direct, overt competition between individuals or units representing a school or institution; individual performance is directly and officially assessed, recognized and rewarded.	Bowling, archery, rifle shooting, individual track and field events, individual swimming events.
COACTIVE DEPENDENCE	Individual participants are dependent on a common but external source for initiation and control of their actions rather than on each other; members perform similar tasks simultaneously; a collective performance contributes directly to team effectiveness.	Rowing, tug-of-war.
REACTIVE-PRO-ACTIVE DEPENDENCE	*Proactive Dependence* — one member initiates the action but must depend on others to complete the action. *Reactive Dependence* — the individual must wait for the completion of the task of other positions in order to perform and complete his task.	Football quarterback, baseball pitcher. Football pass receiver, baseball catcher.
INTERACTIVE DEPENDENCE	Members are mutually dependent on each other; there are two way interactions between any two members; continuous interaction between members enhances the opportunity for team success.	Basketball, hockey, soccer.

Table 8.5. Types of coordinative procedures (Adapted from Thompson, 1967).

CATEGORY	DESCRIPTION
COORDINATION BY STANDARDIZATION	A set of rules, regulations, routines is developed which constrain, regularize or limit the actions of individual members. As a result, these actions are synchronized so that they are consistent with those taken by other members within the unit.
COORDINATION BY PLANNING	A set of schedules, objectives, plans-for-action are developed which relate to the performance expectations of group members within the unit.
COORDINATION BY MUTUAL ADJUSTMENT	Preestablished decision rules and plans cannot be developed because of the fluctuating performance demands within the task. Therefore, coordination is achieved through reciprocal adjustments among group members.

competition (i.e., coordination through planning) but during the game mutual adjustments must be made to adapt to differences in pass coverage and pass rush pressures by the defense.

The coordination necessary in coactively dependent tasks can be achieved largely through standardization although some planning may be involved.

Finally, sports involving independent tasks cannot be considered team sports and the issue of coordination is largely irrelevant. However, to the extent that precompetition decisions are required regarding the order in which individuals will compete or the events to which individuals are assigned, coordination is effected by standardization. A summary of this relationship between task interdependence and coordination is presented in Figure 8.2.

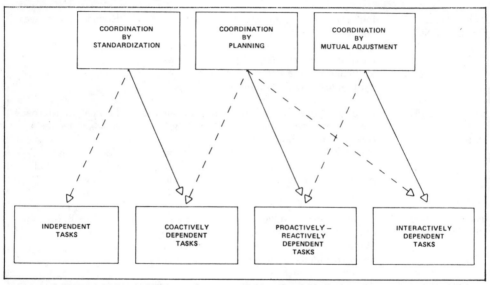

Figure 8.2. The relationship of various methods of achieving coordinative activity to tasks with varying degrees of required performance interdependence. The heavy solid line represents the predominant method utilized (From Carron and Chelladurai, 1979). Reproduced with permission of the publisher.

The final proposition was that *the degree of cohesiveness present in dependent, coactively dependent and proactively-reactively dependent tasks is unrelated to performance success. In tasks requiring interactive dependence, cohesiveness contributes to improved coordination which, in turn, leads to improved performance.* That is, the point emphasized here is that the type of coordination required dictates the extent to which cohesiveness is a factor in performance success. If cohesion is conceptually linked to sport by facilitating effective performance interaction between team members, then the relationship is only applicable in those sports where member initiated interaction and coordination are predominant factors in successful performance. Thus, the level of cohesiveness is irrelevant to performance success in independent and coactively dependent tasks, only minimally involved in proactively-reactively dependent tasks but a major factor in interactively dependent tasks. In fact, the Lenk study with rowing teams (coactively dependent task) and the Landers and Crum study with bowling teams (independent task) show that conflict or tension may be beneficial to performance success. Further, the studies which have shown that cohesion is related to performance have generally involved tasks which are interactively dependent.

In short, and as an overview or summary statement "various sports differ in the degree to which task interdependence is required of participants; the degree of task interdependence present affects the type of coordination necessary; and, the type of coordination necessary affects the degree to which group cohesiveness is a mandatory factor in performance outcome" (Carron and Chelladurai, 1979).

GROUP STABILITY

Whether cohesion is defined as a resistance of the group to disruptive forces or as the forces that attract/bind individuals to the group, one logical consequence of greater cohesiveness should be that group members are more disposed to retain their membership in that group. As Cartwright (1968) hypothesized "if the restraints against leaving are sufficiently weak, the rate of turnover of membership for a group will be negatively correlated with the group's attractiveness and positively correlated with the attractiveness of alternate memberships."

There is some difficulty in testing these hypotheses in the context of organized sport and physical activity. On one hand, normative forces — contracts, transfer rules, etc. — serve to constrain participants (if the athlete wants to compete) within the team irrespective of the team's level of cohesiveness. On the other hand, the eligibility requirements in age group and scholastic competition insures that there is a consistent turnover of group members, again irrespective of the team's level of cohesiveness.

There is some evidence to suggest that team constancy or stability is related to performance success. For example, Essing (1970), in an analysis of 18 soccer teams, obtained correlations of .62, .58 and .47 between team line-up and efficiency, average constant participation by players and team success and the non-use of newly acquired players and team success respectively. Similarly, Viet (1970) also reported that poorer soccer teams made more frequent changes in playing personnel than successful teams. From a slightly different perspective, Ball and Carron (1976) noted that the most effective variable discriminating between successful, moderately successful and unsuccessful intercollegiate ice hockey teams was years of experience in the league.

A note of caution should be interjected though. Despite the findings of Essing, Viet, and Ball and Carron, there is no basis for assuming that cohesiveness was the mediating factor between team stability and team success. It could well be that other factors associated with stability such as having a better general knowledge of the team's system, being more familiar with teammates' skills and capabilities and/or non-participative contingencies such as being settled into and comfortable with the community at large all contribute to a more effective performance.

In addition, another explanation is possible — that it is not stability which causes success but rather a lack of success which causes instability. As Zander (1976) pointed out "poorly performing organizations typically release more members than do organizations that are succeeding — this is demonstrated at the end of a professional sports season when losing teams rid themselves of managers and players, while winning teams leave well enough alone." Thus, in overview, in sport and physical activity, team stability does seem to be related to performance success.

Whether stability contributes to team success or team success contributes to stability (or, the more likely possibility — their relationship is circular) is not clear. Further, although it does seem reasonable that "the longer a team stays together, the more opportunity there will be for cohesiveness to develop" (Donnelly, Carron, Chelladurai, 1978), there is certainly no direct evidence to suggest that team stability results from an increased cohesiveness among team members. Unfortunately, while these overview statements are too open-ended to be of value, the problem is as Zander (1976) stated; namely, that while "the removal of group members and the recruiting of new ones are central processes in the maintenance of a group . . . they receive little study."

Zander (1976) did present a series of propositions and hypotheses dealing with recruitment and removal of group members and some of these are directly applicable to the issue of cohesiveness. For example, it was proposed that as the cohesiveness of a group increases, the tendency to remove unattractive members is stronger. With a strong sense of group unity and integrity, a group becomes more sensitive to the potential threat that unattractive individuals represent. Conversely, groups low in cohesion are more tolerant of unattractive group members.

However, Zander also proposed that the tendency to remove an unattractive member decreases if the removal is potentially harmful to the group itself (i.e., by producing conflict between the individual's supporters and those who wish to remove him from the group) or if the removal decreases valued contributions made to the group. In the latter instance an individual is said to have *idiosyncrasy credit* (Hollander, 1960) if his differences or the reasons for unattractiveness to the group are permitted because of valuable contributions made.

Another aspect of group maintenance is the case of voluntary departures. The "individual resigns when he is not appreciated, recognized, or provided satisfaction by his group" (Zander, 1976). Voluntary departures are, of course, also a predominant feature of sport and physical activity (Orlick, 1973; Orlick and Botterill, 1975). This issue was discussed in the previous chapter. One reason noted by Orlick (1973) was that "for the majority of the children the goals and rewards in terms of positive outcomes are consistently out of reach." Pease, Locke and Burlingame (1971), in contrasting the cutting versus quitting process in athletics (i.e., athletes being "removed" by the coach or "voluntarily departing"), found that incompatibility between the athlete and coach (as assessed through Schutz's (1958) *Fundamental Interpersonal Relations Orientation − Behavior − FIRO − B*) is a factor in the latter instance but not the former.

SATISFACTION

In the context of industrial and management science, considerable attention has been directed toward *satisfaction*, a factor which is somewhat related to cohesion. For example, one similarity lies in the circular nature of the satisfaction and performance relationship: in a manner similar to cohesion-performance, satisfaction may be a cause or an effect of performance (Sheridan and Slocum, 1975).

Another similarity is that both cohesion and satisfaction may be interrelated to performance in a circular fashion. For example, Martens and Peterson (1971) found that teams that were more cohesive were more successful and, in turn, the more successful teams expressed greater satisfaction with participation. It was proposed that a consequence of this satisfaction is increased cohesiveness (see Figure 8.3).

What is more important, however, (at least from the point of view of the present discussion), is their difference. That is, while cohesiveness is conceptually viewed as a *group* property, satisfaction has usually been considered from the perspective of the

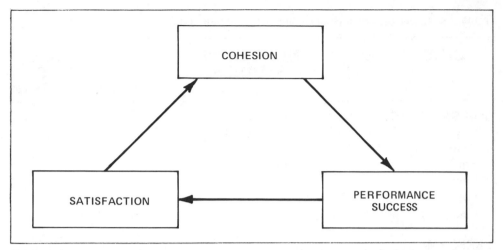

Figure 8.3. The circular relationship between cohesion, success and satisfaction (Adapted from Martens & Peterson, 1971).

individual within an organization; e.g., what factors contribute to employee productivity and satisfaction?

When the relationship between satisfaction and stability is examined within this framework, research has shown that there is either minimal or no correlation between satisfaction and stability measures such as absenteeism or personnel turnover (e.g., Hackman and Oldham, 1976, Oldham, 1976).

A slightly different perspective concerns the relationship of job involvement to satisfaction where job involvement is a commitment to the organizational task, an involvement with work roles and performance. As such, job involvement is similar to task motivation which was discussed earlier. In their analysis of the available research, Rabinowitz and Hall (1977) noted that only minimal relationships have been reported between stability (i.e., absenteeism and turnover) and job involvement. A summary is presented in Table 8.6. Not surprisingly, one of the conclusions arising from their review was that "much of the variance in job involvement remains unexplained" (Rabinowtiz and Hall, 1977).

From a sport perspective, the effect of task and affiliation motivation upon success and satisfaction in intramural basketball teams was examined by Martens (1970). He found that those teams high in task motivation were more successful and more satisfied than were teams low in task motivation. Moreover, teams high in affiliation were not as successful but were more satisfied with team performance than were teams low in affiliation motivation.

Carron, Ball and Chelladurai (1977) also examined the effects of individual orientation (task, self and affiliation motivation) and team success in intercollegiate hockey upon satisfaction with individual and team performance. Differences in success and individual orientation did not have any effect upon the level of satisfaction expressed with individual performance. However, in a finding consistent with that reported by Martens (1970), team success for individuals with increased levels of task motivation led to heightened levels of satisfaction with team performance.

Table 8.6. Correlates of job involvement (Adapted from Rabinowitz and Hall, 1977).

CORRELATES	NUMBER OF STUDIES	APPROXIMATE MAGNITUDE OF RELATIONSHIP
JOB SATISFACTION		
Work	3	.40
Promotion	3	.30
Supervision	3	.35
People	3	.35
Pay	3	.15
Company	1	.40
PERFORMANCE	7	0
ABSENTEEISM	2	0 and .45
TURNOVER	4	.25
SUCCESS	2	+

Note. When correlations were not reported in the literature +, -, or 0 are used to indicate the relationship found.

CIRCULAR ASPECTS OF THE COHESION-PERFORMANCE RELATIONSHIP

An additional aspect of the influence that cohesiveness has upon performance is the impact that performance success has upon cohesiveness. That is, while increased cohesiveness leads to a more effective performance, one consequence of that improved performance is heightened cohesiveness. As indicated earlier, Martens and Peterson (1970) have suggested that this circular relationship is mediated through the factor of satisfaction (see Figure 8.3 again).

An issue which has not received a great deal of research attention in sport is the question "What is the stronger relationship — cohesion leading to performance success or performance success leading to cohesiveness?" It is difficult to answer this question with certainty with any research design since the research's initial observations can never represent the subjects' first experiences together. However, a statistical analysis which does permit strong causal inferences is a longitudinal cross-legged correlation procedure. In order to carry out this analysis, paired serial data for each of the variables is required. The correlations between each of the various variables is then computed. In Figure 8.4, an example is presented in schematic illustration. The correlations r_1 and r_2 represent the test-retest reliabilities for cohesion and performance respectively. The correlations r_3 and r_4 represent the concurrent relationship between performance and cohesion. Finally, the correlation r_5 represents a lead cohesion performance relationship while r_6 represents a lagged performance cohesion relationship. Through a comparison of the magnitude of these correlations — particularly r_5 versus

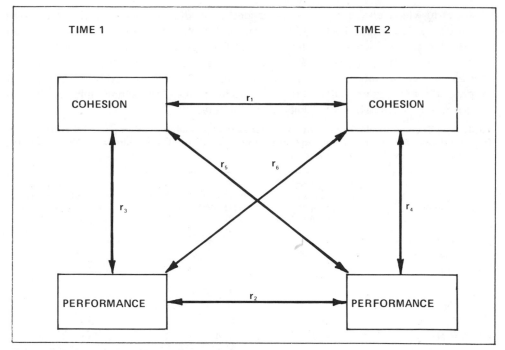

Figure 8.4. A cross-lagged correlation design.

r_6 — it is possible to make inferences on the direction of causality.

Bakeman and Helmreich (1975) used this approach in an excellent, well designed study. Ten teams of aquanauts were observed continually for 182 consecutive days while living and working in an underwater habitat. On the basis of the results, the authors concluded that a stronger case could be made for performance causing cohesiveness than for cohesiveness causing performance success.

However, the applicability of the Bakeman and Helmreich findings for sport and physical activity is questionable for at least three reasons (Carron and Ball, 1977). One is that the isolated, restricted, highly structured working and living environment utilized, coupled with the length of time spent in that situation represents an unique experimental situation, unrelated to anything in sport.

Also, cohesion was defined as the time members of an aquanaut team engaged in conversation during their leisure time. The nature of the experimental environment coupled with the fact that the aquanauts were under continual observation provided for this unique behavioral assessment of cohesion. It would be literally impossible to obtain an equivalent measure with most sport teams but even if it were possible, it is doubtful that the social-interpersonal measure of "time engaged in conversation" could be linked conceptually with performance effectiveness.

A third reason is the Bakeman-Helmreich operational definition used for performance; namely, the percentage of time engaged in work relative to the total time under observation. As Bakeman and Helmreich pointed out, there is a possibility that this measure "taps not performance, but something far simpler, more plodding, and more mundane — the passage of time accompanied by the motions of work." In port, the assessment of performance is not only easier to obtain for a sport team, it is also more objective.

A study which also used the cross-lagged procedure but in a sport context was reported by Carron and Ball (1977). Some of the findings from this study have been outlined in earlier discussions in this chapter. The *Sports Cohesiveness Questionnaire* was administered to intercollegiate hockey teams in early mid and post season. The correlations comparable to the value r_5 of Figure 8.4 are presented in Table 8.7. It is apparent from an examination of the magnitude of these values that the lead cohesion performance relationship is negligible in these data.

Table 8.7. Pearson product-moment correlations (r_{12}) and second order partial@ correlations ($r_{12.3}$) between cohesion and subsequent performance (From Carron and Ball, 1977). Reproduced with permission of the publisher.

COHESION PARAMETER	EARLY SEASON COHESION WITH MIDSEASON PERFORMANCE	MIDSEASON COHESION WITH POST SEASON PERFORMANCE		EARLY SEASON COHESION WITH POST SEASON PERFORMANCE	
	r_{12}	r_{12}	$r_{12.3}$	r_{12}	$r_{12.3}$
FRIENDSHIP	.135	.187	.239	.304	.329
INFLUENCE	-.063	.329	.262	.165	.359
ENJOYMENT	-.194	-.479	.101	.107	.444
BELONGING	-.049	-.248	.116	.028	.112
TEAMWORK	-.464	-.643*	-.136	-.002	.692*
CLOSENESS	-.277	-.434	.034	.073	.511
VALUE OF MEMBERSHIP	-.185	-.116	-.101	.149	-.002
COMPOSITE	-.225	-.391	.056	.072	.431

* $p < .05$

@ The effect of the concurrent performance level was partialed out.

Three sets of correlations were presented to test the performance-cohesion relationship. These are the equivalent of r_3, r_4 and r_6 of Figure 8.4. However, it was noted that "intuitively, the latter would seem to be the most adequate of the three . . . to test the hypothesis" (Carron and Ball, 1977). These correlations are presented in Table 8.8. With the exception of the measures of friendship, influence and value of membership, significant correlations were obtained between performance and the subsequent measures of cohesiveness.

An overview of the results in general is presented in Figure 8.5 using the values for *composite cohesion* (the average of the seven individual measures). This overview simply adds support to a conclusion that the performance-cohesion relationship is considerably stronger than the cohesion-performance relationship.

A final qualifying note which seems appropriate, concerns the relevance of the Carron and Ball findings (and for that matter, the Bakeman and Helmreich findings) to cohesion as a construct representing improved teamwork, unity and coordinative performance. The items in the *Sports Cohesiveness Questionnaire* (with the possible exception of 'teamwork') assess attraction — the interpersonal attraction of individuals to other competitors, the attraction of individuals to the group and the general attractiveness of the group itself. *It does not reflect a task oriented cohesiveness, a cohesiveness represented in enhanced coordination within the group.* Thus, the Carron-Ball and Blakeman-Helmreich conclusions could be paraphrased to read "There

Table 8.8 Pearson product moment correlations (r_{12}) and second-order partial@ correlations ($r_{12.3}$) between performance and subsequent cohesiveness (From Carron and Ball, 1977). Reproduced with permission of the publisher.

COHESION PARAMETER	MIDSEASON PERFORMANCE WITH MIDSEASON COHESION		MIDSEASON PERFORMANCE WITH POSTSEASON COHESION		POSTSEASON PERFORMANCE WITH POSTSEASON COHESION	
	r_{12}	$r_{12.3}$	r_{12}	$r_{12.3}$	r_{12}	$r_{12.3}$
FRIENDSHIP	.054	-.085	-.274	-.475	-.026	-.254
INFLUENCE	.220	.365	-.335	-.740**	-.154	-.608 *
ENJOYMENT	-.657**	-.674**	-.773**	-.553 *	-.815**	-.798**
BELONGING	-.391	-.468	-.721**	-.706**	-.727**	-.851**
TEAMWORK	-.736**	-.645 *	-.799**	-.489	-.875**	-.814**
CLOSENESS	-.564 *	-.563 *	-.600 *	-.313	-.679**	-.602 *
VALUE OF MEMBERSHIP	-.069	.058	-.490	-.585 *	-.634**	-.738**
COMPOSITE	-.528 *	-.556 *	-.770**	-.694**	-.790**	-.900**

Note. The negative signs associated with the correlation coefficients reflect the nature of the scales used. More successful performance was indicated by a larger percentage but greater cohesiveness was indicated through lower scores.

@ The effect of the concurrent cohesion was partialed out.

* $p < .05$

** $p < .01$

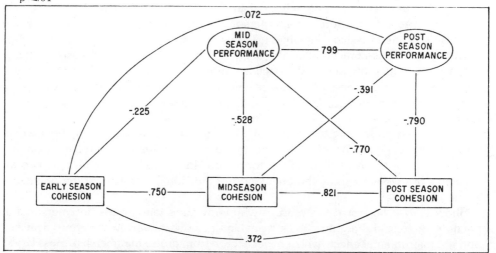

Figure 8.5. Cross-lagged correlations for cohesiveness and performance success in ice hockey. (From Carron and Ball, 1977). Reproduced with permission of the publisher.

is strong support for a conclusion that the level of performance success experienced by the group contributes to an increased attractiveness of that group. There is minimal evidence to suggest that the degree to which a group is found attractive contributes to increased performance success."

What this best highlights is the need to establish what underlying processes the term *cohesion* is thought to represent within sport and physical activity. To date, the only position, one which has been implicitly adopted via the measures of cohesion used, has been the traditional viewpoint that cohesion reflects attraction.

SUMMARY

Cohesion is a complex construct which may be viewed as a dependent variable (i.e., as an *effect*, as for example in the effect of performance success upon cohesiveness) and as an independent variable (i.e., as a *cause*, as for example, in the effect of cohesiveness upon performance success). In addition, it may be viewed as a component variable within a circular system.

As the adhesive property of groups, the force which unites a group, cohesion has been defined in two conceptually different ways: as *the total field of forces which bind members to the group;* and as *the resistance by the group to disruptive forces.* Traditionally, the definition which has received the greatest endorsement has been the former — the total field of forces approach. However, a number of criticisms have been leveled at this approach.

One criticism has been that it focuses on the individual as the unit of reference/analysis rather than on the group itself A second concerns the generality of the definition and the resultant difficulty in converting it into operational terms. Yet a third has been the relatively restricted manner in which cohesion has usually been operationalized by proponents of this definition; namely, as attraction.

Five traditional approaches have been used to measure cohesiveness: the degree of interpersonal attraction among group members, the attractiveness of the group as a whole, the expressed desire to remain in the group, the level of closeness or identification with the group and composite indices which have utilized all of these. This latter technique has been the approach used in the *Sports Cohesiveness Questionnaire* which incorporates measures of interpersonal attraction, influence, sense of belonging, value of membership, enjoyment, teamwork, and closeness.

Cohesiveness-as-attraction has also been subject to criticisms. The reasons advanced have been that interpersonal attraction underrepresents the concept of cohesion; fails to account for cohesiveness under conditions of negative affect; lacks empirical support; and does not account for the improved coordination/teamwork evident in sport.

The process underlying the development of group cohesiveness may be analyzed through the examination of either the motivational bases for group membership-participation or the process of group formation. In the case of the former, two approaches are possible: using the orientation of individual members or the orientation of the group itself.

Shaw (1974) has listed five reasons why individuals join groups: interpersonal attraction, interest in the group goals, social interaction, interest in the group activities, and the instrumental effects which might accrue from group membership. Bass (1963) proposed that three underlying motives for group participation are a task, self and affiliation orientation.

It has been proposed that the forces binding a sport team together are of a task, social and normative nature. The task forces (which evolve from task and self-motives) result in the development of coalitions of maximum resources among group participants which lead to enhanced coordination and a more effective performance. The affiliative forces, on the other hand, lead to the development of cliques which can have a deleterious effect upon performance.

Two group motives have been suggested: the desire for group success and the desire to avoid group failure. It has been hypothesized that groups with a stronger desire for group success perform better than groups with a weaker desire for group success. Also, the desire for group success is more strongly aroused in strong groups (i.e., groups with high unity and cohesiveness) than in weak groups.

Groups may be formed deliberately, spontaneously and as a result of ascription or external designation. Deliberately formed groups may be of six types: work groups, problem solving groups, social action groups, mediating groups, legislative groups, and client groups.

One of the consequences of group cohesiveness which has been examined is its effect upon performance. While the results from research in sport and physical activity have been equivocal, it has been proposed that this equivocation can be resolved if the task dimension is taken into account. That is, different sports differ in the degree to which task interdependence or coordinative activity is required among participants. The degree of task interdependence present effects whether coordination can be achieved through the standardization of performance, by planning prior to the actual competition or must be effected through mutual adjustments by teammates during the competition itself. In turn, the type of coordination necessary effects the extent to which group cohesiveness is a mandatory factor in performance outcome.

Another proposed consequence of cohesion is group stability. Stability has been linked with performance success in athletics. However, there is no basis for concluding whether this success is a result of the increased cohesiveness in stable teams or is due to other factors accruing with stability such as a greater familiarity with the team system.

When the cause-effect nature of the cohesion-performance relationship has been explored, results have led to a conclusion that there is stronger support for the conclusion that performance results in heightened cohesion and not that cohesion leads to improved performance.

SECTION V
THE SPECTATOR

The most beautiful sight in the world is that ball fading through the net, then the sudden silence. It's like taking on 15,000 people at once and beating them all.

Calvin Murphy

I don't like watching golf on television — I can't stand whispering.

Dave Brenner

SOCIAL FACILITATION   9

The pioneer work in the area of social psychology had its origins in a sport context. As Zajonc (1965) noted, the most fundamental form of social influence is "represented by the oldest experimental paradigm of social psychology: social facilitation. This paradigm, dating back to Triplett's original experiments on pacing and competition, carried out in 1897 ... examines the consequences upon behavior which derive from the sheer presence of other individuals."[1]

Triplett (1897), using official data from the Racing Board of the League of American Wheelman, compared cycling times under three conditions: *unpaced* (the cyclist raced alone against time); *paced* (the cyclist raced alone against time but in conjunction with a "pacer"—a tandem bicycle manned by 3-4 confederates); and *paced competition* (the cyclist raced against another competitor but both cyclists were paced).

Triplett noted that the *paced competition* condition and the *paced* condition were 39.55 sec./mile and 34.4 sec./mile faster respectively than the *unpaced* condition. Thus, Triplett found that the presence of others does have a dramatic influence upon performance. When this presence is in the form of a passive audience and/or other performers, the resulting effect has come to be known as *social facilitation*.

DEFINITIONS AND EXPERIMENTAL PARADIGMS

The actual origin of the term *social facilitation* evolved from Allport's (1924) research with coactive groups and the subsequent discussion of his results. Coaction is represented by a situation in which two or more individuals are working simultaneously, but independently, on the same task. Illustrative of this would be the sports of archery and rifle shooting. Allport did note that the presence of others in the form of coactors resulted in performance improvements. He referred to the effect as social facilitation which he defined as "an increase of response merely from the sight or

---

1. Actually, Triplett (1897) noted that, earlier, another cycling enthusiast named Edward Turner had reported differences in elapsed time for paced and unpaced cycling events.

sounds of others making the same movement."

A slightly different perspective was suggested more recently by Zajonc (1965) and this perspective is contained in his quote presented above. That is, social facilitation was viewed by Zajonc (1965) as "the consequences upon behavior which derive from the sheer presence of other individuals."

Two important developments resulted from Zajonc's definition and subsequent review and these should be noted. The first is that the reference to a directional aspect which was contained in Allport's definition (i.e., "an increase of response") was removed. Thus, in current usage, the social facilitation effects refer to those increases/decreases/improvements/decrements, in performance which are a result of the presence of others.

A second consequence which stems largely from Zajonc's (1965) review is that the frame of reference for the term "social facilitation" has been broadened. It now incorporates not only the coaction paradigm which originally gave rise to the term itself, but the audience (spectator) paradigm as well.

However, it should also be noted that as a result of Zajonc's work, specific boundaries or limits were set for the area of social facilitation and, in turn, these boundaries also serve to define the concept. This point was emphasized by Landers and McCullagh (1976) in their review:

> ...in the motor performance literature...confusion is still evident when the term social facilitation is used rather loosely to denote a variety of social factors affecting performance (Singer, 1972). In attempting to assess social facilitation effects, it is important to control other contaminating factors commonly found in sports situations; that is, social reinforcement, including razzing and encouragement by cheering spectators and participants.

Landers and McCullagh presented a schema which serves as an outline for the area of social facilitation and a slightly modified form of this is presented in Figure 9.1.

Thus, social facilitation is viewed as comprising those situations characterized by the mere presence of others—either as coactors or an audience. It does not include those situations in which those present are interacting with the individual (either as coactive

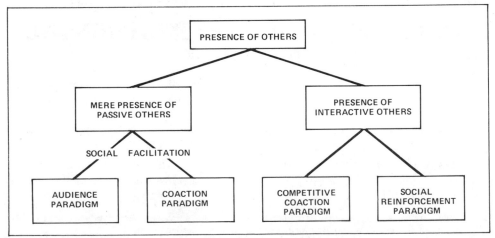

Figure 9.1. Outline of Zajonc's social facilitation hypothesis (Adapted from Landers and Mc-Cullagh, 1976).

competitors[2] or through the medium of encouragement, praise, reproof, and so on). According to Landers and McCullagh, the exclusion of these two paradigms is important since there is a good possibility that the situations represented by them are characterized by different psychological processes. Therefore, while the social facilitation schema presented in Figure 9.1 seems quite restrictive and also is not very representative of the general context of athletics, it does have the advantage of yielding greater experimental control. This factor is particularly important since, as will be apparent from the discussion which follows, the nature and underlying processes of the social facilitation effect are still not clearly understood. If the social facilitation phenomenon can be explained in a relatively restricted context, it may be possible to then utilize this framework in order to account for the complex effects that spectators and competitors have upon the athlete's performance.

HISTORICAL DEVELOPMENT

The current status and level of understanding of social facilitation can be best understood when viewed from a perspective which incorporates the earliest research efforts. In this regard, Landers (1975), in his analysis of social facilitation research, noted that the more recent comprehensive literature reviews (e.g., Cottrell, 1972; Martens, 1975; Wankel, 1975; Zajonc, 1972) have been quite consistent in their summarization of the salient historical developments which have contributed to our current theoretical approach to social facilitation. The important features which have been repeatedly referenced are that:

1) Prior to 1965, the social facilitation area was characterized by equivocal findings. Some studies found that an audience and/or coaction situation improved performance while others reported just the opposite effect. There were no apparent consistent trends within the findings.

2) Very little research attention was directed toward social facilitation problems between 1930 and 1965. Due to an inability to reconcile the contradictory findings, researchers lost interest in this area after the mid 1930s.

3) In 1965 Zajonc proposed a theoretical framework which reconciled these previously equivocal findings. That is, he noticed a pattern in the previous research and was the first to propose a Hullian-Spence drive theory interpretation to account for the social facilitation effect.

However, Landers (1975) noted that *"these statements about the early literature are not very accurate when we are referring to human performance"* (emphasis added). Thus, it would be advantageous at this point to examine (1) the early research in overview (which showed the positive and negative effects under coaction and audience conditions), (2) the manner in which Zajonc (1965) reconciled these apparently contradictory findings, and (3) the misinterpretations of this early work which were identified by Landers (1975).

---

2 . As Landers and McCullagh (1976) pointed out:

...The distinction...between the coaction and competitive coaction paradigms is often times difficult to discern. The difference between these two paradigms appears to be the degree of competition for it is doubtful if competition with others has been totally eliminated in the coaction paradigm. Even at the time the distinction was first made (Allport, 1924), manipulation checks revealed that 80% of the subjects in the coaction paradigm indicated a moderate degree of rivalry.

EARLY RESEARCH

Positive Effects. The introduction of an audience was found to improve performance in a wide variety of tasks. For example, Meumann (1904, cited in Cottrell, 1972) engaged subjects in an ergographic test of muscular effort and fatigue. That is, the arm was strapped to a table, a weight was suspended from the finger and, then, the weight was pulled as far and as rapidly as possible. Although performance initially quickly declined to an asymptotic level, Meumann observed that upon his sudden reappearance into the test room, performance levels showed dramatic improvements. This observation was later confirmed empirically in subsequent experiments.

Another experiment which showed positive effects from the presence of an audience was carried out by Travis (1925). He had subjects practice on the pursuit rotor for 20 trials per day until no performance improvements were shown for two consecutive days. An audience of 4 to 8 people was then introduced for the subsequent performance (which consisted of another 10 trials). Travis then compared performance in the alone condition (the average of the best ten consecutive scores which undoubtedly yielded an inflated estimate of performance) with performance in the audience condition. The results indicated that 18 of the 22 subjects tested showed improvements from the alone to the audience condition, the average group improvement being approximately 3%.

Cottrell (1972) subsequently computed a t-test on the Travis values and noted that this improvement from performance alone to performance in front of an audience was statistically significant. Similarly, Pessin (1933), Bergum and Lehr (1963) and Singer (1965), using nonsense syllable lists, a vigilance task and the stabilometer respectively, also found that when a high level of proficiency was achieved, the introduction of an audience resulted in an improvement in performance.

A number of authors also reported that performance in the presence of a coactor was superior to performance alone. The observations of Triplett (1897) with cyclists have already been introduced. In attempting to account for these improvements in performance under coaction conditions, Triplett considered a number of possible explanations including both physiological and physical factors (a suctioning effect, a sheltering effect) and psychological factors (encouragement, hypnotic suggestion, brain worry). He eventually settled upon a *dynamogenesis theory* which incorporated two dimensions. The first was that "the bodily presence of another rider is a stimulus to a racer in arousing the competitive instinct ... another can thus be the means of releasing or freeing nervous energy for him that he cannot of himself release" (Triplett, 1897). The second dimension was that the sight of movement in another racer could suggest a higher rate of speed and serve as an inspiration to greater effort.

Triplett (1897) then tested this theory in a laboratory experiment in which young boys engaged in a reel winding task. It was reported that the dynamogenesis theory was supported—performance was improved under coaction. More recently, Landers and McCullagh (1976) computed a t-test on Triplett's values and noted the coaction condition was significantly faster than the alone condition. However Wankel (1975) cautioned that:

> ...it is important to note that Triplett's laboratory study did not accurately represent the cycling field situation where he made his initial social facilitation observations. Whereas, in the cycling situation competition against time was present in all situations and the differences were in terms of the coactor, i.e., no coaction, a pacer or a competing racer; in the laboratory study, the two conditions were con-

trol (no coaction - no competition) and competition (coaction + competition). In other words, coaction was completely confounded with competition in the experimental study. Another problem was the manner of testing (i.e., alone-together-alone-together). It is highly unlikely that such a sequential procedure would in fact produce the conditions desired as there would be a carry-over from the competitive condition to the alone condition. Thus, while Triplett suggested that the study did support his dynamogenic theory, it is quite apparent, regardless of the equivocal results, that he did not in fact accurately test the theory. It was left for future researchers to test the utility of his two factor theory of the facilitating effects of others.

A field study which supported the view that the presence of coactors results in an improvement in performance was reported by Lorenz (1933, reported in Dashiell, 1935). He compared the speed of performance of women factory workers from a shoe-assembly line operation working alone versus while at a 6-person table. It was observed that on the average, output increased from 43 to over 60 pairs of shoes per day under the coaction situation.

The comprehensive contributions of Allport (1920, 1924) were among the most significant of the early period. Using a variety of verbal/mental tasks (e.g., chain association learning, vowel cancellation, multiplication, problem solving and reversible perspective figures), he contrasted a "pure" coaction situation (see Figure 9.1 and Footnote 2 again for the distinction between coaction and competitive coaction) with performance alone. This attempt at achieving coaction without competition was achieved by eliminating any comparisons of the results with coactors or investigators.

Allport found that while the coaction situation enhanced speed of performance, the quality of performance was frequently negatively affected. Thus, he concluded that "it is the overt responses, such as writing, which receive facilitation through the stimulus of coworkers. The intellectual or implicit responses of thought are hampered rather than facilitated" (Allport, 1924).

Allport also attempted to account for why an improvement in performance occurred. Two factors were proposed:

...the first of these is social facilitation. The movements made by others performing the same task as ourselves serve as contributory stimuli, and increase or hasten our own respones. This process is accompanied by a consciousness of impulsion. The second is rivalry. Its occurrence is in direct proportion to the competitive setting of the group occupation, though a certain degree of rivalry seems natural to all co-activity [Allport, 1924].

Negative Effects. In contrast to those studies which reported positive effects from the presence of others are a number of studies (e.g., Dashiell, 1930; Gates, 1924; Husband, 1931; Moore, 1917; Pessin, 1933; Pessin and Husband, 1933; Wapner and Alper, 1952) in which performance was detrimentally affected by the presence of spectators. For example, Pessin and Husband (1933) found that an audience condition resulted in more trials being required to learn a finger maze (17.1 versus 19.1, a difference of 11.7%). In addition, a greater number of errors were noted when the audience was present (a 20.1% difference).

Also, when Pessin (1933) examined the learning of nonsense syllables, he found that an alone condition was superior to an audience condition. Subjects practicing in front of a spectator required more trials to learn a seven-syllable list (11.3 versus 9.8, a 15.3% difference). Similar results were reported by Dashiell (1930) and Moore (1917) with a multiplication task; Gates (1924) with a naming-adjectives problem; and Wapner and Alper (1952) with a word pairing task. And, as indicated previously, Allport (1920, 1924) also reported that in coaction situations the quantitative aspects of some tasks were enhanced whereas the qualitative aspects were negatively affected.

If little research attention was directed toward social facilitation problems after the 1930s (until Zajonc's review in 1965), a significant event marking this turning point would be Dashiell's review in 1935. He summarized the previous work by noting that:

> ...little has been added to Allport's analysis, that little being mostly of the nature of reminders that to get pure 'alone' or pure 'co-working' (and we may add, pure 'spectator' or pure 'competing') situations is extra-ordinarily difficult [Dashiell, 1935].

Thus, Dashiell considered the area of social facilitation to be characterized by unresolved and largely unresolvable issues.

A REANALYSIS OF THE EARLY RESEARCH

As stated earlier, Landers (1975) pointed out that recent literature reviews by Cottrell (1972), Martens (1975), Wankel (1975a), and Zajonc (1972) are characterized by their endorsement of a series of generalizations: namely, that (1) prior to 1965 the area of social facilitation was marked by equivocal findings; (2) very little research attention was directed toward social facilitation problems between the 1930s and 1965; and (3) the theoretical framework to reconcile these divergent findings was originally proposed by Zajonc. But, it was also pointed out that Landers questioned the accuracy of these generalizations—particularly with reference to research with human subjects. A number of factors were listed by Landers which formed the basis of his proposal.

First, the results of early research were not as equivocal as was suggested. Some generalizations which were known and clearly supported by the early work were that:
— performance speed is enhanced by the presence of others,
— social facilitation effects are small and dissipate as the individual becomes habituated to the situation,
— actual presence (i.e., as contrasted with a presence which is implied by virtue of the experimental instructions given to the subjects — an example of this would be videotaping for future viewing) was not necessary to obtain the effect,
— the presence of other coactors results in a leveling effect—an improvement in performance by individuals of lower ability accompanied by a slight decrement in performance by subjects of higher ability.

Secondly, the purported decline in research from the 1930s to 1965 was mainly in studies with animals. Research with human subjects did not show any appreciable decrease.

Thirdly, on the basis of his analysis of the early research, Landers concluded that while there have been recent studies which have demonstrated that *learning* is detrimentally affected by the presence of others, this was not the case in the early research (which is, of course, contrary to the conclusion reached by Zajonc in his 1965 review). While trends were present indicative of an impairment in learning resulting from the presence of others (e.g., the studies of Allport, 1920, 1924; Dashiell, 1930; Gates, 1924; Pessin[3], 1933; Pessin and Husband, 1933; and Wapner and Alper[3],

---

3 . Landers (1975) did find that while some treatment comparisons showed significant differences, the "alone" versus "physically present audience" comparison did not.

1952), when these trends were analyzed by modern statistical methods, no significant effects were obtained.

Finally, Zajonc (1965) was not the first author to propose Hullian-Spence drive theory in an attempt to account for the social facilitation effect. Church (1962) utilized drive theory in the discussion of his results on competitive coaction. Landers (1975) emphasized that "even though Zajonc was not the first ... there is no doubt that it was his amplication and extension that attracted the attention of the scientific community." In short, while this final point is important in terms of placing early research into perspective (and giving Church his due), it in no way detracts from the significance of Zajonc's work.

ZAJONC'S (1965) PROPOSED RECONCILIATION FOR THE DIVERGENT RESULTS

After reviewing previous human and animal research which had utilized the audience and/or coaction paradigm, Zajonc proposed that there was a subtle consistency or generalizability inherent in the apparently equivocal findings:

> ...the generalization which organizes these results is that the presence of others, as spectators or as coactors, enhances the emission of the dominant responses [Zajonc, 1965].

Thus, consistent with drive theory expectations, two main hypotheses were advanced:

(1) in unlearned tasks, the habit strength for the correct response would be weak, the dominant habit would be incorrect and, therefore, the presence of others would be disruptive to performance;

(2) in well learned tasks, the habit strength for the correct response would be strong, the dominant habit would be the correct one and, therefore, the presence of others would lead to performance improvement.

This proposal is illustrated in Figure 9.2. The underlying rationale is explicitly contained within the overview of drive theory presented in Chapter 3 and will not be repeated here. Suffice to say that drive theory with its intervening variables of *drive* and *habit strength* has been the principal general theoretical model utilized to examine the social facilitation phenomena.

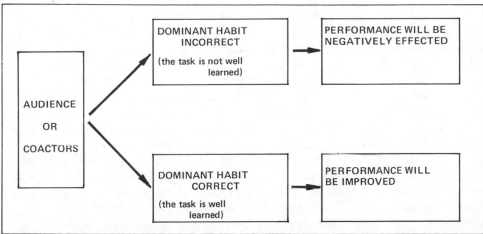

Figure 9.2. Zajonc's generalizations relating to the influence of an audience or coactors upon performance.

THE MEASUREMENT OF DRIVE IN SOCIAL FACILITATION RESEARCH

THE NATURE AND ASSESSMENT OF DRIVE

Although it is generally not consistent with current practice, Zajonc (1965) used the terms *drive, arousal* and *activation* interchangeably to reflect a level of emotional excitement. Commenting upon this Wankel (1975a) suggested that this:

> ...substitution of arousal for drive is important in that while drive is purely a hypothetical construct, arousal has an underlying neurophysiological basis which facilitates independent measures of this energizing construct (cf. Hebb, 1955; Duffy, 1962). By using arousal rather than drive, Zajonc was able to refer to studies of arousal changes due to social influences to support his suggested arousal interpretation of social facilitation.

Arousal, or energy mobilization, may be assessed in three ways: using *electrocortical, autonomic* and *behavioral* measures (Martens, 1974). The electrocortical technique consists of obtaining EEG recordings for the level of neural excitation from the cortex of the brain. While it is a particularly effective technique, it has not been used in social facilitation research to date.

The most widely used physiological measures of activation-arousal include those processes which are under the direct influence of the autonomic nervous system. In social facilitation research, a variety of these indices have been used including heart rate (Evans, 1971; Henchy and Glass, 1968; Landers and Goodstadt, 1972; Wankel, 1973,) palmar sweating (Cohen and Davis, 1973; Martens, 1969a, 1969b) and muscle tension (Chapman, 1973, 1974). However, there has not been any clear pattern to the results. Some studies have shown that the presence of others result in increased autonomic arousal but others have reported that there is no effect.

This lack of clear agreement among the various results suggests either of two conclusions. One is that the presence of others does not universally lead to an increase in arousal. On the other hand, another plausible (at least at this point in social facilitation research) conclusion is that the problem lies within the various measures themselves. For instance, it has been repeatedly demonstrated that the autonomic responses are quite specific (Lacy, 1967); there is very little relationship between the different measures. In short, given the same stimulus event (e.g., the presence of others), the heart rate and galvanic skin response for three different people might be markedly different. While one individual might show an elevated heart rate and galvanic skin response, a second could show no effect in either while the third could show an increase in one but a decrease in the other. Obviously if indices such as heart rate and sweating which are thought to reflect the same underlying process (i.e, arousal) do not show agreement among themselves, the researcher is faced with a dilemma: did the audience fail to increase arousal level or was the particular physiological measure utilized inappropriate for that individual in that situation? As a result, most behavioral scientists would advocate the use of a battery of physiological tests to measure arousal.

The third method of assessing arousal level has been to use *self report inventories* such as the Spielberger (1970) *State-Trait Anxiety Inventory (STAI)* and Thayer's (1967) *Activation-Deactivation Adjective Checklist (AD-ACL)*. Using the STAI, Carron and Bennett (1976) reported increased state anxiety under coaction conditions while Landers, Brawley and Hale (1977) found that neither a coaction nor audience condition produced increased arousal as measured by the STAI. McCullagh and Landers (1976) and Thayer and Moore (1972), using the AD-ACL, found that an audience condition resulted in heightened activation scores but Landers, Brawley and Hale (1977) reported no effects from either audience or coaction.

By way of overview then, it can be stated that the attempts to objectively verify increased arousal as a result of the presence of others has not been particularly successful. However, this could be partly attributed to the present limitations in our ability to measure those parameters thought to be associated with increased arousal.

DRIVE VIA "MERE PRESENCE" VERSUS "EVALUATION APPREHENSION"

The most contentious issue in social facilitation theory and research insofar as the issue of drive is concerned evolved from Zajonc's (1965) suggestion that the *mere presence* of another individual is a sufficient condition for producing increased arousal or activation (drive). Initially, no attempt was made to elaborate upon or define this phrase. However, in a subsequent paper, Zajonc (1972) stated that:

> ...when we speak of 'mere' presence in the context of social facilitation, we must mean that performance effects that are associated with the presence of others can be obtained even though all other factors and processes that are commonly associated with the presence of others are eliminated. That is, presence of others can have performance effects even though there is no chance of imitation, even though competition is ruled out, even though the spectator or the companion does not control the performer's reinforcement, and even though the companion's presence does not signal potential rewards or punishment.

In essence, Zajonc assumed that there is an innate, biologically based mechanism which leads an organism to respond with increased arousal/activation simply as a result of the bodily presence of another.

However, a second view which is generally associated with Cottrell (1972) is that the presence of others is a learned drive—the presence of others is associated through experience with evaluation and it is the anticipation of the evaluation process which results in increases in level of arousal. The underlying mechanism is that of classical conditioning. This was elaborated on by Cottrell (1972):

> ...it is assumed that at birth the stimuli produced by the mere presence of another organism are motivationally neutral; they neither increase nor decrease the individual's general drive level. Various aversive and gratifying events that serve to increase the individual's general drive level occur throughout the individual's life. Many of these events are spatially and temporally contiguous with the presence of others. For example, frequently others are present when an individual is praised or rewarded for his performance, and also when he is criticized or punished ... With an increasing number of such encounters, the stimuli from the mere presence of others gradually become through classical conditioning, sufficient to increase the individual's drive level. Through experience the individual learns to anticipate subsequent positive or negative outcomes whenever others are merely present and not overtly doing anything that has motivational significance for him. It is these anticipations, elicited by the presence of others, that increase the individual's drive level. The mere presence of others is not a sufficient condition to increase drive; this presence must also elicit anticipation of positive or negative outcomes.

There have been two methodological approaches which have been used to empirically analyze the "mere presence" versus the "evaluation apprehension" viewpoints: the *early social learning approach* and the *situational approach* (Landers and

McCullagh, 1976).

Early Social Learning Approach. In the early social learning approach, an attempt is made to control for the degree of social learning of anticipated evaluation from the presence of others. That is, by controlling the extent to which the organism has been subjected to previous social experiences, it should also be possible to control the extent to which the presence of others is represented as a potentially evaluative situation.

Cottrell (1972), in support of his evaluative apprehension hypothesis, pointed out that animals reared in isolation do not exhibit characteristic social facilitation reactions in the presence of other animals. Obvious ethical considerations eliminate this isolation design from being used with humans but a number of more indirect individual difference measures have been used to examine the role of prior social learning. These include a preselection of subjects on the basis of differences in *personality* (e.g., Cox, 1966, 1968; Ganzer, 1968; Meglino, 1976), *birth order* (e.g., Quarter and Marcus, 1971), and *culture* (Carment and Hodkin, 1973).

In Ganzers's (1968) study, the personality dimension of test anxiety was used. If it can be assumed that a concern felt for taking tests and having performances evaluated is acquired, then individuals differing in level of test anxiety could be expected to differ in the degree to which the presence of others is arousal-producing. Ganzer had high-, moderate- and low-anxious subjects learn a list of nonsense syllables either alone or in front of a spectator. It was observed that with the introduction of the spectator, the greater the anxiety level, the greater the decrement in performance.

Another personality dimension utilized has been dominance. Meglino (1976) proposed that "since personality dimensions have associated behavioral characteristics ... one could say that the behavior characteristic of high scorers on that dimension has been well learned, and the behavior characteristic of low scorers has been poorly learned." He then used a 2 x 2 experimental design in which high and low dominant individuals were tested in a leadership situation under evaluation—videotaping for subsequent viewing by an expert audience—or no evaluation conditions. When the number of direct verbal commands (the dependent variable used) was examined, a significant interaction was noted; under evaluation conditions, high dominant leaders behaved more dominantly while low dominant leaders behaved less dominantly. These results are illustrated in Figure 9.3. Thus, indirect support was provided for the evaluation apprehension viewpoint.

Quarter and Marcus (1971) tested subjects of different birth order on a verbal recall task either alone or in the presence of two spectators. The underlying rationale for using birth order was that different types of social experiences are characteristic of different birth orders so that first borns and only children are more responsive to social pressures and potential evaluation than later born children. The authors reported that under the audience condition, recall performance was detrimentally affected only for first born children while first born and later born did not differ in the alone condition.

And, finally, Carment and Hodkins's (1973) cross-cultural comparison of students from India and Canada showed that the latter were more affected by coaction setting than the former. Thus, by way of overview, it appears that when the results from studies of animals reared in isolation are taken along with the results from those studies in which individuals from different social learning backgrounds (as assessed by personality, birth order or culture) are compared, there is greater support for Cottrell's

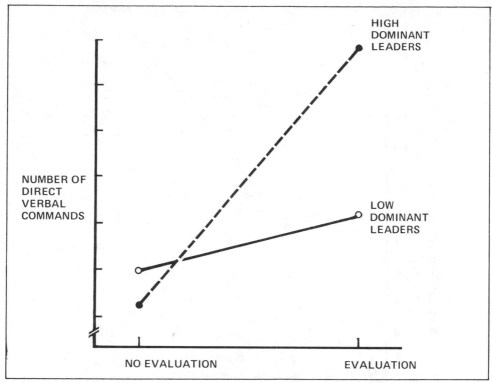

Figure 9.3. Verbal commands given by high dominant and low dominant leaders under evaluation versus no evaluation conditions (Based on data from Meglino, 1976).

view that the presence of others is a learned source of drive.

The Situational Approach. The second methodological approach which has been used to compare the "mere presence" with the "evaluation apprehension" viewpoints is situational in nature—an attempt is made to control for the extent to which others present in the performance situation can serve an evaluative function.

In support of his contention that the mere presence of other individuals is not sufficient to produce increased arousal, Cottrell (1972) reported the results of a number of studies in which the potential for evaluation was manipulated (Cottrell, Wack, Sekerak and Rittle, 1968; Henchy and Glass, 1968; Paulus and Murdoch, 1971). In the Cottrell, Wack, Sekerak and Rittle (1968) study, subjects were tested on a pseudorecognition task (see page 276) under one of three conditions: alone; in the presence of a audience of two passive spectators; or in mere presence condition in which two individuals were again present in the test room but were blindfolded. The results were consistent with an evaluation apprehension viewpoint (see Figure 9.4)—the mere presence condition did not differ from the alone condition.

The interpretation placed on these results was that the blindfolded audience were not potentially evaluative and consequently did not contribute to an increase in arousal level. Subsequent studies by Henchy and Glass (1968) and Paulus and Murdoch (1971) with the pseudo recognition task, and Martens and Landers (1972) with a roll-up motor task obtained similar findings. Thus, there is again strong support for a conclusion that if individuals are present in the performance situation but represent a

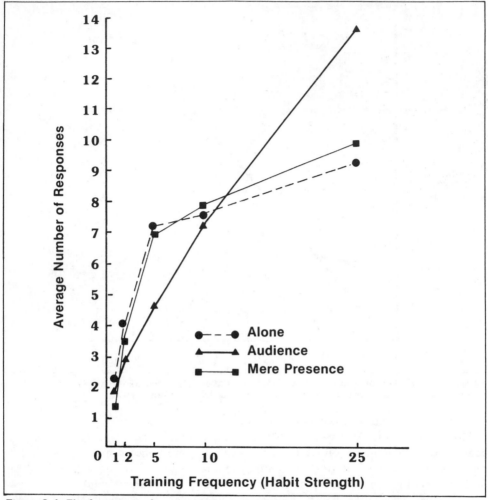

Figure 9.4. The frequency of response emission on a pseudorecognition task as a function of training frequency and conditions of testing.
From: Cottrell, N. B., Wack, D. L., Sekerak, G. J. and Rittle, R. H. Social facilitation of dominant responses by the presence of an audience and the mere presence of others. *Journal of Personality and Social Psychology*, 1968, 9, 245-250. Copyright, 1968 by the American Psychological Association. Reprinted by permission.

low potential for evaluation, arousal level is not measureably increased.

Landers and McCullagh (1976) in their review of the "mere presence" versus "evaluation apprehension" issue, concluded that:

> ...there is agreement among investigators (as the evidence amply demonstrates) that drive is enhanced by permitting access to channels of evaluation, or making evaluation more salient to subjects. The use of the evaluative apprehension evidence as supportive of the conclusion that social facilitation is a result of a learned drive remains controversial. Some investigators (i.e., Crandell, 1974) believe that this line of evidence merely indicates that subjects must at least believe that others are present. . .Rather than considering mere presence and evaluation apprehension to be an all-or-nothing phenomenon which is inextricably linked with physical presence, some investigators (Chapman, 1974) argue that drive created by the presence of others is more appropriately placed on a continuum of 'psychological presence.' The acceptance of this interpretation can reconcile the debate by simply considering evaluative audiences as high in psychological presence and those situations approaching the 'mere presence' end of the continuum as low in psychological presence.

THE PRESENCE OF OTHERS: AROUSING OR RELAXING?

When Zajonc (1965) initially advanced the proposal that the presence of others results in an increase in arousal level, he also cautioned that there may be some instances such as in highly stressful situations where the presence of others could produce a *lowered arousal level*. Schachter's (1959) work on affiliation is quite consistent with this suggestion. An individual who is highly concerned in a particular situation will seek out the company of others. In turn, the presence of these others has a reassuring/calming/relaxing effect which serves to lower level of arousal.

An *intermediate arousal level* hypothesis was advanced by Cottrell (1968) in an attempt to reconcile these contradictory possibilities. "If the initial motivational level of the individual is low, then introducing others in the situation should increase his drive level. If on the other hand, the individual is in a high drive state, then the presence of others should reduce his drive level" (Cottrell, 1968).

Shaver and Liebling (1976) provided a slightly different perspective to the facilitation-affiliation paradox. While they did not completely reject Cottrell's hypothesis, they pointed out that research in the Zajonc tradition has had a completely different focus than has the research in the Schachter tradition. As a result, it is difficult to compare the two paradigms. That is, social facilitation research has studied *task performance* — what affect does the presence of others have upon performance effectiveness? On the other hand, the affiliation research has focused on *people's decision to affiliate* when awaiting an unpleasant experience — what are the parameters which mediate decisions to affiliate? Therefore, while the increased drive evident in the former instance may be considered task relevant (anticipation of evaluation), the increased drive in the latter case is task irrelevant (anticipation of an unpleasant situation).

Shaver and Liebling (1976) did attempt to reconcile the contradiction between affiliation and facilitation research. In a 4 x 2 design, four groups of college students practiced on simple and complex mazed (see page 280). In two of the groups, the subjects practiced alone: one of these (High Fear, Alone) was made anxious prior to beginning performance when they were informed that a blood sample would be taken at the conclusion of the experiment; the second was not given these instructions (Low Fear, Alone). The other two groups were also given the blood sample instructions: one in the company of an anxious confederate who was to share the same fate (High, Fear, Worried Observer); the other in the company of a calm observer who was also to share the same fate (High Fear, Calm Observer).

Shaver and Liebling, using a drive theory orientation, predicted that the task irrelevant fear would have a drive-like effect upon task performance with the High Fear, Worried Observer condition showing the greatest effect; the Low Fear, Alone condition, the least; and High Fear, Calm Observer and High Fear, Alone conditions being intermediate. The results for the complex maze were consistent with these predictions with the number of errors being 143.1, 67.4, 102.0 and 103.1 respectively.

CHARACTERISTICS OF OTHERS PRESENT AND THE RESULTANT DRIVE EFFECTS

A number of investigators have manipulated various *subject characteristics* within the audience and/or coaction situation in an attempt to vary the drive level of the performer. These include the number, sex and expertise of others present.

Size. The underlying rationale for varying the size of the audience or the number of coactors present lies within the *summation principle*. Discussing this principle in relation to audience size, McCullagh and Landers (1976) noted that "since a learned drive can be aroused by spectators' presence, the intensity of this audience-induced drive may be increased merely by varying the number of spectators."

Using a ball roll up task and a reaction time task, McCullagh and Landers (1976) systematically varied audience size from one through six. When the relative levels of activation were assessed (using Thayer's (1967) AD-ACL) a linear trend was found: nervousness and activation increased as audience size increased. However, these differences in drive level were not reflected in performance differences in either of the two tasks.

Brenner (1974) used a Psychological Stress Evaluator to assess the degree of arousal indicated through voice patterns in public speaking situations. His results also supported a summation effect in that the level of stress was a power function $(X^{0.47})$ of the audience size (varied from 0 to 2, 8 and 22 spectators).

The results from coaction studies have not shown any definite trends. For example, Martens and Landers (1969), using a muscular endurance task (the dominant leg was held horizontal for as long as possible), found that performance was better for individuals tested in tetrads than for either dyads or alone. However, Burwitz and Newell (1972) reported poorer performance scores on a ball roll up task for tetrads than for dyads or alone. In the Martens and Landers (1972) study with a ball roll up task, increasing performance impairment was found under direct evaluation in alone, dyads, triads and tetrads. And, finally, Hillery and Fugita (1975) reported that increasing the coacting group size from one through ten resulted in a corresponding increase in performance on manual and finger dexterity tasks.

Sex. Sex has also been systematically varied as an independent variable in order to determine whether the psychological presence provided by same- or opposite-sex audiences and/or coactors represents a different motivational situation for the performer. On the basis of the results which are available, it does appear that this is not the case. For example, Bird (1975), using manual dexterity and hand steadiness tasks; Cox (1966), using a marble dropping task; Harney and Parker[4] (1972), using a ball roll up task; and Rikli (1974), using hand steadiness and grip strength tasks, found that the sex of the task performer and the sex of the audience had no impact upon performance.

On the other hand, there is some evidence which suggests that males are less susceptible to social facilitation effects than are females—the presence of others during task performance has a greater tendency to increase drive level in females. Both Carment (1970), using a level pulling task, and Hunt and Hillery (1973), using maze learning, noted that the performance of females was facilitated by a coaction situation while the males was not (i.e., males performed similarly in the alone and coaction situations). Landers, Brawley and Hale (1977), using simple and complex maze tasks, obtained a significant interaction between sex and dominant response; females required significantly more trials to reach the criterion than males.

---

4 . Harney and Parker were actually examining social reinforcement rather than social facilitation (see Figure 9.1 again).

Expertise. When the expertise of others present has been manipulated, the resultant performance effects have been consistent with drive theory predictions. That is, a more expert audience increases arousal level and enhances the emission of the dominant response. For example, Henchy and Glass (1968) reported that an expert audience had a greater effect upon performance in a psuedoword recognition task than a nonexpert audience. Similarly, Bergum and Lehr (1963) noted that a more expert audience produced greater social facilitation effects in the performance of a well learned vigilance task. And, finally, the research literature reviewed earlier under the heading *Situational Approach* is also pertinent here. In sum, the available research contributes to a conclusion that the more expert the audience, the greater their potential for evaluation and the greater their potential as a source of drive to the performer.

THE MEASUREMENT OF HABIT STRENGTH IN SOCIAL FACILITATION RESEARCH

The intervening variable of habit strength, like drive, must be inferred from observed events. And like drive, the manner in which habit strength is operationally defined is of critical importance. But as Carron and Bennett (1976) observed, there are:

> ...inherent limitations in the use of motor tasks if Hullian-Spence drive theory is used as a theoretical model. The major limitation lies in the difficulty of assessing the habit hierarchy for motor tasks. That is, the number and relative strengths of the competing response tendencies (i.e., the 'correct' response versus the 'incorrect' response or responses) either cannot be determined or can only be assessed indirectly and imprecisely. Many authors have apparently simply ignored this problem when examining social facilitation effects on motor tasks.

But obviously, since Zajonc's (1965) proposal was that the presence of others enhances the emission of the *dominant response*, some method of estimating which response is dominant is necessary in order to effectively examine his proposal.

The general methodological approaches which can be used to control for habit strength differences may be classified within three broad categories: *prior training of a dominant response; mapping the dominant response from subject preferences;* and by *using population values to determine the dominant response* (Cottrell, 1972). While all three of these are relatively effective, the first method has been the most frequently utilized in motor skills research.

PRIOR TRAINING OF A DOMINANT RESPONSE

As indicated in Chapter 3, a habit hierarchy refers to the relative strengths of the correct response versus the incorrect response or responses. A dominant habit may be created experimentally in a hierarchy through a differential pretraining of responses. This methodology in its basic form involves the "relatively frequent presentation of one response alternative versus the infrequent presentation of the other response alternatives" (Carron and Bennett, 1976). In recent research reports, two variations have been evident: the *learning phase versus performance phase approach* and the *differential reinforcement approach*.

Learning Phase versus Performance Phase. As a comparison of Figures 3.2 and 3.3 in Chapter 3 illustrates, habit is the learning component within the Hullian-Spence theory. Early in learning, incorrect habits are dominant. However, with repeated practice and reinforcement, there is learning—the bond between the stimulus and the correct response becomes stronger—and the correct response assumes a position of dominance within the hierarchy. Thus, a number of authors have designated the acquisition phase of practice as a *learning or incorrect response dominant phase*. On the other hand, the stage in practice in which scores have leveled off and the performance curve appears asymptotic is designated as a *performance or correct response dominant phase* (see Figure 9.5).

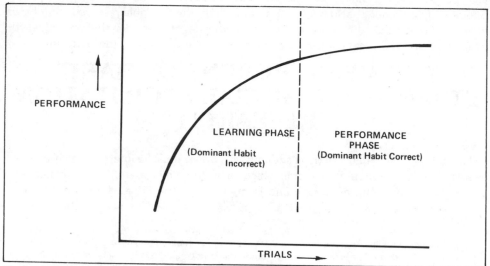

Figure 9.5. Practice curve subdivided into two components: a *learning phase* (the dominant habit is incorrect) and a *performance phase* (dominant habit is correct).

This paradigm was used by Martens (1969a) in an experiment involving a coincident timing task. A criterion for performance effectiveness was established (i.e., the learning phase) and when the subjects achieved this standard for three consecutive trials, it was assumed that the learning stage was over and the performance stage had begun. An alone and an audience condition (which consisted of 10 passive spectators) were utilized during both the learning and the performance phase. The results are illustrated in Figure 9.6. The results were consistent with drive theory predictions—the audience condition caused performance decrements in the learning phase but led to a facilitation of performance in the performance phase.

A similar technique was utilized by Haas and Roberts (1975) with a mirror tracing task. Again, there was support for a drive theory prediction since the audience condition improved performance in the performance stage but led to performance decrements in the learning stage.

Differential Reinforcement. In the differential reinforcement approach, the practice session is subdivided into two components: a *pretest* (or *training* phase) and a *test* phase. In the pretest or training phase, habits of different strengths are established via differential presentation and/or reinforcement. A habit hierarchy is established in this way and is then utilized in the test phase to examine social facilitation issues.

A study by Cottrell, Wack, Sekerak and Rittle (1968) which utilized the pseudoword recognition task illustrates this particular approach. In the pretest phase, subjects prac-

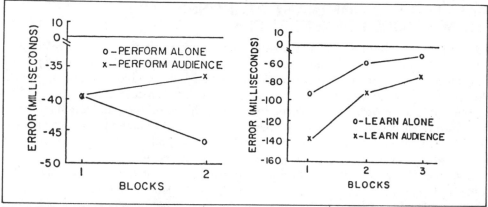

Figure 9.6. Arithmetic error during the learning phase (figure on the left) and arithmetic error intravariance during the performance phase (figure on the right) of coincident timing practice Source: Martens, R. Effects of an audience on learning and performance of a complex motor skill. *Journal of Personality and Social Psychology*, 1969, *12*, 252-260. Copyright, 1969 by the American Psychological Association. Reprinted by permission.

ticed each of ten nonsense words (e.g., *Afworbu*) which were presented with varying frequency. Thus, a habit hierarchy was established among the ten responses. During the test phase, words were successively flashed on a screen and the subjects were required to identify the specific word on each trial. A total of 160 trials were given but 120 were actually pseudorecognition trials—the stimulus duration was insufficient to allow for recognition of the word. As a consequence, each of the ten nonsense words were in competition during these 120 trials. The results were in line with drive theory expectations: relative to an alone condition, the presence of evaluative spectators enhanced the emission of the dominant response (see Figure 9.4 again).

The pseudoword recognition task involves verbal-mental skills. Research which ultimately contributes the most to our understanding of sport and physical activity must utilize tasks which have predominantly motor requirements. But, unfortunately, as Carron and Bennett noted:

> ...most motor tasks are not suitable when it is necessary to control for or assess the relative tendency/probability of a spectrum of possible responses. A task that involves more than one virtually identical stimulus-response alternative is necessary. The critical issue is that the response alternatives be highly similar or identical to each other. Otherwise, the 'total task' is nothing more than a series of discrete independent motor responses, each of which has its own unique habit hierarchy. Choice reaction time (RT) represents an excellent example of the type of task required. The habit hierarchy can be viewed as a function of the number of possible response choices. [Carron and Bennett, 1976].

A four-choice reaction time task was used by Carron Bennett (1976). A 60-trial pretest phase was used to establish three different habit hierarchy conditions. For the no-dominant-habit-condition, each of the four alternative responses appeared equally and randomly in the pretest phase. For the dominant-habit-correct condition, the response which appeared predominantly in the test session was presented in 40 out of the 60 pretest trials while for the dominant-habit-incorrect condition, one of the nontest responses appeared in 40 out of the 60 trials. However, there was no support for the hypothesis that coaction would interact with the habit strength condition producing an improvement in performance for the habit-correct group and a decrement in performance for the habit-incorrect group.

MAPPING THE DOMINANT RESPONSE FROM SUBJECT PREFERENCES

When the dominant response is assessed through the response preferences of the subject, the experimental design again involves two stages of practice: a pretest phase and a test phase. In the pretest phase, the individual is exposed to a number of possible response alternatives and asked to select one. This process is then repeated a number of times in order to establish a habit hierarchy comprising the dominant (i.e., most frequently chosen) and nondominant response(s). During the test phase, an audience or coactors are introduced to test the Zajonc hypothesis that the presence of others serves to enhance the emission of the dominant response.

Goldman (1967) used this methodology to examine the influence of coactors upon color preference. During the 30-trial pretest phase, subjects wrote out which of five color samples was preferred at the moment. One half of the subjects were tested alone in the 30-trial test phase while the other half were examined with four coactors. The results showed that the presence of the coactors led to an increase in selection of the dominant response. Unfortunately, this technique does not appear to have been used in motor skills research.

USING POPULATION VALUES TO DETERMINE THE DOMINANT RESPONSE

A predominant characteristic of the two previously discussed general strategies is their reliance on two stages of practice: a pretest phase when a habit hierarchy of dominant and nondominant responses is established and a test phase when this habit hierarchy is utilized in a social facilitation paradigm. In a third approach, the pretest phase is not required. The habit hierarchy is known through either *population norms* or the *characteristics of the task*.

Population Norms. Cottrell, Rittle and Wack (1967) tested subjects alone or in front of a passive audience of two spectators on a competitional and noncompetitional paired associates list originally developed by Spence, Farber and McFann (1956). The 12 synonym pairs in the competitional list were designed to maximize the extent to which there were competing response tendencies present (e.g., barren-fruitless, arid-grouchy, etc.). On the other hand, the 15 synonym pairs in the noncompetitional list were designed to minimize the degree of association between different pairs and, therefore, minimize the competing response tendencies present (e.g., barren-fruitless, adept-skillful, etc.). On the basis of drive theory, it was hypothesized that the presence of an audience would lead to improvements in paired-associates learning of the noncompetitional list but decrements with the competitional list. The results, which are presented in Figure 9.7, supported this hypothesis.

Another approach has been to control initially for differences in habit strength by preselecting subjects from the total sample according to their extreme scores—that is, the individuals with high and low ability—on the task to be used. The assumption underlying this procedure is that high ability reflects a dominant habit correct condition while low ability reflects a dominant habit incorrect condition (e.g., Hitchman, 1975; Wankel, 1973).

Characteristics of the Task. When the task consists of a fixed number of discrete, independent responses set in series and the total number of possible responses (i.e., the *population* of responses) can be determined, then it is possible to estimate the relative

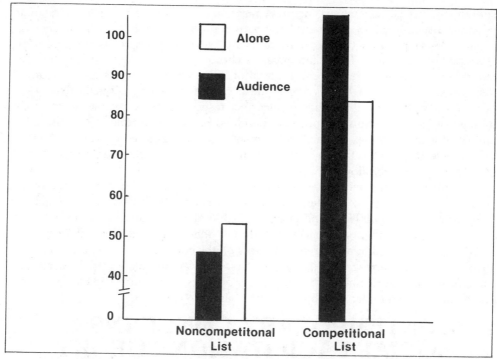

Figure 9.7. Paired-associates performance on a competitional and noncompetitional list under alone versus audience conditions (From Cottrell, 1972, based on data from Cottrell, Rittle and Wack, 1967). Reproduced with permission of the publisher.

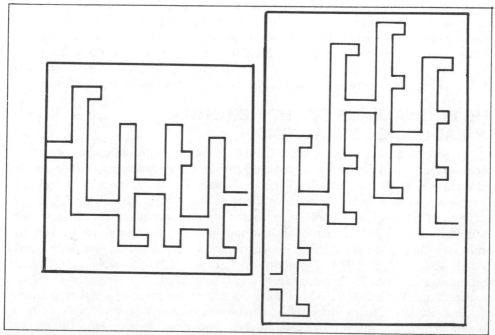

Figure 9.8. A *simple* (two-choice) and *complex* (four-choice) maze task.

strength of the correct versus incorrect responses. Also, it is possible to estimate whether a subject is in a dominant habit correct phase or a dominant habit incorrect phase. The simple and complex maze tasks are excellent examples (see Figure 9.8).

In the complex maze, four alternatives or choices are available at each of five different levels—on any trial there are a total of 20 possible responses or 15 incorrect responses. A dominant habit correct phase can then be operationally fixed as a percentage of the actual number of incorrect responses made relative to the total number of incorrect responses possible. Landers, Brawley and Hale (1977) used this approach with a complex maze. A 50 percent criterion was selected (i.e., 7.5 out of the possible 15 errors) as the point at which the incorrect habit dominant phase changed into a correct habit dominant phase.

A number of investigators have used the simple and complex maze tasks (e.g., Hunt and Hillery, 1973; Landers, Brawley and Hale, 1977; Shaver and Liebling, 1976; Williams, 1977). Hunt and Hillery (1973) and Shaver and Liebling (1976), in accord with drive theory expectations, found that increased drive through the presence of others led to an increase in errors on the complex maze but a decrease in errors on the simple maze. Similarly, Landers, Brawley and Hale (1977), using the complex maze, reported an increased number of errors in audience and coaction conditions during the dominant habit incorrect phase.

CONTEMPORARY CONCERNS IN SOCIAL FACILITATION THEORY AND RESEARCH

A number of authors, after evaluating the progress made in social facilitation theory and research since Zajonc's article in 1965, have highlighted points of concern and/or suggested alternate research strategies which might be pursued. Foremost among this work would be the commentaries by Landers, McCullagh and Wankel (Landers, 1975; Landers and McCullagh, 1976; McCullagh and Landers, 1975; Wankel, 1975a, 1975b). An overview of their suggestions and discussions is as follows:

THE EQUIVALENCE OF THE COACTION AND AUDIENCE PARADIGMS

A longstanding assumption in social facilitation theory and research has been that there is an equivalence between the coaction and audience paradigms—both coactors and audiences result in an identical behavioral effect. However, the underlying basis for this assumption may be questionable (Landers and McCullagh, 1976; McCullagh and Landers, 1975). For example, a number of researchers have not obtained similar performance effects from coactors and an audience with the same task. In fact, in some instances, performance effects under coaction versus audience have been in opposit directions (Bird, 1973; Carment and Latchfor, 1970; Dashiell, 1930; and Martens and Landers, 1972 versus Sasfy and Okun, 1974).

Landers and McCullagh (1976) pointed out that others present, whether as coactors or spectators, can produce evaluation apprehension. However, the coaction situation is unique in that it contains a number of additional factors. For example, in coaction, performance may be enhanced either by the sight and sound of the coactor's activity or via directive cues relating to the most effective performance strategy to use. Also, performance may be detrimentally affected from the distracting impact of the presence of others and their performance. "It may be these 'extra ingredients,' inherent in the coaction paradigm, that contribute either singly or conjointly to produce a lack of correspondence" (Landers and McCullagh, 1976).

Although the question of the equivalence of coaction and audience effects has not been specifically examined, it will have to be pursued in future research.

LEVELING EFFECTS UNDER COACTION CONDITIONS

A second, somewhat related issue is that leveling effects are characteristic of coaction situations—the presence of others may improve performance in subjects of lesser ability but more competent individuals show slight regressions (Landers, 1975; Landers and McCullagh, 1976; McCullagh and Landers, 1975). This issue has not been as readily apparent in recent research reports since investigators tend to report group data (i.e., means and standard deviations for the total sample) rather than the scores for individual subjects. However, the leveling effect is quite evident in earlier work (e.g., Hurlock, 1927; Lorenz, 1933; Triplett, 1897; Whitemore, 1924).

On the basis of these results, it has been suggested that individuals practicing in coaction situations should not be considered independent (McCullagh and Landers, 1975). Even though the individuals are working independently and even though rivalry, competition and comparison are reduced or eliminated, performance under coaction can be viewed as interrelated. A variety of techniques are available and, if used, would reflect this interrelatedness. One method would be to match coactors according to initial ability. A second technique would be to either use the data from only one member of the coacting unit while a third would be to treat the coacting group as a unit of analysis (that is, obtain a sum or mean score of the total unit). Finally, since coaction situations are so prevalent in sport and physical activity, it would be beneficial to determine *why* and under what circumstances the leveling process occurs—what are the underlying mechanisms?

ALTERNATE MODELS FOR SOCIAL FACILITATION RESEARCH

It has also been suggested that alternate models should be examined in place of drive theory for social facilitation research (Landers and McCullagh, 1975; Wankel, 1975b). The two most frequently cited have been the inverted-U model and the attribution model. Although both were outlined in some detail in Chapter 3 (and, therefore, are not repeated here), the discussion on the attribution model was largely restricted to the role it plays in postdictively explaining performance outcomes. Wankel (1975b) has also presented an outline of how attribution theory might also be used in a prior context as a motivational framework to examine performance.

In Weiner's (1972) model for attribution, a stimulus event or situation elicits predictive causal cognitions which, in turn, produce affective responses and goal expectancies that determine subsequent behavior (see Figure 9.9). Wankel pointed out that the presence of others as coactors or an audience (i.e, the stimulus event) and the subsequent apprehension of evaluation produce an affective anticipation—the anticipation of pride or shame. This anticipated effect could influence subsequent performance in a number of possible ways.

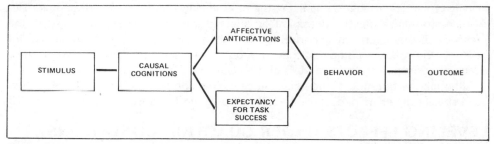

Figure 9.9. Components of an attribution model of motivation (Adapted from Weiner, 1972).

"One possibility is that the increased affect, due to the presence of evaluative others, leads to an increase in the subject's expected subjective utility of an act and in turn his intended effort on the task" (Wankel, 1975b). Thus, the individual who anticipates experiencing pride with success or shame with failure tries harder. The improvements in performance resulting from the presence of others are a product of this increased effort.

Duval and Wicklund (1972) attributed the decrements in performance resulting from the presence of others to the poorly skilled individual's attempts to perform beyond his abilities. However, Wankel discounted this explanation in favor of a distraction hypothesis—the individual is motivated toward exerting more effort on the task but his attention is distracted under the high affect conditions. Consequently, the actual task relevant effort is less and performance suffers.

The final possibility suggested was that the mere presence of others "causes the subject to either lower his estimate of his task related ability or to raise his estimate of the difficulty of the impending task. Either of these cognitions would lead to a raising of the subject's intended effort for less difficult tasks but at the same time would lower the cutoff-point at which he judges his effort on difficult tasks to be futile—hence, he would stop trying sooner on difficult tasks" (Wankel, 1975b).

To date, there has not been any research directed toward an attributional explanation of social facilitation effects in motor skills. Thus, it is difficult to evaluate its utility as an alternate explanatory model.

SUMMARY

Social facilitation may be defined as the effect that the mere presence of others has upon task performance. Consistent with this reference to "mere presence," social facilitation does not include those instances where there is overt competition, interaction or communication between the performer and those others present. Two specific experimental paradigms have been used to examine social facilitation: audience and coaction.

Historically, a significant milestone in the development of this area was the Zajonc article in 1965. In it he proposed that the confusing picture in previous research could be reconciled through the use of a drive theory explanation—the presence of others increases arousal level and enhances the emission of the dominant response.

Drive, which was equated to arousal/activation, can be assessed independently in three ways: using electrocortical, autonomic and behavioral measures. The latter two have been most frequently used but there has not been any clear trend in the results. While some studies using these techniques have shown that an audience (or coactors) increases arousal, other studies have not. These discrepancies may reflect limitations in the measurement techniques themselves.

The most contentious issue in social facilitation research has been the question of whether the mere presence of others is a sufficient condition for increased drive or whether this presence must be accompanied by the anticipation (apprehension) of evaluation. There has been considerable support for the latter viewpoint from studies of animals reared in isolation; studies in which the early social learning experiences of humans are indirectly accounted for (i.e, via individual differences in personality, birth order or culture); and studies in which the amount of direct evaluation present is manipulated. However, it has also been suggested that mere presence and evaluation apprehension are points along a continuum of "psychological presence." The latter is potentially more arousing than the former.

Another issue which has arisen is the social facilitation-affiliation paradox. Whereas research in the former area has indicated that the presence of others is arousal producing, research in the latter area has indicated that the presence of others is relaxing. One explanation may be an intermediate arousal level hypothesis—if initial motivation level is low, the presence of others is motivating, but if initial motivation level is high, the presence of others is relaxing. Another proposal has been that the two paradigms are not comparable as they currently exist. Concern in the social facilitation area has been with task performance while the focus in the affiliation area has been on the basis for individuals' decisions to affiliate in stressful situations.

A number of investigators have manipulated various subject characteristics within the audience and coaction paradigms in an attempt to vary drive level. There is reasonable support from this work to conclude that: increasing the size or expertise of the audience leads to an increase in drive level; the sex of the spectator(s) does not influence drive level; and, males are less susceptible to social facilitation effects than are females.

There are inherent limitations in the use of motor tasks if Hullian-Spence drive theory is adopted because of the difficulty of assessing the habit hierarchy. The three general approaches adopted in previous research include: the prior training of a dominant response; mapping the dominant response from subject preferences; and, using population values to determine the dominant response.

A number of unresolved issues are present in the area of social facilitation. One of these concerns the assumption that the coaction and audience paradigms are equivalent. There is some evidence which suggests that they are not. Another question raised has been with the adequacy of drive theory as an explanatory model for social facilitation. Alternate models have been proposed including the inverted-U hypothesis and the attribution theory. Neither of these alternate models has received serious attention at this point.

REFERENCES

Adams, J.S. Toward an understanding of inequity. *Journal of Abnormal and Social Psychology*, 1963, *67*, 422-436.

Adams, R.S. and Biddle, B. J. *Realities of teaching: Explorations with video tape*. Holt, Rinehart and Winston, 1970.

Alderman, R. B. *Psychological behavior in sport*. W. B. Saunders, 1974.

Alderman, R. B. Incentive motivation in sport: An interpretative speculation of research opportunities. In *The status of psycho-motor learning and sport psychology research*, (B. S. Rushall, Ed.). Sport Sciences Associates, 1975.

Alderman, R. B. Strategies for motivating young athletes. In *Sport psychology: An analysis of athlete behavior*, (W. Straub, Ed.). Mouvement Publications, 1978.

Alderman, R. B. and Wood, N. L. An analysis of incentive motivation in young Canandian athletes. *Canadian Journal of Applied Sport Sciences*, 1976, *1*, 169-176.

Allen. V. L. Social support for nonconformity. In *Advances in experimental social psychology*, Vol. 8, (L. Berkowitz, Ed.). Academic Press, 1975.

Allen, V. L. and Levine, J. M. Social support and conformity: The role of independent assessment of reality. *Journal of experimental social psychology*, 1975, *7*, 48-58.

Allport, F. H. The influence of the group upon association and thought. *Journal of Experimental Psychology*, 1920, *3*, 159-182.

Allport, F. H. *Social psychology*. Houghton Mifflin, 1924.

Allport, G. W. *Personality: A psychological interpretation*. Holt, 1937.

Allport, G. W. *Pattern and growth in personality*. Holt, Rinehart and Winston, 1964.

Anderson, G. J. *The assessment of learning environments: A manual for the Learning Environment Inventory and the My Class Inventory*. Atlantic Institute of Education, 1973.

Anderson, W. G. Teacher behavior in physical education classes. Part I: Development of a descriptive system. Unpublished manuscript, Teachers College, Columbia University, 1975.

Anderson, W. G. and Barrette, G. T. Teacher behavior. In *What's going on in gym: Descriptive studies of physical education classes*, (W. G. Anderson and G. T. Barrette, Eds.), Monograph 1. *Motor Skills: Theory into Practice*, 1978.

Ansorge, C. J., Scheer, J. K., Laub, J. and Howard, H. J. Bias in judging women's gymnastics induced by expectations of within-team order. *Research Quarterly*, 1978, *49*, 339-405.

Argyle, M. *The psychology of interpersonal behavior*. Penguin Books, 1967.

Argyle, M. *Social interaction*. Tavistock Publications, 1969.

Argyle, M. and Kendon, A. The experimental analysis of social performance. *Advances in Experimental Social Psychology*, 1967, *3*, 55-98.

Argyle, M., Lallje, M. and Cook, M. The effects of visibility on interaction in a dyad. *Human Relations*, 1968, *21*, 3-17.

Arkes, H. R. and Garske, J. P. *Psychological theories of motivation*. Brooks/Cole Publishing Co., 1977.

Arkin, R. M., Gleason, J. M. and Johnston, S. Effect of perceived choice, expected outcome and observed outcome of an action on the causal attributions of actors. *Journal of Experimental Social Psychology*, 1976, *12*, 151-158.

285

Arnold, G. E. and W. F. Straub, W. F. Personality and group cohesiveness as determinants of success among inter-scholastic basketball teams. Proceedings — Fourth Canadian Symposium on Psycho-Motor Learning and Sport Psychology. Health and Welfare Canada, 1972.

Aronson, E. Some antecedents of interpersonal attraction. In Psychological dimensions of social interaction: Readings and perspectives, (D. E. Linder, Ed.). Addison-Wesley, 1973.

Asch, S. E. Effects of group pressure upon the modofication and distortion of judgements. In Groups, leadership and men (H. Guetzkow, Ed.). Carnegie Press, 1951.

Asch, S. E. Social psychology. Prentice-Hall, 1952.

Asch, S. E. Studies of independence and conformity: I. A minority of one against a unanimous majority. Psychological Monographs, 70, No. 9 (Whole No. 416), 1956.

Atkinson, J. W. Motivational determinants of risk taking behavior Psychological Review, 1957, 64, 359-372.

Atkinson, J. W. (Ed.) Motives in fantasy, action and society. Van Nostrand, 1958.

Atkinson, J. W. An introduction to motivation. Van Nostrand, 1964.

Atkinson, J. W. and Feather, N. T. A theory of achievement motivation. Wiley, 1966.

Atkinson, J. W. and Litwin, G. H. Achievement motivation and test anxiety conceived as motive to approach success and motive to avoid failure. Journal of Abnormal and Social Psychology, 1960, 60, 52-63.

Atkinson, J. W. and Raphelson, A. C. Individual differences in motivation and behavior in particular situations. Journal of Personality, 1956, 24, 349-363.

Axelrod, H. S., Cowen, E. L. and Heilizer, F. The correlates of manifest anxiety in stylus maze learning. Journal of Experimental Psychology, 1956, 51, 131-138.

Backman, C. W. and Secord, P. F. The effect of perceived liking on interpersonal attraction. Human Relations, 1959, 12, 379-384.

Badin, I. J. Some moderator influences on relationships between consideration, initiating structure and organizational criteria. Journal of Applied Psychology, 1974, 59, 380-382.

Bakeman, R. and Helmreich, R. Cohesiveness and performance: Covariation and causality in an underseas environment. Journal of Experimental Social Psychology, 11, 478-489, 1975.

Baker, R. F. The effects of anxiety and stress on gross motor performance. Unpublished doctoral dissertation, University of California at Los Angeles, 1961.

Bale, P. Somatotyping and body physique. Physical Educator, 1969, 61, 75-82.

Bales, R. F. Interaction process analysis: A method for the study of groups. Addison-Wesley, 1950.

Bales, R. F. How people interact in conferences. Scientific American, 1955, 192, 31-35.

Bales, R. F. Task roles and social roles in problem-solving groups. In Role theory: Concepts and research. (B. J. Biddle and E. J. Thomas, Eds.). John Wiley & Sons, 1966.

Bales, R. F. and Borgatta, E. F. Size of group as a factor in the inter-action profile. In Small groups: Studies in interaction, (A. P. Hare, E. F. Borgatta and R. F. Bales, Eds.). Knopf, 1955.

Bales, R. F. and Strodtbeck, F. L. Phases in group problem solving. In Group dynamics: Research and theory (D. Cartwright and A. Zander, Eds.), 3rd Ed., Tavistock Publications, 1968.

Ball, D. W. Ascription and position: Comparative analysis of 'stacking' in professional football. Canadian Review of Sociology and Anthropology, 1973, 10, 97-113.

Ball, D. W. Replacement processes in work organizations: Task evaluation and the case of professional football. Sociology of Work and Occupations, 1974, 1, 197-217.

Ball, J. R. and Carron, A. V. The influence of team cohesion and participaton motivation upon performance success in intercollegiate ice hockey. Canadian Journal of Applied Sport Sciences, 1976, 1, 271-275.

Bandura, A. Principles of behavior modification. Holt, Rinehart & Winston, 1969.

Banta, T. J. and Nelson, C. Experimental analysis of resource location in problem-solving groups. Sociometry, 1964, 27, 488-501.

Barrow, J. C. Worker performance and task complexity as causal determinants of leader behavior style and flexibility. Journal of Applied Psychology, 1976, 61, 433-440.

Basler, M. L., Fisher, A. C. and Mumford, N. L. Arousal and anxiety correlates of gymnastic performance. Research Quarterly, 1976, 47, 586-589.

Bass, B. M. The orientation inventory. Consulting Psychologists Press, 1962.

Bass, B. M., Dunteman, G., Frye, R., Vidulich, R. and Wambach, H. Self, interaction, and task orientation inventory scores associated with overt behavior and personal factors. Educational and Psychological Measurement, 1963, 23, 101-116.

Bass, B. M. and Klubeck, S. Effects of seating arrangements on leaderless group discussions. *Journal of Abnormal Social Psychology*, 1952, *47*, 724-727.

Bateson, N. Familiarization, group discussion and risk taking. *Journal of Experimental and Social Psychology*, 1966, *2*, 119-129.

Bavelas, A. A mathematical model for group structures. *Applied Anthropology*, 1948, *7*, 16-30.

Bavelas, A. Communication patterns in task-oriented groups. *Journal of the Acoustical Society of America*, 1950, *22*, 725-730.

Bavelas, A. An experimental approach to organizational communication. *Personnel*, 1951, *27*, 367-371.

Bavelas, A., Hastorf, A. H., Gross, A. E. and Kite, W. R. Experiments on the alteration of group structure. *Journal of Experimental Social Psychology*, 1965, *1*, 55-70.

Baytor, D. Children's enjoyment in competitive sports. Unpublished Master of Arts Thesis, University of Western Ontario, London 1978.

Beckman, L. J. Effects of students' level and patterns of performance on teachers' and observers' attributions of causality. *Journal of Educational Psychology*, 1970, *61*, 76-82.

Behling, O. and Schreisheim, C. *Organizational behavior: Theory, research and application.* Allyn & Bacon, 1976.

Bem, D. J. Self-perception theory. In *Advances in experimental social psychology*. (L. Berkowitz, Ed.), Vol. 6. Academic Press, 1972.

Bennis, W. Organizational developments and the fate of bureaucracy. *Industrial Management Review*, 1966, *4*, 41-55.

Bergum, B. O. and Lehr, D. J. Effects of authoritarianism on vigilance performance. *Journal of Applied Psychology*, 1963, *47*, 75-77.

Berkowitz, L. Group standards, cohesiveness and productivity. *Human Relations*, 1954, *7*, 509-519.

Berkowitz, L. and Macaulay, J. R. Some effects of differences in status level and status stability. *Human Relations*, 1961, *14*, 135-148.

Berlyne, D. E. *Conflict, arousal and curiosity.* McGraw-Hill, 1960.

Bird, A. M. Effects of social facilitation upon females' performance of two psychomotor tasks. *Research Quarterly*, 1973, *44*, 322-330.

Bird, A. M. Cross sex effects of subject and audience during motor performance. *Research Quarterly*, 1975, *46*, 379-384.

Bird, A. M. Team structure and success as related to cohesiveness and leadership. *Journal of Social Psychology*, 1977, *103*, 217-223. (a)

Bird, A. M. Development of a model for predicting team performance. *Research Quarterly*, 1977, *48*, 24-32. (b)

Birney, R. C. Burdick, H. and Teevan, R. C. *Fear of failure motivation.* Wiley, 1969.

Blake, R. R. and Mouton, J. S. Conformity, resistance and conversion. In *Conformity and deviation* (I. A. Berg and B. M. Bass, Eds.). Harper, 1961.

Blau, P. M. *Exchange and power in social life.* Wiley, 1964.

Block, J. R. Motivation, satisfaction and performance of handicapped workers. Unpublished doctoral dissertation, New York University, 1962.

Bonner, H. *Group dynamics: Principles and applications.* Ronald Press, 1959.

Bonney, M. E. Relationships between social success, family size, socioeconomic home background, and intelligence among school children in grades III to V. *Sociometry*, 1944, *7*, 26-39.

Boulding, K. General systems theory: The skeleton of science, *Management Science*, 1956, 197-208.

Bowers, D. G. and Seashore, S. E. Predicting organizational effectiveness with a four factor theory of leadership. In *Groups and organizations* (B. L. Hinton, Ed.). Wadsworth Publishing Co., 1971.

Bowers, K. S. Situationism in psychology: An analysis and a critque. *Psychological Review*, 1973, *80*, 307-336.

Brawley, L. R., Landers, D. M., Miller, L. and Kegras, K. F. Sex bias in evaluating motor performance. *Journal of Sport Psychology*, 1979, *1*, 15-24.

Brenner, M. Stagefright and Stevens Law. Presented at the Eastern Psychological Association Meeting, 1974.

Brody, N. N. achievement, test anxiety and subjective probability of success in risk-taking behavior. *Journal of Abnormal and Social Psychology*, 1963, *66*, 413-418.

Brown, J. S. *The motivation of behavior*. McGraw-Hill, 1961.

Brown, R. W. *Social psychology*. Free Press, 1965.

Burwitz, L. and Newell, K. M. The effects of the mere presence of coactors on learning a motor skill. *Journal of Motor Behavior*, 1972, *4*, 99-102.

Butcher, H. J. *Human intelligence: Its nature and assessment*. Harper Torch Books, 1968.

Byrne, D. Attitudes and attraction. In *Advances in experimental social psychology*, (L. Berkowitz, Ed.), Vol. 4, Academic Press, 1969.

Campbell, J. P., Dunnette, M. D., Lawler, E. E. and Weick, K. E. *Managerial behavior, performance, and effectiveness*. McGraw-Hill, 1970.

Caplow, T. A theory of coalitions in the triad. *American Sociological Review*, 1956, *21*, 489-493.

Caplow, T. Further development of a theory of coalitions in the triad. *American Journal of Sociology*, 1959, *64*, 488-493.

Carder, B. The relationship between manifest anxiety and performance in college football. Unpublished master's thesis, University of California at Santa Barbara, 1965.

Carment, D. W. Rate of simple motor responding as a function of coaction competition and sex of the participants. *Psychonomic Science*, 1970, *19*, 342-343.

Carment, D. W. and Hodkin, B. Coaction and competition in India and Canada. *Journal of Cross Cultural Psychology*, 1973, *4*, 459-469.

Carment, D. W. and Latchford, M. Rate of simple responding as a function of coaction, sex of participants, and the presence or absence of the experimenter. *Psychonomic Science*, 1970, *20*, 253-254.

Carron, A. V. Motor performance under stress. *Research Quarterly*, 1968, *39*, 463-469.

Carron, A. V. Reactions to 'anxiety and motor behavior.' *Journal of Motor Behavior*, 1971, *3*, 181-188.

Carron, A. V. Personality and athletics: A review. In *The status of psychomotor learning and sport psychology research* (B. S. Rushall, Ed.). Sports Sciences Associates, 1975.

Carron, A. V. Role behavior and coach-athlete interaction. *International Review of Sport Sociology*, 1978, *13*, 51-65.

Carron, A. V. and Ball, J. R. Cause-effect characteristics of cohesiveness and participation motivation in intercollegiate hockey. *International Review of Sport Sociology*, 1977, *12*, 49-60.

Carron, A. V., Ball, J. R. and Chelladurai, P. Motivation for participation, success in performance and their relationship to individual and group satisfaction. *Perceptual and Motor Skills*, 1977, *45*, 835-841.

Carron, A. V. and Bennett, B. B. Compatibility in the coach-athlete dyad. *Research Quarterly*, 1977, *48*, 671-679.

Carron, A. V. and Chelladurai, P. Psychological factors and athletic success: An analysis of coach-athlete interpersonal behavior. *Canadian Journal of Applied Sport Sciences*, 1978, *3*, 43-50.

Carron, A. V. and Chelladurai, P. Cohesiveness as a factor in sport performance. Accepted, *International Review of Sport Sociology*, 1978.

Carron, A. V. and Garvie, G. T. Compatibility and successful performance. *Perceptual and Motor Skills*, 1978, *46*, 1121-1122.

Carron, A. V. and Leavitt, J. L. The effect of practice upon individual differences and intravariability in a motor skill. *Research Quarterly*, 1968, *39*, 470-474.

Carron, A. V. and Marteniuk, R. G. An examination of the selection of criterion scores for the study of learning and retention. *Journal of motor behavior*, 1970, *2*, 239-244.

Carron, A. V. and Morford, W. R. Anxiety, stress and learning. *Perceptual and Motor Skills*, 1968, *27*, 507-511.

Carter, J. E. L. The physiques of male physical education teachers in training. *Physical Educator*, 1964, *56*, 66-76.

Carter, J. E. L. Th physiques of female physical education teachers in training. *Physical Educator*, 1965, *57*, 6-16.

Cartwright, D. The nature of group cohesiveness. In *Group dynamics: Research and theory*, (D. Cartwright and A. Zander, Eds.), (3rd ed.). Harper and Row, 1968.

Cartwright, D. and Zander, A. *Group structure: Attraction, coalitions, communication and power*. (D. Cartwright and A. Zander, Eds.), (3rd ed.). Harper and Row, 1968.

Cartwright, D. C. and Zander, A. *Group dynamics: Research and theory*. Harper and Row, 1953.

Cartwright, D. and Zander, A. *Group dynamics: Research and theory*. Row, Peterson & Co., 1960.

Cartwright, D. C. and Zander, A. *Group dynamics: Research and theory*, 3rd. ed., Tavistock Publications, 1968.

Castaneda, A. Reaction time and response amplitude as a function of anxiety and stimulus intensity. *Journal of Abnormal and Social Psychology*, 1956, *53*, 225-228.

Castaneda, A., Palermo, D. S. and McCandless, B. R. Complex learning and performance as a function of anxiety in children and task difficulty. *Child Development*, 1956, *27*, 327-332.

Cattell, R. B. Concepts and methods in the measurement of group syntality. *Psychological Review*, 1948, *55*, 48-63.

Cattell, R. B. *Personality: A systematic, theoretical and factual study*. McGraw-Hill, 1950.

Cattell, R. B. New concepts for measuring leadership in terms of group syntality. In *Group dynamics: Research and theory*, (D. C. Cartwright and A. Zander, Eds.). Row, Peterson, 1953.

Cattell, R. B. *Personality and motivation structure and measurement*. World Books, 1957.

Cattell, R. B. *The scientific analysis of behavior*. Penguin, 1965.

Cattell, R. B. and Butcher, H. J. *The prediction of achievement and creativity*. Boobs-Merrill, 1968.

Cattell, R. B. and Eber, H. W. *Handbook for the Sixteen Personality Factor Questionnaire*. Institute for Personality and Ability Testing, 1962.

Cattell, R. B., Eber, H. W., and Tatsuoka, M. M. *Handbook for the Sixteen Personality Factor Questionnaire*. Institute for Personality Ability and Testing, 1970.

Chapman, A. J. An electromyographic study of apprehension about evaluation. *Psychological Reports*, 1973, *33*, 811-814.

Chapman, A. J. An electromyographic study of social facilitation: A test of the "mere presence" hypothesis. *British Journal of Psychology*, 1974, *65*, 123-128.

Cheffers, J. T. F., Amidon, E. J. and Rodgers, K. D. *Interaction analysis: An application to nonverbal activity*. Association for Productive Teaching, 1974.

Cheffers, J. T. F. and Mancini, V. H. Teacher-student interaction. In *What's going on in gym: Descriptive studies of physical education classes*, (W. G. Anderson and G. T. Barrette, Eds.), Monograph 1. *Motor Skills: Theory into Practice*, 1978.

Chelladurai, P. A multidimensional model of leadership. Unpublished doctoral dissertation, University of Waterloo, Waterloo, Ontario, 1978.

Chelladurai, P. and Carron, A. V. A reanalysis of formal structure in sport. *Canadian Journal of Applied Sport Sciences*, 1977, *2*, 9-14.

Chelladurai, P. and Carron, A. V. *Leadership*. Canadian Association for Health, Physical Education and Recreation, 1978.

Chelladurai, P. and Haggerty, T. R. A normative model for decision styles in coaching. *Athletic Administrator*, 1978, *13*, 6-9.

Chelladurai, P. and Saleh, S. D. Preferred leadership in sport. *Canadian Journal of Applied Sport Sciences*, 1978, *3*, 85-97.

Church, R. M. The effects of competition on reaction time and palmar skin conductance. *Journal of Abnormal and Social Psychology*, 1962, *65*, 32-40.

Cialdini, R. B., Bordon, R. J., Thorne, A., Walker, M. R., Freeman, S., and Sloan, L. R. Basking in reflected glory: Three (football) field studies. *Journal of Personality and Social Psychology*, 1976, *34*, 366-375.

Clore, G. L. and Byrne, D. A reinforcement-affect model of attraction. In *Foundations of interpersonal attraction*, (T. L. Huston, Ed.). Academic Press, 1974.

Cockerill, I. Personality of golf players. Unpublished thesis, University of Leeds, Institute of Education, 1968.

Cofer, C. N. and Johnson, W. R. Personality dynamics in relation to exercise and sports. In *Science and medicine of exercise and sport*, (W. R. Johnson, Ed.). Harper, 1960.

Cohen, J. L. and Davis, J. H. Effects of audience, status, evaluation and time of action on hidden problems. *Journal of Personality and Social Psychology*, 1973, *27*, 74-85.

Coleman, J. S. *The adolescent society: The social life of the teenager and its impact on education*. Free Press, 1961.

Collins, B. E. and Guetzkow, H. *A social psychology of group processes for decision-making*. Wiley, 1964.

Collins, B. E. and Raven, B. H. Group structure: attraction, coalitions, communication and power. In *The handbook of social psychology*, 2nd ed., (G. Lindzey and E. Aronson, Eds.), Vol. 4. Addison-Wesley, 1969.

Comrey, A. L. Group performance in a manual dexterity task. *Journal of Applied Psychology*, 1953, *37*, 207-210.

Comrey, A. L. and Deskin, G. Further results on group manual dexterity in men. *Journal of Applied Psychology*, 1954, *38*, 116-118. (a)

Comfrey, A. L. and Deskin, G. Group manual dexterity in women. *Journal of Applied Psychology*, 1954, *38*, 178-180. (b)

Comfrey, A. L. and Staats, C. K. Group performance in a cognitive task. *Journal of Applied Psychology*. 1955, *39*, 354-356.

Cooley, C. H. *Social organization*. Charles Scribner's Sons, 1911.

Cooper, L. Athletics, activity and personality: A review of the literature. *Research Quarterly*, 1969, *40*, 17-22.

Costello, J. and Laubach, S. A. Student behavior. In *What's going on in gym: Descriptive studies of physical education classes*, (W. G. Anderson and G. T. Barrette, Eds.), Monograph 1. *Motor Skills: Theory into Practice*, 1978.

Cottrell, N. B., Rittle, R. H., and Wack, D. L. Presence of an audience and list type (competitional and noncompetitional) as joint determinants of performance in paired-associates learning. *Journal of Personality*, 1967, *35*, 425-434.

Cottrell, N. B. Social facilitation. In *Experimental social psychology*, (C. G. McClintock, Ed.). Holt, Rinehart & Winston, 1972.

Cottrell, N. B., Rittle, R. H., and Wack, D. L. Presence of an audience and list type (competitional and noncompetitional) as joint determinants of performance inpaired-associates learning. *Journal of Personality*, 1967, *35*, 425-434.

Cottrell, N. B., Wack, D. L., Sekerak, G. J. and Rittle, R. H. Social facilitation of dominant responses by the presence of an audience and the mere presence of others. *Journal of Personality and Social Psychology*, 1968, *9*, 245-250.

Cowen, J. E. Test anxiety in high school students and its relationship to performance on group tests. Unpublished doctoral dissertation, Harvard University, 1957.

Cox, F. N. An assessment of the achievement behavior system in children. *Child Development*, 1962, *33*, 907-916.

Cox, F. N. Some effects of test anxiety and presence or absence of other persons on boys' performance on a repetitive motor task. *Journal of Experimental Child Psychology*, 1966, *3*, 100-112.

Cox, F. N. Some relationships between test anxiety, presence or absence of male persons and boys' performance on a repetitive motor task. *Journal of Experimental Child Psychology*, 1968, *6*, 1-12.

Crandell, R. Social facilitation theories and research. In *Explorations in psychology*, (A. Harrison, Ed.). Brooks/Cole, 1974.

Cratty, B. J. *Social dimensions of physical activity*. Prentice-Hall Inc., 1967.

Cratty, B. J. *Psychology and Physical activity*. Prentice-Hall Inc., 1968.

Cratty, B. J. *Psychology in contemporary sport*. Prentice-Hall Inc., 1973.

Croner, M. D. and Willis, R. H. Perceived differences in task competence and asymmetry of dyadic influence. *Journal of Abnormal and Social Psychology*, 1961, *62*, 705-708.

Crossman, E. R. F. W. Information processing in human skill. *British Medical Journal*, 1964, *20*, 32-37.

Danielson, R. R. Contingency model of leadership effectiveness: For empirical investigation of its application in sport. *Motor Learning, sport psychology, pedagogy and didactics of physical activity*, Monograph 5. Quebec City, 1976.

Danielson, R. R., Zelhart, P. F. and Drake, C. J. Multidimensional scaling and factor analysis of coaching behavior as perceived by high school hockey players. *Research Quarterly*, 1975, *46*, 323-334.

Danzig, E. R. and Galanter, E. H. *The dynamics and structure of small industrial work groups*. Institute for Research in Human Relations, 1955.

Darley, J. M. and Latane, B. Bystanders intervention in emergencies: Diffusion of responsibility. *Journal of Personality and Social Psychology*, 1968, *8*, 377-383.

Dashiell, J. F. An experimental analysis of some group effects. *Journal of Abnormal and Social Psychology*, 1930, *25*, 190-199.

Dashiell, J. F. Experimental studies of the influence of social situations on the behavior of individual human adults. In *A handbook of social psychology*, (C. Murchison, Ed.). Clarke University Press, 1935.

Davis, J. H. *Group performance*. Addison-Wesley, 1969.

De Charms, R. C. and Dave, P. N. Hope of success, fear of failure, subjective probability and risk taking behavior. *Journal of Personality and Social Psychology*, 1965, *1*, 558-568.

De Charms, R. C. and Carpenter, V. Measuring motivation in culturally disadvantaged school children. *Journal of Experimental Education*, 1968, *37*, 31-41.

Desiderato, O. Effect of anxiety and stress on reaction time. *Psychological Reports*, 1964, *14*, 51-58.

Deutsch, M. A theory of cooperation and competition. *Human Relations*, 1949, *2*, 129-152. (a)

Deutsch, M. An experimental study of the effects of cooperation and competition upon group process. *Human Relations*, 1949, *2*, 199-231. (b)

Deutsch, M. The effects of cooperation and competition upon group process. In *Group dynamics: Research and theory*, 3rd. ed., (D. Cartwright and A. Zander, Eds.). Tavistock Publications, 1968.

Diehl, B. The effects of emotional stress upon motor performance of anxious and nonanxious subjects. Unpublished master's thesis, University of California at Santa Barbara, 1965.

Donley, R. E. and Winter, D. G. Measuring the motives of public officials at a distance: An exploratory study of American presidents. *Behavioral Science*, 1970, *15*, 227-235.

Donnelly, P. An analysis of the relationship between organizational half-life and organizational effectiveness. Paper completed for an Advanced Topics course, Department of Sport Studies, University of Massachusetts, Amherst, 1975.

Donnelly, P., Carron, A. V. and Chelladurai, P. *Group cohesion and sport*. CAHPER Sociology of Sport Monograph Series, 1978.

Duffy, E. *Activation and behavior*. Wiley, 1962.

Dunkin, M. J. and Biddle, B. J. *The study of teaching*. Holt, Rinehart and Winston, 1974.

Dunn, R. E. and Goldman, M. Competition and noncompetition in relation to satisfaction and feeling toward own-group and nongroup members. *Journal of Social Psychology*, 1966, *68*, 299-311.

Dunteman, G. and Bass, B. M. Supervisory and engineering success associated with self, interaction and task orientation scores. *Personnel Psychology*, 1963, *23*, 101-116.

Duquin, M. E. Attributions made by children in coeducational sport settings. In *Psychology of motor behavior and sport* (D. M. Landers and R. W. Christina, Eds.). Human Kinetics Publishers, 1977.

Duthie, J. H. and Roberts, G. C. Effect of manifest anxiety on learning and performance of a complex motor task. Paper presented at 2nd International Congress of Sport Psychology, Washington, 1968.

Duval, S. and Wicklund, R. A. *A theory of objective self-awareness*. Academic Press, 1972.

Edwards, H. *Sociology of sport*. Dorsey Press, 1973.

Eisman, B. Some operational measures of cohesiveness and their correlations. *Human Relations*, 1959, *12*, 183-189.

Eitzen, D. S. Athletics in the status system of male adolescents: A replication of Coleman's *The Adolescent Society*. In *Sport sociology: Contemporary themes*, (A. Yiannakis, T. D. McIntyre, M. J. Melnick and D. P. Hart, Eds.). Kendall/Hunt Publishing Co., 1976.

Eitzen, S. D. and Yetman, N. R. Managerial change, longevity, and organizational effectiveness. *Administrative Science Quarterly*, 1972, *17*, 110-116.

Endler, N. S. and Hunt, J. MCV. Sources of behavioral variance as measured by the S-R Inventory of Anxiousness. *Psychological Bulletin*, 1966, *65*, 338-346.

Endler, N. S. and Hunt, J. McV. S-R inventories of hostility and comparisons of the proportion of variance from persons, responses, and situations for hostility and anxiousness. *Journal of Personality and Social Psychology*, 1968, *9*, 309-315.

Endler, N. S. and Hunt, J. McV. Generalizability of contributions from sources of variance in the S-R Inventories of Anxiousness. In *Readings in Personality*, (H. N. Mischel and W. Mischel, Eds.). Holt, Rinehart and Winston, 1973.

Endler, N. S., Hunt, J. McV. and Rosenstein, A. J. An S-R Inventory of Anxiousness. *Psychological Monographs*, 1962, *76*, No. 17 (Whole No. 536), 1-33.

Entwhistle, D. R. To dispel fantasies about fantasy-based measures of achievement motivation. *Psychological Bulletin*, 1972, *77*, 377-391.

Erickson, E. H. *Identity, youth and crisis*. W. W. Norton, 1960.

Escovar, L. A. and Sim, F. M. The cohesion of groups: Alternative conceptions. Paper presented at the Meetings of the Canadian Sociology and Anthropology Association, Toronto, 1974.

Essing, W. Team lineup and team achievement in European football. In *Contemporary psychology of sport: Proceedings of the second international congress of sport psychology*, (G. S. Kenyon, Ed.). The Athletic Institute, 1970.

Evans, J. F. Social facilitation in a competitive situation. *Canadian Journal of Behavioral Science*, 1971, *3*, 276-281.

Farber, I. E. and Spence, K. W. Complex learning and conditioning as a function of anxiety. *Journal of Experimental Psychology*, 1953, *45*, 120-125.

Farber, I. E. and Spence, K. W. Effects of anxiety, stress and task variables on reaction time. *Journal of Personality*, 1956, *25*, 1-18.

Feather, N. T. and Simon, J. G. Causal attributions for success and failure in relation to expectations of success based upon selective or manipulative control. *Journal of Personality*, 1971, *39*, 527-541.

Feather, N. T. and Simon, J. G. Attribution of responsibility and valence of outcome in relation to initial confidence and success and failure of self and other. *Journal of Personality and Social Psychology*, 1971, *18*, 173-188.

Feather, N. T. and Raphelson, A. C. Fear of success in Australian and American student groups: Motive or sex-role stereotype? *Journal of Personality*, 1974, *42*, 190-201.

Feltz, D. L. and Landers, D. M. Informational-motivational components of a model's demonstration. *Research Quarterly*, 1977, *48*, 525-533.

Festinger, L. A theory of social comparison processes. *Human Relations*, 1954, *7*, 117-140.

Festinger, L. Informal group communication. In *Group dynamics: Research and theory*, 3rd. ed., (D. Cartwright and A. Zander, Eds.). Tavistock Publications, 1968.

Festinger, L., Schachter, S. and Back, K. *Social pressures in informal groups*. Harper, 1950.

Fiedler, F. E. Assumed similarity measures as predictors of team effectiveness. *Journal of Abnormal and Social Psychology*, 1954, *49*, 381-388.

Fiedler, F. E. *A theory of leadership effectiveness*. McGraw-Hill, 1967.

Fiedler, F. E. Personality and situational determinants of leader behavior. In *Current developments in the study of leadership*, (E. A. Fleishman and J. G. Hunt, Eds.). Southern Illinois University Press, 1973.

Fiedler, F. E. and Chemers, M. M. *Leadership and effective management*. Scott, Foreman and Co., 1974.

Fiedler, F. E. and Leister, A. F. Leader intelligence and task performance: A test of a multiple screen model. *Organizational Behavior and Human Performance*, 1977, *20*, 1-14.

Fineman, S. The achievement motive construct and its measurement: Where are we now? *British Journal of Psychology*, 1977, *68*, 1-22.

Fisher, A. C. In search of the albatross. Paper presented at North American Society for the Psychology of Sport and Physical Activity Convention, Anaheim, Calif., 1974.

Fisher, A. C. and Driscoll, R. G. Attribution of attitudes toward physical activity as a function of success. In *Mouvement* (J. Salmela, C. Bard, R. Desharnais, D. Drouin, M. Fleury, Eds.), 1975.

Fisher, A. C., Horsfall, J. S. and Morris, H. H. Sport personality assessment: A methodological re-examination. *International Journal of Sport Psychology*, 1977, *8*, 92-102.

Fishman, S. A procedure for recording augmented feedback in physical education classes. Unpubished doctoral dissertation, Teachers College, Columbia University, 1974.

Fishman, S. and Tobey, C. Augmented feedback. In *What's going on in gym: Descriptive studies of physical education classes*, (W. G. Anderson and G. T. Barrette, Eds.) Monograph 1. *Motor Skills: Theory into Practice*, 1978.

Fitts, P. and Posner, M. I. *Human performance*. Brooks/Cole, 1967.

Flanders, J. P. and Thistlethwaite, D. L. Effects of familiarization and group discussion upon risk taking. *Journal of Personality and Social Psychology*, 1967, *5*, 91-97.

Flanders, N. A. *Analyzing teaching behavior*. Addison-Wesley, 1970.

Fleishman, E. A. A leader behavior description for industry. In *Leadership behavior: Its description and measurement*, (R. M. Stogdill and A. E. Coons, Eds.). The Ohio State University, 1957. (a)

Fleishman, E. A. *The Leadership opinion questionnaire*. In *Leadership behavior: Its description and measurement*, (R. M. Stogdill and A. E. Coons, Eds.). The Ohio State University, 1957. (b)

Fleishman, E. A., Harris, E. F. and Burtt, H. E. *Leadership and supervision in industry*, (Educational Research Monograph No. 33). Ohio State University Personnel Research Board, 1955.

Foder, E. M. Group stress, authoritarian style of control and use of power. *Journal of Applied Psychology*, 1976, *61*, 313-318.

Forsythe, B. and Schlenker, B. R. Attributing the causes of group performance: Effects of performance quality, task importance, and future testing. *Journal of Personality*, 1977, *45*, 220-236.

Freishchlag, J. Basis considerations in changing attitudes toward physical education-credibility-success, consequences, and self-discovery. *The Physical Educator*, 1973, *30*, 19-21.

Freize, I. Causal attributions and information seeking to explain success and failure. *Journal of Research in Personality*, 1976, *10*, 293-305.

Freize, I. and Weiner, B. Cue utilization and attributional judgements for success and failure. *Journal of Personality*, 1971, *39*, 591-605.

292

French, E. G. Development of a measure of complex motivation. In *Motives in fantasy, action, and society,* (J. W. Atkinson, Ed.). Van Nostrand, 1958.

French, J. R. P. and Raven, B. The bases of power. In *Studies in social power,* (D. Cartwright, Ed.). Institute for Social Research, 1959.

Freud, S. In *The standard edition of the complete psychological works of Sigmund Freud,* (J. Strachey, Ed.). Hogarth Press, 1955.

Fromm, E. *Escape from reality.* Rinehart, 1941.

Gamson, W. A. A theory of coalition formation. *American Sociological Review,* 1961, *26,* 373-382.

Gamson, W. A. Experimental studies of coalition formation. In *Advances in experimental social psychology,* (L. Berkowitz, Ed.), Vol. 1. Academic Press, 1964.

Ganzer, V. J. Effects of an audience presence and test anxiety on learning and retention in a serial learning situation. *Journal of Personality and Social Psychology,* 1968, *8,* 194-199.

Gates, G. S. The effects of an audience upon performance. *Journal of Abnormal and Social Psychology,* 1924, *18,* 334-342.

Gent, P. *North Dallas forty.* The American Library, Inc. 1973.

Gerard, H. B. and Greenbaum, C. W. Attitudes toward an agent of uncertainty reduction. *Journal of Personality,* 1962, *30,* 485-495.

Gerard, H. B., Wilhelmy, R. A. and Conolley, R. S. Conformity and group size. *Journal of Personality and Social Psychology,* 1968, *8,* 79-82.

Gilmor, T. M. and Minton, H. L. Internal versus external attribution of task performance as a function of locus of control, initial confidence and success-failure outcome. *Journal of Personality,* 1974, *42,* 159-174.

Glanzer, M. and Glaser, R. Techniques for the study of group structure and behavior: II. Empirical studies of the effects of structure in small groups. *Psychological Bulletin,* 1961, *58,* 1-27.

Goldberg, L. R. and Werts, C. E. The reliability of clinicians' judgements: A multitrait-multimethod approach. *Journal of Consulting Psychology,* 1966, *30,* 199-206.

Goldberg, S. C. Three situational determinants of conformity to social norms. *Journal of Abnormal and Social Psychology,* 1954, *49,* 325-329.

Goldman, M., Stockbauer, J. W. and McAuliffe, T. G. Intergroup and intragroup competition and cooperation. *Journal of Experimental Social Psychology,* 1977, *13,* 81-88.

Graen, G. Alvares, K., Orris, J. B. and Martella, J. A. Contingency model of leadership effectiveness: Antecedent and evidencial results. *Psychological Bulletin,* 1970, *74,* 285-296.

Grice, G. R. Discrimination reaction time as a function of anxiety and intelligence, *Journal of Abnormal and Social Psychology,* 1955, *50,* 71-74.

Griffen, M. R. An analysis of state and trait anxiety experienced in sports competition by women at different age levels. *Dissertation Abstracts International,* 1972, *32,* 37-58.

Gross, N. and Martin, W. On group cohesiveness. *American Journal of Sociology,* 1952, *57,* 533-546.

Grusky, O. The effects of formal structure on managerial recruitment: A study of baseball organization. *Sociometry,* 1963, *26,* 345-353.

Grusky, O. Managerial succession and organizational effectiveness. *American Journal of Sociology,* 1963, *69,* 21-31.

Guetzkow, H. and Simon, H. A. The impact of certain communication nets upon organization and performance in task-oriented groups. *Management Science,* 1955, *1,* 233-250.

Guilford, J. P. *Personality.* McGraw-Hill, 1959.

Gullahorn, J. T. Distance and friendship as factors in the gross interaction matrix. *Sociometry,* 1952, *15,* 123-134.

Hass, J., and Roberts, G. C. Effects of evaluative others upon performance of a complex motor task. In *Proceedings of the Fourth Canadian Psychomotor Learning and Sports Psychology Symposium,* (I. D. Williams and L. M. Wankel, Eds.). Department of National Health and Welfare, 1973.

Hackman, J. R. and Oldham, G. R. Motivation through the design of work: Test of a theory. *Organizational Behavior and Human Performance,* 1976, *16,* 250-279.

Hagstrom, W. O. and Selvin, H. C. The dimensions of cohesiveness in small groups. *Sociometry,* 1965, *28,* 30-43.

Hall, E. T. *The silent language.* Doubleday & Co., 1959.

Halpin, A. W. and Winer, B. J. A factorial study of the leader behavior description. In *Leader behavior: Its description and measurement,* (R. M. Stogdill and A. E. Coons, Eds.). The Ohio State University, 1957.

Hammer, W. H. A comparison of differences in manifest anxiety in university athletes and nonathletes. *Journal of Sports Medicine and Physical Fitness,* 1967, *7,* 31-34.

Hammer, W. H. Anxiety and sport performance. Paper presented at 2nd International Congress of Sport Psychology, Washington, 1968.

Hammes, J. A. and Wiggins, S. L. Perceptual motor steadiness, manifest anxiety and color illumination. *Perceptual and Motor Skills*, 1962, *14*, 59-61.

Hancock, J. G. and Teevan, R. C. Fear of failure and risk taking behavior. *Journal of Personality*, 1964, *32*, 200-209.

Hardman, K. The personality differences between top class games players and players of lesser ability. Unpublished M.ED. thesis, University of Manchester, 1968.

Hardman, K. A dual approach to the study of personality and performance in sport. In *Personality and performance in physical education and sport*, (H. T. A. Whiting, K. Hardman, L. B. Hendry and M. G. Jones, Eds.). Henry Kimpton, 1973.

Hare, R. Current physical activity patterns and motives towards participation as a function of the degree of former minor hockey participation. Unpublished M.A. Thesis, University of Western Ontario, London, 1976.

Harney, D. M. and Parker, R. Effects of social reinforcement, subject sex, and experimenter sex on children's motor performance. 1972, *43*, 187-196.

Harris, D. V. *Involvement in sport: A somatopsychic rationale for physical activity*. Lea & Febiger, 1973.

Harris, D. V. Assessment of motivation in sport and physical education. In *Sport psychology: An analysis of athlete behavior*, (W. F. Straub, Ed.). Mouvement Publications, 1978.

Hatfield, B. D. and Landers, D. M. Observer expectancy effects upon appraisal of gross motor performance. *Research Quarterly*, 1978, *49*, 53-61.

Healey, T. R. and Landers, D. M. Effect of need achievement and task difficulty on competitive and non-competitive motor performance. *Journal of Motor Behavior*, 1973, *5*, 121-128.

Hearn, G. Leadership and the spatial factor in small groups. *Journal of Abnormal and Social Psychology*, 1957, *54*, 269-272.

Hebb, D. O. *The organization of behavior*. Wiley, 1949.

Hebb, D. O. Drives and the C.N.S. (Central Nervous System). *Psychological Review*, 1955, *62*, 243-254.

Heider, F. Social perception and phenomenal causality. *Psychological Review*, 1944, *51*, 358-374.

Heider, F. *The psychology of interpersonal relations*. Wiley, 1958.

Helmreich, R. and Spence, J. T. Sex roles and achievement. In *Psychology of motor behavior and sport*, Vol. 2, (R. W. Christina and D. M. Landers, Eds.). Human Kinetics Publishers, 1977.

Hemphill, J. K. and Coons, A. E. Development of the *Leader Behavior Description Questionnaire*. In *Leader Behavior: Its description and measurement*, (R. M. Stogdill and A. E. Coons, Eds.). The Ohio State University, 1957.

Henchy, T. and Glass, D. C. Evaluative apprehension and the social facilitation of dominant and subordinate responses. *Journal of Personality and Social Psychology*, 1968, *4*, 446-454.

Hendry, L. B. Assessment of personality traits in the coach-athlete relationship. *Research Quarterly*, 1968, *39*, 543-551.

Hendry, L. B. The coaching stereotype. In *Readings in sports psychology*, (H. T. A. Whiting, Ed.). Henry Kimpton, 1972.

Hendry, L. B. The 'physical educationist' stereotype. In *Personality and performance in physical education and sport*, (H. T. A. Whiting, K. Hardman, L. B. Hendry, M. G. Jones, Eds.). Henry Kimpton, 1973.

Hendry, L. B. Human factors in sports systems: Suggested models for analyzing athlete-coach interaction. *Human Factors*, 1974, *16*, 528-544.

Hersey, P. and Blanchard, K. H. Life cycle theory of leadership. *Training and Development Journal*, 1969, 26-34.

Hersey, P. and Blanchard, K. H. *Management of organizational behavior* (3rd. edition). Prentice-Hall, 1977.

Herzberg, F. *Work and nature of man*. World Publishing Co., 1966.

Heusner, W. V. Personality traits of champion and former champion athletes. Unpublished M.A. Thesis, University of Illinois, 1952.

Hilgard, E. R. and Bower, G. H. *Theories of learning*, Prentice-Hall., 1966.

Hill, R. E. Interpersonal compatibility and work-group performance. *Journal of Applied Behavioral Science*, 1975, *11*, 210-219.

Hill, W. A. and Hughs, D. Variation in leader behavior as a function of task type. *Organizational Behavior and Human Performance*, 1974, *11*, 83-96.

Hill, W. F. and Gruner, L. A study of development in open and closed groups. *Small Group Behavior*, 1973, *4*, 365-381.

Hillery, J. M. and Fugita, S. S. Social facilitation in employment testing. *Educational and Psychological Measurement*, 1975, *35*, 745-750.

Hitchman, M. The learning-performance dichotomy of social facilitation. In *Psychology of sport and motor behavior*, (D. M. Landers, D. V. Harris and R. W. Christina, Eds). The College of Health, Physical Education and Recreation, The Pennsylvania State University, 1975.

Hollander, E. P. Conformity, status and idiosyncrasy credit. *Psychological Review*, 1958, *65*, 117-127.

Hollander, E. P. Competence and conformity in the acceptance of influence. *Journal of Abnormal and Social Psychology*, 1960, *61*, 365-370.

Hollander, E. P. Some effects of perceived status on responses to innovative behavior. *Journal of Abnormal and Social Psychology*, 1961, *63*, 247-250.

Hollander, E. P. *Leaders, groups and influence*. Oxford University Press, 1964.

Hollander, E. P. *Principles and methods of social psychology*. Oxford University Press, 1967.

Hollander, E. P. *Principles and methods of social psychology*, 2nd ed., Oxford University Press, 1971.

Hollander, E. P. and Julian, J. W. Contemporary trends in the analysis of leadership processes. *Psychological Bulletin*, 1969, *71*, 387-397.

Hollander, E. P. and Willis, R. H. Conformity, independence, and anticonformity as determinants of perceived influence and attraction. In *Leaders, groups and influence*, (E. P. Hollander, Ed.). Oxford University Press, 1964.

Hollander, E. P. and Willis, R. H. Some current issues in the psychology of conformity and nonconformity. *Psychological Bulletin*, 1967, *68*, 62-76.

Holtzman, W. H. Recurring dilemmas in personality assessment. *Journal of Projective Techniques and Personality Assessment*, 1964, *28*, 144-150.

Homans, G. C. *The human group*. Routledge & Kegan, Paul, 1951.

Homans, G. C. *Social behavior: Its elementary forms*. Harcourt Brace, 1961.

Hopkins, T. K. *The exercise of influence in small groups*. Bedminister Press, 1964.

Horner, M. S. Sex differences in achievement motivation and performance in competitive and non-competitive situations. Unpublished doctoral dissertation, University of Michigan, 1968.

House, R. J. A path-goal theory of leader effectiveness. *Administrative Science Quarterly*, 1971, *16*, 321-328.

House, R. J. and Dessler, C. The path-goal theory of leadership: Some post hoc and a priori tests. In *Contingency approaches to leadership*, (J. A. Hunt and L. L. Larson, Eds.). Southern Illinois University Pres 1974.

House, R. J. and Mitchell, T. R. Path-goal theory of leadership. *Journal of Contemporary Business*, 1974, *5*, 81-97.

Hovland, C. I., Janis, I. L. and Kelley, H. H. *Communication and persuasion*. Yale University Press, 1953.

Hull, C. L. *Principles of behavior*. Appleton, 1943.

Hull, C. L. *Essentials of behavior*. Yale University Press, 1951.

Hull, C. L. *A behavior system: An introduction to behavior theory concerning the individual organism*. Yale University Press, 1952.

Hunt, P. J. and Hillery, J. M. Social facilitation in a coaction setting: An examination of the effects over learning trials. *Journal of Experimental Social Psychology*, 1973, *9*, 563-571.

Hurlock, E. B. The use of group rivalry as an incentive. *Journal of Abnormal and Social Psychology*, 1927, *22*, 278-290.

Hurwitz, J. I., Zander, A. and Hymovitch, B. Some effects of power on the relations among group members. In *Group Dynamics: Research and theory*, (D. Cartwright and A. Zander, Eds.), 3rd ed., Tavistock, 1968.

Hurwitz, R. Review. In *What's going on in gym: Descriptive studies of physical education classes*, (W. G. Anderson and G. T. Barrette, Eds.) Monograph 1. *Motor Skills: Theory into Practice*, 1978.

Husband, R. W. Analysis of methods in human maze learning. *Journal of Genetic Psychology*, 1931, *39*, 258-277.

Hutcheson, D. E. Relationships among pupil-teacher compatibility social studies grades, selected factors. Unpublished PhD Dissertation, University of California, Berkeley, 1963.

Inciong, P. A. Leadership styles and team success. Unpublished doctoral dissertation, University of Utah, 1974.

Indik, B. P. Organization size and member participation: Some empirical tests of alternate explanations. *Human Relations*, 1965, *18*, 339-350.

Ingham, A. G., Levinger, G., Graves, J. and Peckham, V. The Ringlemann Effect: Studies of group size and group performance. *Journal of Experimental Social Psychology* 1974, *10*, 371-384.

Issacson, R. L. Relation between achievement test anxiety and curricular choices. *Journal of Abnormal and Social Psychology*, 1964, *68*, 447-452.

Iso-Ahola, S. A test of the attributional theory of success and failure with Little League baseball players. In *Mouvement* (J. Salmela, C. Bard, R. Desharnais, D. Drouin and M. Fleury, Eds.) 1975.

Iso-Ahola, S. Determinants of evaluation of team performance. *Scandinavian Journal of Psychology*. 1976, *17*, 292-296.

Iso-Ahola, S. Effects of team outcome on children's self-perception: Little League baseball. *Scandinavian Journal of Psychology*, 1977, *18*, 38-42. (a)

Iso-Ahola, S. Immediate attributional effects of success and failure in the field: Testing some laboratory hypotheses. *European Journal of Social Psychology*, 1977, *7*, 275-296. (b)

Iso-Ahola, S. Effects of self-enhancement and consistency on causal and trait attributions following success and failure in motor performance. *Research Quarterly*, 1977, *48*, 717-726. (c)

Iso-Ahola, S. and Roberts, G. C. Causal attributions following success and failure in an achievement task: A test of self-enhancement. In *Psychology of Sport and Motor Behavior*, Vol. 2, (D. M. Landers, Ed.). Pennsylvania State University Press, 1975.

Iso-Ahola, S. and Roberts, G. C. Causal attributions following success and failure at an achievement task. *Research Quarterly*, 1977, *48*, 541-549.

Iverson, M. A. Personality impressions of punitive stimulus persons of differential status. *Journal of Abnormal and Social Psychology*, 1964, *68*, 617-626.

Jackson, D. N. *Personality research form manual*. Research Psychologists Press, Inc., 1967.

Jackson, J. Personality and rock climbing. Unpublished dissertation, University of Leeds Institute of Education, 1967.

Jackson, J. M. Reference group processes in a formal organization. *Sociometry*, 1959, *22*, 307-327.

Janis, I. L., Mahl, G. F., Kagan, J. and Holt, R. R. *Personality dynamics, development and assessment.* Harcourt, Brace and Jovanovitch, 1969.

Jones, C. M. *Tennis: How to become a champion*, Faber, 1968.

Jones, E. E. and Davis, K. E. From acts to dispositions: The attribution process in person perception. In *Advances in experimental social psychology*, Vol. 2, (L. Berkowitz, Ed.). 1965.

Jones, E. E. and Nisbett, R. E. The actor and the observer: Divergent perceptions of the causes of behavior. In *Attribution: Perceiving the cause of behavior*, (E. E. Jones, D. E. Kanhouse, H. H. Kelly, R. E. Nisbett, S. Valins, B. Weiner, Eds.). General Learning Press, 1972.

Julian, J. W., Bishop, D. W. and Fiedler, F. E. Quasi-theraputic effects of intergroup competition. *Journal of Personality and Social Psychology*, 1966, *3*, 321-332.

Julian, J. W. and Perry, F. A. Cooperation contrasted with intra-group and inter-group competition. *Sociometry*, 1967, *3*, 79-90.

Kamin, L. J. and Clark, K. W. The Taylor scale and reaction time. *Journal of Abnormal and Social Psychology*, 1957, *54*, 262-263.

Kane, J. E. Personality and physical ability. In *Proceedings of the International Congress of Sport Sciences*, (K. Kato, Ed.). Japanese Union of Sport Sciences, 1964. (a)

Kane, J. E. Psychological correlates of physique and physical abilities. In *International research in sport and physical education*, (E. Jokl and E. Simon, Eds.). Charles C. Thomas, 1964. (b)

Kane, J. E. Personality profiles of physical education students compared with others. Paper presented at the First International Congress of Sport Psychology, Rome, 1965.

Kane, J. E. Personality description of soccer ability. In *Research in Physical Education*, 1966, *1*, 54-64.

Kane, J. E. Personality and physical ability. In *Contemporary psychology of sport*, (G. S. Kenyon, Ed.). The Athletic Institute, 1970.

Kane, J. E. Personality, body concept and performance. In *Psychological aspects of physical education and sport*, (J. E. Kane, Ed.). Routledge and Kegan Paul, 1972.

Kane, J. E. Personality and performance in sport. In *Sports medicine*, (J. Williams and P. Sperry, Eds.), Arnold, 1976.

Kane, J. E. Personality research: The current controversy and implications for sport studies. In *Sport psychology: An analysis of athlete behavior*, (W. F. Straub, Ed.). Mouvement, 1978.

Katz, D., Maccoby, N., Gurin, G. & Floor, L. *Productivity, supervision and morale among railroad workers.* University of Michigan Survey Research Center, 1951.

Katz, D., Maccoby, N. & Morse, N. *Productivity, supervision and morale in an office situation.* University of Michigan Survey Research Center, 1950.

Kelley, H. H. Attribution theory in social psychology. In *Nebraska symposium on motivation* (Vol. 15), (D. Levine, Ed.). Nebraska University Press, 1967.

Kelley, H. H. *Attribution in social interaction.* General Learning Press, 1971.

Kelley, H. H. The process of causal attribution. *American Psychologist,* 1973, *28,* 107-128.

Kelley, H. H. and Thibaut, J. W. Group problem solving. In *The handbook of social psychology,* (G. Lindzey and E. Aronson, Eds.), 2nd ed., Vol. 4. Addison-Wesley, 1969.

Kelley, H. H., Thibaut, J. W., Radloff, R. and Mundy, D. The development of cooperation in the "minimal social setting." *Psychological Monographs,* 1962, 76 (19, Whole No. 538).

Kelman, H. C. Three processes of social influence. In *Current perspectives in social psychology* (E. P. Hollander and R. G. Hunt, Eds.) 3rd ed. Oxford University Press, 1971.

Kendall, P. Medical education as social process. Abstract, American Sociological Association, 1960.

Kennedy, J. L. and Travis, R. C. Prediction and control of alertness: II. Continuous tracking. *Journal of Comparative and Physiological* 1948, *41,* 203-210.

Kenyon, G. S. Six scales for assessing attitudes toward physical activity. *Research Quarterly,* 1968, *39,* 566-574. (a)

Kenyon, G. S. *Values held for physical activity by selected students in Canada, Australia, England, and the United States.* U.S. Government Printing Office, 1968. (b)

Kerr, S., Schreisheim, C. A., Murphy, C. J. & Stogdill, R. M. Toward a contingency theory of leadership based upon the consideration and initiating structure literature. *Organizational Behavior and Human Performance,* 1974, *12,* 62-82.

Kidd, J. S. Social influence phenomena in a task-oriented group situation. *Journal of Abnormal and Social Psychology,* 1958, *56,* 13-17.

Kipnis, D. M. Interaction between members of bomber crews as a determinant of sociometric choice. *Human Relations,* 1957, *10,* 263-270.

Kjeldsen, E. K. M. An investigation of the determinants of effectiveness in small task-oriented groups. Unpublished PhD Dissertation in progress, Department of Sociology, University of Massachusetts, Amherst, 1975.

Klavora, P. Application of the Spielberger trait-state anxiety model and the STAI in precompetition anxiety research. In *Psychology of sport and motor behavior,* Vol. 2, (D. M. Landers, Ed.). Pennsylvania State University Press, 1975.

Klavora, P. An attempt to derive inverted-U curves based on the relationship between anxiety and athletic performance. In *Psychology of motor behavior and sport,* (D. M. Landers, and R. W. Christina, Eds.). Human Kinetics Publishers, 1977.

Klein, M. and Christiansen, G. Group composition, group structure and group effectiveness of basketball teams. In *Sport, culture and society,* (J. W. Loy and G. S. Kenyon, Eds.). Macmillan, 1969.

Kling, J. W. and Schlosberg, H. The relationship between tension and efficiency. *Perceptual and Motor Skills,* 1959, *9,* 395-397.

Klinger, E. Fantasy need achievement as a motivational construct. *Psychological Bulletin,* 1966, *66,* 291-308.

Klinger, E. Feedback effects and social facilitation of vigilance performance. *Psychonomic Science,* 1969, *14,* 161-162.

Kluckhohn, C. and Murray, H. A. *Personality in nature, society and culture.* Knopf, 1949.

Kogan, N. and Wallach, M. A. *Risk taking: A study in cognition and personality.* Holt, 1964.

Kolsa, B. J. *Introduction to behavioral science for business.* John Wiley & Sons, 1969.

Korten, D. C. Situational determinants of leadership structure. *Journal of Conflict Resolution,* 1962, *6,* 222-235.

Kroll, W. Sixteen Personality Factor profiles of collegiate wrestlers. *Research Quarterly,* 1967, *38,* 49-57.

Kroll, W. Current strategies and problems in personality assessment of athletes. In *Psychology of motor learning,* (L. E. Smith, Ed.). Athletic Institute, 1970.

Kroll, W. Psychological scaling of the AIAW Code-of-Ethics for Players. *Research Quarterly,* 1976, *47,* 126-133.

Kroll, W. and Carlson, B. R. Discriminant function and hierarchical grouping analysis of karate participants. *Research Quarterly,* 1967, *38,* 405-411.

Kroll, W. and Peterson, K. H. Personality factor profiles of collegiate football teams. *Research Quarterly*, 1965, *36*, 433-440.

Lacy, J. I. Somatic response patterning and stress: some revisions of activation theory. In *Psychological stress: Issues in research*, (M. H. Appley and R. Trumball, Eds.). Appleton, 1967.

Landers, D. M. Social facilitation and human performance: A review of contemporary and past research. In *Psychology of sport and motor behavior*, Vol. 2. (D. M. Landers, Ed.). Pennsylvania State University Press, 1975.

Landers, D. M. Motivation and performance: The role of arousal and attentional factors. In *Sport Psychology: An analysis of athlete behavior*, (W. F. Straub, Ed.). Mouvement Publications, 1978.

Landers, D. M., Brawley, L. R. and Hale, B. D. Habit strength differences in motor behavior: The effects of social facilitation paradigms and subject sex. In *Psychology of motor behavior and sport*, (D. M. Landers and R. W. Christina, Eds.). Human Kinetics, 1977.

Landers, D. M. and Crum, T. The effects of team success and formal structure on interpersonal relations and cohesiveness of baseball teams. *International Journal of Sport Psychology*, 1971, *2*, 88-96.

Landers, D. M. and Goodstadt, B. E. The effects of S's anonymity and audience potential to evaluate S on rotary pursuit performance. In *Proceedings of the Fourth Canadian Psychomotor Learning and Sport Psychology Symposium*, (I. D. Williams and L. M. Wankel, Eds.). Department of National Health and Welfare, 1973.

Landers, D. M. and Luschen, G. Team performance outcome and the cohesiveness of competitive coacting teams. *International Journal of Sport Sociology*, 1974, *9*, 57-71.

Landers, D. M. and McCullagh, P. D. Social facilitation of motor performance. In *Exercise and sport science reviews*, Vol. 4, (J. F. Keogh, Ed.). Academic Press, 1976.

Landers, Donna M. Observational learning of a motor skill: Temporal spacing of demonstrations and audience presence. *Journal of Motor Behavior*, 1975, *7*, 281-287.

Landers, Donna M. and Landers, D. M. Teacher versus peer models: Effects of model's presence and performance level on motor behavior. *Journal of Motor Behavior*, 1973, *5*, 129-139.

Latane, B. and Darley, J. M. Group inhibition of bystander intervention in emergencies. *Journal of Personality and Social Psychology*, 1968, *10*, 215-221.

Latane, B. and Darley, J. M. Bystander "apathy." *American Scientist*, 1969, *54*, 244-268.

Laubach, S. The development of a system for coding student behavior in physical education. Unpublished doctoral dissertation. Teachers College, Columbia University, 1974.

Lawler, F. E. and Porter, L. W. The effect of performance on satisfaction. *Industrial Relations*, 1967, *7*, 20-28.

Leavitt, H. J. Some effects of certain communication patterns on group performance. *Journal of Abnormal and Social Psychology*, 1951, *46*, 38-50.

Leavitt, H. J. and Knight, K. E. Most 'efficient' solutions to communication networks: Empirical versus analytical search. *Sociometry*, 1963, *26*, 260-267.

Lemann, T. B. and Solomon, R. L. Group characteristics as revealed in sociometric patterns and personality ratings. *Sociometry*, 1952.

Lenk, H. Top performance despite internal conflict: An antithesis to a functionalistic proposition. In *Sport, culture and society*, (J. W. Loy and G. S. Kenyon, Eds.). Macmillan, 1969.

Leuba, C. Toward some integration of learning theories: The concept of optimal stimulation. *Psychological Reports*, 1955, *1*, 27-33.

Levinger, G. and Schneider, D. J. Test of the "risk is a value" hypothesis. *Journal of Personality and Social Psychology*, 1969, *11*, 165-169.

Lewin, K. *A dynamic theory of personality*. McGraw-Hill, 1935.

Lewin, K. *Resolving social conflicts*. Harper, 1948.

Liddell, W. W. and Slocum, J. W. The effects of individual-role compatibility upon group performance: An extension of Schutz's FIRO theory. *Academy of Management Journal*, 1976, *19*, 413-426.

Likert, R. "Foreward" In *Productivity, supervision and morale in an office situation*. University of Michigan Survey Research Center, 1950.

Littman, R. A. Motives, history and causes. In *Nebraska symposium on motivation*, Vol. 6, (M. R. Jones, Ed.). Nebraska University Press, 1958.

Lonergan, B. G. and McClintock, C. G. Effects of group membership on risk-taking behavior. *Psychological Reports*, 1961, *8*, 447-455.

Lorenz, E. Zur psychologie der industriellen gruppenarbeit. *Z. exp. angew. Psychol.*, 1933, *45*, 1-45.

Lorsch, J. W. and Morse, J. J. *Organizations and their members: A contingency approach.* Harper & Row, 1974.

Lott, A. J. and Lott, B. E. Group cohesiveness as interpersonal attraction: A review of relationships with antecedent and consequent variables. *Psychological Bulletin,* 1965, *64,* 259-302.

Lowin, A. and Craig, J. The influence of level of performance on managerial style: An experimental object-lesson in the ambiguity of correlational data. *Organizational Behavior and Human Performance,* 1968, *3,* 440-458.

Loy, J. W. The nature of sport: A definitional effort, *Quest,* 1968, *10,* 1-15.

Loy, J. W. Where the action is: A consideration of centrality in sport situations. Paper presented at the Second Canadian Psychomotor Learning & Sport Psychology Conference, Windsor, Ontario, 1970.

Loy, J. W. and McElvogue, J. F. Racial segregation in American sport. *International Review of Sport Sociology,* 1970, *5,* 5-24.

Loy, J. W. and Sage, G. H. The effects of formal structure on organizational leadership: An investigation of interscholastic baseball teams. Paper presented at the 2nd. International Congress of Sport Psychology, Washington, D.C., 1968.

Loy, J., Theberge, N., Kjeldsen, E. and Donnelly, P. An examination of hypothesized correlates of replacement processes in sport organizations. Paper prepared for presentation at an International Seminar for the Sociology of Sport, University of Heidelberg, 1975.

Luschen, G. The interdependence of sport and culture. *International Review of Sport Sociology,* 1967, *2,* 127-141.

Luthans, F. *Organizational behavior.* McGraw-Hill, 1973.

Lynn, R. An achievement motivation questionnaire. *British Journal of Psychology,* 1969, *60,* 529-534.

Maddi, S. R. *Personality theories: A comparitive analysis.* Dorsey Press, 1968.

Madsen, M. C. and Shapira, A. Cooperative and competitive behavior of urban Afro-American, Anglo-American, Mexican American and Mexican village children. *Developmental Psychology,* 1970, *3,* 16-20.

Mahone, C. H. Fear of failure and unrealistic vocational aspiration. *Journal of Abnormal and Social Psychology,* 1960, *60,* 253-261.

Malmo, R. B. Activation: A neuropsychological dimension. *Psychological Review,* 1959, *66,* 367-386.

Mann, R. D. A review of the relationship between personality and performance in small groups. *Psychological Bulletin,* 1959, *56,* 241-270.

Marin, V. Experience as a factor in pro-football success. Paper completed for an undergraduate course on the Sociology of Sport, Department of Physical Education, UCLA, 1969.

Marquis, D. G. Individual responsibility and group decision involving risk. *Industrial Management Review,* 1962, *3,* 8-23.

Marteniuk, R. G. Motor performance and induced muscular tension. *Research Quarterly,* 1968, *39,* 1025-1031.

Marteniuk, R. G. Two factors to be considered in the design of experiments in anxiety and motor behavior. *Journal of Motor Behavior,* 1971, *3,* 189-192.

Marteniuk, R. G. *Information processing in motor skills.* Holt, Rinehart and Winston, 1976.

Martens, R. A social psychology of physical activity. In *Sport sociology: Contemporary themes,* (A. Yiannakis, T. D. McIntyre, M. J. Melnick, D. P. Hart, Eds.), Kendall/Hunt Publishing Co., 1976.

Martens, R. Effects of an audience on learning and performance of a complex motor skill. *Journal of Personality and Social Psychology,* 1969, *12,* 252-260. (a)

Martens, R. Palmar sweating and the presence of an audience. *Journal of Experimental Social Psychology,* 1969, *5,* 371-374. (b)

Martens, R. Influence of participation motivation on success and satisfaction in team performance. *Research Quarterly,* 1970, *41,* 510-518.

Martens, R. Social reinforcement effects on preschool children's motor performance. *Perceptual and Motor Skills,* 1970, *31,* 787-792.

Martens, R. Anxiety and motor behavior. *Journal of Motor Behavior,* 1971, *3,* 151-179.

Martens, R. Internal-external control and social reinforcement effects on motor performance. *Research Quarterly,* 1971, *42,* 107-113.

Martens, R. Social reinforcement effects on motor performance as a function of socio-economic status. *Perceptual and Motor Skills,* 1972, *35,* 215-218.

Martens, R. Arousal and motor performance. In *Exercise and sport science reviews,* Vol. 2, (J. H. Wilmore, Ed.). Academic Press, 1974.

Martens, R. *Social psychology and physical activity,* Harper and Row, 1975.

Martens, R. The paradigmatic crises in American sport personology. *Sportwissenschaft*, 1975, *5*, 9-24.

Martens, R. *Sport competition anxiety test*. Human Kinetics, 1977.

Martens, R., Burwitz, L. and Newell, K. M. Money and praise: Do they improve motor learning and performance? *Research Quarterly*, 1972, *43*, 429-442.

Martens, R., Burwitz, L. and Zuckerman, J. Modeling effects on motor performance. *Research Quarterly*, 1976, *47*, 277-291.

Martens, R. and Gill, D. L. State anxiety among successful and unsuccessful competitors who differ in competitive trait anxiety. *Research Quarterly*, 1976, *47*, 698-708.

Martens, R., Gill, D. L. and Scanlan, T. K. Competitive trait anxiety, success-failure and sex as determinants of motor performance. *Perceptual and Motor Skills*, 1976, *43*, 1199-1208.

Martens, R. and Landers, D. M. Effect of anxiety, competition and failure on performance of a complex motor task. *Journal of Motor Behavior*, 1969, *1*, 1-10. (a)

Martens, R. and Landers, D. M. Coaction effects on a muscular endurance task. *Research Quarterly*, 1969, *40*, 733-737. (b)

Martens, R. and Landers, D. M. Motor performance under stress: A test of the inverted-U hypothesis. *Journal of Personality and Social Psychology*, 1970, *16*, 29-37.

Martens, R. and Landers, D. M. Evaluation potential as a determinant of coaction effects. *Journal of Experimental Social Psychology*, 1972, *8*, 347-359.

Martens, R., Landers, D. M. and Loy, J. *Sports cohesiveness questionnaire*. AAHPER Publications, 1972.

Martens, R. and Peterson, J. A. Group cohesiveness as a determinant of success and member satisfaction in team performance. *International Review of Sport Sociology*, 1971, *6*, 49-61.

Maslow, A. Dynamics of personality organization. *Psychological Review*, 1943, *50*, 514-539.

Matarazzo, R. and Matarazzo, J. D. Anxiety level and pursuitmeter performance. *Journal of Consulting Psychology*, 1956, *20*, 70.

Matarazzo, J. D., Ulett, G. A. and Saslow, G. Human maze performance as a function of increasing levels of anxiety. *Journal of General Psychology*, 1955, *53*, 79-95.

McClelland, D. C. Methods of measuring human motivation. In *Motives in fantasy, action, and society*, (J. W. Atkinson, Ed.). Van Nostrand, 1958.

McClelland, D. C. *The achieving society*. Van Nostrand, 1961.

McClelland, D. C. Toward a theory of motive acquisition. *American Psychologist*, 1965, *20*, 321-333.

McClelland, D. C., Atkinson, J. W., Clark, R. W. and Lowell, E. L. *The achievement motive*. Appleton-Century-Crofts, 1953.

McClelland, D. C. and Winter, D. G. *Motivating economic achievement*. The Free Press, 1969.

McClintock, C. G. Group support and the behavior of leaders and nonleaders. *Journal of Abnormal and Social Psychology*, 1963, *67*, 105-113.

McCullagh, P. D. and Landers, D. M. Size of audience and social facilitation. *Perceptual and Motor Skills*, 1976, *42*, 1067-1070.

McCullagh, P. D. and Landers, D. M. Compatibility of the audience and coaction paradigms in social facilitation research. In *Psychology of sport and motor behavior*, (Vol. 2), (D. M. Landers, D. V. Harris and R. W. Christina, Eds.). College of Health, Physical Education and Recreation, The Pennsylvania State University, 1975.

McCurdy, H. G. and Lambert, W. E. The efficiency of small human groups in the solution of problems requiring genuine cooperation. *Journal of Personality*, 1952, *20*, 478-494.

McGrath, J. E. The influence of positive interpersonal relations on adjustment and effectiveness in rifle teams. *Journal of Abnormal and Social Psychology*, 1962, *65*, 365-375.

McMurray, R. W. The case for benevolent autocracy. *Harvard Business Review*, 1958, *36*, 82-90.

McNally, J. and Orlick, T. Cooperative sport structures: A Preliminary analysis. In *Mouvement*, (J. Salmela. C. Brad, R. Desharnais, D. Drouin and M. Fleury, Eds.), 1975.

McPherson, B. D. Personnel turnover and organizational effectiveness. Paper presented at the First Canadian Congress for the Multidisciplinary Study of Sport and Physical Activity, Montreal, 1973.

Medow, H., and Zander, A. Aspiration for the group chosen by central and peripheral members. *Journal of Personality and Social Psychology*, 1965, *1*, 224-228.

Meglino, B. M. The effect of evaluation on dominance characteristics: an extension of social facilitation theory. *The Journal of Psychology*, 1976, *92*, 167-172.

Meisels, M., Youssef, Z. I. and Doran, M. J. Levels of anxiety, dominant tendency and mirror-tracing performance. *Psychonomic Science*, 1967, *9*, 193-194.

Merton, R. K., *Social theory and social structure*. Free Press, 1957.

Milgram, S. Liberating effects of group pressure. *Journal of Personality and Social Psychology*, 1965, *1*, 127-134.

Milgram, S. Some conditions of obedience and disobedience to authority. *Human Relations*, 1965, *18*, 57-76.

Milgram, S., Bickman, L., and Berkowitz, L. Note on the drawing power of crowds of different size. *Journal of Personality and Social Psychology*, 1969, *13*, 79-82.

Miller, D. T. and Ross, M. Self-serving biases in the attribution of causality: Fact or fiction? *Psychological Bulletin*, 1975, *82*, 213-225.

Miller, L. K. and Hamblin, R. L. Interdependence, differential rewarding, and productivity. *American Sociological Review*, 1963, *28*, 768-777.

Mills, T. M. *The sociology of small groups*. Prentice-Hall, 1967.

Mischel, W. *Personality and assessment*. Wiley, 1968.

Mischel, W. Toward a cognitive social learning reconceptualization of personality. *Psychological Review*, 1973, *80*, 252-283.

Mischel, H. N. and Mischel, W. *Readings in personality*. Holt, Rinehart and Winston, 1973.

Moore, H. T. Laboratory tests of anger, fear and sex interest. *American Journal of Psychology*, 1917, *28*, 390-395.

Morgan, W. P. Physical fitness and emotional health: A review. *American Corrective Therapy Journal*, 1969, *23*, 124-127.

Morgan, W. P. Sport psychology. In *The psychomotor domain: Movement behavior*, (R. N. Singer, Ed.). Lea & Febiger, 1972.

Morgan, W. P. Sport personology: The credulous-skeptical argument in perspective. In *Sport psychology: An analysis of athlete behavior*, (W. F. Straub, Ed.). Mouvement, 1978.

Morgenegg, B. An analysis of the pedagogical functions of physical education teachers. Unpublished doctoral dissertation, Teachers College, Columbia University, 1978.

Morgenegg, B. Pedagogical moves. In *What's going on in gym: Descriptive studies of physical education classes*, (W. G. Anderson and G. T. Barrette, Eds.), Monograph 1. *Motor Skills: Theory into Practice*, 1978.

Morse, J. J. Person-job congruence and individual adjustment and development. *Human Relations*, 1976, *28*, 841-861.

Moxley, S. and Butcher, J. The effect of arousal induced by competition on learning and performance of a motor skill. In *Mouvement*, (J. Salmela, C. Bard, R. Desharnais, D. Drouin and M. Fleury, Eds.), 1975.

Mulder, M. Group stucture and performance. *Acta Psychologica*, 1959, *16*, 356-402. (a)

Mulder, M. Power and satisfaction in task-oriented groups. *Acta Psychologica*, 1959, *16*, 178-225. (b)

Mulder, M. Communication structure, decision structure and group performance. *Sociometry*, 1960, *23*, 1-14.

Murray, H. A. *Explorations in personality*, Oxford University Press, 1938.

Murray, H. A. *Thematic Apperception Test Manual*. Harvard University Press, 1943.

Myers, A. E. Team competition, success, and adjustment of group members. *Journal of Abnormal and Social Psychology*, 1962, *65*, 325-332.

Mynatt, C. and Shermen, S. J. Responsibility attribution in groups and individuals: A direct test of the diffusion of responsibility hypothesis. *Journal of Personality and Social Psychology*, 1975, *32*, 1111-1118.

Nash, E. L., Phelan, J. G., Demas, G. and Bittner, A. Effects of manifest and induced anxiety and experimenter variability on simple reaction time. *Perceptual and Motor Skills*, 1966, *22*, 483-487.

Nelson, D. O. and Langer, P. Getting to really know your players. *Athletic Journal*, 1963, *39*, 88-93.

Nelson, P. D. Similarities and differences among leaders and followers. *Journal of Social Psychology*, 1964, *63*, 161-167.

Newcomb, T. M. Social psychological theory. In *Social psychology at the crossroads*, (J. H. Roher and M. Sherif, Eds.). Harper, 1951.

Newcomb, T. M. *The acquaintance process*. Holt, Rinehart & Winston, 1961.

Nicholls, J. G. Causal attributions and other achievement-related cognitions: Effects of task outcome, attainment value and sex. *Journal of Personality and Social Psychology*, 1975, *31*, 379-389.

Nicholls, J. G. Effort is virtuous, but it's better to have ability: Evaluative responses to perceptions of effort and ability. *Journal of Research in Personality*, 1976, *10*, 306-315.

Nichols, K. A. Preparation for membership in a group. *Bulletin of the British Psychological Society*, 1976, *29*, 353-359.

Nordholm, L. A. Effects of group size and stimulus ambiguity on conformity. *Journal of Social Psychology*, 1975, *97*, 123-130.

Oaklander, H. and Fleishman, E. A. Patterns of leadership related to organizational stress in hospital settings. *Administrative Science Quarterly*, 1964, *8*, 520-532.

Ogilvie, B. C. Psychological consistencies within the personality of high level competitors. *Journal of the American Medical Association*, 1968, *205*, 780-786.

Ogilvie, B. C. Quoted in J. Jares, We have a neurotic in the backfield, doctor. *Sports Illustrated*, 1971, *34*, 30-34.

Ogilvie, B. C. and Tutko, T. A. *Problem athletes and how to handle them*. Pelham Books, 1966.

Ogilvie, B. C. and Tutko, T. A. Self perceptions as compared with measured personality of selected male physical educators. In *Contemporary psychology of sport*, (G. S. Kenyon, Ed.). The Athletic Institute, 1970.

O'Neil, H. F., Spielberger, C. D. and Hansen, D. N. Effect of state anxiety and task difficulty on computor assisted learning. *Journal of Educational Psychology*, 1969, *60*, 343-350.

Orlick, T. D. The athletic drop out: A high price for efficiency. A paper presented at the First Canadian Congress for the Multi-Disciplinary Study of Sport and Physical Activity, Montreal, 1973. (a)

Orlick, T. D. Children's sports: A revolution is coming. *Journal of the Canadian Association for Health, Physical Education and Recreation*. 1973, *39*, 12-14. (b)

Orlick, T. D. The athletic drop-out: A high price to pay for inefficiency. *Journal of the Canadian Association for Health, Physical Education and Recreation*, 1974, *40*.

Orlick, T. D. Games of acceptance and psycho-social adjustment. Paper presented at the AMA Conference on the Mental Health Aspects of Sport, Exercise and Recreation, Atlantic City, 1975.

Orlick, T. D. and Botterill, C. *Every kid can win*. Nelson Hall Publishers, 1975.

Orlick, T. D. and Botterill, C. Why eliminate kids? In *Sport sociology: Contemporary themes*, (A. Yiannakis, T. D. McIntyre, M. J. Melnick and D. P. Hart, Eds.). Kendall/Hunt Publishing Company, 1976.

Orlick, T. D., Partinton, J. T., Scott, H. A. and Glassford, R. G. The development of the skimetric differential inventory: A childrenistic approach. In *Mouvement*, (J. Salmela, C. Bard, R. Desharnais, D. Denis and M. Fleury, Eds.), 1975.

Osborn, R. N. and Hint, J. G. An adaptive-reactive theory of leadership: The role of macro variables in leadership research. In *Leadership frontiers*, (J. G. Hunt and L. L. Larson, Eds.). Kent State University, 1975.

Ostrow, A. C. Goal-setting behavior and need achievement in relation to competitive motor activity. *Research Quarterly*, 1976, *47*, 174-183.

Oxendine, J. B. Emotional arousal and motor performance. *Quest*, 1970, *13*, 23-32.

Palermo, D. S., Castaneda, A. and McCandless, B. R. The relationship of anxiety in children to performance in a complex learning task. *Child Development*, 1956, *27*, 333-337.

Paulus, P. B. and Murdoch, P. Anticipated evaluation and audience presence in the enhancement of dominant responses. *Journal of Experimental Social Psychology*, 1971, *7*, 280-291.

Pease, D. A., Locke, L. F. and Burlingame, M. Athletic exclusion: A complex phenomenon. *Quest*, 1971, *16*, 42-46.

Peckham, V. A study of the relationship between personnel succession and organizational effectiveness. Paper completed for a Special Problems Course, Department of Sport Studies, University of Massachusetts, Amherst, 1970.

Pepinsky, P. N., Hemphill, J. K. and Shevitz, R. N. Attempts to lead, group productivity, and morale under conditions of acceptance and rejection. *Journal of Abnormal and Social Psychology*, 1958, *57*, 47-54.

Percival, L. The coach from the athlete's viewpoint. *International Symposium on the Art and Science of Coaching*. The Fitness Institute, 1971.

Pessin, J. The comparative effects of social and mechanical stimulation on memorizing. *American Journal of Psychology*, 1933, *45*, 263-270.

Pessin, J. and Husband, R. W. Effects of social stimulation on human maze learning. *Journal of Abnormal and Social Psychology*, 1933, *28*, 148-154.

Peterson, J. A. and Martens, R. Success and residential affiliation as determinants of team cohesiveness. *Research Quarterly*, 1972, *43*, 62-76.

302

Peterson, S. L., Ukler, J. C. and Trousdale, W. W. Personality traits of women in team and women in individual sports. *Research Quarterly*, 1967, *38*, 686-690.

Pinneo, L. R. The effects of induced muscular tension during tracking on level of activation and on performance. *Journal of Experimental Psychology*, 1961, *62*, 523-531.

Plimpton, G. Bozo the Bruin. *Sports Illustrated*, 1978, *48*, 54-60, 62, 64. (a)

Plimpton, G. Lord, no more than five. *Sports Illustrated*, 1978, *48*, 32-38. (b)

Precker, J. A. Similarity of valuings as a factor in selection of peers and near authority figures. *Journal of Abnormal and Social Psychology*, 1952, *47*, 406-414.

Price, H. G. Anxiety and failure as factors in the performance of motor tasks. Unpublished doctoral dissertation, State University of Iowa, 1951.

Purdon, J. Athletic participation and self-esteem. Unpublished M.A. Thesis, University of Western Ontario, London, 1978.

Quarter, J. and Marcus, A. Drive level and the audience effect: A test of Zajonc's theory. *Journal of Social Psychology*, 1971, *83*, 99-105.

Rabinowitz, S. and Hall, D. T. Organizational research on job involvement. *Psychological Bulletin*, 1977, *84*, 265-288.

Ramuz-Nienhuis, W. and Van Bergen, A. Relations between some components of attraction-to-group: A replication. *Human Relations*, 1960, *13*, 271-277.

Raynor, J. O. Future orientation and motivation of immediate activity: An elaboration on the theory of achievement motivation. *Psychological Review*, 1969, *76*, 606-610.

Raynor, J. O. Relationship between achievement-related motives, future orientation, and academic performance. *Journal of Personality and Social Psychology*, 1970, *15*, 28-33.

Reddy, W. B. and Barnes, A. Effects of interpersonal group composition on the problem solving behavior of middle managers. *Journal of Applied Psychology*, 1972, *56*, 516-517.

Rettig, S. Group discussion and predicted ethical risk taking. *Journal of Personality and Social Psychology*, 1966, *3*, 629-633.

Revelle, W. and Michaels, E. J. The theory of achievement motivation revisited: The implications of inertial tendencies. *Psychological Review*, 1976, *83*, 394-404.

Rikli, R. Effects of experimenter expectancy set and experimenter sex upon grip strength and hand steadiness scores. *Research Quarterly*, 1974, *45*, 416-423.

Roberts, G. C. Effect of achievement motivation and social environment on performance of a motor task. *Journal of Motor Behavior*, 1972, *4*, 37-46.

Roberts, G. C. Effect of achievement motivation and social environment on risk taking. *Research Quarterly*, 1974, *45*, 42-55.

Roberts, G. C. Win-loss causal attributions of Little League players. In *Mouvement*, (J. Salmela, C. Bard, R. Desharnais, D. Drouin and M. Fleury, Eds.), 1975.

Roberts, G. C. and Martens, R. Social reinforcement and complex motor performance. *Research Quarterly*, 1970, *41*, 175-181.

Rogers, C. R. Toward a modern approach to values: The valuing process in the mature person. *Journal of Abnormal and Social Psychology*, 1964, *68*, 160-167.

Rosenbaum, L. L. and Rosenbaum, W. B. Morale and productivity consequences of group leadership style, stress, and type of task. *Journal of Applied Psychology*, 1971, *55*, 343-388.

Rosenberg, L. Group size, prior experience, and conformity. *Journal of Abnormal and Social Psychology*, 1961, *63*, 436-437.

Rosenshine, B. and Furst, N. The use of direct observation to study teaching. *Second handbook of research on teaching*. Rand McNally Publishing Co., 1973.

Rotter, J. B., Chance, J. E. and Phares, E. J. An introduction to Social learning theory. In *Applications of a social learning theory of personality*, (J. B. Rotter, J. E. Chance and E. J. Phares, Eds.). Holt, Rinehart and Winston, 1974.

Rushall, B. S. Personality profiles and a theory of behaviour modification for swimmers. *Swimming Technique*, 1967, October, 66-71.

Rushall, B. S. An evaluation of the relationship between personality and physical performance categories. In *Contemporary psychology of sport*, (G. S. Kenyon, Ed.). The Athletic Institute, 1970.

Rushall, B. S. The status of personality research and application in sports and physical education. Paper presented at Physical Education Forum, Dalhousie University, Halifax, N.S., 1972.

Rushall, B. S. *Inventories for the Psychological Assessment of Swimmers*. Halifax, 1974.

Rushall, B. S. Psychodynamics and personality in sport: Status and values. In *Readings in Sport Psychology*, (H. T. A. Whiting, Ed.). Lepus, 1975.

Ryan, E. D. The questions we ask and the decisions we make. *Paper presented at the North American Society for the Psychology of Sport and Physical Activity Convention, Anaheim, Calif., 1974.*

Ryan, E. D. and Lakie, W. L. Competitive and noncompetitive performance in relation to achievement motivation and manifest anxiety. *Journal of Personality and Social Psychology*, 1965, *1*, 344-345.

Ryan, T. A. Multiple comparisons in psychological research. *Psychological Bulletin*, 1959, *56*, 26-47.

Sage, G. H. An occupational analysis of the college coach. In *Sport and social order*, (D. W. Ball & J. W. Loy, Eds.). Addison-Wesley, 1975.

Sage, G. H. An assessment of personality profiles between and within intercollegiate athletes from eight different sports. *Sportswissenchaft*, 1972, *2*, 409-418.

Sage, G. H., Loy, J. W. and Ingham, A. G. The effects of formal structure on organizational leadership: An investigation of collegiate baseball teams. *Paper presented at the American Association for Health, Physical Education and Recreation National Convention, Seattle, 1970.*

Samuel, W., Baynes, K. and Sabeh, C. Effects of initial success or failure in a stressful or relaxed environment on subsequent task performance. *Journal of Experimental Social Psychology*, 1978, *14*, 205-216.

Sapolsky, A. Relationship between patient-doctor compatibility, mutual perception and outcome of treatment. *Journal of Abnormal Psychology*, 1965, *70*, 70-76.

Sasfy, J. and Okun, M. Form of evaluation and audience expertness as joint determinants of audience effects. *Journal of Experimental and Social Psychology*, 1974, *10*, 461-467.

Scanlan, T. K. The effects of success-failure on the perception of threat in a competitive situation. *Research Quarterly*, 1977, *48*, 144-153.

Schachter, S. Deviation, rejection and communication. *Journal of Abnormal and Social Psychology*, 1951, *46*, 190-207.

Scheer, J. K. and Ansorge, C. J. Effects of naturally induced judges' expectations on the ratings of physical performances. *Research Quarterly*, 1975, *46*, 463-470.

Scheer, J. K. and Ansorge, C. J. Influence due to expectations of judges: A function of internal-external lows of control. *Journal of Sport Psychology*, 1979, *1*, 53-58.

Schein, E. H. *Organizational psychology*. Prentice-Hall, 1965.

Schelling, T. C. Strategy of conflict: Prospectus for the reorientation of game theory. *Journal of Conflict Resolution*, 1958, *2*, 203-264.

Schlenker, B. R. Group members' attributions of responsibility for prior group performance. *Representative Research in Social Psychology*. 1975, *6*, 96-108.

Schlenker, B. R. and Miller, R. S. Egocentrism in groups: Self-serving biases or logical information processing? *Journal of Personality and Social Psychology*, 1977, *35*, 755-764.

Schlenker, B. R., Soraci, S. and McCarthy, B. Self-esteem and group performance as determinants of egocentric perceptions in cooperative groups. *Human Relations*, 1976, *12*, 1163-1176.

Schmidt, R. A. The case against learning and forgetting scores. *Journal of Motor Behavior*, 1972, *4*, 79-88.

Schreisheim, C. A. and Murphy, C. J. Relationship between leader behavior and subordinate satisfaction and performance: A test of some situational moderators. *Journal of Applied Psychology*, 1976, *61*, 634-641.

Schurr, K. T., Ashley, M. A. and Joy, K. L. A multivariate analysis of male athlete characteristics: Sport type and success. *Multivariate Experimental Clinical Research*, 1977, *3*, 53-68.

Schutz, W. C. *FIRO: A three dimensional theory of interpersonal behavior*. Holt, Rinehart and Winston 1958.

Schutz, W. C. *The interpersonal underground*, 5th ed., Science and Behavior Books, 1966.

Schwab, D. P. and Cummings, L. L. Theories of performance and satisfaction: A review. *Industrial Relations*.

Schwartz, G. *A comparative analysis of succession, size and success among professional sport organizations. Paper completed for a graduate course on the Sociology of Sport, University of Massachusetts. Amherst, 1973.*

Schwartz, S. M. *Words, deeds and the perception of consequences and responsibility in action situations. Journal of Personality and Social Psychology*, 1968, *10*, 232-242.

Schwartz, S. M. and Clausen, G. T. Responsibility, norms, and helping in an emergency. *Journal of Personality and Social Psychology*, 1970, *16*, 249-310.

Scott, J. *Athletics for athletes*. Quality Printing Service, 1969.

Scott, J. *The athletic revolution*. The Free Press, 1971.

Secord, P. F. and Backman, C. W. Interpersonal congruency, perceived similarity and friendship. *Sociometry*, 1964, *27*, 115-127.

Shaban, J. and Jecker, J. Risk preference in choosing an evaluator: An extension of Atkinson's achievement motivation model. *Journal of Experimental Social Psychology*, 1968, *4*, 34-45.

Shapira, A. and Madsen, M. C. Cooperative and competitive behavior of Kibbutz and urban children in Israel. *Child Development*, 1969, *40*, 609-617.

Shapiro, D. Psychological factors in friendship, choice, and rejection. Unpublished PhD Dissertation, University of Michigan, 1953.

Shaver, P. and Liebling, B. A. Explorations in the drive theory of social facilitation. *Journal of Social Psychology*, 1976, *99*, 259-271.

Shaw, M. E. Communication networks. In *Advances in experimental social psychology*, Vol. I, (L. Berkowitz, Ed.). Academic Press, 1964.

Shaw, M. E. *An overview of small group behavior.* General Learning Press, 1974.

Sheldon, W. H. and Stevens, S. S. *The varieties of temperment: A psychology of constitutional differences.* Harper and Row, 1942.

Sheridan, J. E., Downey, H. K. and Slocum, J. W. Testing causal relationships of House's path-goal theory of leadership effectiveness. In *Leadership frontiers*, (J. G. Hunt and L. L. Larson, Eds.). Kent State University, 1975.

Sheridan, J. E. and Slocum, J. W. The direction of the causal relationship between job satisfaction and work performance. *Organizational Behavior and Human Peformance*, 1975, *14*, 159-172.

Sherif, M. A study of some social factors in perception. *Archives of Psychology*, 1935, *27*, No. 187.

Sherif, M. Group conflict and cooperation. In *Group processes*, (P. B. Smith, Ed.). Penquin Books, 1970.

Sherif, M., Harvey, O. J., White, B. J., Hood, W. R. and Sherif, C. W. *Intergroup conflict and cooperation: The Robbers Cave Experiment.* University of Oklahoma Book Exchange, 1961.

Simmel, G. The significance of numbers for social life. In *Small groups: Studies in social interaction*, (A. P. Hare, E. F. Borgatta and R. F. Bales, Eds.), Rev. ed. Knopf, 1965.

Simon, H. A. *The new science of management decisions.* Harper and Row, 1960.

Simon, J. G. and Feather, N. T. Causal attributions for success and failure at university examinations. *Journal of Educational Psychology*, 1973, *64*, 46-56.

Sinclair, E. D. Personality and rugby football. Unpublished thesis, University of Leeds Institute of Education, 1968.

Singer, R. N. Effects of spectators on athletes and non-athletes performing a gross motor task. *Research Quarterly*, 1965, *36*, 473-482.

Singer, R. N. Athletic participation: Cause or result of certain personality factors. *Physical Educator*, 1967, *24*, 169-171.

Singer, R. N. *Coaching, athletics and psychology*, McGraw-Hill, 1972. (a)

Singer, R. N. Introduction to the psychomotor domain. In *The psychomotor domain: Movement behavior*, (R. N. Singer, Ed.), Lea and Febiger, 1972. (b)

Singer, R. N. Social facilitation. In *Ergogenic aids in muscular performance*, (W. P. Morgan, Ed.). Academic Press, 1972. (c)

Singh, N. P. Anxiety and sensory-motor learning. *Psychological Studies*, 1968, *13*, 111-114.

Sistrunk, F. and McDavid, J. W. Sex variables in conforming behavior. *Journal of Personality and Social Psychology*, 1971, *17*, 200-207.

Smith, L. E. Personality and performance research — new theories and directions required. *Quest Monograph*, XII, 1970.

Sommer, R. Spatial factors in face-to-fact interaction. In *Current perspectives in social psychology*, (E. P. Hollander and R. G. Hunt, Eds.) 3rd ed. Oxford University Press, 1971.

Sommer, R. Leadership and group geography. *Sociometry*, 1961, *24*, 100-110.

Spence, J. T. What can you say about a twenty-year-old theory that won't die? *Journal of Motor Behavior*, 1971, *3*, 193-203.

Spence, J. T. and Spence, K. W. The motivational components of manifest anxiety: Drive and drive stimuli. In *Anxiety and behavior*, (C. D. Spielberger, Ed.). Academic Press, 1966.

Spence, K. W. *Behavior theory and conditioning.* Yale University Press, 1956.

Spence, K. W. A theory of emotionally based drive (D) and its relation to performance in simple learning situations. *American Psychologist*, 1958, *13*, 131-141.

Spence, K. W. Behavior theory and selective learning. In *Nebraska symposium on motivation*, (M. R. Jones, Ed.), Vol. 6. Nebraska University Press, 1958.

Spence, K. W. Anxiety (drive) level and performance in eyelid conditioning. *Psychological Bulletin*, 1964, *61*, 129-139.

Spence, K. W., Farber, I. E. and McFann, H. H. The relation of anxiety (drive) level to performance in competitional and non-competitional paired-associates learning. *Journal of Experimental Psychology*, 1956, *52*, 296-305.

Spielberger, C. D. Theory and research on anxiety. In *Anxiety and behavior*, (C. D. Spielberger, Ed.). Academic Press, 1966.

Spielberger, C. D. Conceptual and methodological issues in anxiety research. In *Current trends in theory and research*, (C. D. Spielberger, Ed.), Vol. 1. Academic Press, 1972.

Spielberger, C. D., Gorsuch, R. L. and Luschene, R. E. *The state-trait anxiety inventory*, Consulting Psychologists Press, 1970.

Spielberger, C. D., O'Neil, H. F. and Hansen, D. N. Anxiety, drive theory and computor assisted learning. In *Progress in experimental personality research*, (B. A. Maher, Ed.), Vol. 6. Academic Press, 1971.

Spink, K. S. Win-loss causal attributions of high school basketball players. Unpublished master's thesis, University of Western Ontario, 1977.

Spink, K. S. Win-loss causal attributions of high school basketball players. *Canadian Journal of Applied Sport Sciences*, 1978, *3*, 195-201.

Spink, K. S. Correlation between two methods of assessing causal attribution. *Perceptual and Motor Skills*, 1978, *46*, 1173-1174.

Steiner, I. D. *Group process and productivity*. Academic Press, 1972.

Steinzor, B. The spatial factor in face to face discussion groups. In *Small groups: Studies in interaction*, (A. P. Hare, E. F. Borgatta & R. F. Bales, Eds.). Alfred A. Knopf, 1955.

Stevenson, H. W. Social reinforcement with children as a function of CA, sex of E, and sex of subject. *Journal of Abnormal Social Psychology*, 1961, *63*, 147-154.

Stevenson, H. W. Social reinforcement of children's behavior. In *Advances in child development and behavior*, Vol. 2, (L. P. Lipsitt and C. C. Spiker, Eds.). Academic Press, 1965.

Stevenson, H. W. and Allen, S. Adult performance as a function of E, and sex of S. *Journal of Abnormal Social Psychology*. 1964, *68*, 214-216.

Stogdill, R. M. *Individual behavior and group achievement*. Oxford University Press, 1959.

Stogdill, R. M. *The handbook of leadership*. The Free Press, 1974.

Stotland, E. and Hilmer, M. L. Identification, authoritarian defensiveness, and self-esteem. *Journal of Abnormal and Social Psychology*, 1962, *64*, 334-342.

Strauss, G. and Sayles, L. R. *Personnel: The human problem of management*. Prentice-Hall Inc., 1960.

Strodtbeck, F. L. and Hook, L. H. The social dimensions of a twelve-man jury table. *Sociometry*, 1961, *24*, 397-415.

Taylor, J. A. A personality scale of manifest anxiety. *Journal of Abnormal and Social Psychology*, 1953, *48*, 285-290.

Taylor, J. A. Drive theory and manifest anxiety. *Psychological Bulletin*, 1956, *53*, 303-320.

Teichner, W. H. Effects of foreperiod, induced muscular tension and stimulus regularity on simple reaction time. *Journal of Experimental Psychology*, 1957, *53*, 277-284.

Thayer, R. E. Measurement of activation through self-report. *Psychological Reports*, 1967, *20*, 663-678.

Thayer, R. E. and Moore, L. E. Reported activation and verbal learning as a function of group size (social facilitation) and anxiety inducing instructions. *Journal of Social Psychology*, 1972, *88*, 277-287.

Theberge, N. Personnel succession and organizational effectiveness in professional baseball. Paper completed for a graduate course on the Sociology of Sport, Department of Sport Studies, University of Massachusetts, Amherst, 1973.

Thibaut, J. W. and Kelley, H. H. *The social psychology of groups*. Wiley, 1959.

Thibaut, J. W. and Kelley, H. H. Performance interdependence. In *Role theory: Concepts and research*, (B. J. Biddle and E. J. Thomas, Eds.). John Wiley & Sons, 1966.

Thomas, E. J. Effects of facilitative role interdependence on group functioning. *Human Relations*, 1957, *10*, 347-356.

Thompson, J. D. *Organization in action*. McGraw-Hill, 1967.

Tolman, E. C. and Honzik, C. H. Introduction and removal of reward and maze performance in rats. *University of California Publications in Psychology*, 1930, *4*, 257-275.

Tolman, E. C. and Honzik, C. H. "Insight" in rats. *University of California Publications in Psychology*, 1930, *4*, 215-232.

Travis, L. E. The effect of a small audience upon eye-hand coordination. *Journal of Abnormal and Social Psychology*, 1925, *20*, 142-146.

Triandis, H. C. *Attitude and attitude change.* John Wiley, 1971.

Triplett, N. The dynamogenic factors in pace-making and competition. *American Journal of Psychology*, 1897, *9*, 507-533.

Tuckman, B. W. Developmental sequence in small groups. *Psychological Bulletin*, 1965, *63*, 384-399.

Underwood, W. J. and Krafft, L. J. Interpersonal compatibility and managerial effectiveness: A test of the Fundamental Interpersonal Relations Orientation theory. *Journal of Applied Psychology*, 1973, *58*, 89-94.

Vanek, M. and Cratty, B. J. *Psychology and the superior athlete.* The MacMillan Co., 1970.

Vaught, G. M. and Newman, S. E. The effects of anxiety on motor steadiness in competitive and non-competitive conditions. *Psychonomic Science*, 1966, *6*, 519-520.

Veit, H. Some remarks upon the elementary interpersonal relations within ball game teams. In *Contemporary psychology of sport: Proceedings of the second international congress of sport psychology,* (G. S. Kenyon, Ed.). The Athletic Institute, 1970.

Veroff, J. and Peele, S. Initial effects of desegregation on the achievement motivation of Negro elementary school children. *Journal of Social Issues*, 1969, *25*, 71-92.

Vinacke, W. E. Variables in experimental games: Toward a field theory. *Psychological Bulletin*, 1969, *71*, 293-318.

Vincent, M. F. Attitudes of college women toward physical education and their relationship to success in physical education. *Research Quarterly*, 1967, *38*, 126-131.

Vos, K. and Brinkman, W. Succes en cohesie in sportgroepen. *Sociologische Gios*, 1967, *14*, 30-40.

Vroom, V. H. Some personality determinants of the effects of participation. *Journal of Abnormal and Social Psychology*, 1959, *59*, 322-327.

Vroom, V. H. & Yetton, P. W. *Leadership and decision making.* University of Pittsburg Press, 1973.

Walker, E. L. Psychological complexity as a basis for a theory of motivation and choice. In *Nebraska symposium on motivation*, Vol. 12, (D. Levine, Ed.). Nebraska University Press, 1964.

Wallach, M. A. and Kogan, N. The roles of information, discussion, and consensus in group risk taking. *Journal of Experimental Social Psychology*, 1965, *1*, 1-19.

Wallach, M. A., Kogan, N. and Bem, D. J. Group influence on individual risk taking. *Journal of Abnormal and Social Psychology*, 1962, *65*, 75-86.

Wallach, M. A., Kogan, N. and Bem, D. J. Diffusion of responsibility and level of risk taking in groups. *Journal of Abnormal and Social Psychology*, 1964, *68*, 263-274.

Wallach, M. A., Kogan, N. and Burt, R. B. Can group members recognize the effects of group discussion upon risk taking? *Journal of Experimental Social Psychology*, 1965, *1*, 379-395.

Wankel, L. M. Competition in motor performance: An experimental analysis of motivational components. *Journal of Experimental Social Psychology*, 1972, *8*, 427-437.

Wankel, L. M. The interaction of social reinforcement, audience presence and initial ability level upon performance of a motor task. Presented at the First Canadian Congress for the Multidisciplinary Study of Sport and Physical Activity, Montreal, 1973.

Wankel, L. M. Social facilitation: A review of theory and research pertaining to motor performance. In *The status of psychomotor learning and sport psychology research,* (B. S. Rushall, Ed.). Sport Science Associates, 1975.

Wankel, L. M. A new energy source for sport psychology research: Toward a conversion from D-C (drive conceptualizations) to A-C (attribution cognitions). In *Psychology of sport and motor behavior,* (D. M. Landers, D. V. Harris and R. W. Christina, Eds.). College of Health, Physical Education and Recreation, The Pennsylvania State University, 1975.

Wankel, L. M. The effects of social reinforcement and audience presence upon the motor performance of boys with different levels of initial ability. *Journal of Motor Behavior*, 1975, *7*, 207-216.

Wapner, S. and Alper, T. G. The effect of an audience on behavior in a choice situation. *Journal of Abnormal and Social Psychology*, 1952, *47*, 222-229.

Weiner, B. Need achievement and the resumption of incompleted tasks. *Journal of Personality and Social Psychology*, 1965, *1*, 165-168.

Weiner, B. Achievement motivation and task recall in competitive situations. *Journal of Personality and Social Psychology*, 1966, *3*, 693-696.

Weiner, B. *Theories of motivation: From mechanism to cognition.* Rand McNally, 1972.

Weiner, B., Freize, I., Kukla, A., Reed, L., Rest, S. and Rosenbaum, R. M. Perceiving the causes of success and failure. In *Attribution: Perceiving the causes of behavior*, (E. E. Jones, D. E. Kanhouse, H. H. Kelley, R. E. Nisbett, S. Valins and B. Weiner, Eds.). General Learning Press, 1971.

Weiner, B. and Kukla, A. An attributional analysis of achievement motivation. *Journal of Personality and Social Psychology*, 1970, *15*, 1-20.

Weiner, M. Certainty of judgement as a variable in conformity behavior. *Journal of Social Psychology*, 1958, *48*, 257-263.

Welford, A. T. *Aging and human skill*. Oxford, 1958.

Wenar, C. Reaction time as a function of manifest anxiety and stimulus intensity. *Journal of Abnormal and Social Psychology*, 1954, *49*, 335-340.

Werner, A. C. and Gottheil, E. Personality and participation in college athletics. *Research Quarterly*, 1966, *37*, 126-131.

Weston, P. and Mednick, M. T. S. Race, social class and motive to avoid success in women. *Journal of Cross Cultural Pyschology*, 1970, *1*, 284-291.

Whiting, H. T. A. and Hendry, L. B. A study of international table tennis players. In *Acquiring ball skill*, (H. T. A. Whiting, Ed.), Bell, 1969.

Whiting, H. T. A. The human performance model. In *Readings in human performance*, (H. T. A. Whiting, Ed.). Lepus Books, 1975.

Whittemore, I. G. The influence o competition upon performance. *Journal of Abnormal and Social Psychology*, 1924, *19*, 236-254.

Wiest, W. M., Porter, L. W. and Ghiselli, E. E. Relationship between individual proficiency and team performance and efficiency. *Journal of Applied Psychology*, 1961, *45*, 435-440.

Wiggins, J. A., Dill, F. and Schwartz, R. D. On 'status liability.' *Sociometry*, 1965, *28*, 197-209.

Wiggins, S. L., Brokaw, J. R., Heckel, R. V. and Salzberg, H. C. Manifest anxiety and perceptual motor steadiness. *Perceptual and Motor Skills*, 1962, *15*, 759-762.

Wilder, D. A. Perception of groups, size of opposition, and social influence. *Journal of Experimental Social Psychology*, 1977, *13*, 253-268.

Williams, J. M. Effects of evaluative and nonevaluative coactors upon male and female performance of simple and complex motor tasks. In *Psychology of motor behavior and sport*, Vol. 2, (R. W. Christina and D. M. Landers, Eds.). Human Kinetics, 1977.

Willis, R. H. Two dimensions of conformity-nonconformity. *Sociometry*, 1963, *26*, 499-513.

Willis, R. H. and Hollander, E. P. An experimental study of three response modes in social influence situations. *Journal of Abnormal and Social Psychology*, 1964, *69*, 150-156. (a)

Willis, R. H. and Hollander, E. P. Supplementary note: Modes of responding in social influence situations. *Journal of Abnormal and Social Psychology*, 1964, *69*, 157. (b)

Winch, R. F. *Mate-selection: A study of complementary needs*. Harper & Row, 1958.

Winterbottom, M. R. The relation of childhood training in independence to achievement motivation. Unpublished doctoral dissertation, University of Michigan, 1953.

Wolosin, R. J., Sherman, S. J. and Till, A. Effects of cooperation and competition on responsibility attribution after success and failure. *Journal of Experimental and Social Psychology*, 1973, *9*, 220-235.

Wood, C. G. and Hokanson, J. E. Effects of induced muscular tension on performance and the inverted-U function. *Journal of Personality and Social Psychology*, 1965, *1*, 506.

Wortman, C. B., Costanzo, P. R. and Witt, T. B. Effect of anticipated performance on the attributions of causality to self and others. *Journal of Personality and Social Psychology*, 1973, *27*, 372-381.

Wright, J. H., Gescheider, G. A. and Battig, W. F. Performance on a motor learning task as related to MAS scores. *Perceptual and Motor Skills*, 1963, *16*, 368.

Yaffe, M. The psychology of soccer. *New Society*, 1974, pp 378-380.

Yerkes, R. M. and Dobson, J. D. The relation of strength of stimulus to rapidity of habit-formation. *Journal of Comparative and Neurological Psychology*, 1908, *18*, 459-482.

Yukl, G. Toward a behavioral theory of leadership. *Organizational Behavior and Human Performance*, 1971, *6*, 414-440.

Zajonc, R. B. Social facilitation. *Science*, 1965, *149*, 269-274.

Zajonc, R. B. Compresence. Presented at the Midwestern Psychological Association Meeting, Chicago, 1972.

Zajonc, R. B. and Nieuwenhuyse, B. Relationship between word frequency and recognition: Perceptual process or response bias? *Journal of Experimental Psychology*, 1964, *67*, 276-285.

Zander, A. *Motives and goals in groups*. Academic Press, 1971.

Zander, A. Productivity and group success: Team spirit vs. the individual achiever. *Psychology Today*, (November), 1974, pp 64-68.

Zander, A. The psychology of removing group members and recruiting new ones. *Human Relations*, 1976, *10*, 969-987.

Zander, A. and Forward, J. Position in group, achievement motivation and group aspirations. *Journal of Personality and Social Psychology*, 1968, *8*, 282-288.

Zander, A., Forward, J. and Albert, R. Adaptation of board members to repeated success or failure by their organizations. *Organizational Behavior and Human Performance*, 1969, *4*, 56-76.

Zander, A. and Medow, H. Individual and group levels of aspiration. *Human Relations*, 1963, *16*, 89-105.

Zander, A., Medow, H. and Efron, R. Observers' expectations as determinants of group aspirations. *Human Relations*, 1965, *18*, 273-287.

Zander, A. and Newcomb, T. Group levels of aspiration in United Fund Campaigns. *Journal of Personality and Social Psychology*, 1967, *6*, 157-162.

Zander, A. and Wulff, D. Members' test anxiety and competence: Determinants of a group's aspirations. *Journal of Personality*, 1966, *34*, 55-70.

INDEX

AUTHOR INDEX

SUBJECT INDEX